pp.

Fall from Grace

us - 284 - ff

601

Memoirs of a
Rebel IAS Officer

£4.00

15/24

Fall From Grace

Memoirs of a Rebel IAS Officer

V. Balasubramanian

AUTHORSPRESS

Worldwide Circulation through Authorspress Global Network
First Published in 2022
by
Authorspress
Q-2A Hauz Khas Enclave, New Delhi-110 016 (India)
Phone: (0) 9818049852
E-mail: authorspressgroup@gmail.com
Website: www.authorspressbooks.com

Fall from Grace: Memoirs of a Rebel IAS Officer
ISBN 978-93-5529-337-4

Printed in India at Thomson Press (India) Limited

Contents

Prologue: *Non Serviam* — 7

1. Early Days—The *'Dhamdupat'* Principle,
   Mexican Wheat and *Bĕ-Chirāg Villages* — 21

2. Earlier Days: Ramayana, Rangoon University and Marx — 37

3. Baptism in the Private Sector in Madras and
   My Passage to Bureaucracy — 56

4. The National Academy of Administration:
   My First Experience in Karnataka Secretariat, and Finding
   my Mentor, G.V.K. Rao—The Institution Builder — 70

5. In the Districts—Shimoga, as Deputy Commissioner and
   District Magistrate: *The Job the IAS Officer Looks Forward
   to and Later Looks Back Upon* — 85

6. Gulbarga—Where Adil Shahi Sultans Once Ruled — 101

7. As DC & DM of Bangalore during Emergency Darkness
   under the Lamp — 126

8. Scooter Fee Causing Closure of Bangalore Cinema Theatres — 142

9. Excise Auctions—How to Beat the Liquor Mafia,
   With Mafia Help! — 148

10. An Encounter with a Dilettante Youth Congress Leader — 156

11. Still in Bangalore and Still Emergency! — 160

12. Family Planning and End of Emergency — 164

13. My Travel on Silk Road Starts — 173

14. Karnataka Silk Project—My First Project for
    World Bank Assistance — 186

15. Back to Gulbarga—Return of the Native   211

16. Secretary to Chief Minister   231

17. My Second Stint in Silk—Central Silk Board and
    Learning from China   255

18. The Fall from Grace: A Kaleidoscope of
    Chief Ministers of Karnataka   275

19. Somanahalli Mallaiah Krishna   350

20. You Only Live Twice: The Second, More Rewarding,
    After Retirement   366

21. I Commit Contempt of Legislature   380

22. Summing Up   393

Prologue
Non Serviam

[*Non serviam* is Latin for "I will not serve". The phrase is traditionally attributed to Satan, who had spoken these words as a refusal to serve God in heaven. In modern times "*non serviam*" developed into a general phrase used to express radical, sometimes revolutionary rejection of conformity, not necessarily limited to religious matters only..... *Quoted by James Joyce in Ulysses (1922) which was banned on both sides of Atlantic!*]

From an unintended gift of being forced to house-arrest by Covid-19 and unable to make my annual visits to the UNESCO Heritage Sites from my Bucket List, I wrote my story in 2021. I thought I was writing my autobiography, the Memoirs of a Reluctant Rebel, having followed the philosophy of *Non Serviam*. I plagiarized "Reluctant Rebel" from the biography of 17th century Anglo-Irish satirist Jonathan Swift by John Stubbs. But halfway through I realized that my story is more than a memoir, it is a commentary on the administration of Karnataka. After all, since 1967 I have worked under a kaleidoscope of Chief Ministers starting from Veerendra Patil from his first term, Devaraj Urs, Gundu Rao, Ramakrishna Hegde (whose Secretary I was for three years), Bangarappa, JH Patel, SM Krishna, *et alia* and with eminent officers like GVK Rao, RJ Rebello, RA Naik, TR Satishchandran, JC Lynn, Jayakumar Anagol and, alas, their antipodes. Being essentially an outsider grafted as an Establishment Insider, I had a vantage point to observe the style and substance of the political leaders and the bureaucrats which few commentators get. My experience with people, bureaucracy and politicians being concurrent, I have re-christened the title to my story to appropriately, *Fall From Grace—Memoirs of a Rebel IAS Officer*. Fall not mine, but of administration!

I have read many Memoirs of civil servants. Most of them are chronologies of boring details of bureaucratic life in Prussian prose inducing sleep. I have not followed this style. There is a Chinese proverb which says, *First rate people discuss Ideas, Second rate people discuss Incidents and the Third rate discuss Other People*. It does not say anything about the Fourth rate who describe their own lives! Ambitiously, I have included all the four. While narrating personal experience in jobs I have held, I have discussed Ideas, Incidents and have praised and also criticized gleefully some Chief Ministers and many civil servants. I have used strong language following the advice of Keynes who said, *Words ought to be a little wild, for they are the assaults of thoughts on the unthinking.* But Keynes, had also said caustically, *I work for a Government I despise for ends I think criminal!*

NAGARJUNA'S "FOUR CORNERS" AND IBN RUSHD'S "KNOWN KNOWNS AND UNKNOWN UNKNOWNS"

Reading should not be a substitute for thinking. René Descartes' saying, *I think, therefore I am,* is explained more by its fuller version, *Dubito, ergo cogito, ergo sum*—'I doubt, therefore I think, therefore I am'. So, thinking is vital, not just reading, but having doubts and finding answers, for leading a 'considered' life. I had a rewarding university education. I stood first class first in Rangoon University in 1962 with Economics and Commerce and received the *U Pu* Gold Medal, which of course none in India have heard of! I was a student of the famous Welfare Economist of the London School of Economics, Dr Hla Myint, the Rector of Rangoon U who taught us Economics and Ronald Findlay of MIT who taught Economic Analysis and who was Professor in the Columbia University, till he passed away recently. The IAS had a great snob value in Tamil Nadu (it still has) and even 'preparing' for the IAS was a much admired activity in the then Madras. When I walked from my home to the bus stop, perfect strangers started greeting me which of course I modestly returned. I am a modest person. In fact I have it so much that I can speak about my modesty for hours! I used to go every Sunday evening to the vast Marina beach of the middle class Triplicane locality where I lived in the 1960's. Looking at the endless, tireless, majestic, breezy lapping waves before me, I would argue in my mind for hours whatever theories I had read during the week—in Economics, Political Thought, General Knowledge, Hindu newspaper reports, Mahatma Gandhi (which was then compulsory reading for IAS), *inter alia*, which formed the crux of my 'preparation'. I would ponder on Mercantilism, Divergence of economic supremacy of India and China from 16th century but shifting to Europe from the age of Exploration and theories of Adam Smith, David Ricardo, Marx, Keynes, Milton Friedman—all in Economics, Thomas Hobbes, David Hume, Harold Laski and others in political thought, Mahatma's not much publicized 'Doctrine of the Sword', the South India's Aryan-Dravidian dialectics and the like. This was highly rewarding in crystallizing my personal philosophy instead of hauled up before the Privileges Committee where I proudly defended myself by sticking to my remarks. The *Kannada Prabha* reported on it daily for a month, even drawing cartoons. The Legislature dropped its futile attempt and I lost an opportunity to appear before the House and commit double contempt! I would consider it an adornment on my imaginary Hero Stone, *Vira Gallu!* So, I have written my experience, not in sandy dry words but in more interesting, even in offending scatological rhetoric, about events and people whom I had the immense pleasure of working with and equally, of ruffling feathers! I am sure those who are curious to read this Memoirs will find me a proud person who has much to be proud of. About my modesty, I have already declared, like Oscar Wilde declaring his genius to the New York Customs!

NEVER A DULL MOMENT

I joined the Indian Administrative Service in 1965 at the age of twenty four after working as an Executive Assistant in the private sector's Tube Investments Company of AM Murugappa Chettiar of AMM-group at Chennai. On joining the IAS, I was allotted to the mild Karnataka State. I retired in 2001 when I was sixty years and worked for ten more years in government related work, notably as Adviser to the Joint Legislature Committee for Preventing Land Grabbing and, subsequently when BS Yediyurappa in an unguarded moment appointed me as Chairman of the Task Force for Protecting Public Lands. I come from a feudal background. My father belonged to the Nattukkottai Chettiar, *Nagarathar*—Towns-people—community who are a minuscule professional moneylenders of South India. Since the time of sea-faring Raja Raja Cholan's son Rajendra Cholan who in early 11th century defeated the Sri Vijaya Kingdom ruler in *Kedar* (today's Palampang in Malaysia), the Chettiar community was trading and money-lending in South East Asian states such as Myanmar, Sri Lanka, Thailand, Indonesia, Malaysia, Indonesia and even upto South of Vietnam. Being pious people they had taken sculptors and Priests to construct Hindu temples and spread colourful mythology which influenced local rulers but fortunately not the caste system. Even today, for the coronation of Cambodia's King, a Brahmin family priest has to pronounce Sanskrit *mantras!*

I studied upto school final in Tamil Nadu, but could not join college as there was a Rule in Madras University that to join college one should have completed 14½ years and I was six months short! So my father asked us to come over to Rangoon in Burma instead of my wasting one year in Madras. In Rangoon, my father put me at once in a 'Commercial

College' to study Accountancy, Commercial Law, Typing and Shorthand instead of being idle. As the only child my mother did not allow me playing with other children (I would be spoiled!) and therefore I became a bookworm since I was eight years old. My father made me study a short, 16-page summary of Ramayana by rote, waking me up at 4 in the cold mornings every day! This made me a child-expert in Ramayana. I also wrote the accounts of my father and found that the interest he charged on farmers was 10%, which is enormous when you realize that it is 10% per month of compound interest! But, as the legal limit of interest under Burma's British law was 18% a year, the 'On Demand' document the farmer would sign would be blank except for his signature (all Burmese, including women were literate in Burmese, thanks to the compulsory Burmese primary schools run by Buddhist monks) and it was my job to write falsely the principal amount sufficiently high so that the 10% per month compound interest on Rs.100 in a year would equal 18% simple interest, in one year! Since my good readers may not be very good in compound interest calculations, let me enlighten: the compound interest alone at 10% per month for 12 months on Rs.100 would be Rs.213.80 compared to Rs.18 simple interest in one year! So I would have to calculate and fill up the principal as at least Rs.1,200 in the blank space while the actual principal received by the farmer was only Rs.100, so that the simple interest on Rs.1,200 would equal the compound interest on Rs.100! (No wonder, when a church-goer asked Einstein, *'Professor, are you not afraid of God?'*, Einstein brightly replied, *'I am terribly afraid of Compound Interest!'*) So, for balancing generational justice, in the very first year of my college in Rangoon U, I immersed myself in the *Communist Manifesto* which is the third largest published book in the world after Mao's Thoughts and the Holy Bible. The delightful lectures of my Economics Professor Ronald Findlay and Rector Hla Myint, seduced me to the fundamental Socialist cause of standing for the underdog. There is a Swedish saying: *If you are not a Socialist in your Twenties, you have no Heart; if you are still a Socialist in your Forties, you have no Head!* But, I rationalized it by convincing myself, *It is better to be Headless than Heartless!*

I idolized A Madhavan of the Indian Foreign Service. He was the First Secretary in the Indian Embassy at Rangoon in the 1960's who gave me his *Economic Analysis* by Kenneth Boulding which he had studied for his 1955 UPSC examination. I followed his advice to join government service by writing the competitive examination. But then as my lecturer Dr Findlay had said, once you are infected with Marx you are never completely cured of the virus because Marx is a 'difficult thing to kill'. Working in government you can never be a revolutionary, as the litterateur UR Anantha Murthy told me in 1973 when the CM Devaraj Urs sent him to Gulbarga to look at its famine from an intellectual's eye and report to him. About this, a lot in a later chapter. But in an elite IAS where you can commit murder and get away with because of the Constitutional protection given in Article 311, you can do many things to help the poor and the weak, all within the Rules if you have the mind to, which was what I had done in all my years of service. No harm will come to you except the pin-pricks of transfer. After my retirement, I was surprised to receive a call one day from the Speaker of Karnataka Legislative Assembly that he was appointing me as Adviser to the Joint Legislature Committee to enquire into the land grabbing in Bangalore Urban district. I realized that though I had not done any favour to any MLA, the all-party JLC had agreed with the Speaker's suggestion because of my offending all parties in equal measure and that where their personal interest is not involved, the elected representatives can even be selectively impartial. During the two years of its functioning, there was not a single instance of the JLC members taking a partisan view in instances of blatant land grabbing which was also due to the strong personality of the Chairman of the JLC, AT Ramaswamy MLA. Because of my work done with the JLC, after the coalition government fell because the CM Kumaraswamy developed severe amnesia and 'forgot' to vacate CM's chair to the BJP according to the 'Gentlemen's agreement' *(he said there were no gentlemen in the two parties, hence there can't be any such agreement, with which everyone agreed!)* and when the new government by BJP was formed after a fresh election, the CM Yedyurappa, in an un-alert moment, appointed me as the Chairman of the Task Force for Removal of Encroachment of Public Land in all the thirty districts of Karnataka. However, this did not end well to government. As I had powers to remove encroachments through the Deputy Commissioners and Heads of Departments, it affected the real estate Mafia, especially in and around Bangalore where land value had shot up 530 times (which is a surreal, head-spinning, yes, 53,000%!) between 1970 and 2010, and the Revenue Minister Karunakara Reddy who as King of Bellary had successfully organized illegal iron ore mining, as revealed in the report of Lok Ayukta Justice Santosh Hegde, beyond the reach of even the Chief Minister because of the central party support to the Bellary Monarchs in the form of 'Mother' Sushma Swaraj, abolished the Task Force without even taking the matter to the Cabinet. But being computer-literate, I prepared within two weeks my Report with the title, *Greed and Connivance*, before the last date of existence of the Task Force, narrating the greed of political leaders and the land Mafia and the connivance of bureaucracy in the theft of public lands, without mincing words. Understandably alarmed, the Revenue Minister refused to print my Report and therefore I got 2,000 copies printed at my cost spending Rs.2,20,000 and freely distributed it to Ministers, MLAs, MPs, the media and the NGOs. I mention these matters because most citizens have the impression that bureaucrats are mercenaries of unscrupulous leaders. While this is largely true, the IAS also has some recalcitrant, anarchic rebels who try to climb waterfalls.

To add glitter to my *resumé,* even after my retirement, in the era of Covid-19 also, I have been busy giving talks and holding webinars on varied subjects as given below, which would greatly impress my readers!

1. Protection of Lakes in Bangalore;
2. The Great Recession of 2008—Its Implications for India;
3. 1857—What Really Happened?
4. India and China—Two Different Paths to Development;
5. The Impending Water Famine in Bangalore;
   (A study on behalf of Azhim Premji U)
6. Is India a Failing State? Is There an Alternative?
7. Corruption and Human Rights;
8. Why Black Money Will Rule India?
9. Money, Black Money and Bank Scams in India;
10. Governance of Bangalore Metropolitan Region;
11. China's Belt and Road Initiative and its Implications for India;
12. Vanishing Accountability of Public Servants in India;
13. The Need for an Inquisitorial System of Justice in India in
14. place of the present Anglo-Saxon Adversarial System.

NON SERVIAM (I WILL NOT SERVE)

In my long official service of forty six years I have always followed my anarchic philosophy, which was also the Natural Law of St Thomas Aquinas: *If my action is morally right, it does not matter that it is legally wrong; per contra, if it is morally wrong, it does not help that it is legally right.* This is blasphemy in the civil service and this had led a colleague of mine who had served in the Indian Army to criticize me that I carry the fight to the enemy's camp which was not terribly wise of me. To this my answer to this ex-armyman was, that was the only way to fight any battle as history and the Israelis have shown. As a result, I had created enemies both among the politicians and, more remarkably, within the IAS. Civil Servants are a placid, conformist lot and dread creating ripples, being consummate diplomats. But, as I have narrated in this memoir, I have rather taken to heart the 19th century Scottish poet Charles Mackay's rebuke:

> You have no enemies, you say?
> Alas! my friend, the boast is poor;
> He who has mingled in the fray
> Of duty, that the brave endure,
> Must have made foes! If you have none,
> Small is the work that you have done.
> You've hit no traitor on the hip,
> You've dashed no cup from perjured lip,
> You've never turned the wrong to right,
> You've been a coward in the fight.

I have sharp edges. I flatter myself that rose has thorns and only the fruit-bearing tree attracts stones. My detractors would say Cactus and Agavé also have thorns. But then, Agavé also produces the potent Tequila, the national drink of Mexico which the Azecs created since 1000 BCE. Besides my experience as an officer of the elite IAS, I have freely commented upon Chief Ministers and some senior bureaucrats with whom I have worked. I have paid tributes where due as in the case of my mentor GVK Rao who was Chief Secretary in Karnataka and later Member, Planning Commission of India, Jayakumar Anagol who was my first boss and Philosopher-Deputy Commissioner in Raichur district and many others. I have admired Devaraj Urs, the only dynamic Chief Minister who boldly tried to shift political power from the dominant Lingayat and Okkaliga communities to the Backward Classes. After him, the old status quo of *Udū* (the strong member of Iguana family which Shivaji's generals used to scale fort walls) grip on power by Okkaligas and Lingayats has of course resumed! As the French say, the more things change, the more they remain the same. I have pulled no punches in finding fault where blame is due. I have also paid encomiums where they were deserved to many of my younger colleagues and officers of other services. My sharp edges have always earned me troubles, more from my IAS Tribal Cains than from the more customarily faulted Machiavellian Politicians. But I have enjoyed these fights with an intellectual masochism, always remembering the remarkable *Paratrooper's Prayer:*

THE PARATROOPER'S PRAYER

I'm asking You God, to give me what You have left.
Give me those things that others never ask of You.
I don't ask You for rest, or tranquility.
Not that of the spirit, the body, or the mind.
I don't ask You for wealth, or success, or even health.

All those things are asked of You so much Lord,
that you can't have any left to give.
Give me instead Lord what You have left.
Give me what others don't want.
I want uncertainty and doubt.
I want torment and battle.
And I ask that You give them to me now and forever Lord,
so I can be sure to always have them,
because I won't always have the strength to ask again.
But give me also the courage, the energy,
and the spirit to face them.
I ask You these things Lord,
because only you alone can give, my God,
What I cannot expect only from myself.

[André Zirnheld was born in 1913, and was killed in action in Libya, in July 1942, during a raid behind enemy lines while serving as a parachutist in the Free French Army. He was a college philosophy professor before the war. Though Lt. Zirnheld never served in the Foreign Legion, all French Paratroopers, the Legion included, have adopted his prayer.]

To the younger officers, to those dwindling army of Knights Templars who have not taken the Faustian bargain, the Paratrooper's Prayer should be the clarion call, like a lion's roar. Even the 'honest' senior officers and the IAS Association will not come to their help in their hour of need. When Vasudevan, an honest officer of Karnataka, was unjustly sentenced to one month's imprisonment by a Supreme Court Judge for contempt of court and the CM Deve Gowda defended Vasudeven and also broke down in the Assembly, yet the President of the IAS Association, who by convention was the second senior-most IAS officer next to the Chief Secretary, vehemently opposed the resolution moved by me in the Executive Committee meeting that the Association members should protest for a day sitting before the Mahatma Gandhi statute opposite the Cubbon Park. This was because he was next in line to become the Chief Secretary and he did not want to jeopardize in the least his chance to ascend the throne *(it was only an imitation leather Featherlite chair!)* Some of us phoned up the younger officers and about fifty, of the 150 direct recruit IAS officers posted in Bangalore, turned up for the protest before the Gandhi Statue. Belonging to the 1965 batch, I was the senior most officer who participated in it. My colleagues of 1965 batch, the seven officers of the 1964 batch, three of the 1963 and two of the 1962 batch—none of them turned up as they were in the 'zone' of the CS-race! Even my seniors from Bengal, the state once reputed for its revolutionary and intellectual fervor, suddenly developed frostbite in the foot and could not reach the Gandhi statue! This is the calibre of the elite bureaucracy which will not come together even to protect its own 'tribal' interest when one of its own honest member is hounded, let alone fighting to protect public interest. *"Every one for him selfe, and the divel for all,"* (John Florio in *First Fruites*, 1578), is the first refuge of even the "neutral" bureaucrats. So, the honest and principled officers are on their own and it should be their rightful glory, worth their suffering. Younger officers having ten or more years of service will face increasing hostility not only from the political class but mainly from their own seniors, the biological wonders with missing vertebrae.

We do not read history, especially after the digital take-over of life. Unlike other Asian countries such as China, Japan, South Korea, Thailand, Cambodia, Philippines, Bangladesh, Pakistan, etc., India is not a 'one language, one genetic-stock, one religion' Nation. Even the diverse Indonesia with 27 crore population of many dialects in over 3,000 islands, of which 87% are Muslims is united by *Bahasa Indonesia* and is still the most secular country with its national carrier named *Garuda* and President Jokovi ending his speeches with the Balinese, *Om Shanthi Om.* Between the death of Aurangzeb in 1707 and the Battle of Palashi in 1757, in fifty years India disintegrated largely due to the bigoted rule of Aurangzeb undoing the unification done by Akbar. The basic centrifugal force in Indian history has again appeared strongly in independent India where we are practicing the immoral, India-patented 'Resort Democracy' of kidnapping MLAs and keeping them in captivity before a no-confidence motion comes up in the Legislature which crime is not seen in any other country, not even in African nations, the cemetery of democracy. With MLAs being routinely auctioned like draught animals—bulls, horses, sheep and goats—all Political Parties have become Poachers Incorporated Private Ltd. Takeover of administration resembling the *'Paleygars'* rule in South India has again resurfaced in the form of MLAs controlling administration. Akbar had established 12 Provinces called *'Subhas'* with its Governor called *Subhedar* and the number of Subhas became 22 in Aurangzeb's time because of expansion of Mughal empire. But with disintegration of the Mughal empire, the *Subhedars* became *Nawabs* not amenable to central control. With weakening of the central authority, the Chief Ministers of 28 states in India (large and small, UP with 20 crore population is the world's 5th biggest *country* in the world and Sikkim has only 6 lakhs), most Chief Ministers have become the *Nawabs* with different degree of independence from the centre. Since these CM-cum-Nawabs have to depend upon their MLAs, the latter have become *Paleygars* and War Lords and the bureaucracy including the Police has become mercenary.

As the Deputy Commissioner and District Magistrate of Gulbarga district, one day in 1973, staying in *Taylor's Manzil*, the Inspection Bungalow with 27 doors, built in 1844 and named after Philip Meadows Taylor, the Deputy Commissioner and British Resident of Raja Nalawadi Venkatappa Naik of Surpur who joined the 1857 Great Mutiny and was crushed, in the Southern-most taluk of my Gulbarga district, I was reading his astounding novel, *Confessions of a Thug*, published in 1839 which became a sensational classic in England and a must-read for Indian Civil Service Officers. From this book, the word 'thug' entered the English language, from the original Sanskrit *Sthaga* (cunning). It described in detail the deceptive and large scale murders and robbery by wandering gangs of 'Thuggees' in central India and the Deccan. As there was no government to maintain law and order these groups of travelling Thugs ruled the land.

Gradually, in India the CMs are losing control and the fragmented Paleygar-structure is replacing central authority and ultimately we may get an anarchy resembling the 'Thug Raj' of Meadows Taylor in 19th century. Already, in the Hindi belt the political leaders maintain their own gangs of 'body guards' with cottage-industry produced pistols. Soon, they will handle AK-47s. This is what has happened to Pakistan's democracy which also inherited the same system of Public Service Commission-recruited Civil Service but which was emasculated by the Army rule starting from Ayub Khan's coup in 1958. Since then it is either the Army or the Army-sponsored politician who is the Prime Minister with the Army Islamized since Zia ul Haq' military rule from 1978 to 1988 when he died in a conspiratorial plane crash. Since then Pakistan is said to be suffering from *Three A's— America, Army, Allah* and with '22 Families' controlling its economy and Bureaucracy rendered irrelevant. With fundamentalism and political chicanery rising and over 2,000 political parties contesting elections in the country (the contesting candidates list in a constituency being as big as a Sunday newspaper) and Bureaucracy becoming Three-Monkeys—See no evil, Hear no evil, Speak no evil—except to carry out the illegal orders of the politicians, India may very well go the same way as Pakistan. As Marx said, History repeats itself as tragedy, the first time. *[The second time as Farce for which we will have to wait!]* It takes over a hundred years for a failing state to become a Failed State as many of the African States demonstrate.

After seventy five years of democracy, most Indians do not have faith in politicians and if some citizens still have some respect for government, it is because of the few remaining honest civil servants and Judges. If this fragile civil service frame despite all its warts, wounds and scabs collapses, there is nothing to hold the polity except the Olive Green uniform. It will be like Pakistan, Thailand, Cambodia and Myanmar which have 'Army-Democracies'. But, there is no need for the few remaining honest civil servants to feel frustrated because the valorous journey they have undertaken is a noble end in itself. The journey is the joy. The world of the corrupt bureaucrats is very small and they live as well-frogs in cold darkness with leeches, the wide sunlit world outside not known to them. The only book most of the corrupt officers have ever read is their bank pass book and the only card they can play in life is their credit card. That is not the case with the few honest officers who are like the brave Greeks, vastly outnumbered by the Persian army, yet defending selflessly the pass at Thermopylae, welcoming martyrdom. In the following pages I have told the story of my experience without embellishments and without holding anything back in the hope it may bring some reassurance to my younger colleagues. And some amusement and, perhaps, a little understanding to all readers.

❖❖❖

CHAPTER 1

Early Days—The *'Dhamdupat'* Principle, Mexican Wheat and *Bĕ-Chirāg Villages*

How to confiscate cabinet minister's tractor and yet get promotion!

It was a crisp January morning in 1967. The North-West monsoon had ended. The *rabi* or the second crop called *hingari* was mainly the rain-fed Jowar (Sorghum), besides Bajra (Pearl Millet) and Groundnut which were the other standing crops, the only greenery to be seen in an otherwise bleak and treeless countryside. The average normal annual rainfall here was hardly 500 mm and also uncertain. I had just completed two months as Assistant Commissioner and Sub Divisional Magistrate of Lingsugur sub-division in Raichur District, one of the then nineteen districts in Karnataka. Right from Akbar's rule when his Diwan Raja Thodarmal had devised the Revenue Administration system of Subha (Province), Zilla (District), Pranth (Sub-division), Tehsil or Taluk and Circle or hobli and below it the villages of India, the Land Administration has remained largely unchanged. I was the AC & SDM in independent charge of three taluks, fourteen revenue circles and about four hundred villages with 300,000 population. In Raichur there were three such sub-divisions. The district headquarters Raichur was 90 km to the east, close to Andhra Pradesh border and its capital Hyderabad and I was left alone in my work, not being in the constant shadow of the Deputy Commissioner of the district who was my boss.

Raichur district was part of Nizam's Dominion till 1947 which was trifurcated in the linguistic Reorganization of States in 1956. It was one of the highly famine-affected areas and backward on all economic indicators. With scanty and uncertain rain the land could support only a sparse population and therefore land-holding by farmers was large. While in the rest of Karnataka the unit of measurement of land is one acre, equal to 4,840 square yards or forty *Guntas*, in the Hyderabad-Karnataka area the common term used was one *Kurigè* which is four acres. I learnt from the villagers that a father would hesitate to give his daughter in marriage to a person who does not own ten *Kurigé*, or Forty acres. Over time, people here had learnt that for a decent and adequate annual food requirement for a joint-family, Jowar *(Sorghum)* harvest from forty acres was needed as only one in three years there will be a good harvest the rest being poor. Even in the inadequate calculation of District per capita GDP (which is just an arithmetic average and does not measure the share of different economic and social groups), Raichur ranked 18th out of the 19 districts in the state then, the last being Bidar, also in Hyderabad Karnataka.

Just before independence, the Tungabadhra Major Irrigation Dam was constructed as a "Protective Irrigation Project" to ensure at least one light-irrigated crop to cover the largest number of farmers, the dominant crops in the district being Jowar, Bajra, Groundnut and minor millets such as Navane and Horse-gram. For a student of Economics and Political Science, this Benthamite Utilitarian principle of the *Greatest Happiness of the Largest Number,* struck me as a progressive irrigation policy for a reputedly Feudal State of Nizam. About 6 lakh acres or one-thirds of the district was to be covered under irrigation with a "Duty of Water" of 120 acres per cubic foot flow per second *(Cusec)* while in most other irrigation projects in India it was only about 80 acres because of Paddy, Sugarcane and other water-guzzling crops, which were forbidden under the Tunga Bhadra Project.

No doubt, the Nizam's Hyderabad Dominion was a feudal state. It had a tradition of *Jagirdars* and *Dhanis,* meaning *"Lords of Wealth"* from pre-British days who owned over a thousand acres, some even five thousand acres of land even after independence. They could administer criminal justice over their subjects inspite of Courts having been established with the Indian Penal Code and Code of Criminal Procedure in place since 1861. As a feudal state the income inequality in the district was extreme. The landed gentry mostly belonged to the Lingayat community in Hyderabad-Karnataka. One such Jagirdar in my sub-division was the "Raja" of Gejjalaghatta who owned huge extent of land, even owning a small island in the middle of Tungabhadra river which bifurcated Raichur from Bellary district. But the person wearing pants in the Raja's household, I learnt, was his smart younger wife Basavarajeswari who was also a cabinet minister, no less, in the then Congress Ministry of Veerendra Patil, the CM.

There was only one problem. Her family owed government Rs 72,000 and not a single instalment had been paid since 1946. The outstanding loans were for two tractors, irrigation pumpsets and even "Fodder Loans" usually given to poor farmers in years of famine to buy Jowar stalks for cattle, at the rate of Rs 100 per acre of land owned! If you were a landless agricultural labourer you got nothing because no land and therefore no cattle, no fodder or any type of loan! No property and you are nothing! In 1967 the outstanding loan of Rani-B was five times its 1946 value. My predecessor BR Prabhakara was two years senior to me, belonging to the 1963 batch of direct recruits and, being a mild-mannered Mysore gentleman, he had issued many polite D.O. letters to the Raja for paying at least some instalments. In officialese, a *"D.O"*. letter is a *demi-official* letter where the officer writes personally to the recipient starting with "Dear" or "My dear" and ends with "Yours sincerely" and signs it himself while all formal, usually offensive Government communications will be addressed as "Sir" and signed as "Yours faithfully" by the Under-Secretary "for the Secretary". In British days, the letters used to end with "Your Obedient Servant" as a mockery by the Masters! The customary official letter in AC's office was signed by the head *Sheristedar,* from Persian *Sarishta-dhār* meaning "Administrative Officer of the Court". The rigid convention is that, a D.O letter should invariably be replied by a D.O letter or immediately acted upon! While the Jagirdhars in pre-independence days knew very well the protocol, in independent India, Rani-B, the cabinet minister, had chosen to ignore them much to the dismay of my predecessor who could not do anything against a cabinet minister.

Unlike my predecessor I was not a gentleman, flattering myself as a Marxist, who would allow a wilful defaulter get away just because of being a cabinet minister. When I assumed charge as AC and SDM, the Deputy Commissioner of Raichur district, Jayakumar Anagol was a 1956 Emergency Recruit officer, the Union government having recruited a large number of officers in addition to the annual recruitment, to fill up large vacancies. Anagol was a well-read person in Philosophy and social sciences and, as an officer, a 'Development-Oriented Disciplinarian'. I will explain this term later. He conducted a Revenue Officers meeting every month. In the first meeting I had attended, he stressed the importance of collection of government loans strictly. He also said the ACs should make personal efforts to collect the dues of big defaulters whom the lower level revenue officers were afraid to handle. For my strong leftist philosophy, this was music. When I called for the big defaulters list, my *Sheristedar* Janardhana Rao brought a few files and I found the name of Rani-B on top, with my predecessor's DO letters remaining unanswered. Then, being careful, I dictated a politely firm letter, drawing attention to her silence to my predecessor's letters, finally ending it by saying if the dues are not paid within one month, I would be rather unhappy to attach the tractors and pumpsets which were mortgaged as security. At this, my good *Sheristedar* showed signs of acute discomfort and whispered that the Rani*sahiba* was a powerful Lingayat leader and now a cabinet minister and please, would the AC-*sab* kindly omit the last sentence! To his dismay I did not and the letter was sent by Registered Post Acknowledgment Due to keep the legal records complete. In the 1960's, Mahatma Gandhi's biography, *My Experiments with Truth* translated by Mahadev Desai, was compulsory reading for IAS and, while I was no Gandhian, one of Mahatma's sayings had struck me and stayed ever since: *Men of Truth should also be Men of Care.* I thought it was Darwinian self-preservation.

When I went into the details of Rani B's loan I found that the principal overdue from the loans in the 1940s, was Rs 36,000 and the simple interest at 6% had also crossed Rs 36,000 but the total dues stopped at Rs 72,000. I asked my *Sheristedar* why this was so and he brought to me an old thick Guard File (important circulars from government since British times were kept in a huge, thick "Guard File" for reference which no other private organization can match) and read out the Urdu *Firmans* (edicts since Ottoman Sultans) of His Exalted Highness—HEH Nizam, in which the Preamble stated that under the ancient Hindu Shastras, the first principle of law was Pious Obligation namely, the debt of a Hindu should be repaid, after his death, by his son and grandson and secondly, **Dhamdupat** which is, while repaying such loan the accumulated interest cannot exceed the principal and that the Government of HEH Nizam follows this ancient principle. (This was indeed very interesting to me, a money-lender's son turned Marx-admirer!) Though in the case of the wealthy Ranisahiba, there was no reason not to charge interest beyond 100% of Principal, the basic reasonableness of the *Firman* following ancient Hindu canons impressed me and my admiration for the Nizam's feudal bureaucracy went up by a few more notches, just as the Protective Irrigation of Tungabhadra Project where paddy and sugarcane were prohibited so that more farmers could grow basic millet crops.

Thus, on that cold morning of January 1967, I collected the jeep of the Block Development Officer (in those days ACs and Tahsildars did not have government vehicles and, under Pandit Nehru's Rural Development Minister Mr.SK Dey, every taluk had a 'Block' Development Officer—cynics said he *'blocked'* development—who was given the rare jeep, and the BDO also worked under the AC.) But, since the BDO's driver immediately developed severe dysentery when he learned that the AC was going to Gejjalagatta to seize the Rani's tractors, I took my ever-reliable driver Jaffar who would not over-take a buffalo (I had a personal Standard Herald car) and started after collecting one more peon, Burhan, from the Taluk office who pretended he knew driving, to drive the tractors as I was sure the Raja and Rani would not happily provide drivers.

I had to pass in front of the Inspection Bungalow which was historically the army mess of the British Captain after the 1857 Mutiny. Lingsugur was a *Chawni* or Cantonment because in 1857 the *Bedava* (Hunter community) Raja of Surpur, which in 1967 was known as Shorapur taluk in Gulbarga District adjoining Lingsugur, was one of the few chieftains in South India who rose against the British and to crush him the British had sent an army contingent which was stationed in Lingsugur, 25 miles south of Surpur, across the Krishna river. My official residence was earlier the Captain's house and ahead was the army mess later converted as the PWD Inspection Bungalow. There was a legend that in its upstairs room the British wife of an officer had committed suicide by hanging on a Christmas Eve. (For good measure, just behind my house was the British cemetery with over hundred tombs, shockingly to me, mostly of little children, so my residence had a perfect Stephen King ambience!) There used to be betting among officers in Lingsugur just before Christmas, as to whether any person can sleep in that suicide-room on Christmas eve. When this was informed to me with eager expectation that the young AC should rise to the challenge, I disappointed them by prudently declining despite my rationalist convictions.

When my jeep was passing in front of the IB on that frosty morning, the District Superintendent of Police NS Vasudevan, who was a Tamilian from the Hyderabad Police Service, promoted to IPS and allotted to Karnataka in the 1956 State Reorganization, was having his tea in the garden outside the IB. He was old school and was on tour in Lingsugur and was enjoying his morning tea in the sun. I greeted him and he was curious to know where I was going so early on a winter morning and invited me for tea. So I explained to him my mission. He was rather concerned and said, *"I say, these people are very powerful, so why are you taking this foolish step?"* But when I stood by my sterling principles and resoluteness to practise them, he gave me up as a gone case but was kind enough to insist on sending two emaciated constables (all were famine affected) in sagging uniform to accompany me.

Thus I went with my jalopies to the stone and wood "palace" of the Raja. Only he was at home. The Rani was in Bangalore attending to onerous state duties. I politely declined his tea and explained that I had come to collect the dues failing which I would have to take away the mortgaged tractors and pumpsets. The poor man came close to a stroke when he realized I was serious. There were of course no mobile phones and land line was not working as usual. He said Rani-Sahiba was in Bangalore and would the AC please contact her? I declined and my team went in search of the two tractors and pumpsets and after an hour my cavalcade started rolling to Lingsugur, leaving the Raja totally shattered. Before that, the Revenue Inspector had to prepare a "Panchnama" signed by five rather terrified witnesses that the tractors were attached by the AC after following due process of law, etc. etc. There were many villagers in the village witnessing this strange spectacle which was a rare occasion for them. I reached my office after noon because Jaffer and Burhan had to negotiate the tractors hesitantly and I had to drive slowly the BDO's whimsical jeep which had a mind of its own. In the Academy at Mussoorie in 1965 there was no training for car-driving, only to ride the dreaded horses. Finally, the tractors were parked outside my office building with a board hurriedly written in big letters, *"Forfeited for non-payment of government loans"*. It was the weekly *'Santhē'*, market day, in Lingsugur and most villagers came to see the tractors. After 1857, Lingsugur was even the district headquarters for some decades and therefore there was an impressive hundred year-old building in which my office and the offices of Tahsidar, Treasury and the Magistrate's Court were situated. Outside this impressive building the confiscated tractors were kept which became a local tourist attraction for days.

Unsurprisingly, the first telephone call I received around 3 pm was from the Revenue Minister which was unusual in those days because the RM would not normally phone anyone less than the Deputy Commissioner. The RM, B Rachiah, was a decent person hailing from the Dalit community of Mysore district who do not have much love for the land owning Lingayat gentry, that too of alien Hyderabad-Karnataka. After ascertaining from me what had happened, he said, *Why don't you get a written undertaking from the Raja that the dues will be paid and release the tractors as this appears to be a prestige issue for the Minister?* I rather cheekily told him, *Sir this is a long pending matter and now forfeited under a specific section of the Land Revenue Act and if the tractors have to be released, would the Revenue Secretary may please issue a Government Order?* I knew the Revenue law sufficiently well that once a Revenue officer by an order attaches the mortgaged property, an appeal can lie only to the then Mysore Revenue Appellate Tribunal and Government had no executive jurisdiction over it if the dues have not been paid. I also pretended that the phone line was unclear and put it down.

After this, the Revenue Minister also spoke to my DC that the upstart AC is expecting a GO to be issued, that it was under DC's directions the officers have taken up a government dues collection drive, starting with big defaulters, etc. My philosopher-DC defended me that the AC had indeed taken action as per law and on DC's general decision to collect dues from big defaulters. In the event, the tractors were not released for over a fortnight. But, meanwhile a curious development took place. Rani-B complained to the CM Veerendra Patil, whose staunch supporter she was, that she cannot show her face in Lingsugur unless the tractors were released at once and the AC is transferred forthwith. But the CM, after ascertaining facts, decided that I need not be transferred for acting only according to law. But, to defuse the situation the Chief Secretary suggested I may be sent on a one month's training course to the National Institute of Community Development, Hyderabad starting in a few days and the Assistant Commissioner of Raichur may be kept in additional charge in my absence and the loan due of Rs.72,000 could be paid by the Minister in three monthly instalments, the first instalment to be paid immediately upon which the seized tractors could be released. The CM found this to be very reasonable. So I was sent to Hyderabad for a month's training during which time the first instalment of the loan was paid and the tractors were released by the in-charge AC. So I remained un-transferred and became a Martian-Hero of sorts among the officers of Gulbarga Division as my fame as VIP tractor-snatcher spread far and wide!

Thus, I had my first visit to Hyderabad and NICD. I had a wonderful time seeing the Salar Jung Museum, Golkonda Fort, Osmania U and other historical sites of the city. As for the Rural Development course there was nothing much to be said as my queries of dialectical materialism horrified the eminent speakers. My real benefit was comparing notes with officers from other states. When I returned to Lingsugur I was welcomed by officers of all departments with great admiration. To my surprise I found that the local Congress MLA, Sangana Gowda, also a Lingayat but opposed to the Minister, called on me and appreciated that strict administration was needed in a backward area like Raichur. Of course his appreciation was mainly because he was also in the running for minister's post but the Rani of Gejjlagatta had upstaged him. Nevertheless, it was comforting to know that officers acting legally were not being punished, especially the Chief Minister not acceding to the request of his cabinet colleague but agreeing with Chief Secretary's formula. I had come out unscathed from my first independent act of defying the establishment from inside. In an important way, this early experience set the rebellious tone for my entire future career. After this incident, I had met Rani-B in various functions. But the consummate politician that she was, she was so polite and respectful to me though my DC Anagol informed me not to be taken by the veneer and told me that she would complain to him often why he was fond of a communist AC! What happened fifty years ago will certainly not happen today even in a comparatively law abiding state like Karnataka. Any ruling party, and Karnataka has had its fair share of musical chairs, would transfer an officer without batting an eyelid if the officer displeases a minister or an MLA.

OF DISCIPLINE AND HOW NOT TO MISS THE BUS; MEXICAN WHEATS, *BÈ-CHIRAG* VILLAGES AND INDIA'S VILLAGE FETISH

Many important things happening to us are just accidents (and no such thing as fate or Karma) and not even by planning. When I had joined the National Academy of Training at Mussoorie in 1965, MG Pimputkar ICS of Maharashtra was appointed as the Director. His terror-trail in Bombay and Delhi Secretariat was legendary. One apocryphal story goes like this: when he was Commissioner of Bombay Municipal Corporation (which was considered then as more important than even the post of Chief Secretary), he once telephoned his home and the maid servant told him, Madam had taken the car out for shopping. Madam did not have a driving licence! So, Pimputkar forthwith telephoned the Commissioner of Police and, giving the car number, asked him to charge her with fine for driving without licence, much to the perplexity of the Police Commissioner. Pimputkar introduced discipline—punctuality, dress code, table manners, full attendance in class, insistence on early morning horse-riding and Physical Training and all such torture, much to the horror of the 110 IAS probationers. It was rumoured he even kept a check of the frequent visitors to the appropriately placed wine shop at the Academy entrance, known as BDS, Bhai Dhan Singh the Gate Keeper, which was second home to many probationers, the first being Hari's canteen hundred yards away!

I was a witness to the rigour of his discipline. Every batch of probationers spends about three weeks in Kashmir, two weeks the full batch visiting historic sites, some days in the house-boats of Dal Lake, and one week of "Military Attachment" later with seven to ten probationers attached to each regiment. In the first leg of the tour, all of us stayed in houseboats from which we were taken every morning by buses to Pahalgam, Khilen Marg, Gulmarg, Sonemarg, Hazratbal Shrine, Shankaracharya hill temple, etc. On our trip, Pimputkar accompanied us ostensibly to observe probationary behaviour. One morning all of us left in three buses to Khilenmarg along with Pimputkar. We had to leave the buses at a distance from the glacier and had to go either by walk or on ponies. Pimputkar told everyone should be back at the buses by 4pm. There were about twenty lady probationers in our batch. Some of them left with a group of admiring Sir Galahad-type probationers. After seeing the glorious sights of Khilenmarg on pony back, I and my close friends (being KTPs—Keen Type Probationers and South Indians, besides) returned to the bus at 3.45pm itself. We were the first except for Pimputkar who was already there. As 4pm approached most of the probationers had returned. Pimputkar said he would give a grace-time of 10 minutes and then we would leave. By 4.15 seven probationers including three ladies had not yet returned and Pimputkar asked the drivers to start. Our pleadings that after 5 pm it gets dark and there are no buses and very few taxis and we cannot leave the lady officers behind, left him unmoved. He sternly told us they are all responsible IAS officers who will have to run the administration of India and they should learn punctuality. So, we returned to Srinagar without them. Most of them straggled in ones and twos till late in the night. The correctness of leaving young lady officers in a new place without transport, I was not very thrilled. But that was Pimputkar. Later, he became the Chief Vigilance Commissioner of India and lived upto his reputation. This however instilled in me an obsession about punctuality. Since then I have always been five minutes early than one minute late.

FIRST EXPERIENCE IN ADIL SHAHI'S BIJAPUR

After selection to IAS in 1965 and joining the Academy, I was allotted Karnataka cadre. On completion of one year's training at the Academy at Mussoorie, I was sent to Bijapur (now Vijayapura) district in Karnataka for one year's field training. The DC was RA Naik, who was himself, I learned surprisingly, the probationer of Pimputkar in Maharashtra earlier. The IAS is a small world. RA Naik too was an extremely strict disciplinarian but was pleasant and very nice to me like most people who have a hard shell but a soft core. The DC's residence in Bijapur was the historic *Adalat Mahal*—Court House—of Adil Shahi Kingdom, a two-storied 16-rooms massive stone building of 15th century and walking distance from the famous *Gol Gumbaz*. [*The great age of Adil Shahis and the Bahmani Sultans is admirably narrated in Manu Pillai's* The Rebel Sultans (2018), *I read much later. Aurangzeb laid siege to Bijapur in 1686 for eighteen months to subdue Sikandar Adil Shah with whose death in 1686 the Adil Shahi dynasty of Bijapur came to an end.*]

RA Naik had in Adalat Mahal his "home office" also, an oxymoron-paradox. Every Collector's residence in India has a Home Office where he works from "home" when he is not in the office. This is a hang-over from British days when the Collector would go riding for inspection of villages in early morning cool, return by noon, go to office to hear cases till evening and return home to attend to file work in the "home Office". He gave me a "suite" of three rooms on the ground floor, which the PWD had refurbished in 1959 when Indira Gandhi had visited Bijapur as Congress President and did not like to stay in the spartan, more open Circuit House. The unintended consequence of her sybarite whim was a blessing to me in an otherwise god-forsaken place like Bijapur though it was the seat of a great kingdom once. Mrs Naik was extremely kind to me and she told me I was expected to take from her fridge upstairs anything anytime without fuss. Enthusiastically I complied. That is how I learnt that adding grapes to green salad improves the taste greatly. Bijapur, having a dry climate, grows a lot of grapes.

RA Naik made me write a Diary of two pages every day in an exercise book as to what I did each day and my opinions without holding back anything and put it up to him every Saturday. Invariably, it would come back to me Monday morning with his remarks, sometimes caustic, on the margin. This was a great experience for me because it made me do some serious observations with whatever department I was with and write a *précis* about it and what is more, my uninhibited views. This actually made me serious about day-to-day observations. His standing instructions were, whenever he went on tour I should accompany him. He had a sturdy 1956 Willys, 5-gear van and his driver Abdul Nabi will knock at my door that Collector-sab is going on tour next day. It so happened there would be a Divisional level meeting in Belgaum, three hours by road, every alternate month. Belgaum was the century old Divisional headquarters for the districts of Belgaum, Karwar, Dharwad and Bijapur. I would accompany the DC every time and would stay at the bachelor apartment of Bipul Bhattacharya who was AC, Belgaum and one year senior to me and Bharat my batch-mate who was probationer like me in Belgaum district. Also, sharing the apartment with them was PS Nagarajan KAS, a fine officer, who was the Municipal Commissioner of Belgaum. Much later, when I became DC & DM of Bangalore district in 1975, he would be my Special Deputy Commissioner and was an authority on land revenue laws, being an LL.M himself and a great help and friend to me.

Following the advice at the Academy, I had this habit of calling on senior officers like the DC, SP, Executive Engineer and District Health Officer of whichever district I visited even though I had no work with them. I had thus met Maharudriah, the elderly DC of Belgaum every time I was in Belgaum. He was a promoted-officer from the State

Cooperation Department and a very fine Lingayat gentleman who was extremely nice to me in the best Lingayat tradition of North Karnataka. This had led to an amusing aftermath. His probationer and my batch-mate Bharat was a polymath and polyglot, a learned, great linguist well-versed in six languages including Urdu and Persian and a quiet introvert. In fact, I met Maharudriah the DC during my visits there many times more than Bharat and he somehow came to think *I was his probationer!* Later, when I was posted to the Secretariat in Vidhana Soudha as Deputy Secretary, Planning Department, Maharudriah was Secretary, Development, Housing, Panchayats and Cooperation (DHPC), and whenever I had dropped into his spacious room which was next to my own cubicle, he would beam and introduce me to his visitors that I was earlier his probationer! Of course, being highly urbane (and highly modest, needless to say!), I would accept it with great grace without correcting him.

RA Naik had asked me to visit and study the Agriculture Research Farm at Hithanahalli village near Bijapur which was the oldest agricultural research station in the State. I spent a week there. It was there I learnt about Dry Farming practices such as Mulching, Soil Conservation, Graded Bunding, Black Cotton Soil properties, water logging and the like. The Scientist there told me that the British had established in the 1850s five Dry Farming Stations in India—at Rohtak in Punjab, Sholapur and Bijapur in the then Bombay Presidency, Raichur in Nizam's Dominion and Hagari in Bellary district of Madras Province. Then he asked me, do you notice, out of these five, three are now in Karnataka and Sholapur is only just across Bijapur's border? Thus, this area is the core of arid zone in India apart from Rajasthan. He told me that next to Rajasthan, Karnataka had the largest area under the Arid Zone. He also gave me the classic, *Dry Farming in India,* by Kanitkar and taught me about *Kharif* (SW monsoon) and *Rabi* (NW monsoon) crops, the traditional Indian farmers' reckoning of 15 fortnightly rains from May to November and many other useful matters. All this was totally new to me and would be of immense help in days to come. Because of RA Naik's insistence on a daily work-diary, I had to take copious notes of what I learned every day. Which is why what we become in our later life depends largely upon the accident of who our DC was when we are posted first as probationers.

MEXICAN WHEAT IN RAICHUR

After my probation in Bijapur, in my posting as Assistant Commissioner and SDM of Lingsugur in 1967-1969, I had opportunity to do a few things much more interesting than attaching tractors of Ministers. The 1960's was the first decade of Green Revolution in India. Norman Borlaug had developed high yielding, disease-resistant dwarf varieties of wheat by genetic mutation in the traditional wheat strains of Mexico. These were quite successful and almost the entire wheat area in Mexico was using these new wheat varieties such as *Sonora* and *Lerma Rojo*. Borlaug was awarded Nobel Peace Prize in 1970 for his contribution to control famine in Central America. In 1965, due to the efforts of MS Swaminathan of Indian Agricultural Research Institute, Pusa, New Delhi and the Union Agriculture Minister C Subramaniam, 100 kilograms of these dwarf wheat seeds were imported to India. After multiplication in the Pusa Institute, two varieties, *Lerma Rojo* and *Sonora* were received in Raichur also in 1967. My philosopher-DC Anagol took initiative to propagate them in the winter-wheat areas of Raichur district. I had the great opportunity to take part in this programme. Anagol had obtained from the US Embassy, a copy of Norman Borlaug's report, *Campaigns Against Hunger* which recorded how the new wheat was propagated in Mexico and he gave it to me after his reading. Such was the intensity of efforts of Anagol which had washed a little on me also. We selected Progressive farmers who planted them and the harvest was significantly higher than from the local varieties. However, the farmers even in those days had observed that the new wheat, when cooked, was not as tasty as the traditional varieties! In fact, as in wheat, new and improved Hybrid Jowar, Groundnut TMV-2 and Rice IR-8 and Taichung Native 2 were all planted as part of the Green Revolution efforts in Raichur district. While the harvest gave significantly higher yields, the general complaint was about the table quality, resulting in lower price per quintal though the yield and income was significantly higher. In course of time, as years went by, the weakness of Green Revolution strategy namely, soil damage due to high doses of chemical fertilizers and pesticides, would be known. But in the 1960s, it was quite exciting to be *green revolutionaries* and indeed it did increase the food production of India. But it was confined to the irrigated area such as Sindanoor taluk in my jurisdiction of three taluks. The dry farming areas of Karnataka did not benefit from it except for migration of landless labour to irrigated taluks.

BÈ-CHIRAG VILLAGES AND JAMABANDHI

There was relative prosperity in the irrigated villages in Sindhanoor taluk in my sub division visible in the form of motor-bikes, textile shops, "Hindu Military" Hotels (non-vegetarian without beef or pork), pharmacies and cinema theatres. But the state of the dry-farming villages had remained unchanged. Many from these rain-dependent villages had migrated to the irrigated areas for work. They had left behind their aged parents in their native villages. Many villages in the unirrigated taluks thus gave a deserted and depressed look. One of the annual Sacred Rituals in the Revenue Administration was called *Jamabandhi*. The system established in Mughal times has continued till 1970's. In 1773 when the Charters Act was passed by Britain and Warren Hastings was appointed as the first Governor General of India at Calcutta, he divided Bengal (including Bihar and Orissa) into six districts and appointed the first "Collectors" to collect land revenue and maintain law and order and retaining the Mughul Revenue framework at Taluk and village levels intact. Ever since, the Collectors and Sub-Collectors visited villages every year and finalized the collection of land revenue and settled land disputes and it was called *Jama-bandhi*. Increasingly, this system was being given up in practice when land revenue itself was abolished in an unwise post-independence political act of throwing the baby with bathwater.

But in 1967, it was still present in tradition-bound Raichur. There is a format for doing *Jamabandhi*. The Report for each taluk starts with the information of the number of total villages, then the number of Inhabited Villages and the Number of *Bēcharaq* villages. I learnt from my Tahsildar that *Bēcharaq* means Un-inhabited, but it was the corrupted form of *Bē-Chirag* or *"Without Light"*. There was no light in the dilapidated houses of these villages because there was no one living in these villages. Why? Because, I learnt, people have left due to floods, plague, cholera, severe famines or sacking by dacoits. Mainly people had left *en masse* because of loss of livelihood and in search of employment. In my sub-division I found about fifteen percent of villages had become *Bē-Chirag* with falling houses and the *Gramthana* or the original Village Site with snakes living in the abandoned huts. In that sense, Harappa-Mohanja-daro is also a *Bē-Chirag* urban settlement of some 40 centuries. Thus, I had in my jurisdiction both *Bē-Chirag* villages, declining old villages in dry-farming areas and new, big Village Settlements in irrigated areas as 'Camps' by Andhra Farmers emerging in a changing economy just before my eyes.

It struck me that villages without economic opportunities going out of existence and new villages or some big villages becoming towns is an inevitable phenomenon in economic development and ultimately villages will disappear. This was very different from the 'Gandhian Economics' of Self-sufficient Village Republics and *Gram Swaraj*, I had read but which now appeared to me as meaningless slogans. My economics background told me we cannot go back in history while rest of the hitherto poor countries are going forward. The interesting information escaping economists, both Gandhian and non-Gandhian, is the following:

POPULATION SIZE OF VILLAGES IN INDIA & KARNATAKA (2011)

Sl.#	TOTAL No VILLAGES	POPN < 200	200 to 500	500 to 1000	1000 to 2000	2000 to 5000	5000 to 10000	> 10000	TOTAL
			I	**N**	**D**	**I**	**A**		
								[Million Population in Brackets]	
	% 100	14	19	24	23	16	3	3	100
1	5,97,483	82,149	1,14,726	1,41,761	1,39,136	96,388	18,641	4,682	5,97,483
	(833.46)	(8.18)	(39.68)	(103.29)	(197.49)	(288.64)	(123.81)	(72.37)	(833.46)
	K	**A**	**R**	**N**	**A**	**T**	**A**	**K**	**A**
	% 100	11	19	26	24	16	3	0.6	100
2	27,397	3,137	5,296	7,039	6,492	4,433	836	164	
	(37.47)	(0.295)	(1.86)	(5.138)	(9.15)	(13.23)	(5.56)	(2.23)	(37.47)

Thus, in Karnataka 56% of the total villages, 15,472 out of 27,397, have population each less than 1,000. As the size of rural families is 4.5 persons (in 2011), these are small villages with less than 220 dwellings. As most of these small villages in Karnataka, which is the second most-arid state after Rajasthan, are also situated in dry-farming areas with low (600mm) and uncertain rainfall, the economic opportunities are also very few. It was Dr Ambedkar who exhorted the *dalits* in the villages to leave for towns and cities because they do not have lands which is the only asset in rural area and secondly, there is less social disability of untouchability and more anonymity in cities. According to Ambedkar, Indian villages are a *'sink of ignorance, superstition, poverty and diseases.'* It struck me that this was in sharp contrast to Mahatma's views who considered Villages to be idyllic Republics and India's salvation. For a student of economics who was also seeing the absolute rural poverty in un-irrigable taluks of Lingsugur and Kushtagi in my charge, I could not understand how these small, feudal, crumbling villages with no possibility of water for irrigation or even for drinking, could ever survive let alone achieve self-sufficiency. All over the world, in all the developed countries, the percentage of rural population depending upon agriculture was less than 10%. Even in China, the only country India should compare itself with for its large population, ancient civilization and historic Western domination, planned urbanization was taking place fast in the form of towns where educational and health facilities were being provided and "production brigades" and "production teams" were using bicycles extensively to reach farms after the collectivization of lands in

1949. As a college student I had read Pearl Buck's *The Good Earth* and Edgar Snow's *Red Star Over China,* both of which were sympathetic to China's problems which were the same as India's. Since 1949 China has developed 600 towns of a million population each and by 2030 one billion (60% of its population) was planned to live in urban area and only 400 million in rural area. In many of these towns housing colonies were already built, but people have not yet moved into them, earning the description "ghost towns" in the Western Press. But, since in China there is no gap between decision making and implementation, by 2030 China will become a 'moderately rich' urbanized economy.

In the 1960s, the policy directions from the then powerful Planning Commission was to provide a school building, a drinking water well and an approach road *to each village* and one Primary Health Centre in each Block under the Community Development Programme. But, on the ground I found that it was more practical and economical to construct and maintain a one 10-Room school building in a big village of 5,000 population instead of ten 1-Room school buildings in ten small villages. When I paid surprise visits to villages as we were asked to, the person most surprised was myself because there was no school teacher present there and, instead, an "outsourced" SSLC-failed boy, usually not much older than the students themselves, would be "teaching" five rows of classes 1 to 5, the first row facing the North wall, the second the South wall and so on. The problem was, no school teacher lived in the small village where her school was but lived in the taluk or district headquarters and would come by bus. But the KSRTC bus would reach the village only by noon and the last bus would leave at 3 pm in the economically backward Raichur district. From her salary of Rs.1,000 or so in 1960s, she found it was easy for her to find a SSLC-pass or failed village boy for Rs.100 a month to teach the students for her. The situation in 2020 is far worse. Every year about 5,000 primary schools are being *closed* in Karnataka when the number of students enrolled in the school falls below 10. And Karnataka faces a tragi-comic situation of having an "excess" of primary school permanent teachers than required! The starting pay of the school teacher in 2020 is Rs.20,000 per month. So, teacher absenteeism and informal outsourcing with proxy SSLC-failed boy teaching the students is rampant.

But, because of rural vote bank politics, we have continued with glorification of villages and neglecting any planned development of small towns. Except, in the natural course of economic forces, especially due to demand for jobs, rural youth have been moving to cities. 49% of Karnataka's urban population lives in Bangalore Metropolitan Region.

But our official policy is still glorification of villages from an un-examined Gandhian fetish. Come first of October I have witnessed the pathetic sight of leaders scrambling for *charakas* from Khadi Gramodyog to spin some yarn (pun intended) for a photo-op the next day. My theoretical ideas about the contrast between the Chinese path to development and India's choice of a mixed or a mixed-up economy got confirmation because of my visiting the villages in my sub-division, especially the declining villages in the dry-farming areas which had no future. I would visit China twice three decades later and would travel in rural areas widely and my views of 1960's about China's achievement vis a vis India's would only be strengthened especially its progress in nutrition, health and education which I would dwell in detail in later chapters. Suffice to say, I had a wonderful basic experience as probationer and Assistant Commissioner & Sub-Divisional Magistrate, thanks to RA Naik and Jayakumar Anagol and not forgetting Rani Basavarajeswaris tractors!

❖❖❖

CHAPTER 2

Earlier Days:
Ramayana, Rangoon University and Marx

If a person is not a Socialist in his Twenties, he has no Heart;
If he is still a Socialist in his Forties, he has no Head.

— *A Swedish Saying*

It is better to be headless than be heartless!

—*An addendum by the Reluctant Rebel!*

I was born in Rangoon, Burma in the middle of second world war. (no, I am not a refugee!) My father belonged to the Nattukkottai Nagarathar (Chettiar) caste of South India. According to *Dr.* Manu of Vedic times, they are a very small, close-knit Vysya Varna of professional money-lenders like the Jews. They provided agricultural credit to Burmese farmers. This has some history. The British annexed Burma in 1824 in the first Anglo-Burmese War when Assam was also ceded to India. The colonization was complete by 1884 when Britain won the Third Anglo-Burmese War and exiled the last Burmese King Thibaw Min to Ratnagiri in Maharashtra. The British has a penchant for such exiling. Napoleon was exiled in 1815 to St Helena in South Atlantic and was probably fed arsenic slowly. The last Moghul Emperor of India, Bahadur Shah Zafar was exiled to Rangoon in 1857 and even his grave was unmarked after his death in 1862 and the ground he was buried under was ploughed by bullocks! So much for Britain's cultural superiority! Eric Arthur Blair, more famously known by his pen name George Orwell who wrote *Animal Farm* and *1984,* served in Burma as an officer of the Imperial Police of Burma for five years based on which he wrote an early novel *Burmese Days.*

Burma is very rich in oil, tin, rubies, timber and rice. It has 20% of the area of India but only 4% of India's population. When it became part of British India, East India Company saw the opportunity to export rice and soon Burma became the biggest exporter of rice in the world. But there was no banking system and the few British banks such as the Chartered Bank and Lloyds Bank would not accept rural land as mortgage. Hence, the British encouraged the Nattukkottai Chettiars to extend agricultural credit. Tamil people have a long tradition of trading with South East Asian countries. From 5th century CE of early Chola and Pallava periods there are inscriptions of *Ainnutruvar Nagarathar* (Association of Five Hundred Nagarathar-merchants), who had traded with Burma, Thailand, Srivijaya Kingdom—today's Malaysia and Indonesia and Vietnam and East Coast of China. In Tamil, the word *"Nagarathar"* means "Persons of the City." There has been a close historical connection between South India and South East Asia. *Boopalan* (Protector of Lands) is the designation of the district officer in Indonesia which is a better job-title than the humdrum 'Deputy Commissioner' or 'Collector' in India. *Malai-ooru* (hill country) was the Tamil Name which later became *Malayu* and later *Malaya.*

Therefore, the money-lending tradition of the Nattukkottai Nagarathar community was obviously even earlier to British times. But, after legally abolishing Slavery in 1835 (Britain paid a compensation of £20 million—£17 *billion* in 2021, to 46,000 ex-slave owners but nothing to the families of 3.1 million ex-slaves transported by Britain to the Americas), the British substituted the system of Indentured Labour to work in the rubber plantations of Malaya and tea plantations of Ceylon in early 19th century. For this they employed Tamil *'Maistries'* known as *Kann-kanis* (literally "eye-see-ers" or Supervisors). To the indentured labour also, the money lenders were the Chettiars. It was thus that my father's great, great grand-father went to Burma with many other Chettiars and started money-lending in early 1900's. My father owned 5,000 acres of paddy land in the delta of Irrawaddy River by 1948 when Burma became independent under Aung San. But my father had never even seen the lands he owned! The *modus-operandi* was: The Burmese farmer is given a loan of *Kyats* (Rupees) 100 in 1930s (which in 2021 is worth Rs.3,500 at 4% inflation). The Burmese are a matrilineal society and men are not hardworking and given to drinking rice-liquor. So, at the end of the year he will not be able to return the principal of Rs.100. No problem, my father would say, take another loan and return next year when harvest is better. The default will continue for a few more years after which the mortgaged land will be redeemed in favour of my father under the colonial law and he becomes the owner of the land. But, my father allows the borrower to cultivate the land as a tenant who would get 50% of the harvest. So, the farmer becomes tenant on his own land. Owning 5,000 acres, my father was only a middle-level land lord. The Raja of Chettinad, who was knighted by the Queen, owned 20,000 acres. My father in law, incidentally, went to Malaya and did money-lending and became owner of a rubber plantation there. Thus the

Chettiar community have a long sea-faring tradition in South East Asia. Taking masons and priests, they built temples of South Indian architecture there and spread Sanskrit culture *sans* the caste system.

The war ended in 1945. One of my earliest hazy recollection is of Netaji Subhash Chandra Bose in uniform giving a speech in a school playground in *Kamayut,* a suburb of Rangoon where we lived. As soon as the war ended we came to India. My father used to move between Rangoon and India. I did my early primary schooling in St. Antony's School in Rangoon. As an only child my mother would not allow me to play with other children and so, books and magazines became my companions. The Tamil magazines, *Ambuli-mama* narrating Indian mythology was my favourite along with *Ananda Vikatan* and *Kumudam* though the latter were full of short stories and for grown-ups though. Thus my precocious, bookworm days started before I was ten years old.

A most interesting development took place in my childhood days in Rangoon. My father got for me a summarized version of *Kamba Ramayanam.* The Tamil Poet Kamban lived in 12th Century Chola kingdom. His Ramayana is not a translation of Valmiki Ramayana but a re-telling of *Ramavatharam* with differences in plot. It is an epic of 11,000 stanzas and 45,000 lines. The 16-page capsule booklet my father gave me contained, however, all the major events in Ramayana. But the most painful part was, I was woken up every morning at 5 am and read it aloud for one hour till I got it to learn by rote and repeat the entire booklet any time I was asked to in front of visitors. Though in rote learning one does not understand the meaning of what one is saying, yet, after some time, one starts to understand what the whole thing is all about. Thus I became a kind of child specialist in Ramayana despite the misery of getting up early. I also became a great admirer of Rama, Lakshmana and Hanuman who were always winning fights. The beautiful illustrations in the fortnightly *Ambuli-mama* stories on Hindu epics also helped.

But this happy faith got completely shattered in my SSLC year when I was fourteen. In the early 1950s, The *Dravidhar Kažhagam* (Dravidian Organization) was a radical movement of *Periyar* EV Ramaswamy Naicker, popularly known as 'Periyar EeVeRa'. A contemporary of the Mahatma, EeVeRa was a Congress leader in Madras Presidency and parted ways on the caste question of inter-dining with the Dalits which EeVeRa advocated and, strangely, the Mahatma objected. In protest, EeVeRa left Congress and joined the Justice Party followed by establishing the Self-Respect Movement. He was an iconoclast and had famously said, *"There is no god, and no god at all. He who created god was a fool, he who propagates god is a scoundrel and he who worships god is a barbarian."* He would agree to preside over the wedding ceremony of only inter-caste couples. He would charge Rs.100 for it, but a concessional rate of Rs.90 if the wedding is performed during *Rahu Kalam,* the inauspicious time of 90 minutes every day! Every year he would launch a new campaign. If it is breaking of *Pillayar* (Ganesha) idols this year, next year it would be cutting the *Poonul* of Brahmins (sacred thread worn by Brahmins from *Upanayanam,* the rite of passage ritual from childhood). It was amusing to see the DK volunteers in their trademark black shirt with scissors in hand chasing after poor Brahmins on the road and the police looking the other way. Such was the hold of EeVeRa on the lower bureaucracy and the poor in Tamil Nadu who were all from backward castes or *Shudras,* now OBCs. Till the 1920s when the Justice Party under EeVeRa formed the provincial government in Madras Presidency, 70% of all posts in government and in colleges were filled up with Brahmins though they were only 3% of the population. EeVeRa introduced reservation for the backward castes and the Dalits under his Justice Party Government which was a point of friction between him and the Mahatma apart from not encouraging inter-dining and EeVeRa ultimately parted ways. Had he continued with Congress Party he would have been the unquestioned leader and CM of Tamil Nadu.

EeVeRa's close younger colleague was CN Annadurai, the great orator. The latter and his younger associates separated from Periyar and formed the DMK (*Dravida Munnetra Kazhagam* or the Progressive Dravidian Organization) in 1949 when they failed to convince EeVeRa that DK should contest general elections as a political party while Periyar wanted DK to remain a Reformist Social Movement. That Periyar married his secretary thirty years younger to him came in handy as a convenient excuse for parting ways. One of DMK's earliest action as a cultural and political movement in the early 1950s carrying the mantle of Periyar, was to publish rationalist literature which included a rendition in rhetoric Tamil, Plato's Republic, Dialogues of Socrates and Aristotle, history of Greeks and Romans, writings of Voltaire, Rousseau, Charles Darwin, Marx, Bertrand Russell, American radical thinker Robert Ingersoll and their like. These books were under 80 pages each, summarized in simple and eloquent Tamil aimed at school students and the not highly educated adults and always priced at One rupee (Rs.33 in 2020). The DMK started as a Rationalist Social and Cultural movement following the *Periyar* and advocating agnosticism and anti-casteism to change the minds of Tamils, especially the younger generation right from school. So, these one-rupee books easily available in mobile vans near schools were a great hit. Some of us pooled our pocket money and bought the books and exchanged among us. It was thus, as a young boy, I could know in my own language what these great thinkers had said without having to read the original which I could not have understood any way. To my knowledge, no other political party in India then or since has done this except to some extent the Communist Party who also confine their publications to Marxist thinkers only. While you do not change your mind overnight after half-understanding Plato, Marx or Ingersoll, seeds of different, rebellious, *foreign* ideas are nevertheless sown in your mind to germinate slowly but surely.

In the final months of my SSLC, one event happened which shook my staunch faith in Ramayana. Periyar EeVeRa had the radical view that Ramayana had the roles wrongly reversed and that Ravana was the real *Deva* and Rama the *Asura*. The famous Madras Pachaiyappa college had arranged a debate between the renowned Tamil scholar Dr.Thae Po Meenakshi Sundaranar and Annadurai on Ramayana—whether the Tamils should revere it or burn it. The debate had ended in a stalemate but the arguments of both were published by the DMK as usual in a one-rupee book titled *Thēē Paravattum*, meaning "Let the Fire Spread." CNA's argument was that South Indians should discard Ramayana as it demeans and demonises Dravidians. It is worthwhile to give the crux of his incendiary argument. After Kaikeyi, the third wife, prevails over Dasaratha to make her son Bharata the King, Rama, Sita and Lakshmana start their journey to the forest for fourteen years of *Vanavasa*. They go south of Vindhya mountains and reach *Kishkindha* in the kingdom of Vali (or Bali, V and B being interchangeable in many languages like L and R) and his younger brother *Sugriva* and friend *Hanuman*. Geographically Kishkindha is on the banks of Tungabadra river, then known as Pampa Sara near Hampi. Ramayana describes it as inhabited by Vanaras ("Tail-Humans", in Tamil—*Vaal* = Tail, *Naran* = Human that is Vaal-Naran or Vanaran). Rama kills Vali in the brothers' dispute by shooting his arrow from behind, striking the back of Vali. To Vali's anguished question, why Rama the Deva kills him, who had no dispute with him, in a cowardly fashion from behind, Rama replies that Vali being a *Vanara*-monkey, according to Kshatriya code, an animal can be killed from any direction. CNA made two points: (1) Ramanyana says people living south of Vindhyas are not human but monkeys; (2) Being of inferior birth, South Indian monkey-people can be killed by superior people from North India in any manner. Besides this, CNA made other points: When approached by Ravana's sister Surpanaka, Lakshmana rebuffs her and also cuts off her nose and breasts. On the other hand, Ravana, keeping Sita as a prisoner after abducting her, seeks her approval to accept him and does not force her, a captive. CNA asked, *In this narration who is Asura and who is Deva?*

Again, Vibhishna, the younger brother of Ravana, changes sides, deserts his brother and joins hands with the enemy Rama and not only is he given the Kingdom of Lanka but is also made a "Chiranjeevi", blessed with eternal youth. CNA eloquently commented, Is this not encouraging immorality in Family and civic life? Again, in the end, after Sita returns with her sons Lava and Kusha to Ayodhya, one day when Rama goes *incognito* in the city to know what is going on in Ayodhya, he overhears a washer-man expressing doubts to his wife about Sita's fidelity and Rama's foolishness in taking her back with two kids born away from Ayodhya. Rama then banishes Sita out of Ayodhya and Sita in the end is taken back by Mother Earth. CNA asked, What are the values of Rama towards his wife and his sense of gender justice that he will simply banish her because of the loose-tongued blabber of an inebriate washer-man? And contrast this with Ravana's not forcing a woman in captivity. CNA concluded that Ramayana is an elaborate plot by the culturally inferior Aryans to enslave the Dravidians, who were the earlier inhabitants of urbanised Harappa and driven south. Delivered in the majestic, guttural alliterative rhetoric Tamil of CNA, the effect on young minds was devastating. Even in cold print it was incendiary. However, Faith does not yield to Reason so easily though seeds of strong doubt were sown in my mind about my convictions of Ramayana learned by rote as a child, like a frequently recurring pain from an embedded broken thorn tip in the palm. That booklet, *Thee Paravattum* (Let Fire Spread) was aptly titled because after reading it a rebellious fire would start smouldering in any young mind.

BURMA AND THE UNIVERSITY OF RANGOON

Then I was dealt with another blow. When I passed the SSLC examination in 1955 securing state's sixth rank and went to the Government College to join Intermediate Class, the then two year course before the graduate course, the clerk dismissed me unceremoniously from his presence saying that since I was "Under-Age" I cannot join the college and I can come next year! Crest-fallen, I learnt that the Madras University had a rule, probably even now it has, that a student should be at least of 14 years and 6 months of age to be admitted to college but I was only 14 years. So, as my education could not be continued for one year, my father asked my mother and me to return to Rangoon. There, I was put in the Burma Standard Commercial College, not a real academic college, to study type-writing, shorthand, Commercial English,

Commercial Law and Accountancy as this institution, not attached to the University and not awarding any degree, had no age-restrictions though I found all my co-students middle-aged! In retrospect, the one year I spent in the BSC College was of great value to me as, later next year when I joined the regular college, I could easily note down important points of the lecturers in short-hand, without missing anything, much to the incredulity of my class-mates. I could join the Rangoon University where Burmese language was not insisted upon as a subject but I could instead take Additional English. So, with my proficiency in commercial subjects, I joined the two-year Bachelor of Commerce graduate course. In the B Com graduate course, Economics was common to both Bachelor of Arts (Honours), and for B Com. The Rangoon University changed my life for ever.

DR.HLA MYINT, RENOWNED
WELFARE ECONOMIST AND RECTOR OF RU

The British established the Rangoon College in 1878 affiliated to the Calcutta University and in 1920 the autonomous Rangoon University was established. Burma was a Province of India till 1937. It is a deeply religious Buddhist country following Therawada School from Srilanka but also having many Hindu (Sanskrit) traditions and temples as many South East Asian countries. The monks known as *Phongyis* are highly revered and the monasteries teach all children including girls the three R's till they are ten years old. Because of this, over 90% of Burmese population including women is literate. The State does not interfere with the monks nor the monks with Government, except in the 2007 "Saffron Revolution" against the repressive measures of the military rule. In all cinema theatres it was compulsory for everyone to stand up when the national anthem was sung with the national flag fluttering on the screen, except for the monks who also go to cinema theatres but can remain seated! Also, the image of the Buddha cannot be shown on the screen and will be blacked out. Many Hindus go to the Pagodas and worship the Buddha and the monks bless them as they bless the Buddhists. The Buddhists in Asia have some affinity with Hindus as Buddha was not killed by Hindus inspite of Buddhism being a protest movement against Hinduism. This is to be contrasted with the Jews crucifying Yesu Christu of Nazareth and some deeply religious Catholics even admiring Hitler for the Holocaust.

The academic standard of the RU was very high and rigorous. While over 90% of the Burmese were literate, the pass percentage in the Matric (school final) was deliberately kept low, less than 10%. Of them, a small portion only was admitted to college which was practically free. The rest of the matric-passed students usually joined Technical Schools. This is unlike India where arranging high pass-percentage in SSLC, producing semi-literate youth for no purpose and more than half of them landing in colleges which ultimately produce unemployable graduates. Most other Asian countries follow the practice of maintaining high standards at matric level and starting many Technical Schools on German pattern, thus producing skilled young people who could be readily employed in non-farm sector. As a result, the standard in the collegiate education was very high in Burma. In the under-graduate years in the RU, if a student fails even in one subject in the first year with less than 40% marks, he will have to study one more year and write all the papers (including the subject in which he had failed and also those in which he had passed) thus delaying his graduation by one more year. Therefore, the students took the subjects and attendance very seriously. 'Notes' were prohibited and all had to read text-books only.

My main subjects were in Economics apart from the commerce subjects. The Rector of the RU was Prof Hla Myint who had studied and also taught in the London School of Economics and was a pioneer in Welfare Economics which was becoming important since the 1950s. I had the good fortune of the Rector himself taking classes for us. I graduated from the RU in 1962. Due to the OG-Brain *(OG is for Olive Green Uniform)* military administration humiliating him, Hla Myint returned to LSE within a year of the military take-over. He was pleasant, with glistening eyes, and always a smiling person who would explain complex economic issues in soft and elegant language which mesmerized us. He also emphasized the need for the developing countries (then called Backward Countries) providing universal health, education and public transport to all citizens by the State to be funded by high tax revenue. From the middle of 20th century many of the Western European countries and Japan had already started doing this. Germany was the first country to introduce unemployment benefit and old age pension to its citizens in 1927. High tax revenue and high public expenditure for universal education, health and public transport is the basis of Welfare Economics by which the State takes care of its citizens from cradle to grave. Hla Myint emphasized the need for the Government in Backward Countries to make free universal education and health available to all citizens because such investment in Human Capital is the surest way to develop with equity. He explained, a high and increasing population is not a weakness but a strength provided political decisions are taken to find resources for everyone's basic needs.

However, we did not realize that within one year, in 1962, General Ne Win would take over the government, not because he wanted to usurp the democratic government of U Nu but because political parties failed in governance by defections and bringing down the elected governments. In 1961 itself U Nu's democratically elected government could not function due to political defections and General Ne Win was *requested* to form an interim government for six months and hold general elections. This he did (as few other Military Generals would do) and U Nu was elected with resounding majority but, again failed within one year to manage a functioning government because of internal quarrels within his Anti-Fascist Peoples Freedom League (AFPFL) party. Because of imploding democracy General Ne Win had to take over the government again but this time permanently which continues for six decades now inspite of elections with one-fourths of seats in the Parliament being reserved for Army nomination. "Military Democracy" with elections as in Myanmar, Thailand, Pakistan and erstwhile Indonesia may be a new model in Asian developing countries. Unfortunately, under the military rule from 1962 Burma became an Autarky and a Closed Economy from which it is only now very slowly recovering. Hla Myint left Burma in 1962 for the London School of Economics again as his advice was never sought by the Burmese government though he became a world authority in Welfare Economics.

"MARX IS A DIFFICULT THING TO KILL"
–DR.RONALD FINDLAY, MY ECONOMICS LECTURER

But the person most influenced me in my college days was my Economics lecturer Dr Ronald Findlay. He was just six years older than me. He was of Anglo-Burman-Indian descent and after doing his BA Economics in RU, joined as Tutor, was sent to MIT for his PhD and returned to RU to be lecturer in 1959 when I had just joined the RU in 1960. For two years he taught us Development Economics, International Trade, Trade Cycles, Keynesian Economics and, very importantly, Marxian Analysis and also its Critique. Universities in the developed countries and in India and other developing countries which emulate the West, consider Marx a *Mlecha*, Untouchable and Marxian economic analysis as Taboo, Voodoo, Witchcraft, if not Satanic Verses. This is because most of the Universities in the West are funded by huge endowments and bequests from the rich and the super-rich—Andrew Carnegie, Cornelius Vanderbilt, Henry Ford, Andrew Mellon, JP Morgan, John D Rockefeller, Leland Stanford, James Buchanan Duke, et al who were all Robber Barons and financial criminals who built fortunes but in later age donated liberally to Education. The British-American slave trader Elihu Yale who became the head of Fort St George, Madras of the East India Company and who amassed wealth illegally (he was removed from President of Fort.St.George after 5 years in Madras) later gave large donation to the Connecticut College in the US after which the College became established as Yale University! The US University managements may profess to be free to teach everything but always stop just short of an objective Marxian analysis. In the US "Socialism" is a dirty, unpatriotic word as 'leper' was in England! This is not the case in Europe in institutions such as the London School of Economics (LSE), Oxford and Cambridge, Sorbonne and other European Universities. But Indian Universities and academia practice the American apartheid against Marx.

It was therefore a pleasant surprise to find the RU being managed by an academic council having its own independent endowments with no restrictions and with very few government representatives on its governing council. It had an open mind about different schools of thought and would leave it to the students to analyse the advantages and disadvantages of each. It was in this background that we could learn the pros and cons of Feudalism, Mercantilism, Capitalism, Keynesianism, neo-Keynesianism, Welfare-Economics and Socialism. It was not as if Hla Myint or Findlay were Marxists. All that they did was to tell about great thinkers in economic history such as Adam Smith, David Ricardo, Thomas Robert Malthus, Karl Marx, Alfred Marshall, Joan Robinson, John Maynard Keynes, Joseph Schumpeter, AC Pigou, the Physiocrats and many others and also a critical analysis on each.

My experience in Creative Accounting of making the legal 18% annual interest equal to the illegal 10% per month compound interest by falsely increasing the Principal had led me obsessively to anti-usury philosophy and to logical socialism even before I joined the RU. I could feel guilty of the injustice and how the Chettiar community cheated the Burmese farmers and could understand why the anti-Indian feeling of the Burmese was strong which originated against Chettiars. The derogatory term the Burmese used for all Indians was *Kalla*, like the pejorative *Gaijin* for foreigners in Japanese. We in India do not realize that none of the South East Asian countries has any traditionally tender feelings for India despite being Buddhist or having Indian-Sanskrit cultural roots even in truly secular Indonesia which was probably because of the sharp practices of early South Indian traders and money lenders and the insular, endogamous caste-culture of Indians.

Dr Findlay appealed immensely to my yearning to expand my horizons. Aided by the atmosphere of socialist fervour among most of the students, I took to reading Marx. The RU had a very good library. It encouraged the teaching staff and students to independent thinking. There was no system of "Notes" for students published by retired professors as in India and we were required to read textbooks and the original authors. Paul Samuelson's textbook (he was no admirer of Marx) on Economics was already popular and Findlay asked us to buy and keep it for life. Also, he advised us to understand the writings of famous thinkers of economics and referred us to Eric Roll's *A History of Economic Thought* and not to get lost in micro-analyses. Thanks to him I could read many of the thoughts of the classical thinkers not just in economics but in other subjects also. I was like a hungry elephant fallen into a lush sugarcane field. My earlier brush with the DMK's Re.1 books giving gist of great thinkers in my high school days also helped. I was struck by TS Eliot's *Little Gidding* in which he said, *We shall not cease from exploration; and the end of all our exploring will be to arrive where we started and know the place for the first time.* It was a pleasure to read at length in English the kernel of ideas I came across in Tamil and to understand them more.

The most exciting thing was searching for Marxian thought as the Economics textbooks do not treat it seriously and give only a passing reference, often derisory. But Findlay told us about various aspects of Marxian economics such as, Primitive Agriculture and Slavery system, Feudalism and its decline, rise of dynamic Capitalism, Labour Theory of Value, Surplus Value, Dialectical Materialism, Capital Accumulation, Trade Cycles and Recurring Crises, Reserve Army of the Unemployed, Pauperization of the Masses and Dictatorship of the Proletariat and its criticism. He emphasized that Marx was primarily a sociologist to start with. Having been banished from his native Germany and from Paris and Brussels for his revolutionary activities against the State, he lived in exile in England as a stateless person from 1849 till his death in 1883. He had famously said, *Philosophers have interpreted the world; the point is we have to change it!* By "we" he meant revolutionaries like him.

The *Communist Manifesto* which he together with Friedrich Engels published in 1848 is one of the very few documents which changed the history of the world. The RU Students Union sold it at a concessional rate and it consisted of just 34 pages. It is a remarkable document starting with the explosive statement *A Spectre is haunting Europe, the Spectre of Communism*, and ending with the clarion call, *Workers of the World Unite, You have Nothing to Lose but Your Chains!* It gives a sweep of history, class struggles, injustices and a hope for the future. It has undergone 2,200 editions and translated to 113 languages. I bought it and read it many times for its seminal thoughts and passionate language which was not lost even in translation to English from its original German and French. It opened up many irrepressible rebellious thoughts.

Materialistic Interpretation of History or Dialectical Materialism had a deep impact on me. Marx introduced an important element to Hegelian Dialectics namely, the Dialectical *Materialism* by which he explained: progress of history can be explained by changes in the Means of Production. From Pastoralism to Agriculture to Feudalism to Mercantilism to Capitalism to Socialism, it is the means of production—its methods and inventions, technology, devices—and the ownership of those means of production which explains progress in living standards and the relation among groups or Classes in society and its culture and indeed the march of history. From hunter-gatherers to stable agriculturists, from horse or bullock drawn ploughs to iron ploughs to drillers to tractors, from machines and factory system to assembly line production to artificial intelligence and so on in every aspect of life, it is a relentless march of technological and industrial development and who owns them which is the history of mankind. It is not battles won and lost that decide history in the long run. It is the progress from spears and bows to horse and plough and slaves in feudal age to coal, steam engine and factories in capitalism to welfare-state by high taxation of the rich to provide public health and education to all, to ultimately common state ownership to avoid exploitation by a few owners of Capital (machines, factories, assets) which is the crux of the term Materialist Interpretation of History. The most famous remark of Marx is, *"It is not the consciousness of men that determines their existence, but their social existence that determines their consciousness"*. It takes a few years to comprehend this and then also one may not fully understand it! Even its critics agree that while the Materialist Interpretation of History is not the only interpretation of history, it is nevertheless a seminal analysis.

Similarly, the Labour Theory of Value and Surplus Value are basic tenets of Marxism. The Labour Theory of Value (LTV) was not the invention of Marx but has long been in use since the time of Adam Smith and David Ricardo. In fact, Adam Smith is hailed as the Father of Market Economy though he had added many conditions and precautions such as Perfect Competition, Regulations and State as the Umpire. It was Adam Smith who gave the example: If it takes a person two days to hunt a beaver but only one day to kill a deer, then their 'exchange value' will be One Beaver equals Two Deers. In other words, the value of a product is derived from the labour time required to produce it. Marx only embellished the LTV further and derived Surplus Value from the LTV. The background to this is, in the ultimate analysis there is only one agency or 'Factor of Production' namely, Labour to produce an exchangeable commodity. The convention in Economic theory is that there are four factors of production namely, Land, Labour, Capital and Organization. Land includes all natural resources and Marx held (as also many classical economists, Rousseau and also the Bible) that Land is a Free Gift of Nature and therefore belongs to all and to all generations and there cannot be private ownership of land. For instance, John Stuart Mill of the Utilitarian School *(Largest Happiness of the Highest Number)* had said, *"No man made the land. It is the original inheritance of the whole species"*. Even according to the Old Testament (Leviticus), the Lord had said, *"The Land is Mine and you are but aliens and my tenants."* Capital is Tools and Machines and it is the result of combining Land and Labour and producing them. Organization or entrepreneurship is again only intellectual labour, owning capital and bringing finance and other skills together and organizing production and services and the society itself. Therefore, the only meaningful and indispensable factor making production possible is fundamentally labour and all value is created by labour. *[With Artificial Intelligence coming up, to a large extent repetitive and "unskilled" labour can be replaced with Robots though most economists still say that AI will not result in widespread unemployment. However, AI leading to new Haves and Have-nots, Digital Divides, New Imperialism, etc. are debatable. But this is in the new Millennium and was not in my 1960's college days, much less when Adam Smith, David Ricardo and Marx wrote their theories when Labour and Capital were all-important.]*

Price and Value are not identical. There is Surplus Value available to the capital owning class over and above the wages paid to the labour which created the product. One modern example given by Marxian economist Prof Richard Wolff is: the *Nike* running shoe made in the sweat-shops of Indonesia, Vietnam and Cambodia (there are no strict labour-laws in these countries) employing even child labour and for long hours is priced at $ 60 a pair but the wages paid to the workers (85% are women) to produce that pair of shoes was, in 2017, 20 US cents an hour and the work was for 8 to 10 hours a day for six days a week at a factory temperature of 90°C in tropical climate. In 2018 Nike's profit was over $ 15 billion while the direct labour cost was less than 10% of the total cost. So, the Surplus Value of the product made by the workers goes to Nike at Portland, USA in the form of design fees, financing, marketing and above all profits to be paid as dividend to shareholders and high salaries and bonus to Key Management Personnel. The salary disparity between the lowest and highest rungs in the US is 1 to 350. Contrary to popular belief that in developed countries most of the population holds shares, it is actually only 1% of the population which owns 65% of the *total value* of the shares and bonds. Professor Thomas Piketty's *Capital in the 21st Century* (2014) shows that income inequality and wealth ownership inequality between workers and the rich has been growing during the past few decades and Capitalism has become *Patrimonial* Capitalism in which most of the income is from inherited wealth and such income inequality under Capitalism is not an accident but is structural.

But, for me these would be learning in the future. Back in the RU baptism, I learned about conditions prevailing in Europe and in England in 19th Century of Charles Dickens with factories employing children in cotton and woollen mills under inhuman conditions and the poverty of the workers and the luxuries of the rich. Friedrich Engels, friend, collaborator and benefactor of Marx, was himself the owner of a textile mill in Manchester, having inherited it from his father and therefore he and Marx were aware of the working conditions of labour in England in 19th century. Also, Findlay told us as a very useful caution that in Economic theory there is this famous assumption referred to as *Ceteris Paribus* which is Latin for "Other things being Equal". To simplify a theory, economists usually use *ceteris paribus* so that only one or two variables are examined while keeping all other variables constant and not affecting the theory. This is rather unrealistic because in real life situations, there are many variables and every variable has an effect on other variables. For instance, economic theory says if bank's interest rate on loans is decreased, more loans will be sought and the economy will grow. This is not necessarily true because there are other factors— variables—such as raw material cost, changing technologies, changes in immigration laws, import-export policies, stock market speculations, epidemics, etc. all have effect on a firm's actual borrowing and not just the interest rate. In climatology, for instance, it is not easy to predict the weather accurately because there are too many variables and each variable can have an effect on *other variables* in real time so that *Ceteris Paribus* becomes meaningless. The popular saying is, a butterfly takes off in Beijing and there is hurricane in Florida. Findlay asked us to be aware of the complex, chaotic real life situations and not to be carried away by assumptions to simplify reality to reach elegant mathematical models.

"CAPITALISM WILL FAIL NOT DUE TO ECONOMIC REASONS BUT DUE TO CULTURAL REASONS"—JOSEPH SCHUMPETER

I also learnt about other thinkers who differed with Marxian analysis. One such important sociologist-economist was Joseph Schumpeter. His most popular book is *Capitalism, Socialism and Democracy,* the first line of which starts with the line, *"Can Capitalism survive? No, I do not think it can".* But his reasons were different from Marx's. Schumpeter said that due to innovations by Entrepreneurs and big businesses, Capitalism continuously renews itself by a *Gale of Creative Destruction.* New methods of production make previous methods obsolete and this process goes on. In his analysis, he distinguished Inventions from Innovations and pointed out that innovations go well beyond inventions as innovation also includes new ways of production, new products, and new forms of organization. Capitalism would eventually perish because of its own success, giving way to some form of public control or Socialism, not because of its failure as Marx predicted but because of its success. He explained, ultimately entrepreneurs will run out of innovations and motivation and they will be replaced by bureaucratic Managers and intellectuals. Automation and de-personalization takes root, capitalist motivation of saving for future generations comes to a halt, concept of Family and Private Property which evolved with stable Agriculture changes and discontent rises. Intellectuals and, contrary to Marx, not the Proletariat, become the voices of disenchantment. Thus Capitalism perishes not due to economic reasons as Marx predicted but due to cultural reasons, according to Schumpeter.

THE MACRO-ECONOMICS OF JOHN MAYNARD KEYNES

I learnt much about the Macro-Economics of Keynes. He was no Marxist but an ardent advocate of state intervention in times of economic crises and vehemently opposed the views of *laissez faire* economists that free market will solve by itself its economic crises. During the Great Depression of 1930s unemployment reached 25% in the developed economies. The concrete steps of government policies to save the economies from Economic Depression as advocated in his *magnum opus* "The General Theory of Employment, Interest and Money" were for increasing public expenditure manifold as the visible hand to lift the economy and not depending upon the Invisible Hand of free market advocates. In the US, followed by the western developed countries, the stock markets had crashed in 1929. Keynes said, *"It is generally agreed that casinos should, in the public interest, be inaccessible and expensive. And perhaps the same is true of Stock Exchanges".* Since the private Corporate sector was not able to employ labour and increase production inspite of factories lying idle, the reason being there was a slump in the purchasing power, the *Effective Demand*—demand backed by money purchasing power to buy and not just mere wish of the people to buy— the answer lies in Government stepping in and spend on public works and increase the purchasing power of the people which will trigger the demand for products which will enable the corporate sector to reopen factories and produce goods and services and employ more people. Keynes famously said, *The government should pay people to dig holes in the ground and then fill them up because this will put money in their pockets with which they will start buying things which will increase demand for products which the idle factories will start to produce.* The basic concepts of Keynesian macro-economics viz, Income (Y), Consumption (C), Saving (S) and Investment (I) and their inter-relationships was explained to us by Findlay with the simple example of "Robinson Crusoe" economy.

In Robinson Crusoe's island, when he shipwrecks and is alone (before Man-Friday joins), he has to catch fish with bare hands daily to survive. Assume he can catch four fish a day of 8 hours of fishing and consumes two for lunch and two for dinner. This happens every day with stagnant standard of living. After a few days, Crusoe reckons he can catch 8 fish a day (instead of just 4) if he can make a fishing net. But he has to devote say 2 hours a day for ten days to make a durable coir net in 20 hours. So, he fishes for six hours a day and catches 3 fish (instead of 8 hours and 4 four fish) and eats two fish for lunch and one fish for dinner *reducing* his consumption by one fish for dinner. At the end of tenth day he has the finished net and from 11th day he can catch 4 fish in half day of 4 hours. So, his consumption is restored to 4 fish and he has his afternoon of 4 hours free which he can use to construct a bamboo hut with thatched roof for shelter. So, his comforts as the asset of hut goes up with the same consumption level. So, if a country has to increase its standard of living, in macro-economic terms, it has to forego some part of present consumption and invest it in production of capital goods. Acquisition of the capital good (like Crusoe's fishing net) increases labour productivity of the country.

Thus the macro-economic theory explains how the economy works or should work better than micro-economic theory of a single firm and Utopian Invisible Hand. Findlay explained to us the rescue of capitalism from the Great Depression of 1930's by Keynesian policies of increasing public expenditure by government and how President Roosevelt's New Deal was all about the major program of public works by hiring more than 8.5 million workers who built 650,000 miles of highways and roads,

125,000 public buildings as well as bridges, reservoirs like the Hoover Dam, irrigation systems, parks, playgrounds and so on.

It is not only the Marxian Analysis and Keynesian Macro-economics that we were exposed to. Other streams of thought such as the role of Protestantism in Europe as explained by Max Weber's *The Protestant Ethics and the Spirit of Capitalism* and especially Richard Tawney's *Religion and the Rise of Capitalism* were explained to us. Findlay also cautioned us that the basic assumption in economic theory that people and firms behave in a rational way is not always true. He said that even Keynes had indicated that individuals and companies behave on many occasions in an irrational, exuberant manner (called 'Animal Spirit') which causes speculations in stock market resulting in booms and crashes.

THE GREAT DIVERGENCE BETWEEN WESTERN EUROPE AND INDIA, CHINA AND THE ISLAMIC COUNTRIES

We also had very interesting discussions as to why China, India and the Ottoman Empire of Turkey which had higher level of economic development in 15th and 16th centuries started stagnating and were overtaken by West European countries, mainly England, Holland, France, Italy and Germany since then. Even in Western Europe why was it England where Industrial Revolution occurred first and not in Germany, France, Portugal, Spain or Italy. There were various explanations: Discovery of Americas by Columbus in 1492, discovery of sea route via Cape of Good Hope by Vasco da Gama in 1498 enabling an alternative sea route to India and the Far East, Age of Exploration started by Ferdinand Magellan in 1519, Atlantic slave trade starting in early 16th century as a source of cheap labour to produce sugar and cotton, comparatively smaller populations in Western European countries and better governance, abundance and proximity to coal in England, invention of steam engine and spinning "mule", Dutch invention of Limited Liability Company system enabling merchants and mercantilism and capitalist factory system, need for new markets to sell leading to imperialism, the Protestant ethic of commitment to hard work and thrift, law protecting private property, keeping books of account by double entry system and enabling trust, the State maintaining law and order, above all a ruthless imperialist colonialism ensuring large markets for manufactured goods—these reasons for Western Europe diverging ahead and India and China being left behind, were all thought-provoking ideas.

ALL GOOD THINGS MUST COME TO AN END....
AND MAY BEGIN AGAIN

The years 1960 and 1961 which I spent in the Rangoon University's graduate course were my happiest and exciting times. My mental horizons and my world had expanded greatly in RU. I realized that it is not large amount of material possessions but a large knowledge that makes my mental world richer. In the final examination I came First Class First in the University and was awarded the U Pu Gold medal. I was told by the RU Administration that the Department of Economics can appoint me as Tutor and there was a chance I would be sent to the London School of Economics on condition that on my return I will serve in RU as Lecturer for at least five years. But there was one problem. I must become a citizen of Burma as the RU cannot offer employment to a foreign citizen on permanent basis. Had I accepted it my life and career would have been very different. My convocation award of degree was to be in 1961. But within six months General Ne Win took over the administration due to the democratic disintegration of the U Nu Government. I had no intention to become a Burmese citizen because I had by then, during my second year in the RU, met Madhavan, IFS of the Indian Embassy, Rangoon through my classmate Chidambaram who had earlier worked in the Indian Embassy for some time. It was this that changed my career and life. Madhavan told me, with my good grades I should write the competitive examination of UPSC for IAS and join government service where one could be of great service to the poor. The RU may welcome me with Burmese citizenship, employment in the RU and send me to LSE for higher studies, but my skin colour will still remain the same and I would never *look and think* as a Burman. In retrospect I find my decision was correct because within three years even Dr Findlay was disillusioned as he was not made Professor in the RU inspite of his MIT doctorate due to his Anglo-Burman-Indian origin and *looking* Indian. Race, skin colour and language are more basic than education which civilization cannot perhaps overcome.

I did not see Findlay again after my two years in RU. In the last class he took for us, he answered an oft-repeated question: With the mature industrialized economies as well as poorer developing economies not showing any signs of throwing capitalism out and embracing socialism, is not Marxism dead? He discussed with us that in developed economies the labour and the unemployed have not become paupers because of the advanced labour laws and welfare measures taken by the governments as insurance. In less developed countries there is no revolutionary political organization to bring about a revolution as it happened in Russia in 1917 or in China in 1949 or Cuba in 1959. But then even in developed economies the economic inequality keeps on growing and wealth gets concentrated in smaller and smaller number of people. Besides, because of the very nature of increasing competition to achieve higher and higher accumulation and profits, there are recurring crises in market economies which cannot be prevented. Because of globalization this would affect less developed economies also. The tendency towards accumulation, search for higher profits by any means, economic and social inequality and recurrence of crises were all predicted by Marx in the capitalist system. And Marx wrote for millennia and not for decades. *Marx is a difficult thing to kill,* was the last remark of Findlay to us. He was Professor in Columbia University for fifty years till 2021 when he died at eighty six. Dr Hla Myint died in Bangkok in 2017 at ninety seven. They were my greatest mentors and yet mortals. With melancholy, I recall the Sonnet of 17th century English poet John Dunne:

> Death be not proud, though some have called thee
> Mighty and dreadful, for, thou art not soe,
> For, those, whom thou think'st, thou dost overthrow,
> Die not, poore death, nor yet canst thou kill me.

❖❖❖

CHAPTER 3

Baptism in the Private Sector in Madras and My Passage to Bureaucracy

My convocation was delayed by about six months due to military takeover by General Ne Win. During this intervel, I happened to meet the biggest Indian auditor, Sitaraman who had as his clients many big Indian companies in Rangoon. He offered me a job as his assistant when he saw my credentials of having secured distinction in all the subjects and I joined his firm. This resulted in an unexpected benefit to me. Among his Indian clients, was the company of AM Murugappa Chettiar Group. When I told him I wanted to work in Madras for some time while preparing for the IAS examination he readily offered to recommend me to Murugappa Chettiar who was the Chairman of the AMM Group and was also his long-time friend. Thus I landed in Madras after six months with a letter to AMM, leaving Burma for ever.

The AMM Conglomerate was big group of companies, manufacturing steel tubes, bicycles, industrial abrasives, banking, real estate, etc. in India. It was not as big as the Tatas or Birlas but in South India it was a big company. Within days of my reaching Madras, I landed at AMM's residence in affluent *Santhome* area. AMM's bungalow was called *Chamundi House* and it had earlier belonged to the Maharaja of Mysore. After independence, most Maharajas ended as paupers and the industrialists were the new Maharajas. The Ministers were yet to join the club. It was a fine palatial building, opening to the Elliots Beach. The Manager of the establishment was in the out-house and, as soon as he saw the letter of Sitaraman he took it inside the house and within a few minutes, I was ushered to the presence of Murugappa Chettiar. He was about sixty years and slightly obese and dark in colour as most Chettiars. He was having his breakfast with his younger brother and his adopted son. He was very kind and told me to have breakfast with him. When I showed him my gold medal, which was now my constant companion, he was greatly impressed. Long story short, after enquiring me about my father and Sitaraman, he told his younger brother, who was the Managing Director of many of his companies, to take me in an executive position in one of the group companies. I thanked him profusely and took leave after a sumptuous Pongal and Idli breakfast. Arunachalam, his brother, asked me to meet him later in the day in his office on First Line Beach Road in Parry's corner, a landmark in Madras.

The name of the company I joined was TI&M Sales, that is, Tube Investments and Murugappa Sales which was the trading wing of all the manufacturing units of the Group, just like the Japanese organizations where every *Zaibatsu* like Mitsubishi or Nissan has a trading subsidiary. Next day Mr Arunachalam was not there but the General Manager of the company, one KNR Nair received me and told me that the MD had spoken to him and I would be the Billing Supervisor of the company! I took out my now inseparable gold medal for such occasions but Nair was not interested whether I had a gold, bronze or tin medal or no medal. He had received his instructions about me and that was that! He called the Chief Accountant and told him I would be the new Billing Supervisor at the Executive Assistant pay scale, next only to the Chief Accountant. He took me to his office and told me I will have to supervise the work of about ten clerks who were attending to the work of dispatching the steel tubes and bicycles and preparing the bills and watch timely payment and also sales tax matters. This was all quite new to me and very far from my academic achievements but I decided to learn life in real time. Thus began my employment with India's Corporate sector. I am narrating this in some detail just to show that in private sector, decision making is so quick and without much ado! The only protocol was what the top man wants! Because, after a month, when I went to office, on way to my desk I had to pass the cabin of KNR Nair and I found about ten well-dressed youngsters in the waiting room. I asked the Chief Accountant what was going on. He told me with a smirk that, according to the government rules, every vacancy had to be informed to the Employment Exchange who will send ten names for each post who will have to be interviewed for selection by the company. The waiting persons had come for the interview of the post to which I was already appointed! He laughed and told me, Don't worry, your job is safe, all these persons will be found unsuitable for the job and therefore, as conveniently permitted by the rules, the Management is free to appoint any one it chooses! This was all very intriguing for me to say the least.

My job was soul-killing and was very routine. It had nothing to do with all my academic excellence. But there were a few interesting experience for me. I was also in charge of the Sales Tax matters of the company in which capacity I had to see that the accounts for all sales were finalized and given to the Commercial Tax Officer who had to finalize the Sales Tax Assessment for each year. The Chief Accountant took me the first time to the CTO and introduced me to him. The CTO's office was dingy and it was my first experience with a government officer. He was polite enough and the assessment discussions went off well. But a few weeks later the CTO told me to inform the Chief Accountant to meet him. To my puzzled enquiry whether any further tax information is required he said, *No, everything is OK, just ask him to meet me!* When I told my Chief Accountant, he just laughed and told me, *Do you know why he wants me to meet him? He wants his 'mamool'!* That was the first time I heard about *'Mamool'* and he told me he will take care of it. Later he told me that a bribe of Rs.1,000 (current value Rs.20,000) was paid and he gave me the finalized assessment copy! I asked him why any such *'mamool'* is given when everything was alright with the accounts. He said this is the way it is done and you can't change the system! I asked him how this payment would be accounted for. He said it would be treated as 'entertainment expenditure' of the GM which is permissible on self-receipting!

My second experience was also very amusing. One day, my stenographer told me, next day he would be coming only in the afternoon as he had some work to attend to. I asked him why don't you take half day's casual leave to which he replied it is not his private work but official work. When I probed, he said he was asked by the GM to attend the Board meeting the next day. I asked whether he is taking down the proceedings of the Board meeting and he said, *No I am attending the Board meeting as Director!* I was shocked to know that my stenographer who was getting Rs.200 a month as salary was a Director of the Board of the Company. I was indeed learning how Capitalism works! I decided that I must start seriously preparing for the IAS examination and get out of the private sector job at the earliest.

PREPARING FOR THE IAS EXAMINATION

In Madras there was a great snob-value for the IAS, especially for the "Collector" more than for Secretary to Government or even Chief Secretary! Most Tamils in the districts had not heard of the Chief Secretary, but knew the Collector and treated him as demi-god! This was a long-held tradition. Fort St. George and the Madras *Black Town (George Town)* were established by the East India Company in 1644. In 1772 Warren Hastings, the Governor of East India Company devised the institution of Collector and District Magistrate, to start with in six districts of Bengal. The Madras Presidency also soon followed this system, the most famous Collector of the Presidency being Sir Thomas

Munro. The salary of the Collector of Burdwan, the biggest district in Bengal then was Rs 27,000 yearly which in 2020 was worth Rs 4 crore at 3% annual inflation! The starting salary of an ICS officer in a Madras sub-division in 1940 was Rs 500 a month which in those days was a fortune considering one Rupee had 16 *annas* and one *anna* had 12 *pies* till 1957 when the rupee was decimalized to 100 *naya paisas*. Prices were low. In an interesting photograph of one Café Madras in Bombay which celebrated its 75th Anniversary in 2015, it charged the 1940-price of 95 pies (rounded off to One Rupee!) for a full breakfast of 3 idlis, one upma and one filter coffee. This was in Bombay city with wartime inflation and in Madras sub-divisions in rural areas living cost was much lower! The Madras districts had Deputy Collectors, Tahsildars and Village Officers. The Tahsildar who was also the Taluk Magistrate was and continues to be a highly respected officer in Tamil Nadu. Even now in villages elderly people say, *Does he think he is a big man, is he doing Tahsildar job?* This was because the Tamils by tradition were a law-abiding people and before the institution of Collector in the 1770's, there was only the arbitrary enforcement of a mixture of Sharia law and customary unequal Hindu practices under the Arcot Nawab. Only when British system was introduced, there was orderly enforcement of clear-cut laws which the Collectors enforced strictly and without caste discrimination, except in the case of white people. The law abiding Tamil population therefore viewed the Collector, two levels above Tahsildar, as a local God even till the 1970's when the DMK-AIADMK Party rule alternating each other came to be established, politicising the post. In 1963 when I started preparing for the examination, my neighbours would speak to me with great respect as even "preparing for IAS" was a remarkable thing for the middle-class families in Madras then! When I walked from my house to the bus-stop, even strangers started greeting me profusely!

Selection by UPSC was strictly according to total marks from written papers and interview. The minimum qualification to write the examination was a Graduate degree. In the 1960s about 30,000 candidates wrote the examination of whom about 900 were short-listed according to merit and called for interview for fifteen central services including IFS and IAS. From this 900, about 15-20 were chosen for IFS and about 100-120 for the IAS in the joint merit-list. Another about 300 were chosen for allied central services such as the Police Service, Income Tax, Audit and Accounts, Customs, Ordnance, Railway Accounts, Defence Accounts Services, etc. So, altogether about 500 were selected out of the initial 30,000 which was less than 2%. One could write the examination between the age 22 to 24 and two attempts were allowed.

[This has vastly changed after 1979 because of the large number of aspirants. From 2000, about 6 lakhs actually write the "Preliminary, objective type of papers" of whom about 3,000 are selected for interview from whom about 1,000 are selected for appointment to the 25 civil services. Of this, still only about 120 are for the IAS. Thus the selection to the IAS, 120 from 550,000, is about 0.02% or one in 4,500 who write the examination. Also, while in earlier days graduates with humanities background were dominating, since 1980's more than three quarters of successful candidates are from Engineering, Mathematics and Science background, even medical doctors, where the brilliant can score over 90% compared to a humanities graduate, however brilliant he is, may not score more than 65%. It is therefore more like a lottery, though still based on academic merit, to get into the IAS. Most remarkably, despite the fallen standards across the board, UPSC is the only institution in India against which no corruption charge has been made in 70 years!]

Madhavan IFS had told me I should prepare for the examination for at least one year. His main subject in college was also Economic Theory. Thus began my preparation for the IAS. I had made a time table of fifteen months to prepare since I had to work and could read only after work. My office hours were 9 to 5 and I would be home by 6. I had a rigorous schedule of five hours study every day except Sunday. I had kept Sundays for seeing English movies and for going to the Marina beach for two hours in the evening and think about the various theories I had studied during the week. Sitting in the twilight and cool sea-air with the endless soft metronomic waves teasing my feet, I could think in the serenity of solitude and increasingly realized René Descartes' *Dubito, Ergo Cogito, Ergo Sum,* "I doubt, therefore I think, therefore I am". Dr Findlay had told us, *Reading should not become a substitute for thinking* and his advice has stuck ever since.

For the third Optional paper and the Second Advanced paper I had to study a new subject and I chose Political Thought as Economic History was relatable to it. I promptly became a member of the famous Connemara Library. This was established in 1896 by Lord Connemara who later became Governor of Madras. It was modelled after the British Museum Library in London. When the Haileybury College in England where the ICS officers recruited by the East India Company were trained, was closed after the Great Rebellion of 1857, all its books were transferred to the Connemara Library, Madras. It was one of the four national Depository Libraries in India to which all the publishers of books and journals in India should send one copy compulsorily. It had 600,000 volumes and the oldest book was a 1608 Bible. Though Lord Connemara was a profligate, I admired him because he had built the eponymous Library but for which I might not have got into the IAS. (After 1974 it has also an IAS Study Centre.) For me it was a highly busy two years with work and study. I did not tell anyone in my office about my preparing for the IAS mainly because in its Palakkad Brahmin-ridden atmosphere (about this amazing, malignant species quite a lot later !) no one was on my wave-length and keeping them at arm's length was prudent. In November 1964 I wrote the papers and I knew I had done well. The written examination results came out in January 1965 and I had made it!

THE DREADED I.A.S. INTERVIEW

"Why does the sun rise in the East, why not in the West? Square Root of 0.1, Pakistan, annexing Nepal, Gandhi, and the like"

The IAS interview in Delhi is supposedly the most dreaded part in the UPSC selection. I had never been to Delhi till then. I made some enquiries about hotels and got a single room reserved in Lodhi Hotel on Lodhi Road, South Delhi for one week at Rs.12 per night. (in 2020 it is Rs 15,000!) The interview was in Hyderabad House, about 5 km from my hotel. Being a careful person, one day earlier itself I had reconnaitred the Hyderabad House in the cold Delhi February morning and met some persons who came out of the interview. As it was an interesting interview, I give it below almost verbatim as I remember most of it. What I thought about each question but, prudently, did not venture to reply is also shown in italics as it may be amusing to the readers, most of whom would not have undergone this ordeal!

The Interview Board consisted of the Chairman of UPSC and four members and an outside expert. The normal time for each interview was about thirty minutes. It was a circular shaped table around which members sat and the candidate sits at the opposite end of the Chairman, in a chair similar to the members' chairs, though the candidate may feel it is an Electric Chair! If it is tea-time, the peon serves tea or coffee to the candidate also as for other members. The candidate is not expected to refuse it. I had researched from past records in Connemara Library that from 1949 till the late 1950s about one-thirds of the officers recruited were from Madras, but the single biggest group was from Delhi's St Stephens College (est.1881) who had affluent urban background. Among South Indians many were from the Madras Loyola College (est.1925). Most successful candidates were the children of bureaucrats, defence officers or judges. So, the candidates were socially adept and generally skilled in drawing room culture. A small number like me were not in this privileged group. Therefore, to start with, the kindly Chairman puts all the candidates at ease by asking them familiar questions about their native place, family background and academic qualification. In my case the half-hour interview went like this:

Chairman: I find you were born in Burma and graduated from Rangoon University. How is it you were born in Burma? *[His curiosity was because, out of the 4,000 or so IAS officers in 1965 (still only 6,500 in 2020), those with Burma background would be less than 10.]*

Myself (Reluctant Rebel—RR) : Sir, this was because my parents were in Burma.

Chairman: Why were they in Burma?

RR: My father belongs to Chettiar community whose forebears went to Burma as money lenders around 1900. *[Here I gave a long explanation of his money-lending, exorbitant interest, accumulation of mortgaged lands, my landing in RU and ultimately leaving Burma which was all listened to attentively by all members as seldom a person of such background came before the UPSC. Obviously they thought I was a refugee from Burma which impression I was not keen to correct for strategic reasons!]*

Chairman: You are now working as Building Supervisor?

RR: No sir, it is BILLING—B.I.L.L.I.N.G Supervisor. I am in charge of preparing and sending Invoices for supplies made to dealers all over India. I supervise the work of about ten clerks.

[The initial niceties being over, the real phase started. Under the sympathetic eye of the Chairman, one member started the grilling. Here was the first grenade!]

Member 1 : Why does the sun rise in the East? Why not in the West?

[Actually, this is not a simple question. It has a lot of history. Both Copernicus and Galileo had annoyed the Pope by their Heliocentric theory that Earth which, revolving around itself in 24 hours, is the reason for day and night; the Earth also rotates around the Sun in 365 days which is the reason for seasons. Both Copernicus and Galileo were considered heretics and punished. Even the question was wrong, the Sun does not "rise" in the East, it only "appears" to rise in the East and "sets" in the West. It does not rise or set for almost six months on the poles. But why ask a question from high school physics? But, I decided to be diplomatically factual without offending the Member!]

RR: Sir, the Earth revolves on its axis fully eastwards in 24 hours and this makes it appear as if the sun is rising in the East.

[I waxed eloquent about Earth's and Sun's movements, why it is almost six months darkness and six months twilight at poles and the progress of knowledge of astronomy since Ptolemy which knowledge of Physics by a mere Billing Supervisor duly impressed the querying member but bored others!]

[Then, out of nowhere a second member asked:]

Member 2: What is the square root of 16?

[What has the square root of 16 to do with anything? But then I realized that the "personality test" for IAS is to assess the alertness and reaction of the candidate, ostensibly to know how the officer will handle emergency, law and order situations quite efficiently, if only he could instantly tell the square root of 16!]

RR: Sir, the square root of 16 is 4.

Member 2: What is the square root of 4?

RR: Two.

Member 2: What is the square root of 1?

RR: It is 1, sir.

Member 2 : OK. Tell me the square root of 0.1?

[Beaming, he thought he had caught me. But then he did not know the training of Chettiar boys in mental arithmetic. My father used to mentally multiply fractions of 1/16 called **Veesam and Magani** *which goes upto 1/80 which is 0.0125. Surprisingly, Tamil has a word even for 1/320, known as* **"Mundiri"***! By writing the accounts of my father and listening to the conversations among Chettiars I also had some capacity for fractions, modestly speaking of course! Since I knew, by multiplying a fraction with the same fraction you get a bigger fraction, to get the square root of 0.1, I must multiply two bigger fractions. I did some quick mental gymnastics and knew it should be around 0.3 because the square of 0.3 (or 0.3*0.3) is 0.09, almost 0.1]*

RR: Sir, the square root of 0.1 should be around 0.3.

Member 2: *[Rather disappointed, but still he wouldn't leave me!]*

Tell me, the square root of 16 is 4, square root of 4 is 2 and the square root of 1 is 1. So, the square root of all these numbers are all less than the original number. Then why is the square root of 0.1 more than 0.1?

[He thought he was handing me the **coup de grâce.** *He did not know I was an Achilles Chettiar-boy with chromium-steel clad heels!]*

RR: Sir, when one fraction collides with another fraction, we get a bigger fraction. So, the square root of a fraction should be bigger than the fraction.

Member 2: *[Startled but still disappointed that I was holding up!]* "COLLIDING?" !

RR: *[The moment I said "colliding" I realized I used the wrong word, inspite of spending hours on Wren and Martin Grammar and History of English Rhetoric and Prosody.]* I am sorry sir. I meant "multiplied".

[Finally grumpy Member 2 gave up. Then Member3 took up the attack.]

Member 3: Why did Pakistan demand a separation from India?

RR: It was because of Religion.

Member 3: Just Religion? There was no other reason?

RR: *[I got a chance to show off my reading on the subject. So I carried on pedantically.]* Under Jinnah the Muslim League demanded a separate State for Muslim majority area. The Northwest India and East Bengal had different language, customs, food habits, dress, literature and the only thing common was Islam. So, West Pakistan and East Pakistan was demanded as a separate country. The All India Muslim League was formed mainly on communal lines and after 1935 it strongly demanded a separate state for Muslims in areas with Muslim majority. Under Jinnah's leadership, a Pakistan separated from India became a popular demand. The basis for this movement was religion because the demand was to establish an Islamic Republic of Pakistan.

Member 3 : Have you heard about the Two Nation Theory?

RR: *[The Two Nation Theory is not only for Hindus and Muslims in India but was applied to Britain and Ireland and small countries in Europe in the 19th century. In Political Science, a Nation is different from State. The State should have a Territory, a group of People, a Government and Sovereignty. A Nation on the other hand is a group of people having a common origin, language, literature, habits and* *religion. So within one State there can be two or more Nations; and across two states there can be one 'nation'. While One State-One Nation is applicable to most countries, it can be a disintegrating factor because of ethnic and religious conflicts. Accepting Nation-State is a slippery slope as India has the world's second largest Muslim population in the world, next only to Indonesia, and more than Pakistan or Bangladesh. The logical implication of accepting Nation-State theory is 'One-Nation, One-State' as Vinayak Damodar Savarkar and Madhav Sadhashiv Golwalkar wanted India to become one Hindu Rashtra and not the ideal of a secular Two-Nation-One State Republic. So I had to wriggle out of the troublesome, loaded question of Member3, Mr.Aga. My own reasoning has been, Organized Religion being the "Opiate" of the Masses as Marx had said, in a harmonious State religion and superstition will lose importance and economic development, equality, health and science education will reign supreme and the State will become a Welfare State. But this would be too much to tell Member3, as he may think I thought he was my student which was rather risky to say the least, though may not be totally wrong ! So I said briefly:*

I have read the Two-Nation Theory, sir. But accepting it will lead to the breaking of Indian Union as differences in Religion, Language, Literature, History, Ethnicity, Customs, Geography and Climate, Land-relationship differ widely among Indian states.

[Somehow this did not satisfy Member 3 much. Smugly I thought he knew less of political theory than I! But before he pursued this line of questioning, Member 4 intervened to my rescue, much to my relief.]

Member 4: You said a State can be formed on the basis of religion, like Pakistan. How about India and Nepal? Both have Hindu majorities. Can India therefore annex Nepal because both have same religion?

RR: *[My troubles were not going away!]* No sir. Because historically the British treated Afghanistan and Nepal as buffer states. Afghanistan as buffer against Russia in the Great Game and Nepal as buffer between India and Tibet against China. It will be an act of aggression to annex Nepal under any pretext or reason. India has many problems without adding on more territories.

Member 4: India went to war with Pakistan and there were casualties on both sides. Do you think Mahatma Gandhi with his principle of non-violence would have approved India going to war with Pakistan?

[There was a series of skirmishes between Indian and Pakistan forces since 1947.]

RR: Mahatma Gandhi's non-violence principle was not absolute. He said many things. He had also said about the Doctrine of the Sword. If the alternative to violence is cowardice then he said he would prefer violence. So, I do not think he would have any objection for India going to war with Pakistan to defend its territory.

Chairman:Thank you Mr.Subramaniam. *[Most people leave out the nice 'Bala' from my name, I do not know why !]*

Thus ended my interview which had lasted about 25 minutes. I got a feeling that I did not do that well, especially the Pakistan and Nepal portion. Anyway, I had not panicked and was fully in control of myself. The results were published in the papers in May 1966. I was selected. I had thought I would be within the first ten. But that was not to be. Out of the 110 persons selected I was in 51st position. The first was one Mr SAT Rizvi from UP whom I found later to be a highly cultured person. When I got the mark-sheet I found that I had scored only 45% in the interview. One of my colleagues from Karnataka had got 65% the same year. I asked him what was he asked. He said he does not remember everything except one member had asked him about the state of police investigations in Bangalore and he had replied, *Sir, the Police dogs are doing a better job!* This appeared to have caused some mirth among the canine-loving members since, also, there was no IPS member present! Another batchmate from Bangalore who was quite well-read and knowledgeable, however, got just 15%. A Kerala lady officer next year was asked by KPS Menon, who had retired from IFS by then, about the renowned poet of Kerala, Vallathol. The lady candidate fortunately knew the songs of the poet and so she actually sang one of his famous songs without any hesitation. The interview board was highly impressed by this musical performance and she was given 90% of 300 maximum! It is debatable how within 30 minutes, an interview board, however much its members may have experience in assessing officers, can award marks varying from 15% to 90% (which is 45 to 270 out of 300 marks for IAS) to chance questions like an exotic poet or police and dogs! It is for this reason it was suggested that the marks given should be within a range of say 40% to 60%. But this has not been done. The problem with giving abnormally high marks in the interview is that if the candidate is the son or daughter of a well-known bureaucrat, which is clearly seen from the candidate's application available to the interview board, the natural tendency is to give him a high percentage in the interview which will compensate for a lower percentage of marks in the written examination. I did not lose anything anyway because though my interview mark was only 45%, my written examination mark was 65%. But there is a basic imbalance about the interview marks. Some persons are articulate and have the gift of the gab. Some are introverts but have deep knowledge and commitment. In retrospect, my colleague who got 65% in the interview, later on had his house raided and escaped prosecution only because Bangarappa, the Chief Minister of Karnataka in 1996 asked the Vigilance Commission's DGP to file a "B" Report in the High Court. The other colleague with only 15% but was honest, an introvert and a polyglot retired honourably. So much for the dreaded Interview!

GOODBYE TO MADRAS

In due course I received a shabby, On India Government Service brown envelope from the Ministry of Home Affairs. I opened the shabby cover and found in it the letter informing me that the President of India (no less!) was pleased to appoint me to the Indian Administrative Service and I should report for duty on or before 6 July 1965 at the National Academy of Administration at Mussoorie. I must have read the letter a hundred times dreamily! *THE PRESIDENT OF INDIA! IS PLEASED TO APPOINT....ME....TO THE IAS!! INDEED!!!* Wasn't this good news! Thus, I had achieved my objective.

Next day I went to my office all smug. Wordlessly I showed the letter to the Chief Accountant who was a Palakkad Brahmin to see his surprise. But I was the one who was surprised because his face showed a mixture of shocked distress. Normally, any person would have congratulated a young co-employee as a reflex reaction if he had got through a once in a life time tough examination. But not this Palakkad Brahmin! So I told him gleefully that I would be submitting my resignation in a day or two. He said listlessly, Yes, Yes. So, I prepared a letter of resignation enclosing a copy of my appointment letter and took it to the Managing Director who was sitting in his new, swanky air-conditioned corner room. This MD, Murugappan was the adopted son of late AMM, who had given me a breakfast three years ago in his Santhome beach bungalow. He had obviously been informed about by getting into IAS by the Chief Accountant and so did not show any reaction either. More importantly, he too did not congratulate me. His only query was which state I was going to. Obviously he was well-informed of the IAS. I said I did not know as our state allotment would be known only after we join the Academy. Then he said a strange thing, *I hope you will not come to Madras State!* I could not but compare the generational difference between the patriarch AMM who had given me the job and *Idlis* and his adopted son who was annoyed that I got into the IAS (without his permission?) though joining the IAS was not common for Chettiar boys. I was only the second person from this money-lending community to get into the IAS. He was proof that money does not buy culture nor virtue.

The Chief Accountant had one more parting kick for me. There was a formality of an employee giving one month's notice to the management when he resigns or, in lieu of such notice, one month's pay. As it was the middle of June when I gave the resignation letter and I had to leave by end of the month, there was only fifteen days notice as pointed out by the Chief Accountant. So he informed me half month's pay would be deducted (instead of a farewell party) from my salary! But I was very pleasantly surprised when an Executive Assistant from the Sales Section who belonged to the *Mudaliar* community, which would be technically a Shudra or Other Backward Community (OBC), organized a send-off party in a nice restaurant at the Parry's Corner which was attended by fifty employees but not one from the Accounts Department which, as I had said, was infested with Palakkad Brahmins! They gave me a costly memento and hired a car to drop me at my home after the party. Thus ended my experience with Corporate Sector and Palakkad Brahmins. Anyway I thought so then!

Now, I realize that my animus towards Palakkad Brahmins (Pal-Brams) as a sub-caste of Brahmins on the basis a solitary experience with a Chief Accountant would appear rather paranoiac like anti-Semitism against the Jews. But from my later experience, this was not an isolated incident. I had a co-employee, also a Palakkad-Brahmin, working under the Chief Accountant directly. He was a well-educated person with whom I used to exchange pleasantries and even ideas, though even to him I had not divulged my preparing for the IAS. This was because getting into IAS was a lottery and if I ultimately did not make it, I would become the butt of jokes. But I got through and I showed the General Knowledge paper to this Palakkad person. Surprisingly, he too not only did not congratulate me but after glancing the three page question paper exclaimed, *Is that all, is it so easy to pass IAS?* It was obvious he was belittling my getting into the IAS. So, I told him, this was one paper and there were seven other papers plus an interview and in any case, there was no "passing" the examination, but it was getting higher in rank and in my year to come within the first 110 out of some 30,000 graduates competing, almost all of them being master-graduates and some even PhDs. There were also more such experiences after I got into service which I would narrate as my memoirs make progress. Suffice to say, the Palakkad-Brahmins, driven from Tamil Nadu to North Kerala when Mallik Gafoor invaded Tamil Nadu and after reaching Palakkad, were badly humiliated and discriminated against by the purest of the pure *Namboodiri Brahmins*, and not allowed to perform Pooja in the sanctum sanctorium and were forced to work mostly as lowly cooks to the *Nambbodiris*. Cooking they were allowed because, cooking by any other caste would pollute the Namboodiris and the migrants from Tamil Nadu were in any case Brahmins, so they could not pollute! So, the Palakkad-Brahmins had to necessarily develop a sharpened sense of persecution complex and adopt supreme survival tactics which expressed itself as extreme form of meticulous malevolence, measured misanthropy and monumental meanness towards the lower *Shudras* who were after all only one shade above the unseeable, unhearable, unapproachable and untouchable *Mlechas* and *Chandalas*, described by Dr Manu in 2,694 verses and enforced dutifully by dimwit No.2 *Kshatriya* caste for at least two millennia till recent decades. Dr Manu, the Original Sinner, had said, *inter alia:*

> *"Know that the relationship between a Brahmin ten years of age and a Ksatriya (who is) a hundred years old, is as that of a father to a son, but of these two, it is the Brahmin who is the father."—Manusmriti.*

Having achieved my goal, I happily left the scruffy Corporate Sector and sweaty Madras. I was 24 and it was time to start.

❖❖❖

CHAPTER 4

The National Academy of Administration: My First Experience in Karnataka Secretariat,

And Finding my Mentor, G.V.K. Rao—The Institution Builder

I spent one year of training at the Academy in the sylvan surroundings of the hill station Mussoorie. Horse riding and physical training was a must five days a week which I never cheated on. Some probationers would somehow reserve or bribe docile horses like *Chethak* with Jaggery and I would often be left with the huge black *Nisha* who would take malicious pleasure in stopping just before the 3½-foot hurdle launching me in the air over and across while she would give a triumphant horse-laugh! This happened to me five or six times but I never cringed and each time ran angrily in humiliation back to the horse to get on. Fortunately, I was not injured but one officer was injured severely and had to be hospitalized for weeks. My running back to Nisha to get on the saddle after the falls drew appreciation even from the rustic Nawal Singh, our Horse-Whisperer-Instructor who, some enterprising probationers made research and discovered, was born on a saddle! But, on the whole, life in Mussoorie Academy was an extension of college life. Except one probationer whose probation was terminated because he was found out writing anonymous letters slandering some other probationers. I was allotted to Mysore—the State was renamed Karnataka only in 1973.

After my exciting one year's practical training in Bijapur district and two years' eventful independent charge as Assistant Commissioner and Sub-Divisional Magistrate in Lingsugur sub-division in Raichur district, I got my promotion to senior scale in two years, in July 1969, exactly four years after joining the IAS. I was 28 years old. "Eventful" because inspite of attaching the tractors of the cabinet minister from Lingsugur (there is an obscure provision in the 1859 Code of Civil Procedure which we follow substantially to this day, that 'agricultural implements' cannot be attached for non-payment of loans and tractor can be interpreted as an agricultural implement by a silver-tongued lawyer), I came to no harm and I got my promotion as Deputy Secretary on time. My monthly salary doubled to a princely Rs1,200 (Rs16,000 in 2021 at 5% inflation!)

I was posted as Deputy Secretary in Planning Department. The Planning Secretary was the legendary GVK Rao who was also the Development Commissioner of the State which position was next only to the Chief Secretary and Revenue Commissioner in importance then and he also held the posts of Planning Secretary, Chairman of the State Planning Board and Agricultural Production Commissioner. Everyone called him GVK, except Kengal Hanumanthiah who was earlier the CM and who built Vidhana Soudha (and therefore duly dethroned in 1956 before occupying the CM's room in it), and GVK was his Secretary. Only he called him by his full name, *Gollahalli Venkata Krishna Rao!* I had not met GVK till my posting as his Deputy Secretary. I learnt that my philosopher-DC Jayakumar Anagol who was close to GVK, had recommended me a month earlier that I may be taken either in the Finance or Planning Department. GVK was a confidante of the then Finance Minister Ramakrishna Hegde and Veerendra Patil was the CM (to whose notice I had already come because of my VIP-tractor snatching skills!) So, I joined Planning Department and concurrently as Secretary of the Planning Board in the awe-inspiring Vidhana Soudha and met GVK for the first time. He was close to six feet, almost 200 pounds, had a very pleasing voice and a compelling presence. He was very pleasant to me and asked about my academic background and other personal information. He said Planning was the most important department in the government. It was indeed important in the aftermath of the successive Five Year Plans. He also told me that as Secretary to Kengal Hanumanthiah who was Chief Minister in the 1950's when Five Year Plans were launched and the States were asked to create a Planning Department, he prevailed over Hanumanthiah to keep Planning with CM and GVK also became concurrently the Planning Secretary in addition to being Secretary to CM. Since then whenever GVK moved to other departments, Planning migrated with him till in his present post of Development Commissioner and Planning was still with him. He told me, as Deputy Secretary of Planning and Secretary of the Planning Board, I was actually the Deputy Development Commissioner of the State and my work will be as important as that of Development Commissioner himself!

This was the most delightful part of GVK's man-management. He will boost the spirit of a younger colleague to Olympian heights. In fact, he would tell the Director of Weights and Measures that his is the most crucial job in the State and the same thing to the Director of the

Government Printing Press and Director of Translations all of whom would come calling on him with a lemon in hand which was the courtesy in the old Mysore tradition of Maharaja's government. (Lemon was also being given to mentally ill patients, some GVK-baiters said!) When I asked him what were my duties, he told a gem. *"You decide for yourselves. The whole development programmes of the state is in your hands. You do everything you can. Your capacity will be your limitation! Remember, it is the officer who makes the job, not the job the officer. "*Seldom have I come across such a job chart in any of my subsequent posts.

NATIONALIZATION OF BANKS AND THE ROLE OF PLANNING

A very important event in India's post-1947 history took place in Bangalore in July 1969 within one week of my joining the Planning Department. There was the all-important Congress Working Committee meeting in Bangalore. After the death of Pandit Nehru in 1964, the next most powerful person was Morarji Desai, the Finance Minister, who should have been the obvious choice as Prime Minister. But his mercurial, uncompromising, irascible and overly big-business-friendly trait in an ostensibly-socialistic philosophy of the Congress party had antagonized many MPs and especially the Congress President, the rustic Kamaraj. When he and his close associates who came to be known as the "Syndicate", consisting of Kamaraj, Atulya Ghosh of West Bengal, Nijalingappa of Mysore, SK Patil of Bombay, Biju Patnaik of Orissa and a few other senior congressmen felt that Morarji Desai will not toe their line, they chose the unimpressive, soft-spoken and humble Lal Bahadur Shastri as PM. But, when he unexpectedly died in Tashkent in January 1966, during the Peace talks with General Ayub Khan, the Syndicate under the influence of Kamaraj chose the most unlikely, junior Indira Gandhi, the Minister of Information as the PM, whom Ram Manohar Lohia had once unchivalrously described as *Goongi Gudiya*—Dumb Doll. However, as PM she proved anything but. In 1969 the Congress was becoming unpopular among people. Inflation in double-digits was sky-rocketing and India was dependent on Milo imports from the US under the Public Law-480, the millet given to pigs and poultry in the US. Politically, Mrs Gandhi was hemmed in by the Syndicate. In this background, election to the office of the President was to take place on 19 July 1969 and the Syndicate's candidate was the Lok Sabha Speaker, Neelam Sanjiva Reddy whom Mrs Gandhi despised.

There was the famous Congress Working Committee meeting in Bangalore's majestic Glass House (constructed in 1889 by John Cameron, the Superintendent of Botanical Gardens, Mysore, inspired by the Crystal Palace in London and also called Kew of India) in Lalbaug (equally historical, having been established in 1760 by Hyder Ali). The earlier candidate of Mrs Gandhi for President was Jagjivan Ram, famous for his acute amnesia to file income tax returns, while the Syndicate proposed Sanjiva Reddy. Mrs Gandhi proposed radical economic reforms which was given lukewarm endorsement by the Syndicate. The Home Minister Chavan who had promised support to Mrs Gandhi withdrew his support at the last moment. (Footloose, he would change side when Mrs Gandhi succeeded in defeating the Syndicate!) An enraged Mrs Gandhi took away the Finance portfolio from Morarji Desai on 16 July. She also asked VV Giri who was already the Vice President of India and also the Acting President because of President Zakir Hussein's death in May 1969, to file his nomination for President. Thus the battle lines were clearly drawn. There was an interesting story going on in Bangalore in those days. Jaffer Sheriff who used to be a multi-purpose low level attender, rather like a peon (it was said he used to carry the traditional 'hold-all' night bedding for the railway journeys of Nijalingappa!), was engaged to carry tea-coffee and hot *samosas* to the meetings of the Syndicate in Bangalore at Nijalingapp's house and so he knew all the plots of the Syndicate as in India the mute servants are considered invisible to the point of non-existence. But the shrewd Jaffer Sheriff had sharp eyes and even sharper ears and dutifully kept RK Dhawan, the Man Friday of Mrs Gandhi informed of all the plotting every night. He was duly rewarded for this Mir Jaffar act by being made Congress MP from Bangalore and later Union Railway Minister in Mrs Gandhi's cabinet. (Most of the time the Railways portfolio was reserved for Karnataka MPs!) On returning to Delhi, Mrs Gandhi asked PN Haksar the former IFS Officer who was her key adviser, to prepare immediately an ordinance to nationalize banks. Haksar was no economist and so he consulted Dr KN Raj, the renowned socialist economist about bank nationalization which he wholeheartedly supported. There was a draft legislation as early as 1963, after the economic downtrend following the 1962 Chinese invasion in North East, to nationalize six banks which was however kept in the shelf by the Finance Minister Morarji Desai. The Governor of RBI LK Jha ICS, met Mrs Gandhi with the spruced up draft next day and instead of six banks, fourteen banks were nationalized covering 70% of bank deposits. On 19 July 1969 Mrs Gandhi announced on the All India Radio the government's decision to nationalize major banks. This was the lightning speed with which bank nationalization took place.

It was a land mark event in the economic history of India. A new Banking Department was created in the Finance Ministry and Mrs

Gandhi held the Finance portfolio. The nationalized banks including the State Bank of India which was nationalized in 1955 itself, accounted for about 85% of the total bank deposits and bank credit. But almost all the loans were going to the Big Business. After nationalization, directions were given that 40% of all credit should be extended to the "Priority Sector" namely, Agriculture and Small Scale Industries. Till then Banking was mainly concentrated in urban areas. Henceforth, branches had to be opened in rural areas in large number. While this caused gloom and ultimately total obliteration of the Syndicate in the power struggle, it was a highly popular step among the masses who now believed banks' vaults would be opened to them for non-repayable loans!

When I opened the newspaper on 20 July 1969, a week after joining duty as Deputy Secretary, Planning Department, I was thrilled to read the screaming headlines announcing the nationalization of top 14 banks and the changing priority of lending. This was music to me because of its socialist content. France, under Charles de Gaulle's Provisional Government after the Second World War had nationalized the major banks and the biggest motor car company, Renault. (Later in 1982, Francóis Mitterand nationalized 19 more banks, the energy company Electritě de France and many other manufacturing industries.) In the Academy I had prepared in 1966 a paper for Economics Tutorial with the title *The Need for Nationalization of Banks in India,* much to the delight of our Economics Professor KN Bhattachrya (KNB). So I felt this was a great way to start my stint in the Planning Department. GVK used to come to office by 9.30am, a half hour early and leave promptly at 5pm. So, the next day I left home at 8.30, from my two-bedroomed independent house in Jayanagar 4th 'T' Block, rented for Rs.170 a month with ten months advance rent paid, filled my Standard Herald car with petrol at 72 paise per litre and covered the 8 kilometre distance to Vidhana Soudha in fifteen minutes in relaxed traffic. *(Those were the days!)* As soon as GVK arrived, I went to his room, wished him and told him excitedly, "Sir, banks are nationalized!". *"Yes, what a tragedy!"* was his reaction which totally deflated me. But I persisted, *"But sir, the Banks have deposits of Rs.5,000 crores which can be lent to assist the priority sectors of Agriculture, Animal Husbandry, Power, Water and Small Scale Industries to which 40% of the total bank credit should be extended, as the PM has announced. The Government can now control the Commanding Heights of the Economy."* I did not tell that the phrase was used by Vladimir Lenin because senior Bureaucracy did not want to have anything to do with KDs (Known Depredators!) like Lenin even though Planned Economy was very much a concept implemented by Soviet Union after the 1917 Revolution and Pandit Nehru was a great admirer of Central Planning and Prof PC

Mahalanobis had greatly contributed to the Soviet-style Second Five Year Plan of India 1956-1961 which after all laid the foundation of India's industrial economy which is not sufficiently acknowledged by India's *sarkari* intellectuals today.

"*Commanding Heights of the Economy,* is it? A good way to describe bank nationalization, I say," said GVK noting it in his pad. That day afternoon there was a meeting with the Finance Minister Ramakrishna Hegde about what Government can do with nationalized banks. Both Syndicate Bank and Canara Bank which were in the list of 14, had long been established in South Canara district of Mysore State. This was an important meeting where GVK dominated. He said, *We should now persuade the banks to lend liberally to the priority sector and even give some concrete projects to them. There should be close dialogue between the nationalized banks and the Government.* The term "Institutional Finance" was used by him which should be an addition to government's budget resources. He also introduced me to Ramakrishna Hegde and to other Secretaries present and said, "We have appointed Mr Balu as Deputy Secretary specially to liaison with the Banks", and I drew to my full 5' 4" and politely thanked, even though my appointment was made days earlier when government or GVK had no inkling of the bank nationalization. Then GVK clinched the discussion by saying, "We now have control of the *Commanding Heights of the Economy!*" The FM looked up and said, "I say, that is a good term, I must use it in in my speech in the Assembly," and noted it down! GVK beamed. I admired GVK's remarkable ideological progress within four hours and paid tribute to Lenin silently.

Thus, from "What a Tragedy", the bank nationalization, within hours, became a great state opportunity to GVK. This was his great strength. He never allowed his personal opinions come in the way of influencing government policy. After returning from the FM's meeting, he called me and gave elaborate instructions as to what I should do from then on. I must prepare a list of government schemes and projects to which banks can lend. I asked, how was I to do it? He said, 'Take the Budget document, go through department-wise and scheme-wise and wherever the schemes can be transferred to the State Public Sector Undertakings, prepare proposals for banks funding the PSUs because Banks cannot directly fund government departments. Then, meet the Chairmen of banks, give them a written Note and discuss with them and promise that government will fully support them'. "But sir, the Bank Chairmen are big and busy people, how will they agree to even meet me let alone discuss lending to PSUs with a junior officer like a Deputy Secretary?", I stammered. *Thō Thō Thō* (this was his favourite mild chiding, meaning *No, No, No,* his other catchphrase being *Chày, Chày, Chày,* though I never ventured to ask him what the difference was*), You are not a small Deputy Secretary. You are the Deputy Development Commissioner of the great Mysore state. You prepare the list of possible projects for Institutional Finance by banks, prepare D.O. letters from me* (demi-official letters which are personal letters in government's top protocol of correspondence in thick Bond paper letterhead with State's red logo and it can be quite impressive), *to the Chairmen of the banks and add a last para that I am sending my learned Deputy to explain the proposals and please discuss with him the projects along with your officers. And, don't forget to wear a suit when you meet them."* Now, seldom a government officer directly writes a personal letter to the Chairman of a Bank, much less almost commands him to discuss state projects with his Deputy. But GVK being a realist that he was, he quickly assessed the situation that any Chairman of a nationalized bank will greatly welcome a friendly approach from the Development Commissioner of the State for lending to the Priority Sector now being supervised by the new Ministry of Banking. GVK added that after sending the letters he will personally also speak to them that he is sending his Deputy for a meaningful dialogue. After a few days of my meeting the Chairmen of banks, he would also arrange for them to meet the Finance Minister in Vidhana Soudha.

For good measure, he also told me that I must go to Delhi and call on the Members of Planning Commission, go to Bombay and call on the Deputy Governors of the Reserve Bank of India dealing with the Priority Sectors and also the Chairman of the Agricultural Refinance and Development Corporation (ARDC), Bombay which was established in 1963 to refinance the commercial and cooperative banks to enable their funding the agriculture and allied sectors which later became NABARD—National Bank of Agriculture and Rural Development (though some cynics said it was *Not at All Bothered About Rural Development!)* Thoroughly dazed, I thanked him for the confidence he was reposing in me and took leave unsteadily. While closing the door he stopped me, "Oh, I forgot. Whenever I go to Delhi or anywhere else on tour, you should accompany me!" This was like my old times with RA Naik when I was his probationer. Only this was greatly alarming!

Thus began my three years' learning process under GVK. It was because of his unorthodox method of man-management, I could meet B Sivaraman ICS, Cabinet Secretary, Dr BN Minhas, Member, Planning Commission, Dr RK Hazari, Deputy Governor, RBI, TA Pai, Chairman, Syndicate Bank, KPJ Prabhu, Chairman, Canara Bank and many other celebrities. Inspite of the tight schedule of work during the post-bank nationalization in the Planning Department, when I came to know of a one-month's course on Economic Growth Models in the Institute of Economic Growth, Delhi, taught by Dr Sukhamoy Chakravorti of Delhi School of Economics (he was later made Member of Planning Commission), GVK readily agreed to spare me and I had a useful one month's training at the Institute. At the IEG, Dr TN Dhar who was said to be close to Mrs Gandhi gave regular lectures besides Sukhamoy Chakravorti and I had a lot of time to read at the library of the Delhi School of Economics which was close by. I could even read the methodology of the Second Five Year Plan which used the Input-Output Matrix, the Harrod-Domar Analysis and the like. It was a good learning experience, besides my long arguments with a fellow trainee from Assam who was a *bhakta* of Saibaba and after hearing my intensive blasphemy on godmen he stopped talking to me, much to my relief! I have been an admirer of Bertrand Russell and Richard Dawkins since my college days and had no respect for Sai Babas and similar God-peddlers.

GVK'S STYLE OF MANAGEMENT AND WHAT I LEARNT FROM HIM

"What has Asian Drama to do with Planning?", Finance Dept.

Gunnar Myrdal's *ASIAN DRAMA—An Inquiry into the Poverty of Nations* had just been published in 1968 and there was a book review of it in the *Economic and Political Weekly.* The book said that most Asian countries including India was a "soft state", that is, while the government makes radical welfare laws, it does not take hard decisions to implement them and the State therefore becomes "soft". I took it to GVK and showed him the EPW review. He liked the "soft state" concept and I suggested to him we should buy that book as it was a land mark in economic development of poor countries. He agreed and asked me to send a note to Finance Department for approval as the individual departments did not then have financial powers to buy books on their own beyond Rs.500 and *Asian Drama* (3 volumes) was costing Rs 1,000 even in 1969. So, I sent a brief note to the FD seeking sanction. After a few days the file came back to me with the note of the Under Secretary of FD which read: *Why is the Planning Department interested in Drama and that too in Asian Drama and that too three volumes, won't one volume do? It should be interested in Planning matters and not Dramas!"* So I wrote three pages of what the book was about and took it to Mr Mani Narayanaswamy, the Finance Secretary, who was a fine, suave and liberal person and got his approval. I also wrote a short skit about this, *"However, the FD May Please See",* which was published in the *Deccan Herald* for which I got a honorarium of Rs 100! That was my first earning by writing. GVK had a good laugh when I showed him the Under Secretary's objection and then he told me another gem: *Don't ask prior approval of government. Do it first and seek post-forgiveness! In government, it is better to commit a sin first and then seek redemption than to seek permission first which you will never get!"* I have followed his advice ever since and had never come to any grief.

As to getting *Asian Drama,* the biggest beneficiary was myself. I soaked in it for two months. But the problem was there was little junior bureaucrats like myself could do about its recommendations. Most of the action lay with taking hard policy decisions, passing laws and, more importantly, implementing them boldly. These were mostly in the hands of political leaders at the central level. Since Nobel Myrdal wrote *Asian Drama,* India has gone from Soft State to Jelly to Liquid to Gaseous state and may even wither away in a sense even Marx did not conceive.

'POVERTY IN INDIA' REPORT OF DANDEKAR AND RATH AND STUDY OF DISTRICT-WISE POVERTY LEVELS IN KARNATAKA

In 1971 the famous study of Poverty in India by Professor Vinayak Mahadeo Dandekar and Nilakantha Rath of Gokhale Institute of Politics and Economics of Poona was published which drew the attention to the gigantic poverty problem of India in quantified terms. For the first time it estimated that the 'Poverty Line' for India was the level of food consumption which would give at least 2,250 kcal per person per day and an alarming 54% of Indians were below this Poverty Line. GVK was of the opinion that poverty was not that bad in Karnataka which had a favourable land-man ratio. Being a person from the Old Mysore's 8 districts of the total 19 districts where, because of the benign government of the Maharajas of Mysore State for over two hundred years and able administration of Diwans like Sir M Visvesvaraya and Sir Mirza Ismail, there was no absolute poverty in the old-Mysore region. But GVK had also been the Divisional Commissioner of Belgaum and Gulbarga Divisions and poverty in the traditionally famine-affected districts of Bijapur, Bidar, Gulbarga, Raichur and Bellary was quite severe which he was aware of. Karnataka had a Bureau of Economics and Statistics for a long time which used to coordinate the National Sample Surveys and was bringing out Evaluation Studies of government periodically. I therefore suggested to GVK that the Bureau should take up a quick study of status of economic development in the districts and rank them. This would give the Poverty Index of different districts and special plan funds could be allocated to such districts.

GVK at first demurred because of the political implications of it. This was because when the States Reorganization on linguistic basis took place in 1956, three districts, Bidar, Gulbarga and Raichur with Kannada speaking majority from erstwhile Hyderabad state, four districts of Belgaum, Karwar, Dharwar and Bijapur from ex-Bombay Presidency, and South Canara and Bellary from ex-Madras Presidency integrated and formed the Mysore State. However, cultural and economic integration had not taken place and the Northern districts continued to refer themselves as Hyderabad-Karnataka and Bombay-Karnataka. Besides, the landed gentry's caste dominance which was with the Lingayat community following the great reformist Basavesvara in the Northern districts joining Karnataka and in contrast the Okkaliga community's dominance in the Old Mysore districts got reflected in political power balance. When the new integrated state came into existence in 1956, Kengal Hanumanthiah, an Okkaliga leader from Bangalore district was the Chief Minister after whom, from 1956 to 1971 the Chief Ministers of the State were Lingayat politicians. In the new State, the majority of MLAs were from Northern Karnataka. Since the old Mysore state was a compact area of eight districts with a benign Maharaja's government and efficient Dewans, these districts were economically more developed and, in contrast, the Northern districts, big in size and having larger population, were poorer. Hence, attempts to allocate funds on the basis of backwardness will be unwelcome to the politicians from the Southern districts. But, being a person given to social justice (and the then CM Veerendra Patil and FM Ramakrishna Hegde were from Northern Karnataka and were also impartial) the criteria of poverty as a guideline for plan schemes was accepted in principle. So, GVK agreed for a study of ranking districts in economic development by the Bureau of Economics and Statistics. But it took some time for actual plans to materialize.

GETTING THINGS DONE, GVK STYLE

GVK was a science graduate and a direct recruit to the Mysore Civil Service. The progressive feature of MCS was, Mysore's competitive examination was open to all citizens of India. That was how Mysore had many bright persons from other states entering MCS. GVK did not have any inhibitions about meeting senior Mandarins from North India in Delhi on equal terms. He used to go to Delhi for meetings once a month. Following his instructions, I would go to Delhi two days in advance with a list of important files pending in Central Secretariat, chase them and apprise him when he arrived at Karnataka Bhavan. But then a surprise!

If the file was with an Under-Secretary, GVK would drop into his room with me in tow. Now, in the protocol-obsessed Delhi, no Secretary to Government drops into any subordinate's room. So, the surprised Under Secretary would be overwhelmed at a tall, well-built, Development Commissioner of Union Secretary's rank from Bangalore dropping into his room and enquiring after his health. Nine out of GVK's ten such visits would bear fruit. I still remember his going to the room of SM Murshed, IAS, of West Bengal (the Press called him 'Comrade' Murshed because of his proximity to Jyoti Basu, but ultimately he fell out of favour in 1977 after a quarrel with the FM Ashok Mitra), who was Deputy Secretary in the Ministry of Rural Development, Delhi, in 1970. GVK complimented Murshed for his commitment to the programmes for poor people. Comrade Murshed went all soft and bleary-eyed, immediately ordered coffee and biscuits and GVK got all Karnataka files with him recommended! When I asked GVK why he made it a practice of calling on junior officers, he told me, "Look, that is the best way to get things done as they are the people normally prone to raise objections, so you soften them. Besides, the junior officers of today will be the senior officers tomorrow, so it is better to cultivate them. In Delhi more work will be done if you are nice with the junior officers as they will not raise objections on files!" This was one more advice I followed to the hilt in my career.

MANAGING DEVELOPMENT, BY PENCIL PLANNING!

The Third Five Year Plan (1961-1966) ended in shambles because of the 1962 India-China war and the 1966 war with Pakistan and also the severe drought in 1965. So, there was a Plan "Holiday" for three years from 1966 to 1968 and a new Fourth Five Year Plan (1969-1974) process started in 1969. GVK one day asked me to prepare a one-page table (brevity was his forté) showing each department's Third plan allocation and actual expenditure and one more column under the heading Fourth Plan and leave it blank and bring it to him. He also asked me to bring a pencil with me. Pencil? Puzzled, I said, "Sir I use a Cross ball point pen". He said, "Thō-thō-thō, we have to prepare first a Pencil Plan, bring a pencil." I have known Perspective Planning, Integrated Planning, Sectoral Planning, Annual Plan, Rolling Plan and the like but never a "Pencil Plan". However, this mystery was solved soon. The Planning Commission had given indication that Karnataka's Fourth Five Year Plan can be twice the size of its Third Five Year Plan. GVK took it for granted that we can prepare a Plan of 2½ times, keeping a cushion for bargaining. The total Plan size having thus been indicated, the next step was to put a figure in pencil for twice of what each department had actually spent during the Third plan. The balance amount was kept for new schemes, especially for irrigation and power. Within this criterion, GVK had some favourite departments and some not so liked. Industries department was one which GVK said can take care of itself in the private sector especially since the Industry Secretary, hailing from Gulbarga, Chandappa Patil, a Lingayat gentleman—a very nice person according to me—was however close to Veerendra Patil who was from the same district and was not caring much for the Planning Department as he had a hot line to the CM. So, GVK would give less plan allocation saying that industries could get bank funds. Thus, incredibly, the Fourth Five Year Plan for the State was prepared in thirty minutes indicating the plan allocation for each department *in pencil*. There was no elaborate theoretical analysis of Capital-Output Ratio, Input-Output Matrix, Marginal Rate of Substitution between Capital and Labour, macro-economic trends, anticipated inflation in sectors, etc. which Sukhamoy Chakravarty had painstakingly impressed upon us in the Institute of Economic Growth. Yet, in practice as long as each department was allocated about twice the earlier plan allocation, they were happy because none of the departments had any clue of Planning. It was all a wish-list of projects for them and what their ministers wanted them to include. There would be some bargaining from the heavy-weight departments, but in the end GVK mostly got his way through. But GVK always took care to see that Agriculture, Irrigation and Power, Rural Development and Social Welfare departments got their dues though at the expense of Education and Health, which was quite distressing to me, a student of Dr Hla Myint. I found that at the state level of bureaucracy and political leadership, Development meant Industries, Irrigation, Energy and Tourism and the basic needs of Education and Health took back seat unlike in China.

Being in Planning Department, I could understand the overall macro-issues of the state and also the ground level working of individual departments and their projects. The detailed Fifth Plan document had to be prepared quickly. I was given the task of preparing five chapters including the important Agriculture, Irrigation and Power. But as there were many chapters to be prepared, GVK required two more Deputy Secretaries and took it up with the FM Ramakrishna Hegde who was also the Planning Minister, and got posted two very senior officers, Mr Asvathanarayan of 1959 batch and Mr V.Krishnan of 1960. It was a great pleasure and learning experience for me to work with the urbane, pipe-smoking Mr Krishnan and the very, very hard-working Mr Asvathanarayan. In fact, Asvathnarayan never went home before 8pm.

But I always went home at 5.30pm, after ascertaining GVK's departure at 5pm, taking file boxes with me. Every day I had to pass by Asvathnarayan's room and would peep in to wish him good-night. One day when I dropped into his room at 5.30 as usual I found him packing up to leave. Surprised, I asked, Sir how come you are leaving so early, to which he replied, *I say I am on casual leave today!*

GVK'S CLASSIFICATION: "IS HE NUMBER 1 OR NUMBER 2?"

GVK had practical short-cut icons for complex matters. Often Veerendra Patil used to consult GVK about posting of IAS officers even though it was the domain of the General Administration Department of which the Chief Secretary was the head. But Mysore State, contrary to the tradition of having nice gentlemen as Chief Secretaries like PVR Rao ICS being the first CS after States' Reorganization in 1956 and later Balachandran ICS, RJ Rebello, *et al,* had an insufferable person of highly doubtful integrity, RN Vasudeva, during 1968-1971. It was corridor gossip that he had physically removed his affidavit from his file in the City Improvement Trust Board in which he had affirmed that he did not own a house-site already but which he actually did, while applying for another site from CITB so that he will not incriminate himself. So, the CM and some other ministers would often consult GVK informally for posting of 'good' IAS or KAS officers.

As I was also then the Secretary of the IAS Officers Association *(I used to brag, "There are 13 Secretaries in Vidhana Soudha, 12 of the Government Departments and one of the Association!"),* in which capacity I had come to know the increasing number of younger officers, because from 1964 batch onwards, Mysore started taking 6 to 10 direct recruit officers every year compared to 2 or 3 till then. GVK used to ask me about them, regarding their 'dynamism'. He used to ask me, *Is he No.1 or No.2?* When I asked, What is the difference, he told me, *No.1 refers to being a 'go-getter' officer with initiative, not much bothered about Rules but with heart in the right place while No.2 is one good in writing reports, following rules scrupulously and very obedient, expecting written orders before taking action.* I had read a theory of Empires by historian Arnold Toynbee that an empire gets established and prospers, after the first Conqueror (like Genghis Khan, Timur the Lame, Babur), is adventurous, invades and conquers a territory and its people, and after him, his successor stays within the territory and ensures justice and peace so that he consolidates the empire for a decade or two; and then the third generation successor can annex new territory like his grandfather and the fourth generation ruler again administers peace and trade and consolidates the established, larger empire. This is also known as 'Conquest, Consolidate, Conquest' cycle. While administration is not empire-building, the character of a leader as a builder is needed when a Department requires an expansion and a new era, in other words the No.1, and once this is achieved, there should be a period of consolidating the expanded activities by a calmer, scrupulously rules-following, peaceful No.2. It is not as if No.1 is better and No.2 is no good. Both are required depending upon the stage and need of the concerned department. While this may not be in the syllabus of any Management Institute, its ground-truth is indisputable. Though GVK probably had no theoretical knowledge of Toynbee's theory, he had an excellent practical knowledge of the needs of administration. Since then, I have always remembered his simple moniker-shortcut of being No.1 and No.2 for senior posts.

END OF A MEMORABLE PERIOD IN PLANNING DEPARTMENT

I worked for three excellent years of learning in the Planning Department under GVK. It is not possible to find a better boss than GVK. He believed totally in delegation and therefore found time to read and think. Many able administrators find no time for reading. But GVK found time for both reading and attending functions. At the same time he had full control of his department, which is not a contradiction in terms. For instance, when he told me on my very first day of work, "The objectives are given to you, it is your job to get things done. You are free to achieve your targets by whatever means you think is legal. Your capacity alone will be your limitation. Meet all the important leaders in Banking, Planning Commission, Reserve Bank of India, Universities, go to other states, by sending letters of reference from me signed. Tour ten days a month if necessary. *But once a week keep me informed what you are doing!"* His meetings will not drag on like most government meetings. He had a cardinal rule that none of his meetings will last for more than one hour and will tick off if anyone starts waxing long.

[To digress, this was in total contrast to another fine officer of the State whom I admired, Mr.Zafar Saifullah, topper of 1958 batch who also became Development Commissioner and finally the Cabinet Secretary, the only person from Muslim community, under PM Narashimha Rao. When Mr Saifullah said there is a meeting at 11 o'clock, you have to check whether it is 11 am or 11 pm! Usually, there will be four meetings, all delayed, going on in his chambers simultaneously, one around the main meeting table, the second around his smaller table, the third in his ante-room and sometimes the fourth a standing only meeting just inside the door of his chambers! While going to the airport to catch a plane departing at 6 pm, he will leave his chambers in Vidhana Soudha at 5.15

pm, ask somebody to walk with him the four minutes to the car to discuss an important matter, another officer waiting at the car door to get in and discuss another file till the airport, and from the airport entrance to the security gate his Personal Assistant would be chasing him for signing letters; and Mr Saifulla would be the last passenger jumping into the plane when the ladder was being towed away! He knew all the Indian Airlines' air-hostesses, of course! I was a great admirer of his hard work!]

Later, GVK became the Chief Secretary of the State after which he went to the Centre as Union Agriculture Secretary and, on his retirement, he was appointed as Member, Planning Commission. However, when Emergency was imposed in June 1975, Sanjay Gandhi who exercised extra-constitutional powers, removed him along with many other brilliant bureaucrats, especially from South India and West Bengal, because of his great administrative insight that South Indians were good for routine administration but, for dynamic situations, meaning gross illegalities, government required officers from Punjab! I used to meet GVK after his return from Delhi. He and Mrs GVK would insist that my wife and I should have lunch with them. His was an open house. He used to live in his own house near the Ashoka Pillar in Jayanagar First block. He had a simple life style. I met him last, one month before his passing away. In his last days he was having Parkinson. But he had the same warmth and sharp mind. In my last meeting with him he was reading *The Decline and Fall of the Roman Empire,* the six volume classic of Edward Gibbon and discussed with me some theories for the fall of Roman Empire. To my questioning glance why he was sitting in an angle facing the window, he told me, since he could not move freely, only from his angled chair position he could see the small temple across the street where the poojari would be doing the Pooja six times a day. When I took leave of him, he said contentedly, *I am happy, I am now ready to meet my Maker.* GVK was a great human being. I am proud I worked under him and that he was my mentor. Very few would get such a rare privilege.

❖❖❖

CHAPTER 5

In the Districts—Shimoga, as Deputy Commissioner and District Magistrate

The Job the IAS Officer Looks Forward to and later Looks Back Upon

The beautiful Shimoga district was my first district posting in 1971. I was quite happy at the posting as every direct recruit officer looks forward to this historically highly responsible post. The district posting is the most important early phase in an IAS Officer's career and it is what one looks forward to in early days and later in life what one looks back upon. My boss GVK told me that his district posting was also at Shimoga where the hill-region *(Malè Nadu)* people were quite knowledgeable, cultured and respectful to officers, though argumentative. He advised me to accept functions readily when institutions would approach the DC to be the chief guest. To my query, would it not take away my time from work, he told me that knowing people and their problems was the DC's work and what better way than to meet as many people as possible when they would present their problems in a gathering. Besides, the DC should be "visible" to the people in the district so that by word of mouth people would come to know that the DC is easily approachable and no "middle-man" was needed. *Learn from the politicians, how they maintain their public relations, how the MLAs were meeting people and the CM constantly which is necessary to maintain good relations, "Visibility" is the key,* he said. He also told me to tour as much as possible in the first few months itself instead of being desk-bound. Further, keep on smiling especially to politicians even if he is talking rubbish. You can say No with a smile which will not offend the politician and Yes with a frown which will still irritate him. Egos are critical and as long as you can tickle their egos your adversaries will be soft on you, he mused. With more such useful tips I took leave of him and proceeded to Shimoga.

THE INSTITUTION OF DC AND DISTRICT MAGISTRATE IN INDIA

The office of Deputy Commissioner & District Magistrate is unique to India, the like of which does not exist in any other country. This office never existed in England. It was created by Warren Hastings, the Governor of the East India Company in Bengal in 1772 to administer the *Dhiwani* right of collecting the revenue on behalf of the puppet Mughal Emperor Shah Alam after the Battle of Buxar in 1764 which, more than the Battle of Palashi (Plassey) in 1757, changed the history of India. The title "Collector" significantly indicated that his primary function was 'collecting' land revenue for the Company as Agent of the Moghul Emperor and that the Company was not the real *Ruler* of Bengal, maintaining the myth that the ruler was the Moghul Emperor while in reality he was only a pensioner getting Rs 12 lakhs annually from the Company (Rs 57 crores in 2020) In 1764 Bengal consisted of today's West Bengal, Bangladesh, Bihar, eastern UP and Orissa which was the largest and most prosperous territory in the sub-continent if not in the world. In 1800 Lord Wellesley, the successor to Warren Hastings, established a College at Fort William at Calcutta to train the Collector-recruits. In 1806 the East India College was established at Haileybury in England to train the newly selected civil servants of the Company. It was wound up in 1858, following the adoption of an open competitive examination by London's Kings College for recruitment to the Indian Covenanted Civil Service. The term "Indian Covenanted Civil Service" was abolished in 1887 as a result of the recommendation made by the Public Service Commission popularly known as the Aitchison Commission. Thus, the Indian Civil Service came into existence with the new name. All through these developments, the designation 'District Collector and District Magistrate' remained intact. The DC&DM combined powerful functions of land administration, collection of land revenue and all magisterial functions relating to public order. The only other office which comes close to this is the French *Prefect* system which was created in 1800 by Napoleon Bonaparte, who endowed it with great prestige and influence.

SHIMOGA

In 1971 Shimoga was one of the nineteen districts of Mysore State and it had 8 taluks, four in the Western Ghats (Hills) and four in the *Maidan*, the plains. About 44,000 km^2 or about 28% of Western Ghats lies in Karnataka and North-South it is about 267 km long. The western taluks of Shimoga called *Malénadu* receive high rainfall while the rainfall sharply declines towards the eastern *Maidan* taluks such as Honnali and

Channagiri in the same district which receive a rainfall of only 670mm annually. Thus I found, while Shimoga district was having over 7 *metres* of rainfall in the Western taluks, there was drought in the Eastern taluks when I took charge of the district. The biggest hydro-electric project in Karnataka, the Sharavathy Valley Project with 1,100 MW installed capacity of power harnessing the 900 feet high water fall at Gersoppa, called Jog Falls is in Shimoga.

As can be imagined, Shimoga district, especially the Malnad area, was a tropical paradise. In the winter of 1971 when I joined the district, the monsoon rains were over and the fields were all green with miles and miles of swaying green carpet of standing eye-cooling paddy crop and green-white areca nut gardens. There were ponds with clear water everywhere with pink, blue and white lotus flowers rising from floating dark green leaves on which droplets of water rolling free, like white pearls, reflecting sunlight and it was a sight one cannot forget. Two major rivers, the *Tunga* and *Bhadra* flow through Shimoga apart from Kali, Gangavathi and Sharavathi. Prominent men of letters and poets, KV Puttappa, GS Shivarudrappa, UR Ananthamurthy, KV Subbanna, MK Indira, Na D'Souza and Ha Ma Nayak hailed from this district. It has immense forest wealth, especially sandalwood trees and craftsmen who make intricate designs in sandalwood. It has the Mysore Paper Mills and Mysore Iron and Steel Co and Sandalwood Oil Factory, all started by Sir M Visvesvaraya the Diwan of Mysore from 1912-1919 and the Tungabadra Sugar Factory in the private sector. Altogether it was a prosperous district with nature's bounty. I am waxing eloquent about Shimoga because as my first district, like first love, it made indelible impressions on me.

I reached Shimoga city in my Standard Herald car and took charge the same day. Within an hour my Personal Assistant told me that the SP BN Garudachar, IPS, was on the phone. He welcomed me to the district and asked whether he can call on me whenever it is convenient to me. As I was alone since my wife had gone to Madras expecting our first child, I requested him to drop in at any time and he came immediately. The first meeting between the DC and the SP of the district is always an important matter. The informal protocol is, the SP phones up and calls on the new DC. But in course of time, because of the rivalry between the Indian Administrative Service and the Indian Police Service, some younger generation officers do not follow the protocol and if both officers are status-conscious, there develops a frost between them. But this was not the case with Garudachar who was a fine gentleman, more than a decade elder to me. In fact Shimoga was his last district as SP and he was going on promotion as Deputy Inspector General in a few months' time, while Shimoga was my first district and I was just 30. He could speak Tamil also as his ancestors were from Tamil Nadu and he put me at ease immediately. When he knew I had come alone, he immediately invited me to his house for an informal get together and invited the Executive Engineer, Bore Gowda and one or two district officers which was very nice of him.

My first pleasant experience in Shimoga was the Annual General Body Meeting of the Malnad Arecanut Marketing Cooperative, an organization of 2,000 areca-nut farmers of the district. The DC was the Chairman of the MAMCO. There was another such big Areca-nut Marketing Society in the neighbouring district of Karwar of which a leading farmer who was also an MLA was the Chairman. Ramakrishna Hegde who was the Finance Minister of the state and who hailed from Karwar district, wanted to expand his influence over Shimoga's Malnad landed gentry and wanted them to elect a non-official as Chairman of MAMCO. There were some farmers of MAMCO who supported the proposal while others wanted the DC to continue. The AGM was therefore stormy with both groups arguing their case. I offered to withdraw from the AGM so that they could have a free discussion which was however declined by both groups. Ultimately, the AGM overwhelmingly decided that the DC should continue to be the Chairman of MAMCO because the majority of members did not want the MAMCO to be riven by internal politics and a neutral, time-honoured DC with no political leanings was the best bet for MAMCO. In fact, at the end of the discussions, the small group which wanted a non-official to be the head of MAMCO even apologized to me saying, because of the insistence of the Finance Minister they had supported the proposal and they would be very happy with the DC as Chairman which was the case from the inception of MAMCO. This was an eye-opener for me. I learnt that farmers, left to themselves, could see through the political manoeuvre and decide what is good for them.

THE FIRST CASE I DECIDED—COFFEE PLANTER ENCROACHING FOREST LAND

Though Shimoga was not a major coffee producer, there were a few coffee plantations in Shimoga, bordering Chikmagalur district. The Deputy Commissioner had to hear cases of land disputes which was later transferred to the Mysore Revenue Appellate Tribunal. There was before me a case where one rich Coffee Planter of Shimoga, Shamê Gowda, had been cultivating coffee in 40 acres of government land which was earlier granted to twenty Scheduled Tribe persons who were prevented from occupying it by Shamê Gowda whose own coffee plantation was adjoining the granted land and he was forcibly cultivating coffee in the land granted to ST persons. The petitioners were poor and an advocate of Shimoga bar with CPM leaning had taken up their case *pro bono*. The best procedure in such disputes is to have a 'spot inspection' of the land concerned after giving due notice to all the parties. Therefore, I fixed a date for spot inspection of the disputed land and informed both parties and their advocates to be present. On that date there was a sizeable crowd at the land. The facts of the case were typical of what happens in rural India. After Coffee and Tea were popularized by the British in India, tea in the hilly areas of Assam at first, the Madras, Kerala and Mysore governments granted sizeable forest lands to British planters and their Indian successors expanded plantations, in most cases illegally occupying government Reserve Forest Land also. The coffee and tea plantation lands were all forests once. In most cases such unauthorized occupation by planters were regularized and many cases were under process of regularization. In a few cases, some government lands on the margin of existing plantations were granted to landless persons at 2 acres per family as in this case. But most of these lands granted to the landless were under the illegal occupation of the big planters. The Tahsildar instead of recovering the illegally occupied land and put the twenty landless persons in possession, did not take any action and had allowed the planter to continue. It was this matter which was petitioned before me. The twenty grantees had pursued their case with the Revenue Department officials and had kept their claim alive by paying the concessional grant price fixed for them. It was therefore a clear case of the landless being deprived of their rights by the powerful planter. After hearing the case and after spot inspection, I passed a detailed order holding the continued occupation of the land by the planter as illegal and directed the Tahsildar to restore the land to the tribal grantees with the customary condition that the ST grantees cannot alienate the land before expiry of fifteen years. The planter was rich, belonging to old landed gentry of Malnad Gowda community and also a supporter of the ruling Congress party. My order therefore created a flutter among the community and the legal profession of Shimoga. The planter promptly appealed against my order to the Divisional Commissioner at Bangalore, who belonged to the same Okkaliga community as the planter, gave a stay order. When the advocate for the tribal grantees met me with the stay order, I advised him to file a Writ Petition in the High Court. But the HC did not admit it on the ground that the petitioners should exhaust their legal remedy available to them, namely the appeal pending before the Divisional Commissioner. This was a very early reminder to me that under the Anglo-Saxon Adversarial System of Justice which India adopted from the British, the rights of the weak will not be protected against the claims of the rich and powerful. Of course, the Divisional Commissioner did not hear the case till I was transferred from Shimoga by end of 1972. Much later I learned that the STs failed to get the land.

ILLEGAL SMUGGLING OF ROSEWOOD FROM "MRUGAVADE FOREST" IN THIRTHAHALLI

My next important experience was the case of illegal felling of rosewood in a state reserve forest in Thirthahalli taluk where Tunga river flows. One morning, a few village panchayat members from Mrugavadhe village in Thirthahalli taluk came to my office. Mrugavadhe is deep in the Malnad reserve forest, about sixty kilometres from Shimoga. According to legend, Lord Rama killed the Golden Deer in this forest and hence the name (Mruga for deer and Vadhè for killing). The VP members' complaint was that a forest contractor, George, from Kerala was cutting valuable rosewood trees in the Mrugavadhe forest illegally and transporting to Bangalore. And this was being done with the connivance of all the officials of the Forest Department. Therefore, the Village Panchayat decided to meet the DC. This is what I further gathered from them: In Malnad and in Mrugavadhe area moist deciduous forests cover almost three-fourths of the land. Paddy is the main food crop grown in valleys. Traditionally, the farmers are allowed to collect the leaves in the forest as green manure for their fields, fallen dry branches, honey, wild pepper, non-wood produce and other fallen forest produce without any payment. This is called "usufructuary rights" by the Forest Department which essentially means no right over the trees but only certain customary permission to use its waste-produce. Such rights are also not given in all Reserve Forest area but only those forests adjoining the villages. These are called "Malnad Kan" and considered to be sacred by the village community, each kan having its own deity. Cutting the tree is a taboo and crime against the Deity. But, when coffee was introduced in Malnad, some of these Kans close to the villages came to be under the jurisdiction of Tahsildars. They allotted the marginal Kans for supporting coffee cultivation and came to be called "Hiduvali" Kans, Hiduvali meaning 'under cultivation'. But even in Hiduvali Kans cutting the trees was not permitted as coffee plant requires shade to grow under diffused light. The Kans which were not so given continued to be called Sarkari Kans distinguishing from Hiduvali Kans. According to the

VP members who met me, the Mrugavadhe Forest was not even a Kan but a regular Reserve Forest according to the Forest Department maps. But the village *Patwari* (Village Accountant) of the Revenue Department had suddenly a year ago mentioned in the Land Record—RTC—Record of Rights, Tenancy and Cultivation—as "*Hiduvali* Kan", in the column 'Status of Land' and *entered his own name*. Under this pretext, he permitted the forest contractor to cut the Rosewood Trees standing in twenty acres of land. The Contractor George was doing work for the Forest Department in the neighbouring Chikmagalur district and he had for the past few weeks been cutting down the trees in Mrugavadhe forest and transporting the trunks by trucks. If I go with them immediately they could take me to the actual spot where the rosewood was being loaded.

I readily agreed to go with them and telephoned the Divisional Forest Officer (DF0) in whose jurisdiction Thirthahalli taluk and Mrugavadhe forest were situated, one Ataullah Khan, IFS. Shimoga district having over half of its area under moist deciduous forests, there were three Divisional Forest Officers at Shimoga, Bhadravathi and Sagar. Thirthahalli came under Shimoga Division but as the DFO of Shimoga was on leave, the DFO of Bhadravathi was in additional charge for over a month. So, when I told him that I was proceeding to Mrugavadhe forest and requested him to accompany me, he stalled and said he had to get a report from his subordinate officers which will take time. I told him to suit himself and left with the VP members. It took about an hour and a half to reach the Mrugavadhe village. From there I had to take the jeep of the Block Development Officer and accompanied by the VP members reached the banks of the river. The forest was on the other bank. As the monsoon was long over, the river did not have much water and the VP members took me to a spot where we could walk through the river with only knee-deep water.

When we reached the spot in the afternoon, I saw a few lorries were ready to leave and Contractor George himself standing by them. At the advice of the VP members I had taken with me the Circle Inspector from Thirthahalli. The contractor was quite shocked to see the sudden emergence of the DC with the police, Tahsildar, VP members and many villagers who had by then reached the spot. I checked with the five-year bound-records of RTC forms and found that the Status of the Kan was shown as Hiduvali only for the past two years and prior to that it was shown as "Sarkari kan". In the absence of any grant, it was crystal clear that the entries were illegally written by the Patwari. By this time, the DFO also prudentially reached the spot. So I asked him how the Forest

Transport Permit was given to cut and transport rosewood trees from the forest. He had no answer except that he went by the Revenue Department's record showing it was a Hiduwali Kan. It was clear that instead of protecting the forests he was helping the smugglers to destroy it. It was a 10 ton lorry but carrying 15 tons of timber and even allowing for a high 50% wastage, the rosewood was Rs 4 to Rs 5 crore worth, according to the VP members. And this was his third lorry under the permit for ten lorry loads.

I therefore decided to confiscate the rosewood and the lorry under the powers of the Deputy Commissioner as provided in the Land Revenue Act. The LR Act is a powerful Law coming from ancient days. The legal provision in the LR Act is, any produce illegally removed from a government land can be confiscated including the vehicle removing it. Since forest land was government land, the LR Act will certainly apply in this case. Much to the delight of the villagers of Mrugavadhe and the Taluk Development Board members of Thirthahalli (In 1972 we had the TDBs at the Taluk level and the District Development Council at the District level of which the DC was the Chairman, the Zilla Panchayat with elected officials not having come into force till 1993), I passed a detailed order the very next day. I also sent a report of what had taken place to the Secretary of Agriculture and Forest Department, Bangalore, who was coincidentally Mr RA Naik, my old disciplinarian DC of Bijapur whose probationer I was. He sent it immediately to the Minister of Forest who was KH Patil from Dharwad district and a person known for quick decisions. The DFO was immediately kept under suspension and an enquiry was ordered. He was later sent to Bidar district which was a far cry from the lush green Shimoga district and where it was difficult to find a tree to take shelter under if your vehicle broke down. Criminal cases were also launched against the contractor.

SMUGGLING OF SANDALWOOD IN CHANDRAKAL FOREST IN SHIKARIPUR TALUK

News travels fast in the district, especially when the DC confiscates smuggler's lorries at the initiative of Village Panchayat. By this time the elections to Karnataka State Assembly had taken place in March 1972 and the Indian National Congress headed by Indira Gandhi had an overwhelming majority of 165 seats won compared with only 24 won by Congress-O headed by the Syndicate of Nijalingappa, Veerendra Patil and Ramakrishna Hegde. There were 9 MLAs from Shimoga district of whom 6 were of Congress (I) and, remarkably, the other 3 from Lohia Socialist Party of the late selfless Shanthaveri Gopala Gowda of

Thirthahally. The Malnad constituencies of Sagar, Soraba and Thirthahally elected the three Socialist MLAs of the State. Bangarappa who was an advocate of Shimoga bar and who used to appear before me in some tenancy cases (always unprepared and asking for adjournments) was elected from Soraba taluk. (He would become the Chief Minister in 1990 and would be a disaster to the state. About him a lot, later.) There was thus an almost clear divide between the Malnad political atmosphere and *Maidan* (Plains) taluks.

The DC's anti-smuggling, pro-poor attitude had obviously reached the Panchayats and Taluk Development Boards. Because, within a week of the Rosewood confiscation incident in Thirthahally, a few Councillors of the Town Municipal Council of Shiralkoppa, a small town of hardly 11,000 population in the backward Shikaripur taluk (BS Yediyurappa who would become CM in 2008 was in 1972 the Vice President of the Town Municipal Council of neighbouring Shikaripur Town, a backwater of the prosperous Shimoga district), met me in a delegation and apprised me of a much bigger smuggling operation going on in Chandrakal Sandalwood Forest near Shiralkoppa town. They told me that it was a systematic operation between the higher officials of the Forest Department and the suppliers of sandalwood to the Bombay perfume industry which was using the costly sandalwood oil. But they also warned me that it cannot be a one-time, on-the-spot confiscation of one or two lorry loads. To be effective, the Forest Department which was behind the well-organized crime has to be dealt a severe blow.

With both SP Garudachar and the Executive Engineer Bore Gowda I had become close (we played shuttle-badminton and imbibed beer together afterwards!) from the beginning and I consulted them about the sandalwood smuggling. We agreed to have a joint meeting along with the Forest Department officers and the local Panchayats and villagers near Chandrakal forest. So, I went to Chandrakal and we had an impressive inter-departmental meeting with the people to discuss what was happening and what should be done to stop the smuggling. Unlike villages in the dry farming areas of Raichur and other *maidan* districts, a village in Malnad is more a collection of *hamlets* of ten or fifteen houses spread all over. The villagers took us into Chandrakal forest and what I saw was shocking. *Santalum album* derives its name from Sanskrit *Chandanam* and it is a parasite plant deriving its nutrition from the roots of a host plant. It has a life of over a hundred years and a mature tree produces an oil of immense fragrance which will last over a decade. Because of this, it was used as perfume and the tree is highly valuable. It is a native of South India, eastern Indonesia, Northern Australia and a few other South East Asian countries. It grows to a vertical height of upto fifty feet. It is sacred to Hinduism, Buddhism, Jainism, Sufism, Taoism and Zoroastrianism. Sandalwood is the only tree in the world which is sold by weight and not by volume. The DFO, Sagar who was with us informed that a 10-year old tree would weigh about 600 kg and a 20 year old tree about one ton. In Mysore State it was called Royal Wood and it belonged to Government wherever it stood, even if in private land and could not be cut. In 1972, one kilogram of 20 year old sandalwood was worth Rs.2,000 and one litre of sandalwood oil was costing Rs.50,000 a litre.

When we went into the Chandrakal forest, the scene unfolded before us was distressing. We found stumps of one-foot diameter sandalwood trees at the frequency of every hundred feet. We counted over fifty such stumps in about an hour. The villagers told me that even though the stump of the tree is richest in oil, the smugglers had left them for future extraction because of the abundance of trees available and the ease with which the trunks can be cut with electric saws compared with the difficulty of scooping the stumps. They further told me that every month four or five lorry loads were being transported to Bombay. The lorries were usually 10-tonners with Bombay registration and they learned from the inebriated drivers that they would get Rs 60,000 for one trip. *(present value Rs 6 lakhs.)* I could realize the magnitude of risk and reward in sandalwood smuggling as my take-home pay in 1972 was Rs 1,300 per month and the *super-time* pay of Joint Secretary in Government of India (equivalent to a Secretary in State Government) was Rs 2,500 per month! Crime did pay and how! I smelt the sweet fragrance of sandalwood wafting all around us. When I asked about it, the Tahsildar told that the villagers used the discarded small twigs and branches of the smuggled sandalwood trees left behind, known as "lops and tops", for cooking! This must have been the costliest fuel in the world being used for cooking in the most remotest part in India!

My most interesting meeting on sandalwood smuggling took place with the help of two Petromax lights till 8 pm as there was no electricity in the village. The Tahsildar had arranged a temporary dais with some benches and about five hundred villagers had gathered. The SP, EE and DFO, besides myself and the Shiralkoppa Town Municipal Council President and Vice President were on the dais. Instead of our making speeches, I asked the villagers to speak first about what they knew of sandalwood smuggling and how it could be stopped. Unlike the villagers in the Hyderabad-Karnataka area and Raichur where I had served as AC and SDM, the villagers here were quite articulate and eloquent. They explained how Hindi-speaking persons frequented the area along with the area's Forest and Police officials and how they even generously contributed to the renovation of the local temple and paid for a borewell for the village and how they had smoothly arranged their smuggling operations in the night. I had noticed while coming from Shiralkoppa town to Chandrakal forest, there were some confiscated sandalwood logs in the compound of Shiralkoppa Police Station and had commended the sincere work of the PSI and Circle Police Inspector for checking smuggling. The villagers laughed at this and said that this was the worthless "safety sample" to show on record that small time smuggling was all that was going on here and it was being dealt with according to law! In the total value of the smuggling, this was a very small Insurance Premium. *Which world is the DC living,* an elderly villager even mocked me! When I asked him who are the kingpins who are organizing such grand-scale smuggling, the same old man told me, *What can I say, they are all sitting with you in the stage, Look around you",* he chided me in chaste Kannada.

I returned to Shimoga in the early hours of the morning, quite dazed. With the dynamite of information I had gathered, I wrote a long report on the sandalwood smuggling in Shimoga district and also gave the names of the concerned district level forest officers and sent it to RA Naik, Secretary, Forests Department. After two days he telephoned me and asked what is going on in Shimoga. I gave a full picture of the magnitude of the scandal. Later, he again telephoned me to say that he had shown my report to the Forest Minister KH Patil, who flew into a rage at the disgrace of his Forest Officers. He also wrote a minute to the Chief Minister, Devaraj Urs recommending the suspension of five DFOs, three of whom were then serving in Shimoga and two who were there till two months earlier and also recommended the name of a senior Conservator of Forests of his confidence, Nadgir IFS who hailed from the Minister's district, to conduct a detailed enquiry. He took the file directly to Chief Minister Devaraj Urs along with RA Naik and the CM sent for the Chief Secretary RJ Rebello immediately and the suspension was done forthwith with a press release. RA Naik also told me that the Forest Minister was coming to Shimoga in two days along with Nadgir to see things for himself and he asked me to meet and brief the minister personally.

As promised, the Minister landed at the guest house of the Mysore Iron and Steel Co at Bhadravati, ten kilometres from Shimoga where I met him. There were about twenty persons in his room and none of them officers. I had not met KH Patil till then. The moment I entered, he asked all the local factotum sitting with him to leave as he had some important matters to discuss with the DC. He surprised me by getting up and walking to the door and bolting it. Then he told me very seriously, *You are the father and mother of the district, tell me, who else is involved in this, any of our party people are involved?* I assured him, as far as I know only officialdom had come to my notice. He appeared to be relieved and told me to give all cooperation to the enquiry officer who had also accompanied him. I was a little uneasy about the dramatics of the Minister as he appeared to take decisions too quickly and on impulse. However, the enquiry had been ordered and the best thing was to see that the corrupt officers got punished and the smuggling stopped. Needless to say, thereafter the panicked Forest Department treated me as Royalty!

CHIEF MINISTER'S VISIT TO SHIMOGA DISTRICT

Devaraj Urs made two visits to Shimoga district during my tenure there. Till 1980 the CMs used to travel within the state by car and also by train. There was no helicopter for the CM which practice was extravagantly resorted to later by Gundu Rao. Devaraj Urs used a black and white Mercedes alternatively. The protocol was for the DC and SP to receive the CM at the district border. So, both Garudachar and myself along with our inseparable Bore Gowda the Executive Engineer, went to the border. The border was about 20 kms from Shimoga with the neighbouring Chikmagalur district. The CM's unostentatious cavalcade consisted of just five vehicles, the mandatory Police Pilot jeep, CM's Mercedes, two Ambassador cars of MLAs and the medical van. Urs always sat in front next to the driver and in the back seats there was his Personal Assistant Moinuddin (a Deputy Registrar of the Cooperation Department hailing from Hunsur in Mysore, same as Urs) and the MLA from Bhadravathi who had gone to Chikmagalur to meet the CM. At our border, the CM stopped his car and asked the MLA to come in the car following the Mercedes and asked me to get in. Though surprised, I got in next to his PA in the back seat and travelled upto Shimoga. *En route* for fifteen minutes, Urs quizzed me about the important problems in the district and specifically asked me about what problems the MP and MLAs were creating in the district! I was quite hesitant to get into this topic but Moinuddin whispered to me that the whole purpose of the CM asking the DC to get into his car was for him to know about the administrative problems created by the politicians. The CM disarmingly told me that he was not going to take any immediate action on what I say but was using the DC's informed judgment as an additional source. I told him I had no problems with any of the politicians in the district which he was happy to hear. Indeed, the six Congress and three Lohia Socialist MLAs and the Congress MP TV Chandrasekarappa, a Lingayat gentleman, were all very nice and cordial to me.

A FINAL ACT OF PRO-DALIT LAND GRANT ORDER AND MY DEPARTURE FROM SHIMOGA TO GULBARGA

The Sharavathi river originates at *Ambuthirtha* in Thirthahalli taluk and flows 128 kilometers westwards and joins the Arabian sea. According to mythology Lord Rama shot his arrow to the ground and water sprouted to quench the thirst of Sita and hence the name, *Ambu*-arrow and *thirtha*-water. Sharavati itself refers to *Shara*-arrow. Before joining the sea, the river falls at Jog from a height of about 830 feet. In 1905 when the waterfall was in full splendour without any dam upstream, while an environmentalist would have admired its beauty, Sir M.Visvesvaraya, the celebrated engineer who was working as Superintendent Engineer in Bombay Presidency, saw Jog Falls and wrote in the Visitors Book at the Inspection Bungalow in Karwar district on the Bombay Karnataka side, *"What a Waste!"* In 1964 the huge Linganamakki Dam across Sharavathi was constructed to hold 156 tmc of water and the 1,100 MW Hydro Electric Station was constructed. The huge project submerged about 300 km² (76,000 acres) of forest and cultivated land and displaced 23,000 families. As part of rehabilitating them the government granted land for land as far as possible in other parts of the district in addition to monetary compensation which was meagre. It was called *Mulugade Jameenu,* "(for) submerged land". In Bhadravati taluk which was about 90 kilometres west from the project area, there were government *gomal* (grazing) lands which were coming under irrigation from the Bhadra Project across Tunga river. Some of these lands were given as *Mulugade* land to the land-losers under Sharavathi Hydro-Electric Project.

One day in October 1972, almost a year after my joining the district, Shankaramurthy of *Rashtriya Swayamsevak Sangh* of Shimoga came to meet me with about twenty *Dalits* of Bhadravathi taluk and gave me a petition. (Many years later he would become the Chairman of Karnataka Legislative Council.) He explained that these twenty *Dalits* were cultivating about forty acres of government land for the past ten years. Two years ago these lands became irrigable under Bhadra Project. They had given applications to the Tahsildar of Bhadravati for the grant of the lands they were cultivating as per provisions of the Land Grant Rules. But no action was taken. Meanwhile, the government had issued an order granting this very land to the family members of Minister for Education Badri Narayana Iyengar, MLA of Anandapuram in Shimoga district as *"Mulugade Jameenu"*. He further informed that the Tahsildar has issued an eviction order against the twenty dalit cultivators. As this was very serious, I fixed a spot inspection of the land during which I found that the Minister's brother and his family members had received monetary compensation and in addition the government had granted irrigated land to them. Even legally, the dalit farmers had a strong case as I found that they had been regularly paying *Takrar Takhta (TT)*, which was the penalty levied by the Tahsildar for cultivating the land unauthorizedly. Another factor was, the policy of the new government under Devraj Urs to uplift the historically exploited dalits. The Dalit minister Basavalingappa who was a fire-brand, had taken up many steps to restore dignity to Dalits such as banning of manual scavenging of head-loads of human excreta, granting of free house-sites and regularizing their unauthorized cultivation of government land, etc. During my spot inspection I also ascertained from the farmers of adjoining lands that the Dalits had indeed been cultivating the lands for a long time, from before the lands were coming under irrigable command and they had even hired bullocks from bigger land holders every year for ploughing their lands as they did not own any.

So, I asked the Tahsildar why the lands were not regularized in their names as the law was clear and why he had issued eviction orders against them. He could only show the government order granting the land as *Mulugade Jameenu* to the Anandapuram landlords and also informed that the Education Minister had spoken to him a month ago to put the grantees in possession. It was clear that any eviction of the Dalits who were eligible for being granted the land and favouring the landlords and brothers of the Minister from another taluk who had clearly received monetary compensation for their land, was both against the policy of government and also against the Regularization law. I therefore issued an order under the Land Revenue Act on the petition submitted on behalf of the Dalit occupiers and directed the Tahsildar to put them in possession immediately. Soon after this, when I was just completing one year in Shimoga, I was transferred to Gulbarga.

The Press Club of Shimoga consisting of all journalists of Kannada and English media were well-disposed to me. I had given an unoccupied room on the ground floor in the DC's office to the Press Club at a nominal rent. Shankaramurthy was also a budding journalist then and he showed a copy of my transfer order to his Press Club colleagues. Since my land grant order to the dalits went against the family members of the

Shimoga district minister and his brother, the Press made much of it and reports appeared not only in the Rural, *Mofussil* edition of state level newspapers but also in the city editions. The Minister took this as a personal affront to him. He was not a bad person and even by the more genteel times of 1970's, he was a mild politician. In fact, when he was made a minister—he was the only one from Shimoga and the only Brahmin in the ministry—during his first meeting with me he asked whether it was OK for him to telephone me from Bangalore on any administrative matter and I told him that it would be perfectly alright. He told me that it was likely that some people from Shimoga may come to Bangalore to represent some grievance and he would telephone me in their presence to satisfy them but I was free to take any decision as per Rules as I deemed fit as he would not be knowing the veracity of their claims. This was quite decent of him and can never be expected of any present day ministers. But regarding the Bhadravati lands, he took it quite personally as 40 acres of irrigated land was indeed valuable. Economics always over-rides Ethics.

The press-persons came to me with long faces and the representative of *Kannada Prabha* told me that his colleague from Bangalore had just then telephoned him of my transfer to Gulbarga as DC. This came as a great surprise to me as I had completed just one year and everything was going on well in the district. But the articulate Press of Shimoga took my transfer badly and wrote critically about it. The very next day evening there was a public meeting at the town's central Shivappa Naika circle, in which the Socialist MLAs, Kagodu Thimmappa of Sagar, Sarekoppa Bangarappa of Soraba and Konandur Lingappa of Thirthahally and the Shimoga City Municipal Presedent Jyothi Rao, all spoke criticising the government for transferring the DC and they even mentioned the Minister by name as being responsible for the unjust transfer of the DC for preventing the land grab by his family. The public meeting went on for two more evenings and my personal assistant Shankar used to report it to me after attending the meetings. I waited for two days till I received my transfer order by post and decided to hand over charge the next day and leave. The most touching part was, a few Presidents of the Taluk Development Boards met me and told me sadly that they had gone to meet the CM to retain me in Shimoga to which the CM had told them there was some big problem in Gulbarga which was why I was being transferred and there was nothing political about it. The same day I received a call from the Chief Secretary Rebello that I should immediately handover charge and proceed to Gulbarga as there was a communal disturbance on top of a severe famine situation. He was also good enough to inform me that my transfer was not due to any political reasons but Gulbarga needed a firm hand to deal with the twin problems of communal violence and famine. He also told me to take strong steps to control the communal problem and that government would support me. I therefore left Shimoga next day handing over charge to my Special DC without waiting for any send-off much to the disappointment of the SP, EE and my staff and the Press. That night I also received a call from my wife of the birth of my son Vijay.

It was with mixed feelings I left Shimoga. For one, I liked the beautiful Malnad district with its hills, streams, swaying carpets of green paddy, sugarcane and areca nut gardens, water and flowers everywhere, its mild climate, its highly cultured and educated people and the affection they had shown me. I also had the immense satisfaction of taking action to protect the forests, the interests of Dalits, upholding the prestige of DC & DM in land administration and having excellent cooperation from all the departmental officers and political leaders of all parties.

❖❖❖

CHAPTER 6

Gulbarga—
Where Adil Shahi Sultans Once Ruled

(And where I became a Nawab, almost!)

FROM GREEN PARADISE TO BLAZING INFERNO

I left the blue hills, green valleys, thick woods and sparkling waters of Shimoga and reached the hot, dry, dusty and drab Gulbarga in November 1972. Gulbarga was the second important city in the erstwhile Dominion of Hyderabad. Gulbarga and Bijapur were the biggest districts in Karnataka, Gulbarga having an area of nearly half of Kerala State and four times as big as Goa. The main rain of the district was the North-Eastern 'Return' monsoon from August to November, called *Hingari* and the crops grown known as *rabi*. It so happened that both the 1971 and 1972 monsoon had failed in Gulbarga. In dry, rain-fed areas the effect of monsoon failing two years consecutively is devastating. For instance in the worst, infamous 1772-Bengal Famine, 12 lakh people had died because rains had failed for two years. When I reached Gulbarga, the traditionally last date for *Rabi* sowing namely, 1 November was already over. That year the rainfall in the district was just 40% of the normal annual rainfall, following a less than normal in the previous year and half of the cultivable area was left unsown. Even in the area sown the main food crop White Jowar would not have grain-formation and the plant growth would not even be fodder-worthy for cattle.

It was in this background that I landed at the office of MC Das IAS, the Deputy Commissioner from whom I had to take over charge. Three years senior to me, Das hailed from the lush, paddy growing coastal Andhra Pradesh. He was a good-natured placid person with a liking for good food and did not have much clue to the cumulative effect of famine in the district. In addition to scarcity of food grains and unemployment of landless labour, there was a suspected small-pox death in Gurmitkal town of Yadgir taluk, even though small pox had officially been declared eradicated in the State and even from the country. To add to the problems, there was communal strife in Gulbarga city which had about 35% Muslims out of its population of 2 lakhs. The local MLA was from the Muslim League Party. Gulbarga was the capital of the Bahmani Kingdom till 1425 CE and in 1504 it was annexed to the Adil Shahi Kingdom whose capital was the neighbouring Bijapur. In 1657 it was annexed to Moghul empire by Mir Jumla, the Vizier of Golconda, appointed by Aurangazeb. The Jumma Masjid in Gulbarga had a covered area of 38,000 square feet and unique in the Islamic world.

The communal disturbance had raged for three days and had run its course by the time I reached there. The DC being a peaceful, languid person, was continuing to have negotiations with leaders of both communities. In all such law and order situations, the respectable senior leaders have no role to play and it is the hot-heads who foment trouble on both sides. The lesson the IAS probationers are taught in the National Academy was, during extreme law and order situations, before rowdy elements take control, take severe steps including firing at the earliest time without waiting for any negotiations. The short-hand was "maximum force at the earliest time". This did not happen in Gulbarga and the police on their own had to open fire when the police station was attacked. Gulbarga is a Divisional Headquarters, called *Subhedari*— 'Governorship', during Moghul times and the Divisional Commissioner, Srikantiah a mild-mannered old Myorean gentleman, whose office and residential quarter was in the 19th century *Aiwan-e-Shahi* mansion where the Nizam would stay when he came annually to attend the important *Ürs* of Khaja Bande Nawaz, of the great Sufi saint. For the convenience of accessing the *zenana* of the traveling harem to the mansion, a two kilometre private track was laid all the way from the railway station with a wide platform which still existed, all behind a twenty feet high wall around, away from prying eyes. The VIP guest house with two well-furnished suites and a big Durbar hall was still functional in this mansion. So, I went to call on the Divisional Commissioner in this antiquity. He was a much worried man who told me that the famine, unemployment, no foodgrains, no drinking water, distress sale of cattle and household articles, law and order—all these maladies in Gulbarga were very bad and I should take things very seriously.

In this kind of frightful atmosphere I met Das and since the CS was good to his word in speaking to him, I took charge without any problem. But Das told me he will have to retain the house for a month as he had to still pack things. When I told him I had a fridge coming with other articles, he showed interest and asked me why I was having a fridge! I apologetically explained to him I could keep cool the vegetables, food and water but did not tell him I could keep beer also for fear he may not allow me to use the house for such immoral purposes!

FIRST THINGS FIRST, MISA DETENTIONS
FOR MAINTAINING PUBLIC ORDER

The communal antagonism was still simmering, the SP and the Commandant of Home Guards both met me and warned. The SP, Billimoria, a Parsi, was from old school, having risen from the ranks in the Hyderabad government and promoted to the IPS. The Home Guards Commandant Homi Irani was also a Parsi and a delightful person. Ten years older than me, he was from Poona and had a degree in architecture, surprisingly, from the Stanford University. I could not imagine what a Stanford graduate was doing in the backwaters of Karnataka. He had settled in Gulbarga as he had taken up in the 1960s the construction of the huge 400-bed Gulbarga Government Hospital and after that the Medical College buildings and other government buildings. His high quality of work and strict adherence to principles had impressed Veerendra Patil who was the important leader of Hyderabad-Karnataka in those decades. Homi told me that he attended the 1972 Summer Olympics in Munich where many Israeli athletes were massacred by the terrorists. He had just returned to Gulbarga in October when the riots broke out. Both the SP and Home Guard Commandant being Parsis, they combined well and ensured the handling of law and order with great cooperation. Moreover, the second in command in the Home Guards was my Personal Assistant Ranga Rao, a forty year old, very silent and a very efficient bachelor. Both Billimoria and Homi Irani explained to me the still prevailing latent animosity being actively fanned by the ring leaders of both communities and that violence could again break out any time.

One of the basic advice of Niccolò Machiavelli in *The Prince* (1532), is that when a Prince acquires a new hostile territory, he should unleash harsh punishments at once so that the quarrelling factions can be terrorised and controlled quickly and whatever small concessions the Prince shows gradually later would be welcomed as big mercies. I was no Prince nor Gulbarga the 16th century Italy. But the medieval mentality of the mobs had not changed and Gulbarga in 1972 was still looking medieval both outwardly and inwardly. The Maintenance of Internal Security Act had been brought to force by government in 1971 and it gave enormous powers of detention of persons in the subjective judgment of the District Magistrate. Such detention could extend upto one year unless the detainee was released before the period by a competent authority which was the state government or the High Court. In fact, I had become familiar with the provisions of the MISA in Shimoga itself early in 1972 when some dismissed employees of Karnataka Power Corporation at Sharavathi Hydro Electric Project tried to sabotage the turbines. I had detained them and their outside instigators under MISA which provided for such detention of persons trying to prevent the maintenance of "supplies and services essential to community" and electricity was essential to community.

So, I got the names of Hindu and Muslim instigators, seven each, and sent them to the prison in Bellary as under MISA the DM could detain them anywhere in the state. For Hyderabad-Karnataka people Bellary was *Kalapani,* as traditionally the Bahmani and Adil Shahi Sultans and their army will not cross Tungabhadra and reciprocally, the Vijayanagar Kings will not cross Krishna River. Raichur district between the two rivers called *Doab* was the neutral battle ground and no-man's land. In fact, it was mainly because Aliya Ramaraya, the Regent and son-in-law of the illustrious Krishna Deva Raya crossed the Krishna river with his strong army that the five Bahmani Sultans were forced to join hands for survival and in 1565 defeated the Vijayanagar King at Rakasagi-Tangadgi village on the northern banks of Krishna river, 25 miles from Talikot in Bijapur district and close to Shorapur taluk of Gulbarga. So the trouble-making detainees would be in unfamiliar area with unfamiliar language and unfamiliar food in the infamous mosquito-ridden Bellary jail with difficulty to communicate with their family members 200 kms away, an experience they will not forget in their lifetime even though the MISA detainees would be treated more liberally compared with other prisoners. To satisfy the Review Board, before whom I had to personally appear and explain the reasons for my "subjective satisfaction" I had started to maintain a private, confidential diary of all the observed activities of miscreants the sole objective of which was only to show to the Advisory Board that my detentions were not arbitrary and not all that subjective. In my tenure of six years as District Magistrate in the three districts of Shimoga, Gulbarga and Bangalore I have detained over a hundred persons for economic offences and communal violence but not even one for political reasons, and in all the cases the Advisory Board had approved my detentions. In some cases which went before the High Court also, my detentions were upheld on the strength of my secret but regularly maintained diary. In Gulbarga, I followed up the detentions with convening a meeting of both communities and sternly telling them that if they continue to create problems, I will not hesitate to send more, really more, persons to Bellary prison under MISA detention against which there was no bail.

This had a good effect on both communities and we did not have any communal disturbance for the next three years as long as I was DC & DM there.

FAMINE RELIEF ACTION PLAN

Gulbarga was historically in the core famine area. It took me one week to just go round the eleven taluks to have a geographical feel of the extent of planting and drinking water availability. Then I convened a meeting of the Tahsildars and Block Development Officers in each taluk with the Assistant Executive Engineer and others to know their recommendations of specific action to be taken. I followed this up with a meeting of the district MLAs and Taluk Board Presidents to get their proposals. All of them had the same demands of taking up relief works as there was no work because there was no sowing, opening more fair price shops and making available jowar and other essentials like oil and kerosene, getting fodder for cattle, digging borewells for drinking water which problem will become severe with the temperature increasing in summer months which in Gulbarga district reaches 47°C in April, May and June and stays high for weeks. Thus getting an overall idea of the problems, I got down to specifics by going to the taluk headquarters of each taluk and spending half day with officers of Revenue, Block Development, Public Works and Public Health Engineering who were dealing with water supply. As a result I could prepare a fairly long and detailed Action Plan for each taluk with approximate cost of each work and an overall total cost for each taluk. Adding the rainfall statistics, past famines, fodder availability, prices of foodgrains and other essential commodities and various other statistical information, fortunately available from the District Statistical Officer, the Action Plan for Famine Relief was an impressive looking booklet of about fifty pages for each taluk. I got printed 500 copies of each taluk-booklet in Kannada and English at the government press at Gulbarga. It was not an academic work of high standard but it certainly was an impressive, detailed Action Plan for mitigating the famine for one year. This was prepared in just one month for each of the 11 taluks.

The printed booklets were ready by January 1973 and I sent a detailed report to the venerable Revenue Commissioner, K Balasubramanyam, along with a set of the Action Plan for Gulbarga Famine Relief with copies to the Chief Secretary, Development Commissioner, Finance Secretary and Secretary to the CM. In my letter I estimated the amount required to execute the Action Plan at Rs.11 crores during 1973 till the 1973-Rabi rains (September) and sowing. In

1973 this was a huge amount for one district, its value in 2020 being Rs.126 crores. I had also sent the Action Plan booklet to the MLAs, the MP and the Taluk Development Board Presidents and requested them to study it and to take up the matter with the government for funds. Out of the 11 MLAs elected from Gulbarga district in the 1972 Elections, eight were from Congress (R-Ruling) Party and three were supported by the Congress-(Organization) headed by Veerendra Patil (whose two-storey house was just opposite the Eiwan-e-Shahi.) The TDBs' control was more evenly divided between the Congress (R) and the Congress (O). But, when it came to asking the Government for famine relief funds for the district, all the elected representatives supported the Action Plan and wrote to the Chief Minister, the Finance Minister and the Revenue Minister to approve the Action Plan *in toto* and allot the funds as requested by the DC. Officially enlisting the support of the elected representatives was not the conventional procedure in district administration then but I had to resort to getting all political support in view of the serious nature of the situation.

CM SENDS UR ANANATAMURTHY, ARUMUGAM MLA, KENGAL HANUMANTHIAH AND FINANCE MINISTER M.Y. GHORPADE TO GULBARGA

Stung by the criticism that his government was not handling the famine situation in Gulbarga effectively, Devaraj Urs sent a series of observers ending with the visit of the Finance Minister himself. There was also a background to this. Karnataka politics after the State Reorganization in 1956 had been controlled by the two major landed gentry communities of Lingayats in the Northern districts and Okkaligas in the South, the other communities of Kurubas (shepherds), Other Backwards Communities (OBCs), Dalits and Muslims, playing a subsidiary role. Unlike its neighbouring Tamil Nadu and Kerala, the landed-gentry castes, though in Shudra classification, play an important role in Karnataka's social and political life. The estimated caste and community composition of the State population is given below as this is of fundamental importance in understanding Karnataka's social, economic and political life:

		%
Lingayats	-	9.8
Vokkaligas	-	8.2
Kurubas	-	7.1
SCs	-	16
STs	-	4

Muslims	-	13
Christians	-	1.6
Brahmins	-	2.1
Other Backward Castes	-	38
		99.8

Though the Lingayats and Okkaligas constitute less than one-fifth of the population, economic power, especially in rural area is concentrated in them. The other large communities are the SCs, Muslims and Kurubas. But the largest share of more than two-thirds of the population is a group of non-dominant Other Backward Casts (OBCs), the SCs, STs and Muslims and technically the *Shudras* and Untouchables of Manu. One of the very first acts of Devaraj Urs after coming to power was to constitute a Backward Castes Commission with a well-known advocate, LG Havanur in August 1972 whose Report would be submitted in 1975 which identified 205 OBCs. Devaraj Urs selected a large number of MLA-candidates from the OBCs and their number in the 1972-Assembly doubled to 36 from the 18 in the previous 1967 Elections. Together with 32 MLAs from SC/STs, this was the largest chunk of 68 MLAs in the 212-strong State Assembly from 1972 to 1977. In Gulbarga, only 3 MLAs out of 11 were Lingayats while 5 MLAs were from Backward Castes and one Muslim and Dalit each. Also, the CM had made one Backward Caste and one Muslim MLA cabinet ministers from Gulbarga denying a cabinet post to Lingayats. His strategy which was the novel experiment never tried in Karnataka either before or since, was to form an alliance of Backward Castes, Scheduled Castes and Muslims as a counter-weight to the economically dominant Lingayats and Okkaligas, for the first and only time in Karnataka's history, in which he largely succeeded till he was CM.

The Famine of 1973 came in handy to the disgruntled Lingayat community of Gulbarga which had also suffered because of the famine apart from the landless agricultural labour who constituted about one-thirds of the rural population. The Lingayat community and Congress-O Party in the State was headed by Veerendra Patil from Gulbarga who was the erstwhile CM till 1971. In January 1973 his party started an agitation in Gulbarga against the government by gheroing the DC. On the appointed day a crowd of about 2,000 persons headed by Veerendra Patil and his deputy Chand Mahal Ibrahim (he would change parties many times since then), entered my office room with about ten close associates. I greeted them as I had also known Ibrahim who was from Bhadravathi in Shimoga district and Veerendra Patil as ex-CM had known me as AC. Patil was a very decent person and did not want to indulge in any violence in DC's office. In the morning itself he had sent words to the SP that he and about ten of his close associates would come to gherao the DC and they could be arrested and sent to custody for a day and could be released in the evening while the larger crowd would shout slogans for an hour and would disperse peacefully for lunch! This would give good publicity to the Cong-O Opposition which was their objective. But I told Billimoria we need not arrest them unless there is some violence as I banked upon the gentlemanly behaviour of Patil. The Presspersons were at hand closely watching the proceedings. There was no TV telecast in Karnataka in 1973 which would start with national telecast only in 1982.

There was some drama. I offered glasses of cold water to those in my room and I had also arranged drinking water in big earthen pots outside in the quadrangle for the crowd as a public relations exercise. My PA Ranga Rao, the Deputy Commandant of the Home Guards, later told me that the crowd appreciated this gesture very much. After about ten minutes of general discussion of the famine situation, Ibrahim nudged Patil who asked me, *Well, are you not going to arrest us?* I told him, *No sir, you are only doing a service to the people and asking the government to take relief works which only strengthens the hands of district administration, so why should we arrest you?* He said, *'Look, we have assembled in a large crowd, we are not allowing the DC from doing his work which is an offence under the IPC. So, you should arrest us'.* But I only smiled at him and the Deccan Herald correspondent and his photographer who was close-by caught it in his camera which was published in the next day's paper. As things were not going according to plan, Patil and his associates went out of my room to the large, circular courtyard outside my chambers and started addressing the crowd. To see what was going on and also to make the crowd see the DC (GVK's advice was, the more the people see the DC the better!), I also went out with them and sat on the Visitors bench on the verandah facing the crowd. Ibrahim, known for his mischievous humour and chaste Kannada addressed the crowd that Veerendra Patil will preside over the meeting, who was sitting on the verandah floor and the DC would be the "Chief Guest"! So the meeting went on for about half hour in which Ibrahim abused the government and Devaraj Urs and the ruling party MLAs that they should wear sarees, bras, etc. in his entertaining style. In the end, Patil left me wishing me well and the crowd also left and I went to my office room. But before leaving, Ibrahim went to some inner room in DC's office without my knowing and damaged some tables to mark his scent. All this was noted by the Press and the next day there was a long report in the newspaper in which the district administration was praised for handling the agitation with tact and humour. This was a coordinated agitation in the district headquarters of Raichur, Bidar and Bijapur besides Gulbarga. There were reports of Congress-O leaders having been arrested and some violence in the other three districts. The next day Moinuddin, CM's Special Assistant, telephoned me and said the CM liked the non-arrest and discomfiture of Congress-O leaders in Gulbarga. I used the opportunity to tell him that if I do not receive famine relief funds, the situation will become quite bad in Gulbarga. He said that the CM had taken the matter seriously with the FM for release of funds and he will visit Gulbarga soon.

VISIT OF UR ANANTHAMURTHY AND THE "POLITICS OF FAMINE" (AND THE ORIGIN OF HIS STORY "BARA" WHICH WAS MADE INTO A FILM BY THE SAME NAME)

I got a call from the Revenue Commissioner that UR Ananthamurthy, the famous writer (who received the Jnana Peetha award later in 1994 and who was once shortlisted for the Booker Prize), would visit Gulbarga at the suggestion of the CM for a first hand impartial view of the famine. I had seen in 1971 the movie *Samskara* based on URA's Kannada novel with Girish Karnad in the lead and knew he was a liberal. URA came and stayed for two days visiting villages and meeting college lecturers, the press and also went to Bidar to see its medieval historical monuments. As he was a radical thinker and writer, I called on him as soon as he arrived and had a rewarding, long exchange of views on various matters. He said, his main objective was to see the extent of famine situation and how government was meeting the catastrophe and how the people were viewing it. I told him there are two aspects to what was going on in Gulbarga. A natural calamity like Famine has been a recurring phenomenon in Gulbarga though this time it was quite serious. I gave a long lecture of how it can be mitigated by fairly simple relief works and fair price shops. These are the economic measures which the district administration can do primarily to increase the purchasing power of people, provided sufficient funds were made available. This was just modified Keynesian economics.

I also told URA, that there is but another important aspect to the Famine namely, the political aspect. Following Mrs Gandhi's highly successful slogan *Gharibi Hatao*, the opposition Congress-O in the State was in disarray and the famine in the district was a great opportunity for them to use it against the Devaraj Urs government. In fact, there was an interesting discussion in the District Development Council of which the DC was the Chairman (this was before the advent of Zilla Panchayats with elected representatives at district level replacing DDC) with the MP, MLAs and TDB Presidents attending and presided over by me. The MP Dharma Rao Afzalpurkar though from Congress-I, was a bitter Lingayat critic of the CM. In the meeting he wanted the DC to recommend to government that loans should be given to farmers whose crops were lost or not even planted due to failure of rains. The TDB Presidents, also mostly Lingayat landlords, while appreciating the DC's detailed Action Plan of relief works to be taken up, supported the MP saying that the land owners are not accustomed to do earthwork, unlike the landless labour and therefore loans should be given to landowners. This was because the land-owning class of Lingayats were the backbone of the Opposition Cong-O while the support base of Devaraj Urs' Cong-I was the Backward Classes, scheduled castes, Muslims and other landless. So I gently told the DDC that why should the landless people alone work in the hot sun to earn wages, should not they also get loans like the land owners? I even quoted Lenin to the members, *He Who shall not Work, Neither shall he Eat!* The SC/ST and other Backward Class and Muslim members strongly supported that not only the land lords but the landless workers also should get loans and they need not work, just as the landlords! Mallikarjun Kharge who was just an MLA from Gurmitkal Reserved Constituency strongly supported me! Of course, no such loans were recommended by me to any class.

So I told URA about the Political Aspect of Famine which was a power-game. The political power game in Gulbarga was, there was no Lingayat representation from Gulbarga in the cabinet while the Minister from Gulbarga was Devendrappa Galappa Jamedar, a first-time, obscure, backward class non-entity of fishermen community from Chincholi taluk, which was the native place of Veerendra Patil, who had defeated the Lingayat strongman candidate of Congress-O and there was a demand from the Lingayat community that a person from their community should be made a cabinet minister to deal effectively with the famine. In fact, the Congress-I MLA from Aland taluk, Annarao V Patil, who was a Lingayat strongman was rumoured to have stitched a new teri-cotton buttoned-up suit anticipating his appointment to the cabinet any time! But, Devaraj Urs did not want to yield to the Lingayat lobby and was also delaying release of funds for my Action Plan, to show the Congress-O who was the boss! This was my reading and I told URA that this Politics of Famine should not affect the relief measures to mitigate the genuine distress of the people. This led to a discussion on the dichotomy of Marxism with Indian Democracy as logically Naxalism is the only intellectually honest political solution, as I told him. Recently, starting in 1967 from Naxalbari, the movement by Charu

Mazumdar and Kanu Sanyal was spreading in the so-called Red Corridor and even in Chincholi taluk of Gulbarga which was bordering Telengana's Naxal area. URA smiled and said one cannot be a Marxist and also a practising bureaucrat and in India 'Sabotaging from inside' is a myth and it is the System that will change the idealist and not the other way round. He told me, when the pure water of Ganges joins the sea, it is not the sea water that loses its salt but it was the Ganges which would get salty.

[Little inkling did I have then that at that very moment URA had got the germ of an idea for his famous short-story BARA which was published in Sudha magazine and later made into a film. In fact, from the Sudha short story, it was first attempted as a Hindi film acted and produced by Shashi Kapoor and its draft screenplay was shown to me by Shama Zaidi. But the film never made to the screen because of the emergency censorship. A few years later, after the 21-month Emergency of 1975-1977 was lifted, Bara in Kannada was released. When I called on URA much later at his Bangalore apartment off Richmond Road, he took me for a sumptuous breakfast to the Madras Woodlands Hotel. In the film there is one scene where the politician Bhimoji asks Satish the DC, "Are you a bureaucrat? A revolutionary? You delude yourself that you can be both." This was the exact point URA had made when we had discussed the 'Politics of Famine' at Gulbarga. During our breakfast, a friend of URA dropped at our table and URA introduced me to him as, "He is my hero in Bara"! I would cherish that remark of his as the best certificate, more glowing than any of my senior officers' compliments in any of my Annual Confidential Reports!]

VISIT OF "CM'S ARUMUGAM TO GULBARGA"

There was a three-time MLA, CM Arumugam repeatedly elected from Kolar Gold Fields which had over 90% Tamil population because the gold mining company of John Taylor established in 1881 brought most of the workers from Salem district. KGF had a population of about 1.6 lakhs and CM Arumugam represented them as an Independent. Though he was technically sitting in the opposition benches, he always supported whoever was the Chief Minister. For this reason he was popularly known as "CM's" Arumugam. In the procession of VIPs visiting Gulbarga for famine assessment sent by the CM, it was no wonder that the next was Arumugam. It turned out to be a surprisingly useful visit. Arumugam was born and brought up entirely in KGF and Kolar district had been traditionally one of the most famine-affected area in the South with an annual average rainfall of 700mm and its over thousand tanks drying up every alternate year. So, he knew a lot about famine conditions. He spoke what is popularly called *"Butler* English" and "*Pidgin* Kannada". So, he was very happy when I spoke to him in Tamil (his Tamil was also colloquial, he was one who spoke all languages badly!) I took him around the district a whole day. The first thing he wanted to see was the meats market. I asked him why and he told me that, the price of beef was a good indicator of famine. This was because while beef was generally cheaper than fish, chicken, mutton and pork in that order, in extreme famine conditions, as a last resort, farmers start selling their cattle as they cannot feed them and therefore the price of beef falls enormously as the cattle are worth only their skin-value. So we went to the meat market and found that while there was no fish and a kilogram of chicken was Rs 5 and mutton Rs 4, the beef was a shocking 50 paise a kilogram! The sellers also said that one average sized bullock was being sold for Rs 50 which was its hide-value in distress sale. They also said every day about ten lorries of cattle were going to Bombay. Gulbarga has the sturdy *Deoni* and *Hallikhed* breed of cattle which would cost Rs 10,000 in normal times. The farmers would care and nourish them as their own children. These bulls would be the last thing they would sell. Being costly to maintain, not all farmers could keep them during famine when fodder was not available. Farmers would sell them only if they were desperate and as a last resort like the Family Jewels. This happened in the Gulbarga famine as reflected in the price of beef which I learnt, thanks to Arumugam.

On the road he asked me to stop the car and got out and went inside a few huts and checked how many days' jowar they had. They hardly had any. There was no question of any oil but they had one or two dry onions and some had a few red chillies. This was the only 'vegetable' to go with the *'sukha jolada roti'* a few of which were kept in a bundle for the next few days. In one of the huts there was a coil of aluminium wire. I was puzzled and the villager would not tell me why he had it. Arumugam told me that it was obviously stolen from the Electricity Board sub-station as it could be sold in the market. In another village, our vehicle was stopped by a crowd and they said a villager had died of hunger. We waded through the crowd and found an emaciated body. I wanted to send the body for post-mortem but Arumugam advised me not to do that. He took out a hundred rupee note which was nearly one month's wage then and gave it to the dead person's wife and told her to do a proper cremation. Back in our car, he told me that all normal deaths would also be claimed as Famine Deaths by politicians and I should not worry about it. In some villages we found that there were only a few old people and young children left as all able bodied persons had migrated to Goa, Hyderabad, Bombay and Bangalore in search of work or for begging.

CM Arumugam spent one full day in travelling with me to various villages and the next day he met some of the MLAs and TDB Presidents still available in Gulbarga. Many of the ruling party's MLAs were avoiding Gulbarga because of fear of Congress (O) supporters harassing and *gheroing* them. During the discussions with the MLAs he ascertained that they wanted the Action Plan prepared by the DC should be implemented without any delay to avoid disaster. After that he had discussions with me and went through the Action Plans. He wondered why the government was not allocating funds to take up the works. He himself answered his question, *Perhaps there is politics of Old Mysore versus North Karnataka*!. He told me he will apprise the CM and complimented me for meeting the people and talking to them instead of being office-bound with police protection and took leave.

FINANCE MINISTER'S VISIT AND THE ALLOTMENT OF FUNDS

Obviously the CM took Arumugam and URA seriously because within three days I received a call from the Finance Secretary Satishchandran, who was very upright and highly regarded and the first direct recruit in 1952 to the IAS from native Mysore. He would also later become the Chief Secretary. He told me that the CM had asked the FM, Ghorpade to spend three days in Gulbarga and assess the famine situation. He also told me that Ghorpade had studied economics in Cambridge and belonged to Bellary district's Sandur Samasthan's princely family. He warned me to be ready with all statistical data and not attempt any bluffing as he would find out the truth in no time and my credibility would be gone. He also told me to expect him to be short-tempered with officers! The FM, MYG as he was known, was coming by road from Bijapur which was bordering Gulbarga on the Western side. So, I went to the border of Afzalpur taluk on the banks of Bhima river, a tributary to Krishna. Though protocol did not require it, I wanted to receive him at the border and had decided I would accompany him from his entry to my district till his exit. I found MYG to be a very energetic person. At the Afzalpur IB there was the usual crowd shouting slogans organized by the Congress-O. MYG climbed on to the bonnet of the car (he was then 41 and only ten years older than me) and addressed the crowd that all relief works would be taken up within a week. He also told them that, if necessary people would be employed to dig holes and fill them up and wages would be paid by government. I was pleasantly surprised to hear from MYG this famous saying of Keynes of *"digging and filling holes and being paid for it"* to increase the purchasing power in the economy to come out of the 1930's Depression in the Western countries. While proceeding from Afzalpur to Gulbarga in the car I complimented him for his Keynesian quote. He was surprised and asked me how did I know that. So I briefly explained to him about my economics background and also told him that the Gulbarga situation was crucially different from the 1930's Economic Depression in the West because Gulbarga did not have idle factories and idle workers as in the West, but landless labour had no work due to failure of rains. Not only government had to take up labour-intensive works for the landless, pay wages to create purchasing power but also had to open a large number of Fair Price Shops, arrange supply of foodgrains and other essential commodities as the private sector merchants would take their own time and also we had to take steps to control black marketing. Besides, we had to take up immediate steps to meet the drinking water scarcity which would worsen with the starting of summer which in Gulbarga would be from early March itself. While he was thinking about it, I asked the driver to stop the car and told MYG I would show him a phenomenon he may not have seen anywhere.

Because of the scarcity of Jowar and its high price, many poor people were collecting a kind of coarse wild millet of pink coloured small round grains which was bitter but edible and normally grazed by cattle and sheep. In the grain hierarchy this was below Bajra (Pearl millet or *kambu*), Navane (Fox-tail millet), Milo (red sorghum) which were all given as animal feed in the US. In Gulbarga, this minor wild millet was found just by the side of the road, below the road level where there would be "borrow pits" from which soil would have been taken to put on the road while constructing the road and therefore there will be some residual moisture below these road-side pits and this pink millet grew there. MYG and I got down and I collected some of these grains and showed him that this is what many poor people were collecting. I gave him a few grains which he munched and found it to be bitter. He was shocked and incredulous whether people were really eating it. I told him we will stop in the next village and he can ask the villagers himself. Being a meticulous person and probably checking whether I was bluffing, he stopped the car in the next village and showed the few villagers who gathered the pink grains and asked them whether they know what it is. Some of them told that many Dalit people in the village are eating it but *we Lingayats cannot eat it and we cook only Bili Jola*. This clinched the issue of my credibility with MYG as in all his experience he had not come across people eating such inferior wild grains and he realized my demonstration was not staged.

I travelled with him the next three days and used my experience of what I learned from Arumugam earlier of entering huts at random and showing what little foodgrains they had. I also explained to him, out of 1304 villages in the district there were about 200 where the drinking water problem was severe and many more villages would also become dry as the summer progresses. There were a few private companies in Bangalore, Hubli and Hyderabad owning High Speed Rigs which could drill a 6-inch diameter, 150 feet deep borewell in three days. With scientific geophysical instruments more accurately locating water source instead of the hit and miss false method of Twig-pointing, we could be sure of providing clean drinking water in about 200 problem-villages if I could hire 10 High Speed Rigs for three months, starting immediately.

I showed MYG the Action Plan booklets we had prepared for each taluk which contained specific details of relief work of each category with cost. MYG was quite impressed with the taluk-wise booklets which gave in addition a lot of useful statistical information of each taluk in a compact form. I also told him that when government spends huge amount, such work should also be productive in the nature of Capital Works, that is, small projects which could give long term benefits and not just "digging and filling holes." I also showed him in the booklets the estimate of works which amounted to about Rs.11 crores for the whole district for the period January to December 1973, assuming there will not be a third continuing year of failure of rains.

I also impressed upon him the need for closely supervising the different types of work by the staff under the DC namely, the Assistant Commissioners, Tahsildars and Revenue Inspectors and also other departments. Otherwise, the different departments—especially the PWD who had to execute the works had a notorious reputation for leaking funds. In Gulbarga district there were sixty *Revenue Circles* or *Hoblis* in eleven taluks and for each circle there was a Revenue Inspector called *Girdawar* in Gulbarga. With 15,000 km^2 area and 1,304 villages in the district, each RI had to cover about 250km^2, 25 villages and hamlets and about 24,000 population, and therefore mobility was extremely crucial for the RIs. They had to depend upon KSRTC buses which were few and irregular. Other departmental officers such as the Engineers of PWD, Irrigation Department, Police Department, etc. had jeeps while the Revenue Department did not, even though in a famine situation the Revenue Department's role was the most important. I had therefore worked out a proposal, besides a jeep to every Tahsildar, of providing loan to each RI for the purchase of the sturdy Enfield Bullet motor cycle which he could repay in instalments. In this way, the motorbike becomes the RI's property which he will maintain carefully unlike a government vehicle and for his touring about 800 km a month a fixed monthly travelling allowance of Rs.75 for POL—petrol, oil and lubricants. (In 1973 petrol price was Rs.1.25 per litre and the motorbike would give 30 km per litre). Therefore, after consulting my RIs, ACs and Tahsildars I had arrived at the loan of Rs.6,000 for the cost of the bike and the loan repayable in 60 monthly instalments. The only hitch was, the Mysore Civil Service Rules did not provide for a loan of more than Rs.3,000 to government servants of the rank of RIs and there was no provision for a fixed travelling allowance of Rs.75 monthly. But since the RIs would continue to be in service certainly for more than 5 years and a monthly FTA of Rs.75 was worth the effective supervision for the proper utilization of huge Famine Relief expenditure, I had prepared a reasonable proposal for the government. This also I explained to MYG. Another innovative administrative matter was to strengthen the supervisory powers of the DC by giving him disciplinary powers of suspension and ordering enquiry of field level employees of all the departments in the district (not only of the Revenue Department) of Revenue Inspector rank. This was unheard of till then.

I found MYG was closely listening to me poker-faced. I also found he was keeping a leather-bound black Notebook in which he was scribbling from time to time. On the final third day I put forth my master proposal. As any action to deal effectively with the famine situation will inevitably require government approval for funds and by the time such approvals come from Government, the famine would have run its full course and the calamity would be unprecedented, I told MYG that government should permit the DCs of the three worst famine-affected districts of Gulbarga, Bijapur and Bidar to incur expenditure first and seek approval post-facto. He was leaving the next day to Hyderabad to catch the plane to Bangalore. He invited me to have dinner with him that evening at Eiwan-e-Shai. I went with the anxious expectation of the Last Supper and found him to be sitting alone with his Black Notebook. About his scribbling in the notebook, I had checked with my friend Vasudevan IAS who was Deputy Secretary in the Finance Department and the right hand of Finance Secretary TR Satshchandran. He told me that MYG would have noted down all the things I was telling him and would have cross-checked their correctness. So, at the end of our pre-dinner talk, I was very pleasantly surprised when he said he was convinced about the serious situation in Gulbarga and he entirely agreed with all my proposals—the Action Plans, High Speed Rigs, Jeeps to Tahsildars, Motor Bike loans to RIs, making funds available to DC for various works and giving the DC disciplinary and financial powers. He also asked me to write down all that in the form of a detailed letter addressed to the Finance Secretary and mark a copy to him and also send copies to the Chief Secretary and to the Secretary to CM, JC Lynn. He asked me to send the letter through a messenger the very next day so that it will reach him and others without delay. He told me that I had the unique opportunity of accomplishing a great task in Gulbarga which no Minister or officer ever had. He also complimented me for my commitment and the very cordial relations I had with the MLAs and TDB Presidents in the district and their total agreement to DC's proposals when MYG had discussed the famine matters with them. I did not realize it then, but his good opinion of me had continued for the next four decades till he passed away in 2011. Even after my retirement and long after he himself had left government and politics, he asked me to be on the Board of Directors of his family-owned company, the Sandur Manganese and Iron Ore Company from which I benefited greatly by learning about mining, taking up works like environmental protection, public toilet construction (under the Corporate Social Responsibility— CSR) and, not least, financially by way of sitting fees and Director's Commission. But, more than anything, it was his affectionate nature that impressed me. He was truly a great learned person with total integrity and impatience to achieve.

AFTERMATH OF MYG'S VISIT AND
ACCERELATION OF FAMINE RELIEF WORKS

True to his word, MYG took up the matter with the CM and the Cabinet and one-thirds of Rs.11 crores, the fund I had asked for, was released immediately as the first instalment. In the following nine months I had my hands full in implementing the Action Plan and deal with the deteriorating situation. The most visible impact was, surprisingly, the sight of the Revenue Inspectors driving the gleaming red 350cc Royal Enfield Bullet motorbikes (I had specifically asked the Madras firm to paint it red) in the length and breadth of the district. There is something macho and ruggedly Marlboro about a speeding motor-bike as can be seen in Indian films the hero speeding in a motorbike to save the damsel in distress rather than in a car. The status of RIs skyrocketed in the villages, especially with the women-folk, and among the sister-departments as no other official in the district had these motor-bikes for travelling on government work. The advice of GVK, *'spend-first and seek post-approval'* facility gave the DC enormous flexibility and saving time to attend to emergency work. For instance, I could get ten high-speed rigs as planned from three companies and they took up drilling work in earnest with over 80% success rate because of the geophysical instrument they used to zero in on aquifer source. But, in the district there were about 50 villages severely affected by water scarcity which did not have electricity. Even though the borewells were successful there, submersible electric pumps could not be installed for want of electricity and hand pumps could pump out only a small volume of water. We were using the few high capacity borewells, yielding more than 5,000 litres per hour, apart from providing hand-posts with overhead tanks in the village, also by filling water tankers and transporting to nearby villages. So, I requested the Superintending Engineer of the Karnataka Electricity Board for a discussion. He came and said the KEB could provide electricity to these villages provided the required amount, which came to Rs.15 lakhs (Rs.1.76 crores at present value), was deposited with the KEB. This was, because of the perennial financial problem of the KEB, it could take up works for other departments only on what was called "Deposit Contribution" work. I asked him if I gave funds immediately how long would the KEB take to give electricity to the 50 villages. He said, *Within ten days*. I ordered tea for him (coffee in Hyderabad Karnataka was not drinkable, the joke being, when tasting the hot drink the guest asks the host, *Is this Tea or Coffee? and the host asks how does it taste, the guest says, It tastes like Kerosene, and the host says, then it must be tea because the coffee here tastes like Turpentine!*) and sent for Adviachar. He was my Head Quarters Assistant who was a stupendously efficient officer who lived only for work and would never say *no* or *not possible* for any of my unreasonable proposals. In fact, he would never speak even and when silence was impossible, only in monosyllables. People who criticise government servants for being lazy and incompetent have never met unsung heroes like Adviachars or my then Food Assistant Jayachar. One would not find such persons in corporate sector in any country, World Bank, IMF, WTO, etc. He came with his notebook and I told him the problem and asked whether the DC can deposit Rs.15 lakhs and how soon? He looked at me and the SE and wrote something in his notebook and showed me. He had written "15 minutes"! I nodded and he went. I chatted with the SE over tea for some time after which he was becoming restless and wanted to take leave of me. I told him to please wait for a few more minutes so that he could take the cheque. He did not believe it and asked, *How is it possible, shouldn't I get government approval?* I told him, *No, kindly wait*. True to his word, Adviachar brought the Treasury cheque. When I signed and gave it to the SE, he examined it both sides and wondered whether it was valid and could he present it to the Treasury for encashment? I told him, By all means. Still bewildered, he took leave of me. But before he left I told him that now it is his responsibility to provide electricity to the 50 villages within ten days as he had promised. He did it.

The reason why I am narrating this in some detail is, when it comes to emergencies, the Indian Bureaucracy can function at supersonic speed as nowhere else in the world. Only during normal times, they are chained in red tape. In fact, some of the most acute emergency situations can be handled only by the Indian bureaucracy unthinkable in the corporate sector or governments abroad. The millions of refugees who fled from Tibet, Bangladesh, Burma and Srilanka, the recurring Indian famines and natural calamities, even abroad like Hurricanes Katrina and Sandy which the advanced US could not handle quickly, railway accidents, smooth conducting of world's biggest elections—these are problems which the Indian bureaucracy handles with confidence and aplomb and only in public interest, working long hours without any over-time remuneration. People who deride Indian bureaucracy have no clue as to what it is capable of doing. Only during normal times the Bureaucracy is sluggish! But without its Bureaucracy despite its shortcomings, often discredited as *Babus* by the naïve intelligentsia, India will grind to a total halt. Arm-chair intellectuals who have never administered a district do not know what they say. *[As to the derisory description 'Babus', the well-deserved reciprocal is Bania for Corporates, Kazi for Judiciary, Paparazzi for Media and Neta for Leaders!]*

DEATH OF MP, BY-ELECTION AND CM'S LONG VISIT TO GULBARGA

The MP from Gulbarga, Dharmrao Afzalpurkar died of heart attack during 1973 at the height of the Famine relief operations. (His detractors rather unkindly said this was his only positive contribution!) His followers wanted him to be buried in the Municipal Garden which was the only big public garden in Gulbarga. It had never been used for anyone's burial till then and the City Municipal Council wanted the DC to decide the matter as the land was Revenue Land leased to the CMC. I decided that, respecting the Lingayat custom and tradition, he should be properly buried in a sitting position in his native village and not in a park used every day by the public as many morning walkers may be alarmed to find an extra person walking with them without legs! This was happily accepted by all. The Election Commission had ordered by-election within three months. This was an important election for the ruling Congress-I as it had lost a string of four assembly elections in southern districts in a row. It was essentially a fight between Veerendra Patil and Devaraj Urs. In the 1972 Assembly elections the Congress-I had a resounding victory in Gulbarga district winning 8 out of 11 seats. But Urs did not make any Lingayat MLA a minister. Instead he made a backward caste MLA, Devendrappa Galappa Jamedar, an OBC non-entity from Chincholi, a cabinet minister. So, for the by-election campaign, Devaraj Urs camped in Gulbarga for one week, an unprecedented action by any CM.

It was a high-voltage campaign by both parties. Morarji Desai had come for campaigning for the Congress-O candidate who was a big landlord from Malkhed town (which was once *Manyakheta,* the capital of

Rashtrakutas) and there was a huge crowd to listen to him in the Municipal garden grounds. Seeing the size of the crowd, the Press reported that the Congress-O had an "edge" over the ruling party, forgetting that if in a busy Indian thoroughfare a person simply stands and looks up at sky for sometime, soon a hundred persons will join him to look up and even claim to have seen a flying saucer! There were one or two amusing incidents for me during this election. One week before the polling, the Chief Election Officer of the State Balagopalan who was senior to me by nine years phoned me that he was coming to Gulbarga as the Election Commission, Delhi had asked him to visit Gulbarga to check on the election process in view of the national attention it was drawing. So I sent the district Distinguished Visitor (DV) car to Begumpet airport in Hyderabad and he landed in my office around 1 pm after four hours of road journey. This was in April and Gulbarga was sizzling at 45°C. From Nizam's days, in April and May offices in Gulbarga Division would work from 8.15am to 1.30pm only as afternoons will be too hot and the tar on the road would be melting making it impossible for people to walk and cars to run, the molten tar attaching to the tyres. I sent my peon for a bottle of ice-water to my house which was just a hundred feet and separated from my office only by a wall and gate. My wife was away in Madras expecting our second son. The peon brought a bottle of cold water and I poured for Balagopalan a full, tall glass. He sipped a mouthful. As I was drinking cold water since morning I did not sip any from my bottle. Balagopalan gagged and blurted, *I say Balu, there is something wrong with your water.* As a precaution against jaundice which was reported from some parts of Gulbarga city, we had liberally chlorinated the municipal water supply. So, I told him, *Sir there is some jaundice in the city, so it is the chlorine.* He took one more sip and said, *No, no, this is not Chlorine but something else.* So I took a sip myself from his bottle. It was pure gin! As my wife had gone to Madras, the peon had brought by mistake the bottle of gin, which looked like pure water, from the refrigerator without knowing the difference. I profusely apologized to Balagopalan and told him what had happened and tried to take away his glass and to replace with my bottle of genuine water. Then came the punch line! He hastily withdrew his hand and said, *No, no, this is excellent, I will take it!* So, he drank one full glass of nearly five ounces of pure gin in the half hour he was discussing the by-election seriously with me before I took him for lunch. There are many things we learn from our seniors!

There was another episode though not humourous as the glass of gin at noon. There was an Executive Engineer in the Upper Krishna Project at the Narayanpur dam in Gulbarga district which was the biggest irrigation project in the state under construction. A lot of labour was being employed by the UKP contractors. I had arranged to send over 10,000 landless labour from the famine affected taluks to the project sites for work. There were four Executive Engineers in the UKP area and three were quite cooperative. One EE was not, saying that he could not ask the contractor to employ them as it was the contractor's prerogative to employ whom he wants. While he was technically correct, it was well within his powers to persuade the contractor to employ Gulbarga's landless labour sent by the Tahsildar as done by other EEs. But this EE refused, showing his status and power, and I had kept it in mind and then the by-election came. The Parliamentary Constituency of Gulbarga consisted of six Assembly segments with about 1,100 polling booths, of which about 50 were considered to be "sensitive" and were also in the interior where even jeep would not go and only selected officers were to be posted there as Principal Polling Officers. They had to undergo a special training and would have to visit the village often and be at the Polling Station three days before the polling and stay in the village till end of the polling and bring the ballot boxes to the District Headquarters the next day. There is no such thing as toilet in these villages and equality prevailed in open air defecation. As the District Election Officer we would normally select a person from the Revenue Department not below the rank of Deputy Tahsildar but there was no specific rule about it and the DC could appoint any gazetted officer of sufficient seniority for that work. So, I appointed this recalcitrant Executive Engineer as the Chief Polling Officer for one such sensitive polling booth in the interior of Chincholi taluk which was the farthest from the UKP office of the EE, bordering AP. He took the matter as insulting and wrote to his Chief Engineer that he declines to be a Polling Officer. Now, the Election Law is so stringent that a person refusing to do polling duty can be prosecuted and is liable for imprisonment! The Chief Engineer who was an amiable person contacted me and requested whether the DC could spare the EE from election duty. I told him it can be done as a favour and, by the way, can the CE ask the EE to employ the famine-affected labour whom the Tahsildar would be sending for canal work? Needless to say the CE got the message and the EE wasted no time to ask the Tahsildar to send the workers. There are thus hundred ways a determined DC&DM can get his work done, by request, persuasion and ultimately by veiled threat. The by-election went off without any incident and the Congress-I candidate won in a landslide. The MLAs complimented me and said the impressive victory was because of the extensive relief works, fair price shops and drinking water supply though I knew that it was mainly due to the magical *Gharibi*

Hatao slogan of Mrs Gandhi. While *Gharibi* was not *hatao-ed,* the Congress (O) was certainly *hatao-ed* in Gulbarga!

DEATH OF A DALIT WOMAN IN MLA'S HOUSE

One day the President of the Republican Party of India which had a sizeable following in Gulbarga city came to my office with his followers and gave me a petition. It was quite serious, alleging that a young Dalit female domestic servant was found dead in the house of Congress-I MLA, Subash Patil at Kamalapur which was on the Gulbarga-Bidar highway. The father of the MLA, Shankar Shetty Patil, a Lingayat leader, was the area *Dhani* and was himself MLA earlier. According to the petition, both father and son had prevailed over the Medical Officer of the Primary Health Centre at Kamalapur to give a certificate that it was a case of suicide by hanging. I probed the RPI members further and they pushed in front the parents of the dead girl. They told me that she was beaten up for coming late to work and she died unexpectedly. So, her neck was tied to a rope and she was hung from a beam to make it look like suicide. The RPI President also told me that instead of immediately informing the Police Sub-Inspector, the father of the MLA had gone in search of the Medical Officer who was also a Lingayat obviously posted at Kamalapur at the behest of the MLA. The doctor was on leave and in Gulbarga but went to Kamalapur with the MLA's father, took the body to the PHC and gave a certificate that she died of hanging, apparently a suicide. The girl's parents told me that she was just fifteen and had no reason to commit suicide nor was she ill. This was a very serious matter and had all the ingredients of a heinous crime apart from its political implications namely, suspicious death of a minor Dalit girl in the Lingayat ruling party MLA's house and the Republican Party was taking up the matter. As the law was very clear in case of suspicious death, I constituted a 3-Member Medical Experts Committee headed by the District Surgeon, the District Health Officer and the Principal of Medical College of Gulbarga to exhume her body and conduct the post-mortem again before sunset in the presence of the AC & SDM.

The Exhumation and Post Mortem report was given to me in person by the AC&SDM and the doctors. They had given their finding that the ligature marks were caused after her death and there were injuries on her body which were not from hanging and she was not sexually assaulted. They therefore told me that it was obviously due to beating. The usual procedure was to send the report to the concerned Police Sub Inspector for investigation. But I was none too sure that the

Lingayat Police Sub Inspector would be objective. So, I took the less conventional step of sending my report along with the Medical Experts post mortem report to the District Sessions Judge who had to take the case on his file. He issued an arrest warrant on the MLA and his father and asked the SP personally to conduct investigation. The MLA was in Bangalore and on legal advice came to Gulbarga and surrendered to the Court. This case created a sensation in the State.

[The criminal case went on for six years at the end of which the MLA was acquitted. Under our British Adversarial System of Justice, the Golden Thread of Criminal Law has four important elements namely (1) the accused is innocent until proved guilty, (2) it is for the prosecution to prove the guilt of the accused and not for the accused to prove his innocence, (3) the guilt of the accused should be proved beyond reasonable doubt, and (4) let a hundred criminals go free but let not one innocent be punished. This is markedly different from the Continental Inquisitorial System under the Napoleonic Code where weighing of evidence is not the primary function of the Judge in arriving at a verdict, as under the Adversarial system, but Arriving at the Truth was the objective. In this case it was a fact the girl was killed, the question was who did it and how? Under the Inquisitorial system, the investigation of serious crimes is by the Police is done under the supervision of a Magistrate called the Investigating Magistrate and the duty of the Judge (who is called the Trial Magistrate) is to find out the truth namely, who killed the girl and how. Besides, in France for instance, about 150 law graduates are selected on the basis of a competitive examination annually— just like the UPSC examination in India—and they undergo 33 months training in the Ecolé Nationale de la Magistrature (ENM), after which half of them are posted as Investigating Magistrates and the other half as Trial Magistrates. After three years they exchange posts. Under the British system followed by India, on the basis of evidence given before the judge both by prosecution and defence, only 3% of criminal cases ultimately end in conviction after the seven layers of appeal. The Political Parties, the Judiciary and the Legal Fraternity all are together in this perpetuation of farce.]

FAREWELL TO GULBARGA—THEY SAID IT WITH SCARCE FLOWERS

Fortunately, the 1974 monsoon was normal and the district limped back to sowing crops. The relief works were tapered off by June when the copious rains started. 1975 started with a cold January which was good for standing White Jowar. However, the political and law and order situation in the State and at national level was deteriorating though not in Gulbarga. This was because the people and the opposition political parties were exhausted by the severe famine and the landslide victory of Congress-I in the Parliamentary by-election and the draconian MISA I had happily used against black-marketeers. (The Home Guard Commandant Homi Irani told me that many merchants had shifted their residence to Hyderabad during the duration of the famine!) At the national level, the unrest first started in Gujarat in January 1974 when the students of Gujarat University went on strike against the increase in price of hostel food. Soon it became a popular movement against the Congress-led Chimanbhai Patel government, protesting the high corruption in the government.

By this time I had already spent more than two and half years as DC&DM of Gulbarga after one year in Shimoga. Then I was told by the Chief Secretary that I was being transferred as DC of Bangalore district. Normally, direct recruit IAS officers were not given a third district charge. Karnataka had about 300 IAS Officers and India 5,000, of whom about two-thirds are directly recruited by annual competitive examinations by the UPSC and one-thirds are promoted from State Civil Services and State Departments. Bangalore in 1975 was the biggest district in Karnataka State, population-wise, and had 11 thickly populated taluks. The total population of Bangalore district was 36 lakhs of which 18 lakhs were in Bangalore Municipal Corporation area. It was then the composite Bangalore district which is currently trifurcated as Bangalore Rural, Bangalore Urban and Ramanagaram districts. Being the capital of the state, it was also politically sensitive. I asked the Revenue Commissioner K Balasubramanyam, the DCs being technically working under the Revenue Department, as to why I was being given a third district instead of being posted as a Head of Department. He said while he did not know the exact reason but CM wanted it, because of the difficulties in managing the distribution of essential commodities in Bangalore district as there was a lot of smuggling of foodgrains and sugar to Tamil Nadu whose border was just 20 kilometers from Bangalore. *[He said the CM thought I was good at catching smugglers, and chuckled and asked me "Yakè Nagutheera?"* Why are you laughing *though I was certainly not laughing!]* It was the elderly gentleman's childlike habit to chuckle for no reason and ask you why *you* are laughing even if you are not laughing! He was a delightful person. Karnataka had such fine officers as K Balasubramanyam, RJ Rebello, RA Naik, GVK, most of whom became Chief Secretaries and K Lakshman Rao the then Home Secretary, his brother Narasimha Rau who also became Chief Secretary, KM Mirani, TR Satishchandran, KSN Murthy, TP Issar, JC Lynn, and many other fine officers and gentlemen. Unfortunately, after the coronation of Bangarappa, the Golden Age of Corruption was launched in Karnataka and the State also had, as *'Dhrishti Dosha'* some corrupt mercenaries being made Chief Secretaries and as Secretaries in CM's office, under Bangarappa, JH Patel and SM Krishna, to mention a few till I retired. I will be narrating this Fall from Grace of Karnataka in subsequent chapters.

Thus, I was posted as DC&DM of the Capital Bangalore district in June 1975 with the imposition of Emergency. The officers and leading citizens of Gulbarga district had given me a grand send-off at the Town Hall to which they brought heaps of flower garlands that I never suspected Gulbarga had. I went to Bangalore by train and when the train arrived at Gulbarga station from Sholapur, even the station master took a few minutes to delay the train and tie flower garlands to my compartment and he also garlanded me. I was touched. But the real surprise was when the train reached Yadgir station, thirty minutes from Gulbarga. One Excise Contractor rushed to the platform and into my compartment and garlanded me saying that, he had missed me in Gulbarga and had to garland his DC by chasing the train by car all the way to Yadgir! I was really humbled as I had not favoured any excise contractor in my tenure of thirty three months and by the affection of this Liquor Baron whom I did not know. In most ways, Gulbarga made me the self-confident administrator, even an imperious Knight Templar, a Crusader that I believed I became. It was a great challenge and opportunity to serve in the most famine affected district at that time. But in this I was assisted by a set of brilliant, committed officers, especially my learned AC&SDM Ashok Dubey IAS, Food Assistant Jayachar, HqA Adviachar, my eleven Tahsildars, SP Billimoria IPS, ASP Albuquerque IPS at Yadgir and many of my seniors and citizens. I was given full support by MYG the FM, Devraj Urs the CM, Veerendra Patil (even when he was out of power) and all the political leaders from the district. I could proudly say, I stood up and delivered. Sitting in the speeding night train to Bangalore, with fast vanishing shadows and dimlit sad villages blinking in darkness outside, an unexplainable melancholy engulfed me and I grieved like a Nawab who had lost his kingdom!

❖❖❖

CHAPTER 7

As DC & DM of Bangalore during Emergency Darkness under the Lamp

BACKGROUND

From 1974 there were a series of events leading to the deterioration of law and order in India. The 1973 Oil Shock caused double digit inflation and corruption became omnipresent. *Lok Nayak* Jayaparakash Narayan called for a *Sampurna Kranthi* or Total Revolution. Soon Total Revolution became a one-point programme of *Indira Hatao*, 'Remove Indira Gandhi' from power and then form a Party-less Democracy, whatever Athenian and Roman demagoguery that was. At the same time, George Fernandes the fiery Socialist Party leader—rebel without *Pause*—who was heading the powerful Railway Employees Unions called for a General Railway Strike in 1974 which paralysed the railway transport affecting the movement of essential commodities. In January 1975 the Railway Minister LN Misra was blown up by a bomb planted in the Samastipur railway station platform in Bihar. JP exhorted the students to boycott schools and colleges. In a mammoth public meeting at Delhi's Ram Lila grounds he asked the government employees to stop cooperating with the government and also called the Armed Forces to disobey illegal orders. In June 1975, JP, Morarji Desai and all other opposition parties' leaders called for a huge meeting to surround the PM's residence, prevent her from attending office and force her to resign, though this was hardly a Gandhian formula. JP's call for a "Total Revolution", though would have would have ended in Total Confusion, with "party-less government" something like the direct street democracy of Rome, leading to the rule of Julius Caesar.

But the *coup de grâce* was the judgement of Justice Jagmohanlal Sinha of Allahabad High Court on 12 June 1975 declaring void the 1971 election of Mrs Gandhi to the Rae Bareilly Parliament seat on the election petition of the *Lohiaite* Raj Narain and disabling her from functioning as PM and banning her from contesting elections for six years on comparatively trivial grounds such as use of government resources to build the rostrums at her election rallies, that Yashpal Kapoor her private secretary had become her election agent before his resignation was accepted by the government, not accounting for printing of some propaganda pamphlets, use of electricity from the state electricity department, etc. The *Times of India* sarcastically commented this as, dismissing a head of government for a traffic violation! Nani Palkhiwala, the counsel for Mrs Gandhi filed an appeal in the Supreme Court and Justice VR Krishna Iyer gave a ruling on 24 June 1975 granting a conditional stay that she could not attend Parliament during the pendency of the petition. The next day, the opposition parties announced their plan to organize a large public 'house arrest' of her by surrounding her official residence and preventing her from coming out. The Jan Sangh which was ruling Delhi Municipal Council was ready to provide man power. I thought this was like the crowds surrounding the Winter Palace of the Tsar in Petrograd in 1917. But while Tsar Nicholas II abdicated, the occupant of Delhi's No.1 Safdarjang Road, India's own unrivalled Tsarina, was made of sterner stuff. In the early hours of 25 June 1975 Internal Emergency under Article 352 of the Constitution was imposed following which civil liberties were suspended. Four organizations, Anand Marg, Naxalite Movement, Rashtriya Swayam Sevak Sangh and Jamaat-e-Islami were banned. Immediately after the proclamation of the Emergency about 7,000 persons mostly belonging to RSS, Jansangh, Naxalites and Left parties and DMK were detained. Interestingly, some of the prominent persons who supported Emergency were Vinoba Bhave ("India needs *Anushasan Parva*—Era of Discipline", he said), JRD Tata, writer Kushwanth Singh, Mother Teresa, M Karunanidhi (till his government in Tamil Nadu was dismissed), and MGR. *[A total of about 110,000 were detained during the 21 months Emergency—as many as 40,000 from Shiromani Akali Dal and Shiromani Gurdwara Prabhandak Committee, though Sikhs constituted only 2% of India's population.]*

THE TWENTY POINT PROGRAMME AND THE 'BONZAI' FIVE-POINT PROGRAMME

In this background of JP movement and Emergency I took charge as DC&DM of Bangalore District including Bangalore city. In 1975 Bangalore Municipal Corporation Area had a population of 21 lakhs and the entire district had a population of 32 lakhs, the most populous district in the State. Under the Code of Criminal Procedure the District Magistrate was the Deputy Commissioner and the Commissioner of Police for the city of Bangalore was the Additional District Magistrate.

The detention of political leaders which included important leaders such as Atal Bihari Vajpayee, Lal Kishan Advani, Venkiah Naidu, Arun Jaitley, Veerendra Patil, Ramakrishna Hegde, HD Deve Gowda, PGR Sindhia, Karunanidhi, JH Patel and many others was done by the ADM & Commissioner of Police under direct orders from the Union Home Ministry. Importantly, I had decided that I will not issue any political detention order under MISA except for economic offences. The powers of detention of delegated to the ADM and Commissioner of Police, in addition to the DM&DC helped me in this regard greatly. The proclamation of Emergency was immediately followed by the announcement of a liberal 20 POINT PROGRAMME of:

* Abolition of Bonded Labour by law;
* Liquidation of rural indebtedness and moratorium on recovery of debt from the poor;
* Ceilings on ownership of vacant land, distribution of surplus land among rural poor;
* Bringing down prices of essential commodities;
* Confiscation of lands owned by smugglers;
* Promote austerity in government spending;
* Raising income-tax exemption limit from Rs.6,000 to Rs.8,000;
* Stepping up house site availability to houseless;
* Reviewing laws on minimum agricultural wages;
* Bringing 5 million additional hectares under irrigation and a programme for augmenting underground water;
* Increasing Power Generation;
* Developing handlooms sector and improving quality of people's cloth;
* Effecting socialization of urban land and ceiling on possession of vacant land;
* Special squads for controlling conspicuous consumption and summary trials of economic offenders;
* Liberalizing investment procedures and deterrent laws against misuse of import licences;
* New schemes for workers association in industry;
* National Permit for road transport;
* Essential commodities at controlled prices to students in hostels;

* Books and stationery at controlled prices;

* New Apprenticeship scheme to enlarge employment and training to weaker sections.

Besides the 20-Point Programme there was also the 5-Point Programme of Sanjay Gandhi who held no positon in Government and yet got more importance than any Minister because of his Extra-Constitutional Authority status. This does not happen even in a dynastic monarchy like Saudi Arabia, the only country in the world named after a family—*Saudi,* where the Crown Prince does not exercise such power over the government as Sanjay Gandhi did. There was no public agitation, no intellectuals protesting, no priests condemning. Mrs Gandhi famously said, *"Not even a dog barked"!* More of this later. The 5-Points Programme was:

* Adult Literacy ("Each one, Teach one");
* Tree Planting;
* Radical Family Planning;
* Abolition of Dowry;
* Abolition of Caste system;

On the face of it, these programmes were highly laudable, environment-friendly and helping the poor. I therefore started applying myself to their implementation. The DC&DM, apart from the basic land administration, was the implementing authority for all government programmes in the district.

BONDED LABOUR IN BANGALORE—DARKNESS UNDER THE LAMP

Just two days after the momentous proclamation of Emergency I opened the *Indian Express* along with my morning coffee sitting in the guest house of the Bharat Earth Movers Ltd, off-MG Road (Bangalore was the only district where the DC did not have an official quarters and I was yet to be allotted a house by the House Rent Controller), when I saw the bold heading in the Letters to the Editor page of Indian Express, *What Use Bonded Labour Abolition Act?* which was signed by one Brother George. It said, *While the Prime Minister had announced that bonded labour has been abolished by law, does the government know that right under its nose in this capital city bonded labour is practised in a blatant manner in a quarry within a walking distance of Krishnarajapuram police station and will the government take any action to rescue the bonded labourers?* As the letter gave the precise location of the quarry, as soon as my official vehicle which was a sturdy four-wheel drive Willy's Jeep Station Wagon driven by my equally sturdy driver Govindappa (he was also the President of the State Drivers Union, I learned!) came to pick me up at 9 am, I decided to find Brother George whose Seminary name was also given in his letter which was on the outskirts of KR Puram on the National Highway 4, just 20 minutes then from Bangalore city. So I reached the Seminary and the novice-brothers were surprised at the DC visiting them. They fetched a more surprised Brother George. When I introduced myself and told him my intention was only to know more about the quarry bonded labour and to rescue them, he was happy to come with me to show the quarry. So I took him in my van and when we approached the place he told me to stop and pointed at the quarry. He could not come to the quarry as the contractor was influential and he could harm him and the seminary. So I thanked him and proceeded to the quarry with my Tahsildar of Bangalore East Taluk whom I had collected at KR Puram, on the way.

First, I had a look at the quarry which was very deep at about 200 feet and found many men, women and also children working and a *maistry* supervising. Seeing a government vehicle, he came up and soon some quarry-workers also came up. Not accustomed to being interrogated by the DC, the *maistry* was blabbering. I saw a large prison-like rectangular single storey stone-barrack building within a hundred feet of where we were standing and I asked the *maistry* what it was. Frightened, he said he did not know. By this time I had noticed the loincloth clad stoneworkers were whispering among themselves in Tamil. So I asked them in Tamil what that building was and they answered it was where they lived. So we moved to the building and I found there was only one steel door and it was locked. When the Tahsildar asked the *maistry* to open it, he said he did not have the key. So, Govindappa, with great enthusiasm, broke open the door. When we entered I found there were about 20 children and a few women cooking. By this time all the quarry-workers had also assembled inside the prison-like building and this is what I learned from them: They were a group of nearly 200 stone workers and they belonged to *Oddar* community (a stone-breaking caste) from Denkanikottai in the neighbouring Krishnagiri district of Tamil Nadu bordering Bangalore district. They were professional stone-breakers and the *Yejaman* Rayappa (the Contractor) had one year ago brought the families to this quarry. Each family was given an advance of Rs 200 and they had to work, including children, from 6 am to 12 noon and again from 4 pm till sunset. The more experienced workers were to use *Thottayi,* the Blasting Gelatine to break the rock into small boulders and other men were to break them into still smaller *jelly*-stones and women had to carry them to the top of the quarry and store them. The Gelatine cost would be deducted from the weekly wages. Part of the wages would be deducted from the advance and every Saturday some cash will be given to the workers to go to the weekly *Santhè* (market) in KR Puram to buy essentials. If the male worker goes to the *Santhè* his wife will have to remain behind, if the wife goes the husband had to stay back and if both had to go, the children would remain as hostage. In one year none of the families had repaid the original advance of Rs 200 fully. It may take two more years for them to completely repay the remaining amount, *Yejaman* Rayappa had told them. The *maistry* would be present from 6am to 6pm and when all workers were inside the Barracks he would lock the door and leave. There were two *Dharwans* to guard during the night.

I asked them why no one tried to escape. One young worker pointed to a middle-aged woman and said she was his mother and when once she went to see their relative in another nearby quarry and did not return for two days, the *Yejaman* brought her back to the Barracks, the *maistry* tied her to the tree (he showed me the tree in the courtyard) and branded her with hot-iron just above the left breast. When I was aghast with disbelief he led his mother in front of me and told me to see for myself. *Oddar* women do not wear an upper garment as it would be inconvenient for them when breaking stones with their right hand which was why Rayappa had branded her on the left upper breast. A shining two-inch scar was clearly visible as if she was a branded cattle. I asked him why no one had stopped Rayappa, why he himself being her son did not rush to her rescue. He said, what can we do, we are poor people and *Yejaman* is very powerful, the police are with him and if we protest we will be beaten up. I noticed that while narrating these events neither the woman nor her son was crying as is the norm when villagers explain their hardship to officers. They explained the branding in an expressionless, deadpan, bored voice devoid of all emotion. It then struck me that what I was witnessing was not the humdrum, colourless, listless, vacant life of the extremely poor as I have seen in famine-stricken Gulbarga. This was something of a different genre, not just abject poverty but a category below poverty which can be termed only as *Degradation* which decile is not shown in any economic survey on income inequality tables. In a miserable life, people have to be first promoted to Absolute Poverty from the lowest, unstudied category of Degradation. When a person's mother is being branded by hot iron like an animal, the reflex action of any son, even a poor son, is to attack the perpetrator in a reflex action of primeval mammalian instinct. If this natural instinct was not there to stop Rayappa that day, it was because Degradation had reduced human behaviour below the minimum Line of Human Nature, something like the paralytic, Absolute Indifference of a victim, like a doe in the jaws of a cheetah being eaten alive, giving up life-struggle after some time as one sees in the National Geographic. This was akin to behaviour in the Nazi Concentration Camps where some inmates would even spy upon fellow Jews, to the *Kapos,* to curry favour with the guards. Or some beggars who display deliberately maimed rented babies to get sympathy from people sitting impatiently in cars in traffic junctions willing for the signal to change to green.

By this time, the *maistry* had attempted to slip away but my formidable Govindappa caught him and dragged him to the same tree where the *Oddar* woman was once tied and branded and I asked Govindappa to tie him up to the tree so that he would not run away again. The frightened *maistry* started crying and blabbering, fearing he was going to be branded. From my interrogating him further, more gruesome stories spilled out. The Gelatine to blast rocks was used by the senior workers who were not experts nor had the licence to use dynamite. To save expenses Rayappa was using the workers illegally. Being not technically trained to handle explosives, there were two occasions in the past when the Gelatine had exploded pre-maturely killing two labourers. To escape arrest they were hurriedly buried in the crevices of the quarry. By then, it was already 4 pm and I had spent over five hours in the quarry and the barracks without any lunch but I had more work.

I asked the *maistry* to be untied and proceeded to the Police Station which was just a few minutes from the quarry and on the old Bombay-Bangalore-Madras National Highway-4. The Police Sub Inspector was alarmed at my sudden appearance as it was a rare occasion to get an unannounced visit from the DM. I asked him whether he was aware of the practice of bonded labour in the quarry just four kilometres from his police station. What he told me was still more shocking. He said, there was no such thing as bonded labour in his area and he knew Rayappa the benevolent PWD contractor who had given employment and shelter to Dalit *Oddars!*. It was futile to enlighten him because during my interrogation the *maistry* had confessed that Rayappa was a major contractor supplying stones required for the National Highway. He had also heard Rayappa was constructing the big building coming up at the entrance of 100-Feet Road at Indira Nagar, for the Minister of Agriculture Chikke Gowda from Hosakote which taluk town was just ten kilometres from the quarry on way to Kolar town. It was obvious that Rayappa was a big-time contractor close to the Minister and therefore protected by the government departments including the Police, Mines & Geology and Revenue. It was a case of the Fox being appointed as Watchman to the Poultry Farm. I therefore asked the Tahsildar to write a detailed narration about the quarry which became the First Information Report to the Police and asked the PSI to arrest Rayappa and his three associates for offences under the Bonded Labour Abolition Ordinance. The puzzled PSI asked, *Sir, what is Bonded Labour*

Ordinance, as he did not have a copy of it! So I told the Tahsildar to give a copy to him.

It was already getting to 7 pm. So I decided to leave. But before leaving I made a phone call to JC Lynn who was Secretary to CM as the CM was in charge of 20-Points Programme. Besides, the quarry episode was quite a serious one and the first of its kind in Bangalore and indeed in the State, being just two days after the proclamation of Emergency and there was the possible link of a cabinet minister to the contractor Rayappa. Lynn had himself just reached home when I rang him. After listening to me for fifteen minutes he simply asked me where was I now. I told him I was about to leave the Police Station for Bangalore. He told me, *You go straight to CM's house next to the government Kumara Krupa Guest House, opposite the Golf Course and narrate to him what had happened.* Surprised, I told him I have no appointment with him to meet him in his house at this late hour. Lynn said he would ring up the CM that the DC, Bangalore is coming to inform him of a serious matter, a matter very much a part of Emergency administration. Lynn was five years senior to me and was a highly upright, ethical and bold officer who was Secretary to the CM Veerendra Patil from 1968 to 1971 and when Devaraj Urs became CM he continued with him as Secretary which would last till 1980 when Gundu Rao, a protégé of Sanjay Gandhi, the 'Dark Knight' of Emergency, would become CM, about which later. Lynn served Veerendra Patil and Devaraj Urs ten years, giving them always the right advice however unpopular and, to the credit of both CMs, they appreciated such impartial, albeit often irksome, advice. He was like CM's Conscience Keeper, like the official King's Conscience Keeper from William the Conqueror to Henry VIII in England. Therefore, Lynn immediately understood the significance of my bonded labour narration. Among the Press and the opposition parties there was an animosity against the government because of the suspension of fundamental rights, press censorship, detention of political leaders and a general atmosphere of fear. In such an atmosphere, a humane matter like the release of bonded labour and arrest of one of its practitioners right in Bangalore would put the government in a favourable light. This was probably why Lynn wanted me to go straight to the CM and narrate the quarry bonded labour episode.

So I reached CM's house at 9 pm, dusty, sweaty and dishevelled. One of the PAs at CM's residence received me and rushed me to the CM who was in the dining room with his family members. The CM, his wife Chikkammanni, his younger daughter and her husband Dr Nataraj (even though he had not completed MBBS course!) were all about to start their dinner and the CM asked me to join him and asked me what was such an important matter Lynn was excited about. So I recited the incidents I had rehearsed in my van. He listened to me patiently. Then he shocked me by asking, *Would you like a drink?* Only then I noticed that he and his son in law were having a glass each. Urs was a charming person. He was quite tall and weighed about a hundred kilograms. In his younger days he was a regular wrestler. Surprised, and without thinking, I blurted, *If it is no trouble, sir* and I got a glass served by Dr Nataraj. (That was the first time ever I tasted *Royal Salute*. It was supposed to be the top of the Chivas family!) Devaraj Urs came from a small community close to the Wodeyar Maharajas of Mysore. The word Urs comes from *Arasu* meaning King. After a few minutes he sprang another surprise on me. "Why don't you detain him under MISA?" I had told him that I had ordered Rayappa and his associates' arrest under the Abolition of Bonded Labour Ordinance (the Act was still to be passed) under which imprisonment of 3 years was prescribed when convicted. But MISA was psychologically more forceful and detention was solely on the basis of the subjective satisfaction of the DM. I agreed at once, marvelling at the grasp for drama by a consummate politician. The same night the CM informed the Press about it and it was splashed in the front page of both English and Kannada dailies next day. Thus, I was introduced to Bangalore public and how! I realized that I had the CM's *carte blanche* to use MISA against economic offenders. I passed detention order against Rayappa and three of his henchmen and sent them to Bellary jail which became my favourite state guest house for MISA detainees.

The matter did not end there. If the rescued bonded labour are not rehabilitated they would have to go back to bondage with the same *Yejaman* and on more adverse terms. Fortunately for me, Rayappa was supplying small-size stones called *Jelly* to the National Highway and my old Shimoga friend Bore Gowda was now promoted and was the Superintending Engineer of National Highways at Bangalore! So I telephoned him and he readily agreed to ask his EE to continue to buy the *Jelly* from the ex-bonded labourers provided they could be formed into a collective body. So I got the Deputy Registrar of Cooperative Societies of Bangalore Mr D'Souza who proved to be an excellent organizer. He immediately put his Assistant Registrar to form a Labour Cooperative Society of the ex-bonded labourers and arranged to sell the stone-material without any stoppage. Also, under the 20 Points Programme, People's Housing was important by which houseless persons could be given sites of 30 feet by 20 feet and also a house of ~300 square feet could be built with a grant of Rs 2,500. I therefore asked the the Block Development Officer to allot sites to the fifty families at the quarry and also to construct houses for them immediately. I had to get the mining lease of Rayappa cancelled and transfer it to the Labour Cooperative Society. This caused some delay because the Department of Mines and Geology had a long-standing patronage with traditional contractors and political leaders. I had to gently tell the Director of M & G that MISA does not exempt officers from its reach as the term used in it was *'any person'* which would not exclude the Director! He took the hint and the lease was granted to the Labour Coop Society. Thus, this ended happily for the released bonded labour whose livelihood became better because of the abolition of their unjust debt and their getting own houses. Later, they named their colony of 50 new houses 'Subramanya Nagar'! No monetary incentive can ever equal such appreciation of an officer by the poor.

Following this episode more instances of landless agriculture labour being held as bonded labour in the houses of landlords were discovered. The *modus operandi* of this was: The Dalit landless labourer sends his teenage son to work in the house of the landlord on an annual basis in consideration of four or five bags of *ragi* for a year given to the father at the beginning of the term of bonded labour and the boy will be given free food, shelter and for the festive occasions of *Shankranthi* in April and *Deepavali* in November a set of new clothes. This system was called *'Sambala'*. Customarily, the term of *Sambala* began with the harvest of *ragi* in March-April, that is, on *Ugadi* (new year day in South India) and ended at the next *Ugadi*. After that the arrangement may be either renewed or terminated as agreeable to both parties. I was surprised to find agreements even signed in Rs 10 Stamp Paper and the terms were spelt out in detail and Left Thumb Impression of both parties affixed in the paper along with witnesses' signatures. But these were not registered in the sub-Registrar's office as there was no legal provision for it. But the fact it was on a stamp paper with signatures of both parties and witnesses lent binding in the mind of the dalit father. The duties of the boy were to look after the cattle of the landlord and generally do any work allotted to him by the landlord. The Assistant Commissioners and Tahsildars undertook a campaign to identify such bonded labour in the villages and rehabilitate them by arranging to give bank loans to buy buffaloes or sheep and also to provide house sites and construction of houses under Peoples Housing Scheme. Within three months of Emergency the officers collected over forty such bonds in stamp paper and I sent some of them to the Revenue Commissioner and Chief Secretary as samples which they had not seen before.

"DID YOU PUT THIS THUMB ON YOUR PETITION?"—
THE WRATH OF A LANDLORD

Though Bangalore was not yet India's Silicon Valley in mid-1970s, it was already the fifth biggest metropolitan city in India after Mumbai, Delhi, Calcutta and Madras. There were a number of central public sector undertakings such as Bharat Electronics, Bharat Earth Movers, and Hindustan Machine Tools, the German company MICO-Bosch in the Corporate Sector which was established as early as in 1953, and the Regional offices of big banks and many multi-nationals were shifted to Bangalore. Besides, Karnataka was the first state to start what came to be known as "Donation Colleges" in Medicine, Engineering and other professional courses. Till the 1960s there were only government professional colleges in India. There was thus an explosion of medical and engineering colleges in Bangalore and in other districts due to the liberal attitude of the government though there were also huge bribes to grant permissions to start them. It was common for other states' students to get admission in Karnataka's private colleges by paying high 'donations' to these management seats. One of the reasons for the rapid expansion of industries in Bangalore was this readily available skilled manpower.

Such quick development of Bangalore from the mid-1960's led to an increase in Bangalore city's population from 17 lakhs in 1971 to 30 lakhs in 1981, an incredible increase of 76% in a decade. This had its inevitable impact on land values. In surrounding rural areas of Bangalore the value of agricultural lands sky-rocketed leading to grabbing of land by the powerful. One such extreme form of feudal land grabbing came to my attention just three months into the Emergency. One day about ten *dalits* came to my office who had a gruesome story to tell. Five of them had bandage on their hands. They were from Chikka Jala village on NH 9 in Devanahalli taluk in my district, about 20 km from my office. They were agricultural workers of one landlord Muni Papanna Gowda. Five years earlier, Gowda made them apply for grant of gomal land from government, 5 acres each. Under the Land Grant Rules landless labour could be given upto 5 acres of dry land to each family, the first preference being to persons belonging to Scheduled Castes of the same village. So, Muni Pappanna Gowda pursued their applications with the Revenue Department and got them granted five acres each from the Gomal. (From early times, every village had reserved for cattle grazing—Gomal—at the rate of 30 acres for 100 heads of cattle and six goats being equated to one head of cattle. With urbanization the number of cattle got reduced in villages in Bangalore and so there was *excess*

Gomal from which lands could be granted.) After the land grant, Gowda formed an Agriculture Cooperative Society with the ten Dalit grantees and their 50 acres with himself as Chairman. Then he got loans of Rs 5,000 for one acre each from the Primary Land Development Cooperative Bank of Devanahalli for developing the land. Having received Rs 2.5 lakhs for the 50 acres, Gowda used it to plant the quick growing *Eucalyptus tereticornis* (Mysore Gum) and *Casuarina* (*Sarve gida*) which had a ready market for paper industry and as fuel wood. Both give a yield of about 30 tons per acre every three years. Munipapanna Gowda made the first harvest of cutting just two months ago and sold the wood for Rs.15 lakhs (currently Rs.135 lakhs) to Harihar Polyfibers paper mill.

The ten dalit workers, though they were the title-holders of the fifty acres of wooded land in which they were made to work as labourers by the Gowda, had not received any income from this land except their weekly wages at Rs.30 per male and Rs.20 per female worker. Then, about a month ago, they received notices from the Assistant Registrar of Cooperative Societies that each of them had to pay Rs 1,500 plus interest at 8% plus penal interest for the loan of Rs 25,000 each of them was given for their 5 acres of land each and which they had failed to repay. As they had not received any loan nor any income from the land, all being received by Muni Papanna Gowda, they approached a dalit leader who advised them to approach the Deputy Commissioner. So they got a petition written by the Dalit leader to which the five dalits (out of the ten grantees) affixed their left thumb impression and came to the DC's office two weeks ago and gave the petition to the Reception Clerk in the ground floor of my office for which they got an acknowledgment in Red Card, which system I had introduced for serious matters. Their petition was promptly sent by my office to the Tahsildar of Devanahalli who also visited Chikka Jala three days ago and enquired the matter first with the dailts and then with Gowda.

After the departure of the Tahsildar, Muni Papanna berated the dalits and after ascertaining who had put their LTI in the petition against him, he and his sons pinned the five and cut off their left thumbs, shouting *"Now, let me see how will you give petitions to the DC?"* The five dalits removed the bandage and showed me their left hands. I could see the still blood-stained stumps where their thumbs had been. It took me some time to recover from what I had heard and seen, my fury rising. It was clearly grievous hurt under the IPC with imprisonment from seven to ten years. Besides the victims being dalits, it will attract the penal provisions of the Scheduled Castes and Tribes (Prevention of Atrocities) Act. I therefore sent the dalits to the Government Victoria Hospital along with my Headquarters Assistant. I had telephoned the Superintendent of the Hospital to examine the wounds of the dalits and give a certificate of the cause of injuries after his own examination. My HqA returned with the certificate and the dalits in the afternoon.

So, I decided something more than merely prosecution under the Indian Penal Code should be done. Besides, I was not too sure that the powerful Gowda landlord will ever get punished by our Courts. Firstly, he would get bail, the police would be pressurized, the case would go on for years, the victims would be harassed, the prosecution witnesses would turn hostile, the government advocate may even get 'mamool' from the defence lawyer as is the custom and finally Muni Papanna Gowda will be acquitted as the case was not "proved beyond reasonable doubt" and the already poor dalits would be further demoted to Degradation level. So I decided that in addition to the ritual of police prosecution which could take its own long futile course, I would conduct Externment Proceedings within my own powers as DM as I had learned from my Gulbarga experience where I had externed an Irani Gypsy gang.

Under the Police Act, the DM has powers to extern any person outside his district, who are 'reasonably likely to cause danger or alarm to community'. Many DMs are not even aware of these powers. The Externment order of the DM can of course be challenged before the High Court. Hence I had to follow scrupulously the provisions of natural justice so that the order would stand the scrutiny of the HC when the powerful landlord would move the HC. So, I issued notices to Muni Papanna Gowda and to the dalits that I would be conducting an Inquiry in Chikka Jala village itself and had asked the Tahsildar to arrange its publicity by beating of the drums, tom-toms, in the village daily. I chose to hear the case in the village itself because it was open to all including the entire villager and also the press. Mainly, the advocate representing the accused would be in unfamiliar ground, away from the Kafkaesque atmosphere of Indian Courts, and surrounded by a mass of ill-clad, emaciated poor people with accusing eyes in the dusty village with no other lawyer fraternity in black gowns moving around with supreme self-importance. The crucial point was to remove the advocate from his familiar territory of rarefied court hall and put him in a real-life Indian village. The device of tom-tom in the village is also a highly effective legal method from ancient times when, apart from informing all the villagers including the alleged offenders, it causes incalculable humiliation to the person accused. Such tom-toming seven days in a row made Muni Papanna look powerless and provided mirth to villagers with naked, nose-leaking children running after the tom-tommer! On the appointed day Muni Papanna did not appear before me nor was represented by his advocate but all the dalits and the entire village of some 300 people were present. After ascertaining for the record that the notice was sent to him by registered post as well as pasted on his house inspite of which he was not present, I proceeded to record the statement of each of the ten dalits and also invited some of the villagers including the panchayat members to give their evidence. It took me the whole day to record the evidence of over thirty persons in my hand-writing. Apart from the dalits there were other independent eye-witnesses belonging to other castes who gave their evidence of Muni Papanna's illegal acts including the cutting of the thumbs of the dalits.

The Assistant Registrar of Cooperative Society, the Revenue Inspector and Village Accountant, all gave evidence of the grant of 50 acres of land to the dalits and the planting and cutting of trees by Muni Papanna. I had also taken the precaution of informing the dalit leader who had helped the dalits to prepare their petition to appear before me and he gave evidence that in his opinion the continued freedom of movement of the accused is sure to cause fear and danger to the powerless dalit community and bodily harm and damage to their meagre huts. At the end of the day I had a voluminous file of over a hundred pages of direct evidence. Armed with this I returned and spent a week to prepare a detailed order. But before passing the order, I also took the precaution of issuing another notice to Muni Papanna to appear in my court and give his explanation because it was usual that the High Court would require that a *second chance* of being heard should have been given to the accused in the interest of 'natural justice'. The Indian Judicial system requires only a small technical excuse to acquit the rich and the powerful against the poor and powerless. But this time also, Muni Papanna chose to remain absent. I was intrigued why he was not even being represented by an advocate. So I asked my Tahsildar to find out why he was shy to appear before the DC. What the Tahsildar told me was astounding. The Home Secretary then was a highly influential officer and himself belonging to the *Okkaliga* community and had his farm with a huge, circular, stone-paved, open irrigation well just by the side of the National Highway-9 from Bangalore to Hyderabad passing through Devanahally and close to Chika Jala village. He used to visit his farm every second Saturday of the month and on that occasion many of the important persons of *Okkaliga* community would gather for dinner with goats killed for the *Bada Khana* (as done by the Indian Army in forward areas, one of which I had attended during my military attachment as IAS Probationer.) During the dinner meeting, the grievances of the community, the politics of the area, the attitude of the local officers, etc. would be thoroughly discussed and action points including transfers, filing cases, beating up (!) etc. would all be duly decided. In the last meeting, after my issue of notice to him, Muni Papanna was also present in the dinner meeting and he had raised the danger posed to him and to the community by the DC. The Home Secretary was a consummate diplomat and a realist. He therefore counselled patience to him saying that this was the time of Emergency and the DC as DM had powers of detention under MISA and the Home Secretary had no intervention powers over the DM and besides, the CM approves all action taken by this DC in implementing the PM's 20-Point Programme. He therefore advised Muni Papanna not to appear before the DC and if the DC passes an *ex-parte* order, he can file a Writ Petition before the High Court which powers have not been taken away by the Emergency laws for Police Act offences.

So, I prepared a detailed Externment Order highlighting the background, the gruesome feudal, medieval atrocity of cutting off the thumbs of his own workers from whose lands the landlord benefited instead of the dalits benefiting from land granted to them. For good measure I also commented upon the classical French of *Noblesse Oblige*—meaning Nobility has Obligations and from it the lofty legal principle of *Jural Correlative* which says that if a person has a right over another person, simultaneously he also owes a duty to the other person. My motive in using such high octane legal terms was to impress the Judge when my order was sure to be appealed against and the Judge would be intrigued to go through the legal lexicon and also would appreciate that a mere DM not belonging to the legal fraternity had applied his mind in passing the order! Very often the High Court passes strictures on DCs that they do not pass "speaking orders" and in 'telegraphic language'! With the over-100-page evidence of a large number of persons as recorded in the village itself and recording the fact that enough opportunity was given to the accused who chose to remain absent, mine was not merely Speaking but a *Screaming* order! As the law for externment gave powers to the DM to extern the guilty not only beyond his district but also from districts contiguous to his district and for two years, I royally externed Muni Papanna, feeling like a 10th century Hoysala King, beyond the district limits of Bangalore, Tumkur, Kolar and Mandya for two years. Besides, the Tahsildar had arranged with the dalits to file a complaint with the Devahanalli Police under the Indian Penal Code and the 'Atrocities' Act. In my Externment case the Judge found it was a somewhat unusual 40-page order and the brief facts in the Preamble to the order itself (I always wrote a two-page Preamble so that it catches the attention of the Appellate Judge at once before he starts dozing reading the lengthy order!) showed the seriousness of the offence. Besides, it was rather unusual for the HC to see the DM hearing the case sitting in a village. I had even quoted an old West Bengal pre-independence case where a British Magistrate chose to hear a case on a railway platform because the legal convention was, wherever the Magistrate sits, it becomes a 'Court'. Obviously the High Court Judge took time to read the whole order and in view of what was said in the order and the extreme savagery of facts, he was good enough not to give any stay but only admitted for hearing in the usual course. So, Muni Papanna Gowda had no alternative but to leave his village and Bangalore. I learned he went to stay with his relatives in Dharmapuri district of Tamil Nadu which was not far from Bangalore. But it was no help to him because my order was very clear that if he enters the districts mentioned in the order before two years he will be arrested for violation of the order. The Police and Revenue Department officials had also been strictly informed to be watchful that he does not come into the four districts Karnataka. He could only be escorted by the police in handcuffs as accused to Bangalore only to attend the HC hearings and back to Dharmapuri in handcuffs which was a great humiliation to a powerful landlord apart from advocates fees.

The local and national newspapers gave wide publicity to the externment and the reasons for it. Especially, the Chief Reporter of Deccan Herald, Mr Jagdish, had followed up the case from early on and wrote eloquently about the heinous nature of the crime of the landlord with the photographs of the Dalits' left hands and the externment order which was the first of its kind in Bangalore district in decades. He also got the Press Council's award for his investigative report. In a later government he also became the Press Secretary to the Chief Minister. Muni Papanna could not return to Devanahalli for two years. His petition and the cases against him under IPC dragged on as usual and I learned he had also died before its closure. When I look back upon this episode, I wonder why the DCs who are District Magistrates do not use their Externment powers more often. It is a powerful law in Indian conditions reminiscent of the olden day Kings exiling wrong-doers beyond their kingdoms. The offender is uprooted from his household, friends, property and district familiar to him besides suffering humiliation. This is the normal law since ancient times and has nothing to do with the Emergency when civil rights were suspended and even more drastic than detention under MISA. After all, the British ruled India with only IPC, Cr.PC and Police Act.

❖❖❖

CHAPTER 8

Scooter Fee Causing Closure of Bangalore Cinema Theatres

As DC & DM of Bangalore During Emergency (Contd.)

National telecast by Doordarshan started in Bangalore only in 1982 with the Asian Games held in Delhi. Till then the main entertainment in Bangalore was only cinemas in theatres. The cinema theatres in Bangalore were like palaces—spacious, comfortable with air-conditioning and built aesthetically. There were 72 cinema theatres in Bangalore in 1975. Every day there were three shows, the matinee, evening and night and on Friday, Saturday and Sunday one extra morning show also. Weekend shows would be running house-full. The DM is the regulatory authority for cinema theatres under the Karnataka Cinemas (Regulation) Act which covered Bangalore city. Cinema was a big thing in Bangalore not only because it was highly profitable but because most of the theatre-owners were also Excise Contractors. Before the advent of IT from mid-1980s, liquor was the biggest money-earner and a sizeable earning from liquor industry was unaccounted. Part of this black money went into these picture palaces. All political parties were dependent upon Excise Contractors for electoral survival before real estate boom started in the 1990s. As *quid pro quo,* many liquor barons were made Members of Rajya Sabha—*the Elders*(!), having been nominated to avoid the rough and tumble of tough electioneering. HR Basavaraj, DK Audikesavulu, Vijay Mallya were all liquor barons nominated to the Parliament by political parties in power. Arguably, blood may be thicker than water but liquor was certainly the thickest. Even Lord Balaji Venkateswara could not stop Audikesavulu and Vijay Mallya from being nominated to the Board of Trustees of Tirupathi Tirumala Devasthanam! Suffice to say, Cinema theatres were big business and their owners being mostly liquor lords were law unto themselves even during the Emergency. It was said that the cinema-shows were used for conversion of black money to white as these were not even public limited companies subject to formal audits by chartered accountants. Even if the theatre was half-empty, the management could claim it was running House Full! As the Licensing and Inspection authority of cinema theatres in Bangalore district, I had to inevitably study the legal provisions under the Cinematographic Act meticulously.

It was in this background that when I was holding my weekly Press Meet on a Saturday, one press correspondent complained that the cinema theatre owners of Bangalore had suddenly increased the parking fee for scooters from Rs 2 to Rs 4 and for bicycles from Re 1 to Rs 2 while no parking fee was collected for cars! Obviously, the avid cinema-going Press correspondents were all scooter owners. Though it looked trivial, I thought it was interesting from the point of equality and also to needle the swollen-headed theatre-owners. Legally, it was mandatory for the Cinema management to provide certain number of parking slots for two wheelers and cars *inside the theatre compound wall* in proportion to the number of seats, in addition to the number of urinals and toilets, fans inside the theatre, emergency exits, fire protection, etc. The law did not say anything about charging a fee for such parking. Importantly, I was able to get hold of an old English Privy Council decision where a rich cricket patron went to the Lords Cricket Club to see a match in 1920's, bought the ticket to enter the 'premises' or property of the Marylebone Cricket Club, established in 1814, parked his T-model black Ford car at the allotted space for parking patrons' carriages. While he was enjoying the match, a batsman hit the 5½ ounce cricket ball for a huge six and it sailed over the pavilion and fell on the windshield of the patron's car and broke the glass. The patron claimed damages which the MCC refused as the ball hitting the windshield was an accident and not intentional. The patron appealed to the Privy Council which was the highest court of appeal in England then and it held that when the patron had purchased a ticket to get into the premises of the Lords and had parked his car in the specified space, it was the responsibility of the management to protect it as such protection was implied in the purchase of the ticket and it was not an open public place where the patron's car was parked but it was within the Lords Club 'premises'. That the complainant was also a member of House of Lords helped to make the decision! The crucial legal point was, the purchase of the ticket presumed the responsibility of the MCC to protect the patron's vehicle *for which no extra payment was needed.* In the case of the modern cinema theatre it was more stringent and even mandatory for the management to provide a certain number of parking space for two-wheelers and four-wheelers. Only those who purchased the ticket to see the cinema had access to such designated parking space. The Rules do not authorize charging any fee for it. It was therefore implied that any such fee was already part of the ticket price. Besides, if such fee was allowed for one mandatory condition namely, the parking space, the management can start charging for use of toilet, fans or air-conditioning, drinking water, even for use of seats, etc. which are all mandatory and for which no charging of fee was provided in the Rules.

So, I issued notices to the 22 theatres which were collecting parking fees for scooters to show cause why action should not be taken for violation of Licencing Conditions. The Cinema theatre owners were members of the powerful Karnataka Film Chamber of Commerce and they met me in a delegation headed by M Bhaktavatsala. He was suave, urbane and also a writer and film producer. He tried to impress upon me that the maintenance cost of cinema halls had gone up for the past five years and the theatre owners had no alternative than to increase the parking fee. Also, the fee collection was annually auctioned and it was the successful contractor who actually collects the fee though he pays the auction bid amount to the theatre in a lump sum. But when I pointed out that there was no provision for such collection in the Law, his only explanation, somewhat smugly, was that the matter was discussed in the Film Chamber of Commerce and the fees could not be reduced, much less done away with, at this stage. I told him politely that no such fee can even be collected let alone be increased and that there was a law to that effect and there is also a District Magistrate to implement it and it was not for the Film Chamber of Commerce to decide. Equally politely he said, kindly pass any order as required by law and we will take it up with the government. I found his confidence that the KFCC could get anything done at the government level rather amusing as the orders of the DM had to be appealed to the High Court and could not be reversed by the government.

So, I prepared, by now in my trademark style, a detailed order running to over 20 pages quoting all the Rules, circumstances, reasons and, of course, the Privy Council judgment also. This was because I had seen that the Courts and the advocates were obsessed with citing innumerable precedents and the more ancient the case reference quoted, the more sacred it was and the Judges would be duly impressed. So what could be better than quoting the vintage Privy Council? So, I passed the order and pronounced it in my open court on a Friday afternoon and immediately arranged for its pasting on the 22 cinema theatres and seal the theatres by my quiet and efficient Headquarters Assistant Raghavendra Rao who was also the Additional District Magistrate. He finished the task by 6 pm that day. This came as a shock to the theatre owners and also the weekend public crowding at the theatres. The management of the theatres had to pacify the agitated crowds to come on the following Monday to collect the refund.

One of the big theatres, the Kapali Theatre in the central Subhedar Chatram Road was owned by one Rajagopal who was the brother in law of the Home Secretary. He was also heading the Labour Union of cinema theatre employees. Under his leadership the theatre owners first met the Home Secretary and requested for reversing the orders of the DM. He pleaded his inability as there was no provision in the Act for the Government to over-rule the DM's orders. He advised them to approach the High Court. Led by Excise Contractors they then met the Chief Minister and complained about the high-handed action of the DM. But, when the Home Secretary briefed the CM that there was no provision in the Law for government to overrule the DM's orders, he chuckled and advised them to approach the Court. But the next day after seeing the newspapers, the CM telephoned me and told me that I did a good job of taking up the cause of bicycle and scooter riders. This was because the generally anti-Emergency media was in this case quite favourable to the DM's action. But the CM also asked me why I chose a weekend to close down the theatres which put to inconvenience a large number of common people. I told him that the idea was to precisely cause maximum loss to theatre owners who were also Excise Contractors, to put them in their place as they were getting arrogant and bragging they could get the government pass any orders they wanted. The CM just laughed.

As the High Court was not in full attendance on Saturdays, the theatre owners could not get a stay on my orders. On Monday they petitioned the HC for a stay on my orders. Justice Chandrakantaraj Urs, who was earlier the Advocate General, was the single judge bench before whom the petition came up. As Advocate General he had known me when I was DC of Gulbarga and had represented the government and me in MISA and a few Contempt cases against me. He knew my work well. He went through my detailed order and gave only a conditional interim-order. While he did not stay the collection of parking fees, he ordered that the collection should be kept in a separate Escrow account with details of from whom the fee was collected and not to draw any amount from the account till the petition was finally disposed of. If it was held finally that the fee was legally collectible, then the theatres can take the amount but if the Court was to hold that the fee was not legal, then the amount collected should be refunded to each of the patrons. This was totally impracticable to the theatres because they had to keep laboriously entries of names and addresses in registers for each small amount collected and in case they lost the case, they had to return these paltry amounts to each of the thousands of patrons. As this accounting problem was too cumbersome and they were none too certain they will win the case, they stopped collecting the parking fee altogether, deciding to see what was going to happen to the case in the HC.

Now, the Cinemas (Regulation) Act, 1964 and Rules are extremely stringent in protecting the interest of the patrons. For instance, the number of urinals and commodes in the toilet is fixed according to the seats licenced in the auditorium and there should be always running water and cleaning staff. The number of fans is fixed according to the total seats if there is no central air conditioning. In any case, there should be a generator of sufficient capacity when electricity fails. The distance between two rows of seats is strictly specified and it cannot be reduced even by millimetres to accommodate more number of seats, the staircase shall not be less than 1.25 metres wide and so on and on in scary intimidating details! It was an ordeal even for me to read and certainly a nightmare to the theatre owners. Even Franz Kafka who wrote *The Trial* describing the tortuous Austro-Hungarian bureaucracy would have fainted reading India's Cinematograph Rules!

So, I sent word to the big theatre owners that I would inspect their theatres with respect to each of the legal requirement and for the slightest failure to meet the precise specification, the theatre will be closed till the defect is set right. And I would take up one defect after another on an instalment basis and not all defects at one time. This would keep theatres closed for long periods and would be perfectly legal. I did not actually do this because the message went home to all the petitioners which was my objective. They understood that even if they win the case, the DC would carry out his threat of inspection of their theatres and no theatre was one hundred percent compliant with all the legal requirements. Therefore, one by one the petitioners met me and promised that they would withdraw their petitions from the group which they did.

In my next press meet the journalists jubilantly congratulated me for taking action to show the Excise Contractors-cum-theatre owners their place. More importantly, it was the reporter of *Indian Express,* who had originally raised the issue, wrote a glowing report representing all journalists. The irony was, closing down theatres does not greatly help poor people or a progressive action of any significance like land reforms, rescuing bonded labour or externing tormentors of dalits. But it was this act of defying the liquor barons on a small matter of parking fee for scooters that captured the imagination of the Press. After the 21 months of Emergency when I was finally transferred, instead of drily noting the

Indian version of Italian Mafia, reminding of Al Capone and one of them meeting me just before the auction at my home was certainly not good news. So, I told him, *Well, why not we meet in the auction hall Monday morning, half hour earlier?* Then Sowkar pleaded that what he had to inform the DC in person was going to affect the auction lease-rent and since he had heard that the DC is a straight person who will show no fear or favour to any contractor, he wanted to tell me in confidence an important method in auctioning which will benefit the government. I was intrigued and so told him to come next morning to my house and I will also ask my Excise Superintendent to be present. This was to safeguard myself with a witness! But Sowkar sounded greatly alarmed and said hastily, *No no, please do not ask anyone, especially not the Excise Superintendent as in no time he will go and inform the Excise Commissioner who is a supporter of the powerful Guruswamy-Venkataswamy Brothers and will defeat my purpose.*

So, I agreed to meet him the next day which was Sunday morning and both Sowkar Channayya and his son landed in their Mercedès. Sowkar was in his late fifties, plump, with three fingers of sacred ash horizontally and a big dot of *red kum-kum* on his forehead, a thick gold ring on each of his even thicker fingers, wearing an ivory colour silk suit and a gold-laced silk *pēta* (much more dazzling than our Revenue Commissioner K Balasubramanyam's, as befitting a Mysore Mafia *Don*) and dispensing the aroma of French *eau de parfum* profusely while his young son in Armani suit spoke polite English with an American accent. I used to live in a Rent Control house then as the DC, Bangalore was the only DC in the state having no designated quarters. *[When I complained to GVK, who had by this time become the Chief Secretary, that there was no official quarters to the DC of Bangalore, he dismissed me unceremoniously saying, "Tho tho, why does the DC, Bangalore require a government house, you can get any rent control house you want!"]* The rent control house I got was an old spacious building on Millers Road belonging to a member of the family of the former Maharaja of Mysore. *[A side-story: This irritated a colleague direct recruit IAS officer greatly as he did not succeed in getting the same house he had a fixation on and had even brought political pressure from the Revenue Minister himself who was my departmental boss! But, as DC of Emergency-Bangalore, I beat him! He would later become Director of Industries by bringing yet more political pressure and would keep up a chain-supply of Napoleon VSOP to the Industries Minister! Unfortunately, when his wife left him he could not bring sufficient political pressure to get her back! He should have known, in life you win some, you lose some, so take things stoically. Much about such spicy matters, later.]* I was using one room as the inevitable Home Office in my spacious house. The Sowkar came straight to the point: *Sir, you know the rivalry among excise contractors. In Mysore-Mandya-Bangalore districts, where the consumption is the highest, the competition to get the licence to distribute Rectified Spirit (RS) is between the Gurusway-Venkataswamy brothers and our Sowkar family. The brothers have formed a cartel by registering a company, Sri Sudha & Co, (SSCo), making most of the small contractors their junior partners and have decided to take contract of three districts and wipe out my family. So, it is now a fight for survival for me. One day before the formal auction by the DC in every district, the dominant contractor organizes an informal auction inviting all the contractors. This is the real auction which will take place today evening in Bangalore at the house of Venkataswamy which I will also attend. But I will not agree to SS&Co's proposal to withdraw from bidding in the formal auction by DC on Monday, even though I will be offered an 'honorarium' for abstention. I will attend the informal auction mainly to know how much the SS&Co will bid approximately for the retail shops and plan my strategy.*

The Sowkar then explained to me, assisted by his son in English, what his father's plan was. Bangalore district had about 900 retail liquor shops in its 11 taluks and had the biggest sales in the State and therefore the highest lease-rent, the earlier year's rent crossing over Rs 1 crore. This year, 1976, it will be even more. The auction notification had four parts. It started with the proposed auction of shop by each shop. No one bids for single shop-wise as it was too small a rent for each shop and impractical to manage. Then comes the "Group-wise" auction of about 20 groups, each group having 40 to 50 shops. Then, the Talukwise auction which will have about 70-80 shops each. But, the real interest would be in the "District-level" auction which was for the entire 900 or so shops in one go. Only the big contractors can afford to pay the rent for all the shops in the district and SS&Co was formed by Sowkar's rival Venkataswamy-Guruswamy brothers to take over Bangalore district and thus control most of the Southern districts also. Sowkar was not big enough to take on the SSCo for the entire Bangalore district though he could compete for about 200-300 shops in Bangalore district. The usual procedure was, he said, the DC would pass over Shop-wise and Group-wise list because there will be no bidders and take up Taluk-wise list for which there will be competition and then of course the District-list. After ascertaining the maximum bid amount for district, the DC would call "Once" and if there was no further bid, "Twice", but will not go on to call "thrice" if there was no more bid because by the technical interpretation of the auction procedure, the final calling "Thrice" was reserved for the Government which was the final authority to complete the auction. So the DC could only say "Twice" which for all practical purposes was the final bid because there had been no instance of

Government over-ruling the final bid reached before the DC after he had called "Twice".

Now, the usual procedure was, the DC takes up each Taluk and ascertains the highest bids in the first round and then calls "Once" and if there is no more bids for each taluk, the highest bid will be recorded. But—and this is the key point—the DC does not say "Twice" for the highest bid reached for each taluk because it will make it final at DC's level. As the District-as-a-whole bid is still to be auctioned, after ascertaining the highest bids for each of the Taluks, he adds up the total for all the Taluks in the district to get an idea as to what the rental for the whole district is going to be. Then he takes up the "District" bid which will have the real competition. Most contractors are interested in the District bid and when the bidders give their final bids, the DC calls "Once". If there is no further bid, then he compares the total of final bids for all the taluks and if the district final bid is more than the total amount reached for the Taluks as a whole earlier, then only he calls "Twice" so that all the shops in the district in one lot is given on rent to the successful bidder. Invariably, the District-bid for all the shops will be a little higher than the total for all the taluk-wise shops bids added together.

Now, came the Machiavellian plan of the Sowkar: After ascertaining the highest bid for each "Taluk" and calling "Once" and totalling the amount for all the Taluks, the DC should take up the customary District-as-a-whole bid and ascertain the highest bid and can call "Once". *Then comes the real twist in Sowkar's plan.* Instead of calling "Twice" (as the District bid amount would be invariably higher than the total of all the Taluks' bids), *the DC should go back to the Taluk-wise bidding once again and ascertain for the second time what the highest bid for each Taluk will now be.* Though this was never done before, yet it is perfectly legal because the DC has called for each Taluk only "Once" earlier and nothing stops him to ascertain whether there will be any improvement in the bid amount for each taluk if he takes up Taluks for the second time.

So, when the DC pauses the "District as a whole" auction after saying "Once" and goes back and takes up the 11 Taluks one by one, Sowkar and his men will bid and compete with SSCo for each Taluk. This time the bid amount will keep on going up because the Sowkar can afford to increase the bid to his highest limit knowing what the SSCo's total district bid was and in any case the latter cannot afford to leave out any one Taluk. This is because if Sowkar gets a foothold even in a few Taluks out of the 11, he can create problems to SSCo in many retail shops in SSCo's domain which can purchase from Sowkar's bordering shops. Thus, even if Sowkar does not get a single Taluk, he could still create havoc in SS camp by forcing them to increase their bid amounts in competition with Sowkar. This attrition will enhance the district rental. So the DC has nothing to lose?

Frankly, I did not fully understand what was being said. So the junior Sowkar took me over the entire explanation once more. Finally, I understood that Sowkar's plan was simply to see that his rival pays a much higher rent by this jugglery of going back and forth of Taluk-wise and District-level auction process and by withholding the final bid of calling "Twice" till after the second round of Taluk-wise bidding and then finally the second round of District level bidding. So, I asked the Sowkar why he was doing this because obviously he does not get anything by enhancing government's rental revenue. He frankly told me that if he makes the SS pay an exorbitant rent in the already high-rent Bangalore, Sowkar can bid comfortably in some other remaining districts in the South such as Mysore and Mandya. I did not commit myself to anything and told them we will see next day how it goes. While leaving, the Sowkar told me that when I do not finalize the District-level bid the first time and try to go back to Taluk-wise bidding for the second time, the Excise Commissioner would interfere because he supported SSCo. So, I should be firm as the DC is the top authority in the auction hall and not the Excise Commissioner, nor the Government. More importantly, I should not tell anything to anyone, especially my Excise Superintendent who will immediately go to bite the ear of Excise Commissioner. I told him I will play it by the ear (puns, ad nauseam, intended!)

Next day I reached the majestic Puttanna Chetty Town Hall on JC Road at 9 am itself suited and booted for the 10 am auction. Built by Sir Mirza Ismail in 1935 in the elegant neo-classical Greco-Roman style, The Town Hall on JC Road was a land mark of Bangalore. All the freedom movement's agitations were held in front of the Town Hall and the practice continued after independence also. Inside, it could hold a little more than 1,000 persons in the two floors, the upper one being a balcony. It had a central aisle and a spacious dais at one end. My Excise Superintendent was wearing a new suit for the occasion and his staff were already installing a telephone and I was told that it was the "hotline" to Excise Commissioner. I did not say anything about my previous day's discussion with the Sowkar. There was a festive atmosphere and each side of the aisle was occupied by the smaller contractors of each of the Mafia groups with their inevitable brief cases which, my Excise Superintendent told me, contained 100-Rupee currency note bundles for depositing the one month's Earnest Money as soon as the "twice" was called by the DC to make the final bid binding. It was like a Mafia mega-meeting of Godfather. The Guruswamy-Venkataswamy brothers entered the hall exactly at 10 am and the Sowkar and his son a few minutes earlier. These Mafiosi leaders, all in resplendent gold-laced *petas* and silk suits had a lot of old world charm and the bosses one by one came over to me just below the dais and wished me well before occupying their front rows. It was all gloriously, criminally, resplendent. I felt, I was presiding over a Freemason ritual!

The auction started in the usual pattern, Taluk-wise and then for the district. I found that the total of Taluk-wise bids was about 40% more than the earlier year's rent. The highest bids for each taluk was by SSCo. Then, when the District-level bid was taken up, the bid amount went up by another ten percent. I noticed that, in true Mafia style, the leaders were just sitting poker-faced and their henchmen were actually doing the bidding by just raising their index fingers indicating each time a Rs 10,000 raise. My Excise Superintendent was beaming and whispered in my ears that he had already informed the Excise Commissioner and the EC-*Sab* had conveyed his congratulations. When all were expecting that the auction was over and were expecting me to say "Twice" to the District bid, I took—also with a poker face—the mike and said, *Now, we will go back to Taluk-wise and start the bidding again.* For a moment there was a pin drop silence which was deafening and then all pandemonium broke out. Venkataswamy the younger brother was already sprinting to the dais and my panic-stricken Excise Superintendent was on the point of a cardiac event. Venkataswamy whispered to me that this was not the procedure and I cannot go back to "Taluk-wise" bidding again. I asked him where is it stated that the DC cannot go back to Taluk-wise bidding when he has not pronounced "Twice" to the District-level bid and the auction process was still in progress. He said I should ask the Excise Commissioner for advice. I said the law was clear and there was no bar for me to find out the final bids for the Taluk-wise shops by asking for bidding a second time. By this time Venkataswamy had lost his poker-face and said to me very agitatedly, *Sir this is not the procedure, this is against the Rules.* I told him I do not find anything against the rules in what I was doing. He was a little puzzled and asked me, *Why was I going back to Taluk-wise bid again?* I told him calmly that I was exploring the possibility of whether the Taluk-wise bids can go up in the second attempt. Then he probably understood what the game was and he told me he and his colleagues have to consult their advocates and requested me to adjourn the auction by two hours. I declined and said that I have to complete auction as quickly as possible and according to the plain reading of the Rules, there was no violation. Meanwhile, my profusely sweating Excise Superintendent, his new suit ruined, rushed to me and said that the Excise Commissioner was on the hotline. I told him to please inform the Excise Commissioner that the DC was in the process of auctioning which was a quasi-judicial proceeding and was therefore unable to talk on the phone in the middle and I would talk to him after the auction was over. This increased his sweat-stream to a torrent and he appeared to be close to a collapse!

I started enjoying the day and proceeded as discussed with the Sowkar earlier. True to his word, the Sowkar and his henchmen went on bidding higher and higher for each Taluk only to be surpassed by the exasperated rival to still higher bids. It took three more hours and well past 4 pm to complete the final bid for the District. This was because, I could not say "Twice" to each of the Taluk-shops as I had to arrive at the total of all the Taluks after the second round of bidding. Once the Taluks' total for the second time was reached, I would have to go back to District-level bid again and auction it to know what the final District-level bid would be. If that was lower than the latest total of Taluk-wise bids, I would have to again go back to Taluk-wise bidding and pronounce "Twice" to get the highest amount for each Taluk. I found that in the second round the final bid amounts for the taluks had surpassed the previous year's rent by over 75%! So, I went back to District-level bid and this time got another about 10% higher amount from SSCo who wanted to make sure they got the whole district. They were somewhat bewildered by what was going on. Then I completed the auction and thanked all and closed the proceedings. Compared to the Rs 1.1 crore rent of the previous year, the current year's rent was close to Rs 2.5 crores. At the end, both Venkataswamy and the hitherto silent elder Guruswamy came over to me to the dais and congratulated me saying that even though they and their partners would incur a loss, they had no alternative and I did well to increase the revenue to the government. But they also told me, Sir, we will have to go the Court and get a stay as the procedure the DC had followed today was never done before. I wished them well with a big smile and thanked them for successfully taking the district. In my mind I was greatly relieved that there was no chaos and stoppage of the auction or even a Mafia-style shoot-out which would have been truly historical. When there was pandemonium earlier in the Hall, I had strongly suspected, there may be *John Brownings* hiding in their brief cases under the crisp bundles of currency notes! I must say these elderly Mysore Liquor Barons had an admirable old-world charm the Western Mafiosi could never match!

That evening I prepared a long, confidential report describing how, based on "an anonymous tip" I conducted the auction. I ended the report by saying that this unorthodox procedure of auctioning which was strictly according to the legal provisions resulted in more than doubling of the annual rent for Bangalore district compared to the previous year. I sent the report to the Finance Secretary, SK Warrior since Excise Department administratively came under the Finance Department with a copy to GVK, the Chief Secretary with a polite covering letter "for kind information"! When I tried to contact the Excise Commissioner on the hotline as promised, his PA told me he had become apoplectic and had gone home sick with his ears almost detaching from the rest of his body! Next day Warrior phoned to congratulate me. I also sent a more formal letter to the Excise Commissioner just informing that the auction was conducted as per law and the district rent had gone up by 210% thanks to *his cooperation*. I did not receive any response from him. In the event, SSCo did not go to the Court as they had no case.

❖❖❖

CHAPTER 10

An Encounter with a
Dilettante Youth Congress Leader

[Still in Bangalore and Emergency Continuing]

Well into the second year of my tenure as Emergency DC of the capital district, one day I received a phone call from a factotum in CM's office that one Mr Bhat, a Youth Congress leader, requests for an appointment with me. I told him that my office was open to everyone and no recommendation was needed and in any case he was welcome to meet me the next day. So, Bhat duly swaggered to my office. He was in his early thirties for membership to Youth Congress was then till age 35 and for office bearers upto 40. Even though students' participation in the Congress freedom movement was significant prior to independence, the actual shaping of the Youth Congress, in terms of flag, logo, etc. actually took place after 1950. With the meteoric rise of *Dhuma Ketu* Sanjay Gandhi in Congress politics in 1974-75, the Youth Congress became the Indian equivalent of *Hitlerjugend,* the infamous Hitler Youth. Elected Chief Ministers were scared of Youth Congress. Even though Sanjay Gandhi (b.1946—d.1980) did not occupy any elected position, he became more than an *enfant terrible,* a terror to Chief Ministers. He divided CMs into two categories, the *Airport-going CMs* and those who stayed away. Whenever he went to a state, the entire cabinet with the CM would be waiting to receive him. There was once a famous photograph of the UP CM ND Tiwari holding Sanjay Gandhi's *chappals* when the latter was climbing on to a protesting elephant! Very few CMs resisted the airport homage and Devaraj Urs was a prominent one. So, Sanjay Gandhi became the patron saint of two Youth Congress small time body-guards, Gundu Rao and his mentor Faiz Mohamad Khan (popularly known as Field Marshal Khan and, to Gundu Rao especially, 'Father-Mother-Khan'.) Sanjay Gandhi encouraged them to undermine the authority of Urs. It was in this background that I got the call from CM's office to give an appointment to Bhat.

I had made my enquiries about Bhat as normally any DC would check the pre-existing conditions of a bad character meeting him with pressure from above. He was from South Kanara district and said he was the younger brother of a serving Chief Engineer. He claimed he was writing the biography of Devaraj Urs. More importantly the rumour, obviously spread by him was, he was engaged to be married to the youngest daughter of the CM! This was big time rumour. He was a little overbearing towards me, DC or no DC. So, I asked him curtly what was his purpose in meeting me and he said he wants to start an industry. I said that was indeed highly laudable and asked him, what industry. He said he wanted to make furniture as a lot of private housing projects were coming up in Bangalore and the need for quality furniture was immense. Now, this was a little dicey as there was a large number of small scale furniture makers in Bangalore as could be seen on the famous Infantry Road in the city and also some big firms like the Featherlite, then on Mysore Road. So I told him, Good, you should approach the Industries Department who can assist you. Then he told me the real purpose of his visit. He had already met the Director of Industries and he had his own building. What he required was grant of a licence for allotment of Rectified Spirit to polish high value furniture. As I did not know the relationship between RS and furniture, I asked him why he required RS for his industry. He told me this is what many of the furniture industry abroad uses and he was going to buy basic furniture from small industries and polish them and sell. It appeared to me like a lot of cock and bull story as his basic purpose appeared to be to get hold of RS which was in great demand in the black market for smuggling across the border to Tamil Nadu as Karnataka's border at Attibele was just fifteen kilometres from Bangalore. In any event, I asked him to give an application for me to examine. He gave it and requested me to expedite its sanction. He also bragged about his writing the memoirs of Devaraj Urs and coyly hinted that he was the fiancé of CM's daughter. Frankly, I thought he was lying.

I sent his application to my Excise Superintendent to examine his request for its need, whether government is allotting any RS to furniture industry at all and, if so, how much, the facilities he has for making or polishing furniture, etc. He brought his report in a week. Indeed, a small quantity of RS of about 5,000 litres a month was being allotted to about 500 furniture makers in Bangalore. But, it was not necessary as RS was costly and there were many cheaper alternatives. In any event, the address given by Bhat as his 'manufacturing facility' was the garage of a residential house which could not be used for industrial purpose under the Land Use prescribed by the Town & Country Planning Act. Bhat had applied for 10,000 liters of RS per month which would be 120,000 liters in a year! If that much RS was used for polishing, the whole of Bangalore will not be sufficient for storing furniture! So, I issued an order rejecting his application giving all these reasons and also added for good measure that the application did not appear to be for a genuine purpose. I also sent a copy of the order with a confidential letter to the Home Secretary whom I knew was not getting on well with the Ear-Flopper Excise Commissioner. The Home Secretary belonged to the landed gentry Gowda community while the Excise Commissioner was an uncharacteristic Jain and many things in Karnataka government as always depended upon which caste one belonged. To the credit of the Home Secretary, he told me to be careful of Bhat as he was a bogus person making all kinds of claims and that I did well to deny him the allotment.

But Bhat was determined to pursue his demand. So he filed an appeal against my order to the Excise Commissioner who was the Appellate Authority. I had asked my Excise Superintendent to keep track of the case in EC's office and he was reporting to me every three days the lightning progress of the case. The EC would entertain Bhat during hearings, giving him coffee and Ghee Masala Dosa from the famous MTR and Bhat would bitterly complain about the arrogance of the Bangalore DC at which the EC's ears would twitch violently in excitement. All this the Excise Superintendent learnt from the PA to the EC, sitting in the ante-room. In a record-breaking quick disposal of the appeal, the EC granted Bhat his request for 10,000 litres of RS per month much to my surprise. His order did not discuss any legal issues but just said to encourage industrial development of the state the allotment was made to a young and dynamic entrepreneur! Within two days, Bhat showed his cockiness by appearing in my office, flaunting the orders of the Excise Commissioner. But Bhat did not know how government functions. Under the ultra-Kafkaesque thoroughness of Indian bureaucracy, even though EC could over-rule the DC, the actual *release* of the RS had still to be done by another order of the DC! I had seen that my Release Order could also incorporate a few more conditions against the misuse of RS. So, I told Bhat in my best magisterial frown that RS was a dangerous commodity not just because it was inflammable but it had a big black market since its market price across the border was Rs 12 per litre while the official price in Karnataka was just Rs 3/litre. I would therefore be keeping a round-the clock watch of what was happening to the RS he takes delivery of and if it was not found to be fully used to the last drop in his 'factory' for polishing furniture, for which in any case he did not have any facility in his small garage, I would be obliged to detain him under MISA. I made it clear to him that while the EC may over-rule me under the Excise Act, he can do nothing against my MISA order and I would send him to the Bellary prison where the food given was jowar and not the brown, boiled rice of South Kanara! Besides, I coolly informed him, Bellary in summer reached a temperature of 45°C for two months and even the MISA detainees do not get AC but only fans and there was a relay of 3-hour power-cuts in Bellary and the prison's generator was constantly under repairs! What is more, it was full of bat-sized mosquitoes! Long story short, he left crestfallen and that was the last I saw of him. I learnt later from my Excise Superintendent that Bhat went to the EC long-faced and narrated to him what happened and told him he would not be taking delivery of the RS in view of all the risks involved. In his anger the EC's ears started twitching so violently that his PA was afraid they will detach from the rest of him! It was a great entertainment for me and I was glad I could thwart the arrogance of a Youth Congress low-life and the servility of a senior officer. Such satisfaction is immense in DC's job, not measurable in salary.

❖❖❖

CHAPTER 11

Still in Bangalore and Still Emergency!

Land Reforms and how to Grab 950 Acres of Government Land for Rs.1,000 @ Re.1.05 per acre !

West Bengal and Kerala were the pioneer states in implementing land reforms in India. Abolition of Tenancy and 'Land to the Tillers' was their objective apart from imposing a ceiling on individual ownership and resuming the surplus land and its distribution to the landless. Karnataka too had a Land Reforms Act passed as early as 1961. But it was made more rigorous by an amendment in 1974 by the Devaraj Urs Government, even before the Emergency. According to Section 79 A of the Karnataka Land Reforms Act, the government forbade the acquisition of land by a person with an assured annual income of more than Rs 12,000 from sources other than agricultural lands. Further, Section 79 B laid down that, no person other than a person cultivating land personally shall be entitled to hold land. Implementation of the Land Reforms Act, especially the abolition of tenancy and making the tenant the owner of the land was an historically progressive step in the state. It was one of the most important action-points under the 20-Points Programme in the State. But resumption of surplus land and distributing it to landless was not the strong point in Karnataka's land reforms as high ceiling was allowed in land ownership.

In this background, there was an allegation made in the Legislative Assembly by Kagodu Thimmappa in 1976, one of the three Lohia Musketeers of Socialist Party, that in Bannerghatta near Bangalore there was rampant violation of Land Reforms Act by one Sheriff who had usurped lands of many poor peasants. The CM promised it would be thoroughly enquired and a report would be obtained from the DC, Bangalore. My Special Deputy Commissioner was PS Nagarajan promoted to IAS from KAS who was very upright and highly knowledgeable in law, holding a Master of Law degree. Nagarajan was a great help to me as a colleague with ten years more of valuable experience than me. I had known him from my probationary days in

Bijapaur when I used to go to the Divisional Headquarters at Belgaum where Nagarajan, BK Bhattacharya IAS and my batch-mate Bharat were all sharing an apartment as bachelors where I also would be accommodated to sleep on the sofa during my visits. So I discussed the Sheriff case with Nagarajan and we decided to go to Bannerghatta and make an enquiry.

We reached Bannerghatta which was about 20 kilometers from the city. We settled in the Inspection Bungalow, a little away from the town which had a population of about ten thousand as it was getting urbanized, being close to Bangalore city besides the Bannerghatta National Park having been established in 1974. The Tahsildar had brought all the old records and we examined them in detail. What we unearthed was quite shocking. In 1942, an area of 950 acres of government gomal land in two survey numbers of about 500 acres and 450 acres were granted to about 200 landless families for cultivation of ragi. This land was situated between the Bannerghatta Road and Bangalore-Kanakapura Road. They cultivated the land for about five years but did not pay any land revenue. This was because each family holding's boundary was not demarcated by the Surveyors of the Revenue Department and land revenue for each plot was not fixed. However, after 5 years they discontinued cultivation also as there were no rains. So, the Tahsildar resumed the 950 acres back to government as the Land Revenue Act provided. Then in 1949 a strange thing happened. The Tahsildar auctioned the entire 950 acres. But curiously, according to the records, there were only two bidders in the auction proceedings, one Sheriff from Hyderabad and his wife Begum Sheriff who had given a general power of attorney to her husband for bidding in the auction! So, actually there was only Sheriff present in person to bid! His highest bid was Rs.1,000 (yes, Rupees one thousand) for the 950 acres. *[The market value was Rs.1 lakh per acre in 1949 itself and Rs.2 crores per acre in 1976!]* It was a blatant land-grab. However, there were also some complications because many of the original grantees of the 950 acres had already sold away the lands. In going through the names of buyers I found there was a retired Manager of Canara Bank, Moinuddin the Personal Assistant to the Chief Minister (whom I had met from my Shimoga days; in the Bannergatta land he was breeding pedigree canines and selling each puppy for Rs.1,000!) and, surprise of surprises, the unemployed son of the same ear-twitching Excise Commissioner who had ordered allotment of Rectified Spirit to the Youth Congress Leader over-ruling my orders a few months earlier! These 'sales' were in 25-acre plots. There were also some farmers who had purchased the lands in smaller plots and who were living in Bannerghatta town. I sent for them and they confessed that they did not know anything about the "auction" by the Tahsildar but when they came to know about it, they had complained to the then DC of Bangalore, one Channaraja Urs in 1961 and he had cancelled the auction as being fraudulent. But Sheriff had appealed against the DC's order to the Mysore Revenue Appellate Tribunal where the matter was still pending! Nagarajan located from the voluminous files the order of the former DC cancelling the auction who had plainly called it a fraud. Also, the matter was not pending in the MRAT. After the passing of the Land Reforms Act, the MRAT had referred the matter to the Land Reforms Tribunal headed by the local MLA! In our Anglo-Saxon Adversarial system of legal maze and mud any matter can get lost unless some interested party pursues it in the Courts and Tribunals through strong advocates and by giving the customary bribes to the Court clerks.

It took us some time to digest the whole thing. We decided we should inspect the land to get an idea of the ground reality of the fraud. So we started and found that my Willy's 5-gear Station Wagon could not negotiate the route to the land. The Tahsildar showed the map and I found the lands were situated in the interior on both sides of the rough *Bandi Dhari* (cart road) connecting Bannerghatta to the Bangalore-Kanakapura main road from West to East. So, we walked the distance of about five kilometres and found that the land was sporadically cultivated with maize and ragi. It was gravelly and uneven. But it was good land for building houses and it lay between two main roads and very close to the fast-urbanizing city. At the other end of the land, we found ourselves staring at the huge distillery of Khodays on the main Bangalore-Kanakapura road. [Later, the big Cash and Carry Supermarket would come up opposite the Khodays Distillery.] It was quite intriguing—the Excise Commissioner's son buying 25 acres from that land, the Personal Assistant ro CM also purchasing 25 acres from Sheriff of Hyderabad (Sheriff's father was once the Horse Trainer in Mysore Maharaja's Palace, I later ascertained), and at the end of the road a liquor baron's huge distillery standing. As a person steeped in Alistair MacLean thrillers then, I decided I should investigate the matter thoroughly in the coming days. Meanwhile, I wrote a detailed report to the Revenue Commissioner, K Balasubramanyam with copies to the Chief Secretary GVK and Secretary to CM JC Lynn as the CM had promised he would inform the Assembly about Kagodu Thimmappa's motion on Bannerghatta Land Grabbing Scandal. But then, I found in the next day's papers in the Official Postings Column that the Ear-Flapper Excise Commissioner had been promoted and posted in a newly created post of, shock of shocks, *Special Commissioner for Land Reforms!* Naturally my report would go to him and I could not wait to see his ears falling off when he would come to the part of his unemployed son buying 25 acres of land close to Khoday's Distillery! Bannerghatta town was already becoming a suburb of Bangalore city and Sheriff was retaining over 500 acres for himself and his family members (under the Land Reforms Act, each family member could retain a ceiling of 56 acres of dry, rainfed land), even after selling parcels of land to bureaucrats, political leaders and, very interestingly, to NRI's from Dubai! I learned that the land-grabbers were extremely shrewd to purchase land a little away from the city but could afford to park their black money for a decade till the value of land sky-rocketed. However, I could not pursue this Mother of Frauds to its logical end as my transfer orders came just when the Emergency was coming to an end. My transfer had nothing to do with the Sheriff Land Grabbing case as I will explain later. My successor did not pursue this case as his priorities were different, like that of a maintenance-housekeeper or GVK's *No.2 Officer* ! This is the malady in government. Vital matters involving scandals of the rich and powerful are buried because there is no continuity in probe, which entirely depends upon the initiative and philosophy of the officers posted. Even today, this gigantic land robbery of 950 acres for a total price of Rs.1,000 (Rs.1.05 per acre !, while its market value in 2020 would be Rs.9,500 crores at a conservative guidance value of Rs.10 crores per acre) is still existing gloriously in the form of gated communities and 'Farm Houses' near Bannerghatta, between Bannerghatta and Khodays Distillery—and Metro Cash and Carry on Kanakapura Road. Sheriff's family is still owning about 300 acres which is of course pending in the Land Reforms Tribunal for the third generation! Sheriff has even constructed a mini-Taj Mahal in memory of his *Begum,* imitating Shahjehan! The 'Investigative Report'ing Fourth Estate, the Media and the political parties which are making a lot of noise about assault on the Freedom of Press, Freedom of Expression, Corruption in government and violation of Human Rights, etc. have no clue or inclination to stir out of their offices and go to this Mother of Land Grabbing in Bannerghatta just 20 km from the city centre. This can stir a grand Pandora's Box.

❖❖❖

CHAPTER 12

Family Planning and End of Emergency

And I Leave District Administration After Five Years

Family Planning was one of the 5-Points Programme of Sanjay Gandhi, the *enfant terrible* at 29 though it turned out to be his only programme and became the end-game of Emergency. Devaraj Urs had told us in the DCs' Conference as soon as the programmes were announced that there should not be any compulsion to achieve the Family Planning targets. This was in sharp contrast to the methods used in North Indian states. Family Planning was already an ongoing programme in India since 1952 inspite of the opposition of the ever-impractical Mahatma to birth control. This was, surprisingly, unlike China which did not have a population control policy till late 1970s. In 1949 Mao Zedong had famously said:

"A large population in China is a good thing. With a population increase of several fold we still have an adequate solution. The solution lies in production. The fallacy of the Western capitalist economists like Malthus that the increase of food lags behind the increase of population was long ago refuted in theoretical reasoning by the Marxists; it has also been disproved by the facts existing after the revolution of the Soviet Union and in the liberated region of China."

In 1951 India had a population of 361m while China's was 557m. In 1971 India's population was 439m while China's was 666m. In two decades China's population had increased by 51% while India's increase was 21%. Mao Zedong died in 1976 at the age of 83 and China introduced the one-child policy from 1978. But, unlike China, India realized the importance of family planning from the 1950s. In 1968 Hindustan Latex, a Public Sector Undertaking, was established with Japanese collaboration to produce 144m condoms annually with the brand name *Nirodh* meaning Protection. It was distributed free to couples at the Family Planning centres. In 1972, parliament passed the Medical Termination of Pregnancy Act. Mass Vasectomy Camps were started. Nutrition, maternity and child welfare were brought under the purview of the Family Welfare Ministry. Unlike China which imposed draconian disincentives like restrictions in supply of subsidized rice, housing and free schooling, after the first child, India relied upon incentives in monetary form and free contraceptives. However, India's fertility rate decline was modest compared to China's. The World Bank and IMF had been emphasizing to India the need to accelerate the pace of family planning. It was in this background that Sanjay Gandhi entered the scene with his Youth Congress storm-troopers and strong-arm methods.

From 1972 onwards there used to be Family Planning "camps" when Health Department officials publicized the need for family planning and enlist volunteers among couples having more than two children. For this, the officials used to get an honorarium of Rs.15 for each sterilization and the candidate would get Rs.100 and free medicines. The DC was responsible for organizing such camps involving all departments. So, whenever I had visited the villages in Shimoga and Gulbarga and later in Bangalore I used to seek the support of the village panchayats to conduct these camps. During those discussions, I used to ask them why many of the poor villagers having more than four or five children were not coming forward in large number to these camps. Invariably someone would say, *DC Sayabare, Krishna was the eighth child and he was God. So we should also have eight children !* I also learnt from them the logic for having eight children. Out of the eight, four would be girls on an average and they would go away early to their husband's houses and therefore as good as lost to the parents. Out of the four sons, it was probable that two may not survive childhood which leaves two sons. Out of the two at least one may look after the parents in their old age. So, having more children was a tried and tested insurance policy. The official logic that less children means less expenditure and better standard of living for the fewer number, did not make sense to the villagers because in the starved existence of the poor, the food required to an additional child was very little and, after ten years the child can start doing errands and bring some earning. Therefore, restricting the number of children to two was *economically foolish* in poor rural India. This was the reason we were not succeeding much in inducing the poor to the family planning camps. On the other hand, the small number of middle class couples having no children or just one or two, mostly in the towns, were eager to get free contraceptives to delay or restrict childbirths. I remembered my Rector Hla Myint saying, *As income of a family increases the choice is between a baby and a Baby Austin car.*

We had thus a conflict between the method of implementation of FP programme between the Karnataka government policy of persuasion and inducement and the Sanjay Gandhi acolytes in New Delhi fixing

200% targets and the DMs being responsible to achieve them by any means. Due to the press censorship all over India, there was no way of knowing what were these precise "methods" followed by the DMs, especially in the Hindi-belt, who had achieved 200% and some even 300% of the target in sterilization operations. But it was known that those DMs in UP were given a prize of one free Ambassador car for crossing 200% of the target. By this time the reigning philosophy in Delhi was the need for a "committed bureaucracy" as enunciated by PN Haksar, IFS (who had never administered a district in his life) who was Mrs Gandhi's hitherto Principal Secretary. During the Emergency, Sanjay Gandhi took pride in prematurely repatriating many IAS Officers from the Central Secretariat to their state cadres on the ground that, South Indians were alright for normal times but Emergency requires 'dynamic' officers from the Punjab! Much later in 1977, when the Emergency was over and Janata Party had been swept to power, I had the occasion to visit Varanasi and met the DM who was from the North-East and a few years junior to me. He was DM earlier in another UP district during Emergency. I asked him how did the DMs in UP over-achieve their targets. He drew a sketch for me. If a bus was travelling from East to West and comes at a road crossing from North to South and a family planning camp is going on in a place South of the crossing, the PSI standing at the cross-roads will stop the bus proceeding to the West which was its intended destination and instead will divert it to the South to the FP camp. The passengers will be offloaded and all men and women excluding children will be operated upon. It did not matter whether they were unmarried or did not have children or elderly. A Sterilization Certificate would be issued to those who had undergone the operation and this certificate would be insisted upon for issue of any permission—ration card and No Objection Certificate required by myriad government departments. Thus Sterilization became a necessary pre-requisite for any normal work done. Due to the unpreparedness of the persons to undergo the operation, the general unhygienic conditions and the large crowds collected and poor immunity of poverty, there were many complications to the persons who had undergone the operation and also quite a few deaths too which were never investigated as everyone was busy with the camps and operations. In 1976–1977, the programme led to 8.3 million sterilisations, up from 2.7 million the previous year, an increase of 300%. There were some bizarre instances of excesses. According to Vinod Mehta's *Sanjay Story* (1978), one Shahu Ghalake, a peasant from Barsi in Maharashtra, was taken for sterilization. After mentioning that he was already sterilised, he was beaten for resisting! A sterilisation procedure was undertaken on him for a second time! All this was done under the compulsion to exceed targets and the licence to DMs to use force and their eagerness to win the Ambassador car!

Sanjay Gandhi soon became the most important Extra-Constitutional Authority and came to be described as the Dark Prince of Emergency. His 5-Point Programmed consisted of Literacy, Family Planning, Tree Planting, Eradication of Casteism and Abolition of dowry which were all laudable. But, from inception it became a One-Point Programme of Family Planning and his other programmes receded to the background. There were many excesses and atrocities committed at his initiative, especially in Delhi. The worst was the bull-dozing of slums in Turkman Gate in which 70,000 people were forcibly relocated to outside the city. In the police firing 150 slum dwellers were killed. In and around Delhi 161,000 persons were forcibly sterilized within a short period. The high living, no-brainer, numbskull, low-life, bad characters who became champions of Sanjay Gandhi were, *inter alia,* Jag Mohan, Vidya Charan Shukla, Dhirendar Brahmachari—the Indian version of Grigori Rasputin, RK Dhawan, Rukhsana Sultana and their like. Some of the early high-handed acts of Sanjay Gandhi were: when the urbane Inder Kumar Gujral, the minister for Information and Broadcasting in Mrs Gandhi's cabinet refused to take orders from Sanjay Gandhi, he was summarily replaced by VC Shukla. When the famous actor-singer Kishore Kumar declined to sing for Sanjay Gandhi's Youth Congress, he was banned from the programmes of All India Radio!

In Karnataka, on the other hand, none of the DCs achieved 200% of FP targets and many not even 100% nor, of course, was there any prize of Ambassador Car. Only, those who did the maximum were given a National Small Savings Certificate of Rs.1,000 ! The CM had made it clear that there should not be any high-handed methods in FP implementation. This was mainly because of the advice of Lynn who was Secretary to Devaraj Urs (he had earlier been with Veerendra Patil also and would be in the post of CM's Secretary for twelve years!) He had strong Christian values and behind his back we juniors called him "Brother" Lynn! Because of his moral values and the wisdom of Devaraja Urs to follow his sane advice, Karnataka had a firm policy of non-compulsion in implementing FP programme. I remember one day Lynn telephoning me, *I say what is happening with your AC, Bangalore sub-division?* I did not know the background for his question. He told me that the AC had gone to a village close to Bangalore where there was a big Church and threatened the priest for obstructing the FP programme. I said I did not know and will find out and he ticked me off saying, *Well, the DC should know everything that is happening in his district.* I then checked with the AC what had happened. The AC was an energetic, zesty, dynamo in her twenties in her first posting and was very committed to her work which was then mainly the 20-Point and 5-Point programmes. So, she narrated the argument the priest had with her when she had visited the village to arrange a FP camp. The poor priest had invoked scriptures to criticize the immoral FP programme and even quoted the Mahatma. It was not the only Church-estate in my district. Bangalore city was ringed with many big Churches with large extent of land and Seminaries with great reverence among the local people who were of all religions, not just Christians. I told her we should refrain from compulsion, keeping with state government's policy. So, the problem was settled without much rancour and I reported back to Lynn that all was well which he accepted grumpily.

In perspective, it was the single folly of Family Planning excesses under Sanjay Gandhi's mind-infertile, *Gestapo-goons* in the Hindi belt which caused the landslide defeat of Mrs Gandhi when she lifted Emergency on 18 January 1977 after 637 days. All the opposition leaders were released from prison and during the election held in March 1977, out of the total of 542 Parliamentary seats, Congress was reduced to having just 153 seats (losing 163 seats from the previous election), of whom 92 MPs from the four southern states. The Janata Party's tally was 298 seats and its allies' 47 seats, giving them a massive majority of 345 MPs. Mrs Gandhi and Sanjay Gandhi both lost their seats, as did every one of the Congress candidates in northern states of Bihar, Uttar Pradesh and Punjab and winning just one seat each from Madhya Pradesh and Rajasthan. In contrast, in Karnataka, of the 28 Parliamentary seats, 26 were won by the Congress. In Andhra Pradesh out of 42 seats, 41 and in Kerala out of 20 seats, 15 were won by Congress and its ally LDF. In Tamil Nadu out of 39 seats, 34 were won by Anna DMK and its main ally Congress. It is surprising that the vital reason for this glaring regional divide was not grasped and even was glossed over and suppressed by the post-emergency free press and the *soi-disant,* self-appointed, naïve intellectuals and media of India.

The Opposition parties whose leaders were all in prison and released just about 50 days before election, had hurriedly put up a joint front consisting of Congress-Organization, Jan Sangh, Bharatiya Lok Dal, the Socialist Party, Shiromani Akali Dal, the DMK and a few other regional parties and secured 53% of the votes polled compared with the Congress-Alliance share of 41% mainly because of the support from the Southern states. The Janata Alliance, the media and most of the intelligentsia portrayed the election as a choice between Democracy and Dictatorship. When the Emergency was imposed The Times of India carried an obituary that read, *"Democracy, Beloved Husband of Truth, Loving Father of Liberty, Brother of Faith, Hope and Justice, Expired on June 26"*. The Delhi edition of the Indian Express of 28 June 1975, carried a blank-space for editorial, while the Financial Express reproduced in large type Rabindranath Tagore's poem *"Where the Mind is Without Fear"*. After the 1971 Parliamentary elections in which Mrs Gandhi's Bank Nationalization and *Gharibi Hatao* slogan had won her a majority of 352 seats out of 524, the next election was due in 1976 before which Emergency was proclaimed in June 1975. The Parliamentary election due in 1976 was delayed and it was said that Sanjay Gandhi and his Man-Fridays like *Raksha Mantri* Bansi Lal advised strongly against holding elections when things were going on so well! There was talk of a Long Parliament as in England from 1640 to 1660 and the Indian Parliament was even called the Rump Parliament with many foreign media describing Mrs Gandhi as the "Only Man in the Cabinet". Earlier, the Janata Party called her "That Woman" and *Goonghi Gudiya* (Dumb Doll). The BBC polled her (in 1999) as the Woman of the Millennium. Richard Nixon told Henry Kissinger she was a "Witch" and "Clever Fox". With all the epithets describing her as a Dictator, the fact remains that it was Mrs Gandhi who opted for a free and fair democratic election in 1977 which she lost. It was said that the *Khakhi-*brained "Intelligence" Bureau had reported mass support for her because of imposing emergency!

The result of the election was also hailed as India's emphatic reply to Mrs Gandhi's efforts to suppress freedom of the people. The most surprising omission was the total lack of judgement about the role of Family Planning during Emergency and a blind eye as to why the Southern states voted *en masse* for Mrs Gandhi unlike the North. Press censorship, suspension of fundamental rights and detention of prominent opposition leaders were all very much there in the Southern states also. In fact, after the detention of opposition leaders when there was absolutely no public agitation against Mrs Gandhi, she had famously said, *"Not even a Dog Barked"*! Though this was not quite true as demonstrated by George Fernandes (who was described as a Rebel without a *Pause*), CGK Reddy and a few other socialists in what came to be called the Baroda Dynamite Case. George Fernandes was from Karnataka and his brother Lawrence and associate Snehalata Reddy were arrested and uncared for in Bangalore and Snehalata Reddy died of medical negligence in the Bangalore Prison. So there was loss of fundamental rights very much in the South as in the North. But the loss of civil liberties and detention of political leaders did not affect common, poor people in the South or in the North. What affected the poor in the North was the *"nasbandi"*—Vasectomy programme which was the one programme that did not affect the people of the Southern states as none of them followed the dictacts of Sanjay Gandhi.

My Varanasi DM colleague told me, when I met him after the 1977 elections, of an interesting slogan used in the election. The opposition party leaders did not have funds or time to organize an elaborate campaign against Mrs. Gandhi when they were released from prison to fight the election. Choudhry Charan Singh, the No.2 to Morarji Desai, conceived the slogan *"Indira Hatao, Indriya Bachao" (Remove Indira, Save Indriya-Semen)* which, without much expenditure, was written on the walls and on the surface of tar-roads in water mixed with lime so that they would be clearly visible for a few days *(TN Seshan would come on the scene only in 1990 to stop all these. He terrorized all political parties and they whispered among themselves that Seshan was actually Alsatian in disguise!)* The slogan's emotional appeal was immensely strong not only on men but also, in fact more so, on women because while *"nasbandi"* was thought by men to be destroying manhood, rural women perceived it as depriving them of motherhood. In many villages sterilization was construed as castration. While politics of corruption, hunger to stay in power and all other maladies were the same in all states, both in North and South, the Karnataka CM Devaraja Urs and his southern counterparts had the decency to treat the poor people as human beings with private lives and what could be more private than people's bodies? Obviously drunk with power and relying on reports of desk-bound officers of the unintelligent Intelligence Bureau (*Intelligence* Bureau is a contradiction in terms), Mrs Gandhi had continued with the suicidal Family Planning and called for elections, though vehemently opposed by Sanjay Gandhi (*Did he really slap her?*) and was promptly sent home by the poor people of North India horrified by *Nasbandi*. In the land of *Kama Sutra* and the temple sculptures explicitly displaying sex as nowhere else in the world and the epics of *Mahabharata* and *Ramayana* accepting polyandry and polygamy and millions of *Shivalingas* revering the very act of procreation, the foolhardy Sanjay Gandhi brigade let loose the FP programme and the bureaucracy headed by the mercenary DMs and SPs of North Indian states mindlessly implemented it which was what caused the land-slide defeat of Mrs Gandhi in 1977. Indian *Intellectuals* should take at least belated note of this. It should be realized that there was no pressure on Mrs Gandhi to call for the election before even two years of emergency. In fact, the Supreme Court of India to its everlasting, eternal disgrace had already justified the suspension of fundamental rights taking cowardly shelter, locking itself inside the "four walls of the Reasonable Restrictions provided under Article 21 of the Constitution". *[A constitution bench comprising of five judges of the Supreme Court in ADM, Jabbalpur vs. Shivkant Shukla (1976) reversed the first pro-liberty judgments given by various High Courts and held loftily on appeal that "Liberty is the gift of law and can be forfeited by Law". This was in the highly acclaimed Anglo-Saxon Adversarial juridical tradition of the US Supreme Court's (7 to 2) decision in the Dred Scott v. Sandford (1857) in which the SC held that persons of African descent cannot be US citizens and therefore their slavery in the US was legal !]* The only honourable exception in India was Justice HR Khanna ("So clean a man, he makes angels look dishevelled and dirty", said Khushwant Singh, of all people, who admired Mrs Gandhi and welcomed Emergency!) who dissented for which he was superseded for Chief Justice and Mrs Gandhi elevated an obliging junior Justice MH Beg as the CJI in January 1977 before she lost the elections in March 1977 and Justice Khanna resigned. No other "brother" judge resigned in protest. *In high places we invent virtues where none exist !*

I had by then completed twenty months in Bangalore district and nearly six years as DC in the three districts of Shimoga, Gulbarga and Bangalore. Election was announced in January 1977 and polling was to be held in March. Just before the election, I was transferred as Director of Sericulture. The Indian Express instead of reporting the Official Postings in the usual colourless dry officialese, added a word and said, "Mr.VB....the *dynamic* DC of Bangalore has been transferred and posted as the Director of Sericulture". I considered this as the best Confidential Report I ever received!

SUMMING UP MY EXPERIENCE AS DEPUTY COMMISSIONER AND DISTRICT MAGISTRATE IN THE DISTRICT ADMINISTRATION

While modern district administration was introduced in 1772 by Warren Hastings with six districts in Bengal Province, this unique system has continued till date in India with about 850 districts currently. The role of the DC & DM as the representative of the government at the district level has continued with little change. It is a unique office which does not exist even in UK or anywhere else except for France in the form of *Prefect.* Though the institution of DC&DM has come to be diluted with the advent of democratically elected representatives interfering with the district administration, yet precisely because of the devaluation of democracy and the unethical practices such as 'Resort Democracy' by which MLAs are kidnapped and herded together in resorts for long periods, people have come to disrespect the political leaders and the traditional respect of people to the old institutions of district administration has come to stay. For instance, NT Rama Rao changed the name of Taluk into Mandal and the Tahsildar was renamed *Mandalatipati*. However, after NTR has gone, his *Mandalatipati* has also gone and the 'Tahsildar' has come back. Time-tested and time-honoured institutions in orthodox India do not go away.

Thus ended my great experience as Deputy Commissioner and District Magistrate of Shimoga, Gulbarga and Bangalore for nearly six years. This was my most rewarding experience conforming to my ideology. Throughout this period, Devaraj Urs was the Chief Minister and Lynn his Secretary who always appreciated and supported my work. Few can ask for more.

❖❖❖

CHAPTER 13

My Travel on Silk Road Starts
How to Offend Ministers and Still Get a Better Job

Transfer is a common feature in the lives of bureaucrats and also the most important, stable means of livelihood of MLAs without which life loses its meaning for them. I was overdue for a change as I had already over five years as DC&DM in three districts. In Karnataka, direct recruit IAS officers were seldom given five years to work as DC and rarely a third district. There were two reasons for my transfer. For quite some time the district minister of Bangalore Chikke Gowda who was a big landlord, had been complaining against me to the CM. The usual interferences were there from early on. Though a senior Okkaiga politician and holding the cabinet portfolio for agriculture, he was also petty minded. In my early days in Bangalore, he once telephoned me and asked me *not to* issue licence to an applicant for touring cinema. My usual response to any political interference is not to say an outright *No*, having learnt from GVK. The most valuable advice in the BBC Serial *Yes, Minister* and *Yes, Prime Minister,* reflects the time-tested strategy of not saying "No" at once as it hurts the Spermwhale-sized ego of politicians, but instead, the bureaucrat should say *"Yes" first and then sabotage it in a hundred ways.* That is how the meek, intelligent Bureaucrat inherits his pay check and promotion, if not the Earth!

I had learnt from my Shimoga days that whenever an MLA asks for a favour to be shown, it is better to tell him, *I will check what can be done* and then do what is actually permitted according to rules and propriety. There are three categories of any MLA's requests: Some requests are clearly illegal, some are quite correct which I should have done earlier and the third is within my discretionary powers where the rule is neutral and whether you had a comfortable bowel movement in the morning! I had observed that, if a politician makes 10 requests, four will be illegal, three will be permissible and the remaining three will be discretionary. The impermissible requests one need not of course do, the permissible ones one can do immediately and the discretionary ones depend upon whether doing it would be harmful to any poor people if it is done, and if not harmful, these can be done too. The only problem is, while most politicians will not insist on pursuing the impermissible demands especially if the DC is not malleable, taking comfort that he had accommodated other requests, some politicians, especially in the southern Old Mysore districts, will keep on persisting with a personal vendetta, as in Chikke Gowda's case. The bonded labour contractor Rayappa whom I had detained under MISA was supplying building material for the construction of the Minister's three storey building on the prestigious 100 feet road in Indira Nagar, which I found after completion was rented to the Survey of India. This had already put me in the bad books of the Minister. Next was the murder of a dalit in the minister's Hosakote taluk, just twenty kilometres from Bangalore. When the murder was reported in the newspaper, next day I had proceeded to the village as it involved a dalit and the taluk was known for feudal atrocities. I had sat in the village panchayat office and enquired into the murder and from what the relatives of the murdered person told me, it was clear that some dominant caste persons who were supporters of the minister were involved. I had summoned them and threatened them that if there was a *prima facie* case against them, I would not hesitate to take action on my own to *"gadi par"* them (extern outside the district.)

When I returned to my office after the dalit murder enquiry, there was a call from my Divisional Commissioner who asked me to meet him. Karnataka, like many non-Presidency, Part B States in pre-independence India, has the system of having a Divisional Commissioner (renamed Regional Commissioner as an earth-shaking act of administrative reform of Veerappa Moily!) under whom there would be four or five districts for supervision. In 1976 Bangalore Division had four big districts of Bangalore, Tumkur, Kolar and Shimoga and my Divisional Commissioner was a person promoted from the Mysore Civil Service and belonging to the same Okkaliga caste as the district Minister. I learned that his parents had named him dutifully *Somè Gowda*, but as he found the majority of Mysore Civil Service men were Brahmins, he wisely Brahminized his name to Parthasarathy (Prof MN Srinivas would say, this was *'Sanscritization')* to mean Arjuna's Sarathy! He owed his position to the strong politicians of his community. But he was also a mild-mannered person who would not harm a younger officer who worked according to rules. So, when I met him, hospitable soul that he was, he first asked his Office Assistant *'Giggling* Gowramma' to get a *Special Ghee Masala Dosa* for the honourable *Kasaba* DC from the then famous Prakash Café. With this softening, he advised me that while my prompt action to visit villages to protect the downtrodden and Dalits was admirable, would it not be more prudent if I just kept the district

Minister informed before such visits? I politely told him that I was DC&DM for the whole district of Bangalore and not for Bangalore *minus* the Minister's Hosakote taluk! Finding me rhino-skinned, he was good enough to conclude the discussion by saying, whatever I did, he would support me even if the Minister complains against me. I was none too sure of it!

There was a third instance. I used to make surprise inspections of the work of Revenue Inspectors who are a key functionary in Revenue Administration, about 60 in Bangalore district, being supervisors of the cutting-edge level Village Accountants numbering about 300. When I visited the office of the RI of Bidarahalli revenue circle in Hosakote taluk on complaints from some villagers that he was never to be seen, I too did not find him there. My enquiries revealed that he was always at the house of Chikke Gowda, away from the RI's jurisdiction and attending to the personal and political work of the Minister. I therefore promptly transferred him outside Hosakote taluk as it was within my powers. Next day I received a phone call from the Revenue Minister, no less, asking me to cancel my orders and post him back. The Revenue Minister Hutchamasti Gowda was an elderly, charming old-timer from the neighbouring Tumkur district who had earlier appreciated my famine relief work in Gulbarga. So, he frankly told me that the Agriculture Minister was very upset about the transfer and would I please cancel my order? I politely told the RM that there were complaints against the RI and when I visited his office I did not find him and the villagers had told me that he was always at the residence of the Minister attending to his personal work. I did not change my orders as RI's transfer was within the domain of the DC and I had justifiable reason for what I had done. But, after four days when I returned from a tour, my HqA came to me with a long face and showed me an order of the Revenue Department cancelling my order and reposting the RI to the same Bidarahalli. This was unheard of, where a junior official like RI being transferred by the Revenue Secretariat. But, I did not leave it at that. I allowed one week to pass and went to Bidarahalli again to inspect the RI's office. As usual he was not there. I recorded the statement of a few villagers that the RI was never in his office and he was never available for them and for getting their work done they had to go all the way to the Taluk Office. So, this time I issued an order keeping the RI under suspension for dereliction of duty and appointed the Assistant Commissioner as Enquiry Officer. Now, the legal position was, Government cannot cancel the disciplinary action including suspension order under the KCS Rules when an enquiry has been ordered and all would have to wait for the outcome of the enquiry. Firstly, the enquiry had to be completed and an appeal would lie to the Administrative Tribunal and not to government. During the first six months of suspension the official would draw 50% of his salary and after that 75% till his suspension is ended by the Disciplinary Authority who was the DC. I also added a clause in the suspension order that to draw his half salary every month, he had to stay in his headquarters as required under the KCSR and that the Enquiry Officer should certify that he was staying in his headquarters so that the Tahsildar could release his half-pay every month. I had thus made my point emphatically though it earned me the displeasure of the district minister and also, in addition, of the Revenue Minister.

There was a third episode. The bane of Revenue Administration in the districts was the grass root officials not staying in their jurisdiction. In Bangalore this indiscipline was rampant. As the medical and educational facilities were better in the capital, most of the 300 or so Village Accountants of my district were not staying in their village-jurisdiction but had rented houses in Bangalore or had their own houses in the city and would be visiting their villages as they chose. Because of the unavailability of the Village Accountants, the villagers were put to a lot of difficulties and for every small matter they had to go to the Tahsildar involving travel expenditure and they had to stay in the taluk headquarters two or three days to get their work done. So, to enforce discipline, with the background of the general atmosphere of discipline and fear prevailing during the Emergency, I issued a circular to all the VAs and RIs that they had to stay in their designated headquarters so that they would be available to the people failing which disciplinary action under the KCSR would be taken and they would be dismissed from service. The DC was the Prescribed Authority for imposing Major Punishments which included dismissal from service with future bar on government employment. There were about 300 VAs in Bangalore district and I asked the 11 Tahsildars in the district to check whether the VAs were staying in their jurisdiction with proof of sleeping and cooking food and give a factual report to the three Assistant Commissioners who were appointed as Enquiry Officers. At the end of this exercise I dismissed about 70 VAs for not staying in their village headquarters and therefore proven dereliction of duty and followed it up with advertisements inviting applications from qualified persons to fill up the 70 VA posts reserving 18% for SC/ST candidates. This sent a shock-wave among all the staff of Revenue Department in the State because dismissal from the secure and lucrative government employment is un-heard of in any department. On the other hand this was greatly appreciated by the villagers and also by the Dalit Sangarsha Samithi because, inspite of the rule of 18% reservation for SC/STs, there were very few dalit VAs in the district.

A fourth incident was horrifying, involving a tenant and landlord. Even before the 20 Points Programme under which implementation of land reforms was given priority, in Karnataka Devaraj Urs had implemented the "Land to the Tenant" policy by amending the 1961 Land Reforms Act as soon as he became the CM in 1972. This had created a lot of heart-burning among the feudal land lords. Bangalore district, even though it was fast urbanizing and had the state's capital city, it also had a highly feudal culture. This was like the proverbial dark circle of shadow under the lamp. One of the illegal methods of the powerful landlords was to intimidate the tenants not to apply in the prescribed form to the Tahsildar and claim the tenanted land for ownership. If the landlord successfully prevents his tenants from applying for the tenanted lands, he could claim the land as owner-cultivator upto 56 acres of rain-fed land (defined as 10 Standard Acres) and he could show his entire family (some had even shown the names of their cats and dogs!) as cultivating personally in which case each family member gets 56 acres of land, rendering the Land Reforms meaningless. As Assistant Commissioner of Lingsugur I had seen a "Dhani" (former Jaghirdar) owned 1,500 acres of land which was all irrigable. It had taught me that laws in India had no meaning when not implemented and an eye-wash to continue status quo. It is a 'soft state' as Gunnar Myrdal said in his 1968 *Asian Drama.*

In the feudal Bangalore district there was not even the ancient feudal-honour of the European principle of *Noblesse oblige* ('ancestral nobility has obligations, Privileges entail responsibility') among the landed gentry because of the generations long embedded Dominant Caste Immunity and the economic reason of fast rising price of land. Land value in Bangalore had sky-rocketed by 530 times because of the explosion of population and the consequential high demand for housing. David Ricardo's theory of the "original and indestructible powers of the soil" and of "marginal lands" coming up for cultivation and increasing the "rent" of land-owners of more fertile lands have all been rendered irrelevant with the unprecedented urbanization of Bangalore where agricultural lands were being fast-converted to Non-Agricultural purposes. The land-lords of Bangalore, finding the value of their lands going up, clung to their lands by all means, depriving the tenants of their claims even though the tenants were actually cultivating the lands.

In this background, one day the son of a tenant-farmer from Bangalore North taluk came to my office and insisted on seeing me because the landlord was dangling, *yes dangling*, his father upside down inside a well. This was a rather unusual punishment and I heard him out. He had an incredible, medieval story to tell. His father was a tenant of three acres of *Bagayat* land (growing horticultural and vegetable crops irrigated by an open well) of the landlord for over thirty years on a 60:40 share-cropping basis (40% to the landlord and all expenses being borne by the tenant) in a village which was just 10 kilometers from the city. After the Devaraj Urs government came to power and land reforms became an important programme, his father wanted to file the application for confirmation of the tenanted land in his name. The Gowda landlord discouraged him from filing his claim and had even increased the tenant's share from 60% to 70%. But the tenant filed his application anyway. So, the earlier day evening the landlord and his henchmen had come to the land, caught hold of his father and took him to the well, tied his feet and hands and lowered him head-first into the well from a pulley, his head dangling upside down just inches from the water to teach him a lesson. The son ran to the police station and complained but the police did not help and therefore he had come to the DC. I telephoned the Tahsildar of Bangalore North Taluk whose office behind St Martha's hospital was close to my office and I told him to go to the village along with the son and ascertain the facts and if the complaint was true, to file a police complaint and get the landlord arrested. I also told him I would visit the village in the afternoon. By the time I visited the village the Tahsildar and his officials had rescued the tenant after sixteen hours in this novel *Shirasasana* position and fortunately he had not incurred any serious injuries.

I talked to the still terror-stricken tenant and got his statement recorded. The landlord had disappeared from the village by this time. The wells in Bangalore district were then mostly open-wells and deep bore-hole wells were just then coming into existence. These open wells were normally huge, 60'L x 40'W x 50'deep wells with 10 horse-power electric motor pump sets and also with old stand-by pulleys. More than the pain, the terror of hanging head down close to the water surface the whole night could be imagined. While there was no grievous hurt except some minor scrapes, the psychological trauma was immense. I was quite amazed by the ingenuity and medieval barbarism of the Bangalore landlord class. The tenant was fortunate in not having died of shock and terror. Though the Police Sub Inspector had already come and had recorded the First Information Report and had gone in search of the land lord to arrest him for offences under the Indian Penal Code, I decided that this was a fit case for harsher, long-term, preventive penal action. Land Reforms Act was a law passed by the Legislature to give ownership rights to the tenants. An extreme step like attempt to terrorise the tenant to drown in the well sends message to all the tenants not to exercise their legal rights. I could very well argue this could naturally create agrarian unrest and lead to public disorder. To safeguard against this, a counter-message and action should be taken to detain the land lord from moving around and to teach other landlords a lesson. I therefore passed a detention order under MISA giving reasons for the detention even though it was not required but anyway I thought the order should speak, even scream, for itself. I sent him to the mosquito-infested Bellary prison which had by now become my favourite government resort for economic offenders. I also told the press next day that any one harming the tenants to prevent them from exercising their rights would be proceeded under the draconian detention law.

These incidents I am narrating may appear to be extra-ordinary and unique. But in the district administration involving an economy entirely based on land-ownership, the system was still feudal and had not passed on to the Capitalist state with factory system of production even in the State capital. A big 70% of Bangalore district's rural population was still dependent upon agriculture even in the 1970's though agriculture accounted for less than 20% of district-GDP. It was still more like the Lord and Serf system of medieval times. In the twenty months I was DC and DM of Bangalore I had detained over a hundred economic offenders under MISA but not one of them for political reasons. I was fortunate that the detention orders of the opposition leaders such as LK Advani, Atal Behari Vajpayee, Ramakrishna Hegde, Veerendra Patil, JH Patel, PGR Sindhia and over twenty others were all issued by the Commissioner of Police who was the Additional District Magistrate in Bangalore under direct instructions from the Union Home Ministry.

FROM BEING 'MISA DC', I BECOME THE SILK MAN

Not long after my detaining the landlord for dangling his tenant upside down in the well, I finally got my transfer. A few days before my transfer order came, the Secretary of Industries and Commerce, KSN Murthy telephoned me to meet him. He told me that I was being posted as Director in the Department of Sericulture which came under the Industries Department. I was quite happy that finally I was being made an independent Head of Department though I had doubts whether I was fit for the post because Sericulture was a highly technical subject with botany and zoology dominating the process of silk making which is what mulberry cultivation and silkworm rearing was all about. In India, Karnataka was the earliest state under the Mysore Maharaja's government to have started a separate Department of Sericulture in 1918 who appointed Navaratna Rama Rao of the Mysore Civil Service as its first head, his designation being Superintendent of Sericulture. The other such first in India was the Department of Horticulture in Mysore. Both were followed by the Maharaja's government of Kashmir. Post-independence, the heads of Sericulture Department in Mysore were all technical persons and rightly so. I was being posted on the retirement of Director Venugopalan Nair who was a highly qualified technical expert working all his life in the Department. I therefore expressed some uneasiness to KSN of my qualifications to fit in the new job. He told me that the CM knows all about sericulture as he was earlier the Chairman of the Central Silk Board, appointed by Mrs Gandhi when she was made the Prime Minister by the 'Syndicate' headed by Kamaraj. In Karnataka she chose Devaraj Urs from Mysore who belonged to the tiny Arasu community of loyal associates of Maharaja as shadow CM. Since he was not holding any major elected post, she had appointed Urs as Chairman of Central Silk Board, which was the first Commodity Board created by an Act of the Parliament in 1949 under the Union Industries Ministry. In fact, the first Chairman of the CSB was Prime Minister Pandit Nehru himself, in his capacity as Industries Minister which post he held in 1949 besides being the PM. More importantly, Devaraj Urs was a practising sericulturist in Hunsur of Mysore district where he was the President of the Taluk Development Board and his wife Chikkammani Devi used to rear silkworms in their house till they moved to Bangalore.

So, KSN told me that when the current Director would be retiring by the month end, the senior most person to succeed him was a Joint Director whom the CM knew to be corrupt and a drunkard. He therefore wanted an IAS officer to head the department. Besides, the *Trimurtis* of majority community cabinet ministers, Chkke Gowda of Bangalore, Hutchmasti Gowda the Revenue Minister and Industries Minister SM Krishna had jointly been complaining against the 'vindictive attitude' of Bangalore DC against Okkaliga community and that I was on a 'MISA-spree'. The CM had not yielded to their request for my change for one year but when he wanted an IAS officer to head the Sericulture Department because of his interest in sericulture, it was GVK who had become the Chief Secretary in 1975 who suggested my name for the post as I was overdue for a change already and avoid my collision course with powerful ministers which could only harm me. The CM had readily agreed to this suggestion and the posting orders would be issued in a day or two as told to KSN by GVK. KSN also advised me to meet the CM as he had specific ideas about how the sericulture department should shape up as he was holding the portfolio which was unusual for the CM to handle sericulture amidst his busy schedule. By this time, Sisir Das of 1970 batch who was the Assistant Commissioner of Sagar Sub-division in Shimoga district when I was DC there in 1972 and a close friend of mine, was the Deputy Secretary to CM, assisting Lynn who was (always!) Secretary to CM! Sisir was from Orissa who had studied in Delhi and was superb in man-management with a great sense of humour who could pull the legs of politicians without giving offence but who would themselves enjoy his jokes even if they were at their expense. When I told him I require an appointment with the CM he told me just to come along and took me with him to CM's chambers. Karnataka CM's chambers is a magnificent spacious room with two huge sandalwood doors and two conference tables besides CM's own table and a big ante-room. Sisir told me that CM's chambers was a mad house and appointments go haywire and the only way to meet him was to take me personally to him. So he took me to the CM and told him that he should speak to his new Director of Sericulture. The CM had known me as I had met him as DC many a time. The CM took us to the ante-room wading through the MLAs and there were MLAs even in the ante room. He told them to wait outside and gave me ten minutes alone. After thanking him for posting me to Sericulture Department, when I expressed my concern I may not fit to head a highly technical department, he brushed it aside and said that my duty would be to instil discipline as there was tremendous corruption in the grainages and cocoon markets which was why I was being posted there. He also told me to be careful about the Joint Director who belonged to the major Lingayat community and was a manipulator and who was corrupting the entire department by having a clique. Before leaving, he told me I should extend sericulture in the North Karnataka districts as it was then practised only in five southern Old Mysore districts out of the state's 19 districts. I left somewhat overwhelmed.

I went back straight to KSN and reported. KSN was a very senior officer of 1954 batch, remarkably affectionate, an elegantly dressed debonair-bachelor and a brilliant botany scholar from Pune university whose loss to academia was administration's gain. He warmly welcomed me to the Industry family. He was very much interested in the development of sericulture especially because of its mulberry and botany connection and silk was a very high value commodity. He told me to prepare as soon as possible a project proposal for posing to World Bank assistance. An officer of the Agro-Industries Department of the World Bank was visiting India the next month and KSN had invited him to Bangalore and he could request him to visit some sericulture areas if I prepare at least a brief, 10-page outline of a project proposal to give it to him to set the ball rolling. All this was too quick and too much for me the very first day of my learning of leaving the district as DC. I promised him to do my best. KSN also told me that I can drop into his room any time without an appointment. The Industry Secretary in any state is a very busy person and it was so nice of KSN to tell me that I could meet him any time. Next day my posting order was issued and I took charge from my predecessor.

Thus I left the unique, robust and virtuous domain of DC and District Magistrate after a tumultuous tenure. I learned a lot and grew in self-confidence by administering Famine, Communal Unrest, Emergency and MISA, 20 Point Programme, incurring displeasure of the dominant caste ministers but also getting praise from the Finance Minister and the Chief Minister, above all from the people and the Press. Nothing equalled the mountain of flowers from the citizens of arid Gulbarga. Very few IAS officers would have such rich experience in early stages. TP Issar, who was a very affable, humorous and very senior to me by some twelve years, who would become Chief Secretary in 1991, was passing me in the corridors of Vidhana Soudha when I came out of KSN's chambers. He whispered in my earshot, *'cynosure!'*. It was a fleeting moment and, startled, before I could react he had gone past me. But that moment has lasted me life-long. These are some things which no money can buy, no riches can acquire and no corrupt officer can ever dream of.

LEARNING SERICULTURE

I had to learn sericulture like a new student. I will give some technical information as Silk is exotic and Karnataka produces 70% of India's silk, India itself being the second biggest producer after China. After taking charge as Director, I visited immediately the premier Central Sericulture Research Institute at Mysore and called on the Director Dr Krishnaswamy. He gave me a three-volume FAO publication on Sericulture which he had co-authored. So I went away to my old district Bijapur and stayed for four days in the then remote and quiet new circuit house at Bagalkot and read the manual as much as possible right from the origin of silk. Some 2,000 years ago, a Chinese princess was playing with a silk cocoon and she dropped it accidentally into her tea, which was another Chinese invention. While retrieving it, the silk filament started unravelling because it was moistened and the filament kept coming on and on for hundreds of metres, the longest unbroken filament in nature. The silkworm is a caterpillar and it eats voraciously the highly protein-rich mulberry leaf for about four weeks when it becomes ready for its next stage of metamorphosis. It then stops eating and the protein it has consumed is synthesized into two protein liquids, *Fibroin* and *Sericin*. The silkworm brings out these twin protein liquids through its spinnaret in the form of one thin filament which solidifies in contact with air and it spins the single filament *around itself* which becomes a thick Cocoon as a protective shell. The filament is thus an unbroken length of strong filament which can be upto 500 meters or *half kilometre* long.

There was no sericulture in South India till Tipu Sultan's time. In 18th century Tipu Sultan (1750-1799) dedicated his life to fight the British. He found that the superiority of the Europeans in warfare was because of the muskets and cannons using gunpowder, organizing the soldiers into platoon formation and ensuring continuous firing, cannons mounted on light mobile wheels and fast moving cavalry with matchlock guns. He sought the help of the French and succeeded in making Mysore Rockets. In the Second Anglo-Mysore War he even defeated the British East India Company's sepoys in 1780 at Pollilur, Kanjeepuram near Madras but made the mistake of not pursuing them just 75 km short of Fort St. George and wipe them out. His entire life was dedicated to find ways and means to defeat the British. He wanted to import French arms and Arabian horses for which he had to pay. He found that pearls and silk were in great demand in France and in other European courts which he could export to pay for importing cannons and horses. So he developed pearl fishing in Mangalore and Tuticorin (Thuthukudi) coasts. When he learnt silk fabrics was in great demand in aristocratic Europe and that there was silk production in Bengal, he sent two persons from Trichinopoly to Murshidabad to learn the "silk trade". In two years they came back with silkworm eggs, mulberry cuttings and Charka reeling devices. With their expertise, 13 silk centres including reeling of silk yarn were started in and around Mysore and silk fabrics were produced. Under Tipu Sultan's patronage mulberry cuttings were supplied free to farmers and sericulture flourished in Mysore. Even today, mulberry plant in Mysore district is known as *Sultan-e-kaddi,* "kaddi" referring to cutting as mulberry, like rose, is planted with cuttings. Even after the heroic death of Tipu in 1799 (he was one of the few Indian rulers who fought the British and died in the battlefield, like Rani Lakshmibai of Jhansi later in 1858, while all other Indian princes were pensioners of the Company.) The Wodeyar rulers of Mysore continued with patronage to sericulture, followed by the British Resident Commissioners. During the Second World War, sericulture in Mysore received further impetus from the War Department because parachutes were made of silk fabric due to the strength of silk yarn (DuPont's stronger and cheaper chemical Nylon was invented in 1939 and later replaced silk for parachutes) and the silk producing countries, Italy and Japan were Axis powers and China and Korea were inaccessible to the Allied powers. During the war years, six filatures were established in Mysore district and in Kolar thus increasing the demand for cocoons. Thus, though sericulture was introduced from Bengal to Mysore only in late 18th century, because of royal patronage, Karnataka has been producing over the past hundred years three-fourths of India's silk.

I thus found very early a lesson from history that it is not necessarily the climate, natural resources or even "potential" that is needed for development but organization and government's support in the early stages which is crucial, known as the 'Infant Industry' protection in Economics. After all, Bihar, North Eastern states, Orissa and many other states had the same natural conditions as Bengal but it is the distant old Mysore, not even the Bengal Province, which was the domain of Tipu Sultan which produced three-fourths of India's silk because of the continued support given by the Mysore government over two centuries.

Thus, sericulture is a highly organized, technically tightly controlled agro-industry and not a simple crop like paddy or sugarcane. These technicalities are not the typical administrative matters a generalist IAS officer is normally expected to be familiar with. But to be an effective Head of Department (and be worthy of the legendary Navarathna Rama Rao) I had to 'read while running'. Dr Krishnaswamy of CSB from whom I was learning all this was extremely helpful to me. I went through his three volumes of Sericulture Manual and I kept them always with me! A first cursory reading of it took me a month. It was like back to University and learning a new subject and it was quite challenging. But I had the advantage of reading and seeing in the field the ground reality and also learning from farmers. One of the interesting sentences in the then prohibited Mao's Red Book, *Mao Ze Dong Thoughts,* was *"First, Learn from the Masses before Teaching them"!* In very few commodities is India the second biggest producer in the world. Only in silk India is the second biggest producer after China and Karnataka produced three-fourths of India's silk. And I was the Head of Sericulure Department ! Nothing like it to boost one's ego !

Thus I began my interesting service in sericulture in 1976 at the age of 35. I had the great support and goodwill of my Secretary KSN and GVK who was now the Chief Secretary and above all the greatest CM of Karnataka, Devaraj Urs. No other officer could have dreamed of such patronage. Little did I realize that in four years of my heading the department, KSN and GVK would be gone and Devaraj Urs would be upstaged by a failed wrestler! Thus would start the Fall from Grace by Karnataka.

❖❖❖

CHAPTER 14

Karnataka Silk Project—My First Project for World Bank Assistance

My Journey on Marco Polo's Silk Road Starts!

Following the suggestion of the Industry Secretary KSN, I formed a team with my knowledgeable Joint Director Mahadevappa to prepare an ambitious Sericulture project to double the silk yarn production of Karnataka in five years from its then 2,500 tons a year. I also toured ten days a month visiting grainages, silk farms, cocoon markets, reeling establishments and farmers fields to absorb as much as I could about this fascinating industry. Under the Department there were six industrial units—one Silk Weaving Factory and four Filatures (making yarn from cocoons)—all in Mysore district and one Spun Silk Factory at Channapatna in Bangalore district which used the silk waste from reeling establishments and produced a second quality of silk yarn which also had a good market, especially for silk and woollen carpets. In silk, as in coconut, nothing is wasted. Pricey silk carpets of Jammu and Kashmir, Iran (famous for 'Persian' carpets), Samarkhand and Bukhara of Uzbekistan were all made from the spun silk yarn mostly by children because of their nimble fingers.

The Central Silk Board was the first central Commodity Board formed in 1949 and this was followed by establishing 12 commodity Boards, about 12 such as for Tea, Coffee, Tobacco, Coir, Rubber and Cardamom. The CSB's head office was on Marine Drive in Bombay. Within two months, I attended the quarterly Board meeting of CSB at Bombay. The Chairman of CSB was traditionally a non-official (from the time of Pandit Nehru as PM and Industry Minister) and in 1977 the Chairman was from Karnataka, belonging to a backward community and a staunch follower of Urs. The CSB's Annual budget was only Rs 4 crores and this was to cover not only mulberry silk but also the three other non-mulberry silk called *Tassar, Eri* and *Muga* which are mostly reared outdoors, on the trees, in Bihar, Madhya Pradesh, Orissa and in the North-Eastern States. Only India produced all the four types of silk but the internationally traded was mulberry silk.

One of the subjects discussed in the CSB meeting I first attended was the forthcoming conferences of the International Silk Association at Como, Italy and the International Sericulture Commission at Alès near Marsëilles, France. A 3-member delegation headed by the Joint Secretary, Ministry of Textiles and a Director from the Ministry and the Chairman of the CSB were to attend. As silk exporters were considered crucial in the foreign exchange strapped government then, they were calling the shots in the Ministry of Textiles and also in the CSB. So, there were also about ten exporters in the delegation, bearing their own expenses. I noticed that there was no State Director in the delegation though it was the states, especially Karnataka, which had organized the industry from earlier times. In 1976 Karnataka was producing 77% of India's mulberry raw silk. So, I told CSB that the Karnataka Director was the Director of Sericulture *of India* who was missing from the delegation!

When I returned from the CSB meeting in Bombay, Abdul Samad, MLA from Bangalore met me. He was also the Chairman of the Cooperative Silk Marketing Federation, mainly of reelers in Karnataka and himself a silk exporter. He told me he was attending the conferences in Italy and France on behalf of the Federation and whether I am also attending. When I told him I was not a member the delegation, he said, with three-fourths of India's silk being produced in Karnataka, it would be very useful if the Karnataka Director meets the international silk community. He also surprised me by asking whether I have any objections if he requested the CM to write to the Union Textile Minister to include the Karnataka Director in the delegation. I said of course it would be very nice of him to suggest it but the CM may think I was bringing pressure on him. Samad smiled and said, it was he and other prominent Muslim reelers who were mostly from Bangalore district who had requested the CM that I should be posted as Director as the department officials were getting astray and farmers and reelers were not getting any help. There was a neat division of labour in sericulture as traditionally almost all reelers of cocoons in Mysore state were Muslims and Dalits while the farmers were Hindu land-owning castes because the farmers, having reared the silkworms as their children would not kill by boiling them inside the cocoons while the other two communities had no such inhibition. It was the reelers who unwound the silk filaments from the cocoons using ancient 'charakas' and 100-year old Italian Cottage Basin machines. Samad was a decent person and a respected leader. In fact, shortly the CM would make him the Health Minister. So, he said the CM would be happy if I could increase the tempo of activities in the department which was the reason, knowing the subject well, the CM at the Reelers' recommendation posted me, a non-technical IAS officer, for the first time.

Within three days, Industry Secretary KSN rang me that the CM has sent a letter to the Union Textile Minister to include the Karnataka's Director of Sericulture in the delegation. It was thus that immediately of my joining the Department, I attended the two international silk conferences in Italy and France and met the small, elite family of silk manufacturers and officials of different countries. I was especially impressed by the Chinese delegation to the ISA conference at Como, Italy. It was 15-strong with one of their own interpreter. Even though China was the home of silk, by the time of the Second World War, it was Japan which had become the dominant producer of high quality silk because of its high investment in research and development—and consumption, especially the multi-layered *Kimono* worn mainly by women and aristocrats and its shorter version *Yukata*. I also ascertained from the Japanese delegation that a high-end 12-layer, heavy silk satin, women's kimono would weigh as much as 20 kg and would cost US$ 50,000! Therefore, after the 1960s and with industrialization Japanese had switched over to wearing Western skirts and gowns. It occurred to me that Indian women will never change over to Western skirts and it is the craze for silk sarees which was keeping Indian sericulture growing! Japan's trade surplus in 19th and early 20th century was essentially from export of women's silk stockings to the United States and Europe, *Silk Stockings* referring to aristocratic Western ladies. Japan used its trade surplus wisely in importing machinery and technology from the West and industrialized quickly from the Meiji Restoration of 1868 ending the Tokugawa Shogunate military government—"Meiji" meaning the Enlightened Rule of Emperor Meiji. But after the Second World War, it was China which improved its traditional silk industry and by 1970's became the dominant producer, accounting for 85% of world production of silk yarn. However, the European countries especially, Italy, Switzerland, Germany, France and the United Kingdom were still important manufacturers of silk cloth. But they were all dependent on China for their silk yarn. Even Japan and South Korea, their cocoon and raw silk production having gone down because of industrialization and migration of labour from farming to factories, were dependent upon China for silk yarn. I could see the smug amusement of the Chinese delegation in seeing the Western representatives being solicitous, almost *kowtowing* to China for favourable import terms. *Kowtowing* or approaching the Chinese Emperor on one's knees and also crawling backwards on knees while returning, was the old custom in China, much to the resentment of Europeans till the Opium Wars in 19th century when it was their turn to humiliate China. I also found that India did not count at all in this international conference because while statistically we were second to China in production of silk, no country was interested in importing Indian silk yarn as it was classified as "H" grade after A to G. There was nothing below H grade! All the Indian silk merchants who attended the conferences were traders who were exporting Indian handloom silk garments to Europe while the European delegates were manufacturers looking for importing China's high quality silk yarn. I also found the leader of the Chinese delegation examining the price of silk ties and bristling. I spoke to him through their interpreter (whose English also sounded like Chinese!) and learnt that these silk ties were made in Italian silk mills with imported Chinese silk yarn and were four times costlier than in China. His point was, if China manufactured the finished products, China would get the value added and not Italy. I had no inkling that within a decade China would do this and would become the Workshop of the World, not just in silk but in many others. There were also a few Indian handloom silk garments but I was surprised that these were kept in a shelf reading "Thai Silk", the reason being, Thai Silk was better known in the West because of the marketing efforts of Jim Thompson who revived Thailand's silk industry and helped thousands of poor hand loom weavers and popularized Thai silk all over the world. He disappeared in the rain forest of Malaysia in 1967 at the age of 61 and the mystery was never solved. Interestingly, Thai Airways' official marketing slogan is *"Smooth as Silk"!* However, during my tenure as Director I succeeded in making the Air India and Indian Airlines buy pure Silk sarees made in the Government Silk Weaving Factory, Mysore for air hostesses!

I returned from the two-week European conferences, visiting Italy, France, Germany and UK, armed with the knowledge of international silk situation and the great possibility of India, which meant Karnataka, to increase production of international Bivoltine silk and export of value-added silk fabrics at much lower cost. But I also learned from the Japanese delegates that silk fabrics should not be sold "cheap" because, accounting for only 0.16% that is, one-sixth of one percent of world's natural and artificial fibres, it should always remain the fabric for the rich and the aristocracy and the higher its price the higher its demand, a case of "Backward Sloping" demand curve in economics.

I also learned about saving money while travelling abroad during this very first visit to Europe. Our delegation was headed by Mani Narayanaswamy IAS, who was then Joint Secretary in the Textiles Ministry. He belonged to 1953 batch of Karnataka cadre and a highly suave and fine officer who was earlier the Finance Secretary in Karnataka when I was Deputy Secretary, Planning Department. Our delegation also included a resourceful Sardarji, Dr MS Jolly, from the Research Institute of CSB who had done sericulture courses in both Italy and France and therefore could speak French and Italian. In 1977, the government's total daily allowance to me was a small US$ 90 with the exchange rate of 1 US$ = Rs 4.50! The hotel was usually booked by the Indian Embassy and paid for directly by the Embassy. This was called 'split rate' where the Embassy would pay for the hotel and a small cash allowance for food and transport would be given to us, about US$ 20 per day. Dr Jolly advised me that both of us can opt for drawing our full allowance of US$90 (for Europe) and we can ourselves take care of hotel arrangement. European towns are full of *Pensiones* which are small Lodging houses with only bed, bath, telephone and limited facilities, no swimming pool or restaurant and charge less than half of the tariff of a regular hotel. Thus, both of us got the full $ 90 per diem and I paid just $30 for the *pensione*, thanks to Dr MS Jolly's linguistic skill, and could save the major portion of the allowance and use it for visiting Paris, Lyons, London, Rome and Frankfurt—the air ticket already having covered them without any extra payment as we were allowed to fly Executive Class which covered the 'European Sector'. We had to travel by Air India only. For Executive Class passengers, Air India through its agents arranged two nights' "lay over" in these cities where modest hotel rooms were paid for by Air India.

After returning to Bangalore I called on KSN and GVK, who was now Chief Secretary and explained that the Department had to expand and employ more extension officials and office staff, keeping the future in mind. Graciously, GVK allotted an additional 8,000 sft, meant for another department, for a bigger and more modern office for sericulture. The space thus allotted in 1977 still serves as the department's spacious head office even after four decades. Till then the departmental officers including the key functionaries of 15 Assistant Directors were all working in the five Old Mysore districts of Bangalore, Mysore, Mandya, Kolar and Tumkur. Karnataka had then 19 districts and there was no presence of the department in the Northern districts. But, with abundant sunlight and water mulberry grows much better in any neutral soil. I had also read in FAO's Mulberry Manual that soils with pH value of 6 to 7.5 from slightly acidic (as in Southern districts) to slightly alkaline (as in

Northern area), 6.5 being neutral, are quite suitable for mulberry cultivation. I asked my officers to read the Manual and understand more about mulberry cultivation, silkworm rearing and reeling. Almost all the departmental officers were from Old Mysore districts and their cosy existence close to Bangalore was understandable. Some of them did try through the MLAs to get their transfers to the North cancelled but the CM who was holding Sericulture portfolio brushed aside their approaches.

KARNATAKA SERICULTURE PROJECT GETS SOLD EVEN BEFORE FORMAL SUBMISSION!

Within a month of my returning from the conferences in Italy and France, KSN one day informed me that Ducksoo Lee, Director in the Agro Industries Division of the India Department of the World Bank was visiting Delhi and would also spend three days in Bangalore for some other projects of Karnataka and KSN had requested him to spare some time to visit the sericulture areas around Bangalore and Ducksoo Lee had agreed to spare a half day. Meanwhile, I had prepared a 20-page Outline for a Karnataka Sericulture Project of the size of Rs.80 crores to be implemented in five years. *[In 2020 this would be equal to Rs.600 crores. This was a huge quantum jump for a then small department of Sericulture with an annual Plan Budget of Rs.55 lakhs which would increase to Rs.16 crores annually.]* We had included all ambitious infrastructure facilities such as modern Grainages (to produce high quality silkworm eggs), spacious Cocoon Markets, employment of Extension staff, transport vehicles, laboratory equipment, modernization of silk industries and Research and Development. I made 50 copies of it with comb binding as these small matters are impressive and gave five copies to KSN.

Ducksoo Lee was about 50, stocky, muscular and short as most Koreans are and spoke good English. He told me that he was originally from North Korea but migrated to the South before the 1950 Korean War and was employed in the Silk Filature at a small town called Gimje in the South. Thus, he was quite familiar with sericulture. After the Korean war he migrated to the United States and ultimately landed in the World Bank where he was working for the past fifteen years. It was a lucky coincidence that a senior World Bank official knowledgeable about sericulture had come to Karnataka. When I gave him a copy of my Outline at his West End Hotel, he was quite happy there was some basic paper to read. Next day I took him on the Karnataka's "Silk Road" namely, the Bangalore-Mysore Road upto Channapatna where on both sides of the road there were sericulture farmers, government silk farms, grainages, reeling establishments and a busy cocoon market at Ramanagaram. When Ducksoo Lee learned from the farmers first hand that their net income from one acre of mulberry cultivation, silkworm rearing and sale of cocoons was from Rs 30,000 which was next only to income from Thompson Seedless grapes, he was very much impressed. It was around 2 pm in Channapatna which was midway between Bangalore and Mysore. When I told him we have a first rate Central Sericulture Research Institute at Mysore one hour away, he said he would like to visit it and would not mind returning to Bangalore late. So, I took him to the CSB's Research Institute where he saw the research work being done both in silk worm races development and high quality of mulberry plants. *En route* I also showed him the "cottage basin" reeling establishments using an earlier generation Italian device of silk reeling compared to the modern "automatic reeling" machinery used in South Korea and Japan. Throughout the day-long journey and visits I was explaining to him in the car the need for Karnataka to modernize all aspects of sericulture, from mulberry cultivation till silk cloth weaving which latter I showed him in the Government Silk Weaving Factory at Mysore. Thus what was intended to be a 3-hour visit extended to a 12-hour day. After this very busy visit when I dropped him back at the hotel, he thanked me and asked me whether I could meet him next day and have breakfast with him. This was quite surprising as normally the protocol was, the State entertains the World Bank team at the government Kumara Krupa Guest House and not the other way around. I politely agreed anyway as he was friendly and showed great interest in our project.

But his purpose in inviting me for a breakfast discussion was surprisingly different. He told me that Karnataka sericulture has a great future but it has remained primitive. He had read my Outline and said modernization of the silk filatures in the private sector and in government and the silk weaving factory are essential along with all upstream activities such as silk farms, extension and assistance to farmers, expansion of Bivoltine silk, modern grainages and cocoon markets. He said while the Outline I gave him was a good kick-start, the World Bank would have to send expert consultants from Japan to examine the feasibility in Karnataka to produce high quality cocoons and raw silk. The experts would have to establish both technical and economic feasibility of such a project. Then he totally surprised me by saying, everything depends upon whether Japanese Consultants would technically agree to the possibility of Karnataka sericulture lifting itself to modernity and asked me whether it would be possible for me to go to Japan and South Korea and see the modern methods there and meet

Japanese experts and explain to them about Karnataka sericulture, *before* the World Bank sends its official mission. I could only say that the Chief Secretary would have to agree to this as it was unusual though I would be happy to see the modern methods of sericulture and meet Japanese experts. He said he would speak to KSN and Chief Secretary whom he was meeting later in the day before leaving.

MY FIRST VISIT TO JAPAN AND SOUTH KOREA

Long story short, I was told by KSN to visit Japan for three weeks and South Korea for one week, meet institutions and experts, as a preliminary to prepare a comprehensive Project for WB assistance. So, I met Dr Krishnaswamy of Mysore Insitute of CSB again who had returned from Japan recently. He gave me a list of scientists and institutions in Japan whom I should visit. Especially I should meet Dr Yataro Tajima who was the leading scientist in silkworm genetics and who was heading the National Institute of Genetics in Mishima, Japan.

Before leaving for Japan I read the basic facts and history of Japan. Though Japan had twice the geographical area of Karnataka, only about 12% of it was arable (compared to 65% in Karnataka and in India) and three-fourths of Japan was forests, mountains and otherwise not suitable for cultivation and most land being used for industrial and dwelling purposes. Being prone to earthquakes, volcanic eruptions and Tsunamis and devoid of energy resources of oil, iron and coal, it had only human resources to achieve economic development. Both Japan and South Korea are examples of human resources being the only critical factor in economic development and lack of natural resources did not matter. The famous *Zaibatsus* (family-controlled monopoly conglomerates) were responsible for the pre-war industrialization and militarization of Japan. MacArthur administration's attempts with its U.S. New Deal policy of disbanding monopolies did not succeed and *Zaibatsus* transformed themselves into the new *Kiretsu* Multi-National Corporations. The old conglomerates of Mitsui, Mitsubishi, Sumitomo, Dai-Ichi, etc. continue to dominate Japanese economy.

Thus, when I visited Japan in 1978, it was already the world's second biggest economy. Agriculture contributed just about 4% of its GDP (which has since shrunk to less than 2% in 2020). But, rice and cocoons were the only two "protected" commodities—rice because of the fear that in times of war Japan has to feed its 125 million population with its small area of arable land. Cocoons protection was surprising and could be explained only by the passionate love of the Japanese for sericulture and its traditional silk *kimonos*. Japan continues to be a highly cohesive, fiercely disciplined and neurotically patriotic, closed-culture society revering its Emperor. After the introduction of democracy and a constitution by MacArthur administration, Japan's Parliament, the *Diet* and the government continues to be dominated by a one-party government, the rural based United National Party (UNP) ruling the country for more than six decades. *[It was only from 2009 the United Democratic Party (UDP) challenged the UNP for a brief interregnum.]* But the traditional respect and power of the bureaucracy has continued from the Meiji era. Though Japan did not copy the rigorous Imperial-Scholar examination system of China, yet selection to elite government service was by tough examination, the candidates qualifying being mostly from the prestigious Tokyo University. The Secretary to government was designated as Vice-Minister, next only to the Minister. In the Indian Parliament or Legislatures when the Minister fumbles while replying to supplementaries to the main question by an MP or MLA, the officer concerned sitting in the Officers' Gallery, scribbles a Note and passes on to the Minister through the Marshal. But in the Japanese *Diet*, the Principal Secretary can stand up and answer the question! In a BBC publication *Nippon—The Rise of the Industrial Power Since 1945*, the reasons for Japan's quick development was interestingly discussed thus: As in most countries, Japan's power groups also consist of the Politician, the Bureaucrats and the Business. The difference is, in Japan the Business (or Industry) and Bureaucracy have a rigid convention to discuss first between them what action the government should take in any matter, come to an understanding and then the Bureaucracy puts up the policy to the Minister who approves it. When the Business group meets the Politician it pays a polite gift, *"tsukaimono"*, and the policy is approved and everyone is happy! No government has lasted the full four years and the maximum voting percentage has been 53% even in the literate and disciplined Japan. Most Parliamentary members are elected hereditarily and their success is popularly attributed to the so-called *Sanban* (three "ban"): *Jiban* (a strong, well-organized constituency), *Kaban* (a briefcase full of money), and *Kanban* (prestigious appointment, particularly at the cabinet level). In this way, the whole process is silken smooth. Being Japan, the main difference is, both the Bureaucracy and Industry keep the national interest paramount and once these two arrive at a consensus, the Politician takes his cut and does not meddle with the policy recommended. This was also due to the short tenure of the Politician-Minister which in post-1950 Japan was less than one year on an average while the Bureaucrat lasts till retirement and does not change with change in government. In Japan the Politician and the Business give high respect to the Bureaucracy as the public perceives the

Bureaucracy as more mature, knowledgeable and less corrupt. For this reason, retired senior bureaucrats are in great demand in leading Corporations to be on their Board of Directors and the Japanese even have a special term for it: *"Amakudari"—Descent from Heaven!* The National Democratic Party had tried to reduce this influence of bureaucracy but did not succeed because Industry and the public thinks adherence to tradition is necessary in national interest!

The reason for my mentioning this in some detail is because this Japanese attitude helped me greatly in Japan. The level of general knowledge in Japan is very high, Japan's newspaper readership being the highest in the world. Any important book in any foreign language is translated to Japanese and printed within three months. Before meeting any new person they invariably do a thorough background check. So, they knew about the Indian Administrative Service system and thought that it was close to the Japanese system. I therefore received remarkable respect from all during my stay in Japan. When I landed in Japan, Dr Tajima had kindly sent an assistant who knew a little English to the Narita airport which was about 60 km from the city centre. I was booked in the mid-price Hotel New Japan in the central Akasaka area. The usual financial problem which afflicts Indian officials going abroad on official work was not there for me fortunately. As I had learnt the advantages of drawing the full *per diem* instead of opting for the "split-rate" where the Indian Embassy for its own reasons books and pays for a costlier hotel and only a small balance for transport, food, etc. is given in cash to the visitor by the Embassy, I had drawn the full allowance of US$ 100 per day applicable to Japan for my pay-scale from RBI, Bangalore. I have seen later the plight of some officers who had opted for the split-rate to avoid the trouble of finding a proper hotel by themselves and landing in a star hotel booked by the Indian Embassy in foreign cities with gym and swimming pool which in any event they would have no time to use and three restaurants who over-charge and hanging in the Embassy for days to draw the paltry balance of Incidentals amount. The most pleasant thing was, in 1978 the foreign exchange rate for one US dollar was ¥ 310 and one Indian rupee could fetch ¥ 30. *[In fifty years the Japanese Yen has strengthened against both US Dollar and Indian Rupees, the exchange rates being US$ 1 = ¥ 130 and 1 Re. = ¥ 1.70]* Incidentally, within months Hotel New Japan went up in flames in a major fire in Akasaka area! So, my timing was perfect!

Next day, I called on the Indian Ambassador. Avatar Singh IFS, who was in his late 50's and this was his last posting. When I told him this was my first visit to Japan, he took time to advise me how to conduct myself in Japan. I must wear a suit and tie (even in summer, half sleeves and a tie with the jacket under the arm), must be punctual, must carry my visiting cards which should be crisp and not sweat-smudged and preferably I must take some Indian souvenirs especially if I am meeting important persons. Fortunately, I had fulfilled all these requisites including souvenirs—a few silk ties and scarves from the Government Silk Weaving Factory, some sandalwood soaps from the Government Sandalwood Soap Factory, Bangalore and gift-wrapped a few 200 gram coffee tins which was complimentary from the Coffee Board, Bangalore in addition to small sandalwood handicraft items like Buddha images from the *Gudigar Society,* Sagar in Shimoga. Come to think of it, all these are products of Karnataka which is a state rich in natural resources and all from profit-making Public Sector Undertakings. Only, I could not carry a 10 gram gold biscuit souvenirs from Hatti Gold Mines as I had once apologized to a World Bank Loan Officer a few years later, much to her mirth! (Karnataka produces 100% of India's gold.) After a fruitful learning course, I took leave of the good Ambassador. While seeing me off at the door, he told me, *"Remember, Two Indians means One Minus One, Two Japanese means One Plus One!".* I always remember this gem.

I wanted to call on Dr Tajima the same day but he was at the National Sericulture Institute, Suginami at the outskirts of Tokyo attending a meeting as Chairman of the Committee to select Pure Silk Worm Races. This practice in Japan surprised me. Dr Tajima had retired ten years ago but still the National Institute was using his expertise in regular R&D work. He told me over phone that if I was free I can meet him next day at the Institute in Suginami and discuss over dinner. I readily agreed as it was a great honour to talk to the renowned scientist. Next day I was promptly at the Central Institute half hour early. Dr Tajima was in his early 70's. He was about 5'6", slightly built, sparkling black eyes and his hair was still mostly black. This also I noticed in many Japanese. I had asked about the reason with some Japanese later and they told me it was because of the protein-rich food of fish in addition to sea-weed and plenty of vegetables. As to why most Japanese are sparsely built, the *Sumo* wrestlers notwithstanding, one officer joked that Japan is a country of islands with very little living space and if Japanese are fat they will spill over and drown in the ocean!

Most Japanese scientists and experts do not speak English. Japan is a country of one genetic stock, one language, one culture of almost indistinguishable Buddhist-Shinto-Confucian teachings, absolute loyalty to the emperor, had never been conquered till the end of the second

World War, had defeated Russia in 1904, had occupied Korea and Manchuria, South East Asia and had called all foreigners *Gaijins* which though literally meant 'outside person' came to acquire a pejorative meaning (*peculiar foreigner, pitiable barbarian*) and the term is avoided in TV and print media. It had therefore no eagerness to learn English. Also, after the "Great Divergence" when the West had the industrial revolution with many scientific and technological discoveries and innovations, Japan simply translated foreign books into Japanese and also sent their students to the West to learn and return. Most Japanese use the Subway trains and invariably everyone in the train, whether sitting or standing, was reading a book. And, almost everyone wears glasses.

Japanese, like the Chinese, take dinner early. So, when I met him at 6 pm at the National Institute after his meetings, he asked me whether I would like to go to a good Indian Restaurant like *Maharao* in Ginza. I told him, since I take Indian food every day, it would be nice if we can go to any Japanese restaurant of his choice which pleased him. He consulted his two colleagues and asked me if I am OK with fish and I told him fish was excellent. So the four of us went to a Japanese restaurant where the seating was at the ground level and the dining table was just one foot high. But one could lower one's feet to the pit beneath the table so that one need not sit uncomfortably on haunches. Tajima asked me whether I would have *Saké,* the native liquor made from rice as in most South East Asian countries and also in India's North Eastern States like Manipur and Meghalaya where it is called *Madhu.* *Saké* is served either warm or cold and both were ordered. The warm *Saké* was served in square bamboo mug and the cold in crystal ounce-glass and we said *Kan-pay* and drained the glasses. (*Kan-pay, originally Kam-bay in Chinese,* in Japanese means "dry your glass.") After two rounds with the inevitable toasting by each, the main fish course came which was the speciality of that restaurant. For a South Indian of spice, it was bland. After a while, Tajima asked me how I felt. I told him I was fine and asked why he was enquiring. He then said, the fish I had taken was called *Fugu,* pregnant with eggs and only specially licensed restaurants where licenced cooks alone can prepare it because, if not properly cleaned, it can be highly poisonous. His colleague Dr Omura gleefully told me that only a month earlier a famous Japanese actor had died eating *Fugu* in that very same restaurant! Since nothing untoward was visibly happening to me, they decided to celebrate it with a round of Japan's premium *Suntory* whiskey.

I had taken with me a few cocoons (hot-air dried so that the pupae were dead inside without staining the filaments) of Pure Mysore, Bivoltine and Cross-breed. I took them out and showed one by one to Tajima, and his colleagues, Dr Omura and Dr Miyazaki. The Pure Mysore (PM) is the oldest silkworm race in Karnataka and had a filament length of only about 350 meters and was of deep yellow colour, the foreign Bivoltine race codoon had 900 m filament and the light-yellow Cross Breed 700 m. Tajima said he was familiar with the PM and CB cocoons of Karnataka as he had visited Mandya near Bangalore in the early 1960s as FAO expert to advise India on the Japanese Method of Rice Cultivation which India was popularizing in the fifty or so selected Intensive Agricultural Development Programme districts of which Mandya was one. Being a sericulture geneticist he had then visited sericulture area in Karnataka. In 1960s there was very little BV silkworm rearing in Karnataka and the BV race cocoons I was showing him he had not seen then in Karnataka. He was therefore sceptical whether these BV cocoons were raised by farmers in their rearing houses or in the Research Institute at Mysore. The other two scientists had not been to India and the PM and CB cocoons were somewhat new to them.

Tajima asked me some searching questions about the silk content and silk ratio of the cocoons and the rearing conditions of BV cocoons in Karnataka. Fortunately, I had taken with me some photographs also of the rearing houses of progressive farmers rearing BV cocoons. At the end of their cross-examination, perhaps especially aided by my keeping company for the relay of hot and cold *sake* and more so for consuming and surviving *Fugu*, Tajima grudgingly agreed that he believed me that Karnataka, a tropical region with low income farmers, probably could produce high quality BV cocoons. I pressed my advantage and told him that with Japanese technical expertise under a possible World Bank assistance of US$ 70 million, Karnataka should be able to produce BV silk yarn and could even export silk yearn to Japan. My hosts were scientists, but like most Japanese, they were well-read in history and had a respect for ancient India, the land of the Buddha. Besides, my being a Bureaucrat in the comparable category of the elite Japanese bureaucracy also helped. One of the scientists, Miyazaki took out an atlas and said he could not locate "Karnataka" and I had to politely apologize and showed him "Mysore" in his atlas! Such frequent apologizing in Japan, so alien in Indian culture, was *de rigueur* in Japan and I was sure he noticed it approvingly in a *gaijin!*

When we left the restaurant after three hours, Tajima told Omura to drop me at my hotel. Omura spoke some English and I learned from him that Tajima, who was like a senior guide to all the sericulture scientific community in Japan, had told them to take me to the Japan International Cooperation Agency as both of them were well-known in JICA and were on its panel of experts and introduce me to the senior JICA officials. JICA is a unique organization in Japan where it keeps track of its experts in various fields and periodically sends them to Afro-Asian countries on technical consultancy. Its financing body was the Japan Bank of International Cooperation (JBIC). The next day Omura took me to JICA which was in the 55-storey Mitsui building, the tallest in Tokyo then. Japan is a highly hierarchical society but their Line of Respect is not just according to the official position or the salary and income, it was also by the age and reputation of the person. For instance, I noticed that when I went to the office of the Managing Director of Mitsubishi Corporation dealing with silk machinery, it was the younger MD who first bowed to the elderly driver while taking leave and the driver bowing a split second later. Bowing or *Ojigi* is the time-honoured etiquette for which many companies even give training to their newly recruited employees! To satisfy my curiosity, I checked with my hotel manager the correct way of doing *Ojigi*. He gladly demonstrated it to me by bending 45° from his waist, keeping both hands rigid, flat and straight on either sides of thighs and keeping his gaze on ground in front. He said no smiling or shifting of eyes are allowed and the duration of the rigid position can be more or less than 5 seconds depending upon the respect I wanted to show! In Japan everything was precise and prescribed.

Dr Omura was much bowed to in JICA and he took me to the Chairman Dr Hogan. He was a pleasant elderly bespectacled distinguished-looking person and so I did a perfect *Ojigi* and Hogan was delighted and bowed back. He told me that long ago he was Japan's Ambassador to India and was familiar with Delhi and he had also visited Bangalore. Though no project was yet certain, I impressively told him about my discussions with Ducksoo Lee and the likelihood of the World Bank approaching JICA for sending a team of experts to Karnataka. To my surprise, he told me that Ducksoo Lee had also spoken to him, sounding for a possible team of three experts from Japan to be sent to Karnataka within two months or so. This was indeed great news to me. I never expected the matter would move so fast considering that the World Bank bureaucracy had an out-performing red-tape than Delhi.

My next fortnight in Japan was spent in visiting many sericulture farmers, silkworm egg-producers, reeling filatures, Yokohama Silk

Exchange, Kimono handloom weavers, power-loom silk weaving mills and Research Institutes. Though these visits were quite exhaustive, the opportunity to meet so many persons of expertise was exhilarating. Besides, it was winter and I travelled by the highly comfortable trains of Japan. Between Tokyo and Osaka the *Shinkansein* (Lightning), introduced in 1964, popularly known as the "bullet train" runs at 320 kmph. Between smaller cities the slower *Kodama* (Echo) trains run at 160 kmph. Chaperoned by Tajima's assistant, I travelled extensively by these trains and met the experts. Sericulture was already a sun-set industry in Japan and I rarely found stretches of mulberry garden which are so common in Karnataka. But there were still some senior citizens in rural area who were rearing silkworms from May to October when it was warm. Japan had also excelled in research and development in sericulture in earlier days and continued now supervised by the Central Sericulture Institute at Suginami at the outskirts of Tokyo where I had gone to meet Tajima. But these were the last days of the Sericulture Institute in Tokyo because it was being shifted to the Tsukuba Science City about 50 km from Tokyo. This is a remarkable Japanese city where over 60 National Research Institutes are situated and coordination among them was easier. During my later visits to Japan I visited Tsukuba Science City and the National Sericulture Institute in its new building.

Another management practice I found remarkable was the way the Chairman conducted meetings. I had an important discussion with the Chairman of the big Mitsubishi Corporation regarding our silk factories' modernization. Firstly, anyone who entered the office including Mitsubishi staff from Chairman down removed their shoes and put on the soft slippers kept at the entrance. I also found many of the clerks were sitting with one leg under them on their chairs. When I asked about this practice, I was told it is more comfortable for the person to sit as if he is sitting at home and his productivity increases! In the Board room, the Chairman made me sit by his side and there were two little flags of India and Japan in front of us. This is a practice we do not have in India. His officers were all assembled promptly on time. The meetings would go on for hours during which the Chairman was keeping quiet all the time, allowing his officers to speak freely. Sometimes the officers were even shouting at each other. Only when the voices reached higher decibels the Chairman would gently say a word or two to cool the atmosphere. The pros and cons of every small point would be discussed at length and finally the Chairman would give the consensus very briefly and we would go to the next subject. There was no fixed time to end the meeting. It would start at 8.30 in the morning and will go on till lunch when the Chairman would take all of us to a restaurant where also we would continue discussions and after returning to the office the discussion would again resume. It will go on till 6pm and many a time we would all go to dinner together! Such 12 hour discussions I found very strange and tiring. But this was a common practice in Japan.

SOUTH KOREA

I took leave of my Japanese friends and landed in Seoul on a freezing December morning. Mr Ducksoo Lee had given me the reference to the Sericulture Research Institute in Seoul and of many government officials in the Ministry of Agriculture, Forests and Fisheries—MAFF. Korea followed the same pattern as Japan, not only in sericulture but also in economic model. For instance, like the family *Zaibatsu* monopolies of Japan, Korea encouraged *Chaebols* such as Hyundai, Samsung, Lucky Goldstar, SK Group, Lotte, Daewoe, Doosan, KIA, etc. from 1950 under the Syngman Rhee government. After the *coup d'etat* in 1963 when General Park Chung Hee formed the Third Republic, the *Chaebols* were further strengthened. He was President till 1979 when he was assassinated by an officer of the Korean CIA. Korea became a 'middle income' country primarily because of the military dictator's strong domestic economic policies, especially supporting the 'Infant Industry', namely, protecting the domestic industries in early stages. This does not mean all dictatorships lead to economic development, examples being Burma, North Korea, Cambodia, Pakistan, to name a few. It is more complicated. (Much later I read *The Bad Samaritans: The Myth of Free Trade and the Secret History of Capitalism* [2007] by the South Korean academic Ha-Joon Chang of Cambridge U and a critic of neo-liberalism, where he tells developing countries regarding the 'advices' of Western Economists: *'Do not do as they say, Do as they Do'!*) The S Korean government banned his book as being 'seditious'. It is therefore a 'must read and practice' book for all developing countries, especially India.

In Seoul I stayed at a small hotel near the Han River. That was the time, the late 1970's, when both banks of the Han river were being developed in a big way and I saw a large number of buildings and commercial complexes coming up. This was called the *Miracle on the Han River* under the military dictator Park Chung-hee from 1963 to 1979. Sericulture was still thriving in Korea in the 1970's while it was disappearing in Japan due to industrial development and the shrinking of the primary agricultural sector in the national economy. But South Korea was also showing unmistakable signs of youth gravitating to manufacturing industries and to urban areas. I visited a few of the sericulture farmers, the National Research Institute and the Silk Conditioning and Testing House. Here also I noticed the same Japanese practice of the officials removing their shoes as soon as they reach their office and put on soft slippers and keeping their legs under them on their chairs and sit comfortably. Additionally, in Korean offices I also found piped soft Korean music playing in the background which was supposed to increase productivity. Their offices were invariably small including those of heads of office but very brightly lit and there were only common toilets and no attached toilets in the cabins of even higher officers as also in Japan. After the war Japan was highly cost-conscious and their offices and apartments were very small. In the office they found that a person spends in the toilet just 40 minutes in a workday of 8 to 10 hours and it was wasteful to give a private toilet and keep it vacant 90% of the time! I could not but compare mentally the huge ante-rooms and toilets in Vidhana Soudha and MS Building for Deputy Secretary upwards!

SOME REFLECTIONS ON JAPAN AND SOUTH KOREA

The last two days I spent in Seoul were a week-end in December and as it was heavily snowing, there was no official visits for me. So I spent that time in my room, making notes and collecting my thoughts. Both Japan and South Korea were devastated by war and which started rebuilding only after 1950 and achieved astounding progress because of firstly, authoritarian or one-party rule and defence being taken care of by a foreign super-power so that they could invest in education, health and public transport and follow policies of protection of domestic industries and have export-led growth. This is true of another big country, Indonesia, where General Suharto ruled through the Golkar party for over thirty years and a small island-country Singapore where Lee Kwan Yew ruled by "controlled democracy" for four decades and saw it transform from 'Third World to First World'. The big exception is of course China which was never a client state and regained its 'Middle Kingdom'—Centre of Earth—status by its own efforts. Authoritarian rule by itself does not promote economic and social development as shown by Myanmar, Cambodia (where Hun Sen has a continuing rule of over four decades) and Pakistan, Bangladesh and Thailand have either army or mostly army-sponsored pseudo-democratic rulers. Indonesia, Thailand, Bangladesh, Pakistan, Sri Lanka, Nepal, Cambodia, Laos and Philippines apart from China are all better off on the Global Hunger Index than India. The real comparison should be between India and China. Both have the largest populations (together, one in three in the world), both ancient civilizations, almost the same time both became self-determinant, etc. But in 70 years China has ensured health and education for all and the status of a superpower. We in India claim to be a superpower too while we are actually only super-poor.

BACK TO BANGALORE

I returned to India after a useful tour. Devaraja Urs was still in power though he had fallen out of favour with the meteorically-risen evil *Dhoomakethu* Sanjay Gandhi who preferred, crude, strong-armed and immature, former body guards and bus-ticket booking *lumpen* leaders like Gundu Rao. However, due to his time-consuming political problems, Urs shed his ministerial portfolios including his pet subject Sericulture. But before making his follower from Mysore KB Shiviah the Sericulture Minister, he called me to his chambers when Shiviah was also present and introduced me to him. Urs told him, *"I have no intention of changing him for three years!"*. It was the nicest way of saying that if the new minister and his Director do not get along, the Director will not be changed for three years! Rarely one would come across such an encouragement to a mere bureaucrat in the interest of development of a department. Currently, heads of departments and even Chief Secretaries are transferred for offending an MLA, like changing inner-wares. An apocryphal story in Tamil Nadu goes like this: Despite having a stroke which impaired his speech and movement, the ever-green CM of Tamil Nadu, MGR continued to be the CM for many years, working from the cellar chambers of his private residence at Ramavaram Gardens in Madras. Only his private secretary Paramasivam, an officer promoted to IAS, could meet him in person and even his cabinet ministers had to speak to the CM only on the intercom. One day, the story goes, his television was blurred and MGR tells Paramasivam in slurred Tamil *"TV Antana Sari-illaè, Padmanabanè Poda Sollūngo"*, which meant "TV antenna is not good, ask Padmanabhan to put (make it OK)". Poor Paramasivam did not know that the TV was not working, so he mistook the CM's aphasic instructions as *"TV Antony is not good, ask Padmanabhan to be put!"* Now, TV Antony was the Chief Secretary and Padmanabhan was the Additional CS seven places below in seniority. But then the CM could not be troubled and the obedient Paramasivam sent a note to the General Administration Department that TV Antony should be transferred and Padmanabhan should be posted in his place! It did happen that the much junior Padmanabhan was posted as the CS and TV Antony was shunted to State Planning Commission as its Deputy Chairman! This was what had happened in the state once administered by Rajaji, Kamaraj and Annadurai! Talk of Karnataka's Fall from Grace!

After my fruitful visit to Japan and South Korea and landing in the beautiful Bangalore (we appreciate our own home town only when we return to it), I launched myself fully in the preparation of the Karnataka Sericulture Project and also tried to apply in the field the advanced practices I found abroad. One of the basic reforms required was stopping the exploitation of the reelers who make silk yarn from cocoons. The reelers were poor Muslims and Dalits and the margin from reeling was the least, squeezed between the large number of cocoon producing farmers and the small number of monopolistic silk yarn traders. It was indeed surprising that 75% of India's silk was produced in just five districts of Karnataka, of India's total of 850 districts, and sold entirely to 200 merchants in just one very narrow street called Avenue Road in Bangalore. It was always a broker who brought the reeler to the merchant. He takes charge of the bag containing about 20 kg of silk yarn and shows it to the merchant who is sitting behind a table barely 15 feet from the entrance. Then the broker and the merchant perform a strange, Freemason-like ritual of negotiating the price. The merchant and the broker hold their right hands under a towel. The price is arrived without spoken words but by pressing the fingers. The reeler is told finally a lower price than agreed between the broker and merchant.

Much the same was the position with cocoons with the farmers at the mercy of middlemen and reelers till 1970 when the regulatory Act was enforced and cocoon markets were established where all farmers and reelers had to transact by open auction and without middlemen and weighing was done on Avery machines. So, the urgent need was to bring similar regulation in respect of raw silk yarn. Fortunately, almost all the raw silk produced by about 16,000 reelers in Karnataka came to be bought and sold in Bangalore's Avenue Road. So, it would be feasible to create by law one regulated market for raw silk, a Silk Exchange where all silk merchants and reelers should bring and transact without any middlemen, just as in the case of cocoon markets. Another problem plaguing both the farmers and reelers was the violent fluctuations in the price of raw silk which had a ripple effect on cocoon prices. I had seen in Japan, an organization by Government, the Silk Bank at Yokohama, which had fixed a range of high and low price limit for raw silk under which whenever the price fell below the floor level the organization would buy raw silk at that floor price so that the price will not fall further and, similarly, when the price went up above the ceiling level, the Silk Bank will sell at that price so that the price will not go up further. I thought of a government-owned Company with sufficient funds which would perform this function. For funding this price-stabilization function, I thought of a system of collecting 2% market fee each at the cocoon market from farmers and reelers for every transaction. As the value of cocoons sold in the markets was then about Rs.500 crores annually, the market fee collected would be about Rs.20 crores a year. Similarly, I proposed a 2% each market fee in the Silk Exchange payable each by the merchants and reelers. As the value of the 2,500 tons of raw silk produced in Karnataka in 1979 was about Rs.625 crores, the market fee collected in the Silk Exchange at 4% would be Rs.25 crores. Together, the total market fee collected from the Cocoon Markets and Silk Exchange would be Rs.45 crores annually which could only go up *ad valorem* due to the general inflationary increase in price and higher production. The fee thus collected annually should be credited to a Prize Stabilization and Silk Development Fund which should be used only for the purpose of stabilization of silk prices and sericulture development projects in the state.

These were fundamental reforms and therefore I had to get the approval of government for preparing the legislation. As only the Chief Minister could get such reforms done at government level, I approached my friend Sisir Das again, who was still the Deputy Secretary to CM. As I mentioned earlier, Sisir was a delightful officer. So, when I briefed him my purpose, he told me that this would take at least an hour of CM's time and the only way to do it was to put me in CM's car when the CM would be going on a long tour by road. In those days, there was no helicopter used by the CM (later Gundu Rao bought one helicoptor and over-used it.) Within a few days, Sisir arranged for me to accompany the CM by car when he was going to Mysore. With no mobile phones then, I had a captive audience of the CM and explained to him all my proposals. I sat in the back seat and had the CM's undivided attention for one hour till the car reached the welcome arch for him at the entrance of Ramanagaram. He appreciated the proposal for the Silk Exchange which would eliminate the exploitation of reelers. Besides the economic justice, it also had a political advantage for him as the reelers were mostly Muslims and Dalits which will ensure their support to him. He asked Moinuddin, also sitting in the back, to make a note of speaking to the Minister and Law Secretary to prepare an amendment to the existing Act to provide for the Silk Exchange. So, all my proposals got moving fast, thanks to Sisir putting me in CM's car for an hour which opportunity no other officer would have had.

My Project team headed by Joint Director Mahadevappa also made quick progress within three months of my return from Japan. The Industries Secretary, KSN saw to it that it got included in the "pipe line" of the Projects List of Department of Economic Affairs for discussions with the World Bank. Before the end of 1979, the World Bank sent an Appraisal Mission which was headed by Mr Stern, the Project Officer of the Bank as Ducksoo Lee had moved to another department. He was a pleasant person of Jewish descent who had earlier worked as a British civil servant in Kenya. He knew about IAS and we got along smoothly. In World Bank-funded projects, the most important stage is the Appraisal Mission whose *Yellow Cover* Report decides the fate of the project funding. Fortunately for me the two Japanese Consultants in the team were Omura whom I had already met in Tokyo (and shared *Saké and Fūgū*) and another new JICA expert on Silk Filatures. The project proposal had a smooth sailing with the Appraisal Team and the "Wrap Up" meeting at the Union Textile ministry with Department of Economic Affairs officers and the Appraisal Team went without any glitch.

For regulating the silk yarn sale, the Law Department prepared the required amendment to the existing Act to include Silk Exchange requiring buyers and sellers of raw silk to come to the designated Silk Exchange and transact their business with no secret "under the towel" manoeuvres, middlemen or arbitrary deductions for bag weight and the like. As expected, the merchants of Avenue Road boycotted the Silk Exchange to buy the raw silk. But I had taken advance action of informing the weavers' organzations like the Cooperatives in silk weaving centres at Varanasi, Aarani, Kanjeevaram, Kumbakonam, Dharmavaram etc. that they can come to Silk Exchange and buy raw silk directly from reelers. So some of them had come and bought the silk yarn. But we had already formed the Karnataka Silk Marketing Board with Rs.5 crores as fully paid-up share capital by the government. The KSMB was formed after my return from Japan to stabilize the raw silk prices. Shantanu Consul was a direct recruit IAS officer who was a few years junior to me. He was appointed as the Managing Director of the newly created KSMB. He was a dynamo with a stylized, majestic Italian-sounding spelling of 'Consul' for Kanshal! He was from Rajasthan and awfully hardworking. He sat in the spacious Silk Exchange Building which I could get on lease from the Wakf Board right next to Avenue Road. Shantanu sat among all the mountains of silk yarn for days till the middle of each night and purchased the raw silk from the hundreds of reelers who thronged the Silk Exchange in its support and in the face of merchants' boycott. However, within a week, the merchants and middlemen were able to file a Writ Petition at the High Court against the compulsory nature of Silk Exchange affecting the fundamental right to carry a trade but they did not get a full stay order on the Silk Exchange. The HC only said there is no compulsion that all reelers and merchants must come to the Silk Exchange but those who want to come voluntarily to the Exchange could do so till the Writ Petition was disposed of. So, the reelers who fully supported the Silk Exchange and some weavers' cooperatives and of course the KSMB transacted the business in the Silk Exchange. Shantanu Consul was kept busy every day as the Silk Exchange would function even on Sundays and holidays. I met the Advocate General Byra Reddy who appreciated the objective behind the legislation (it was said he was earlier a card carrying CPM member!) and I attended the HC at every hearing. The two-member bench was headed by Justices Jagannatha Shetty and MN Venkatachaliah (who later became the Chief Justice of India at the Supreme Court) and they took note of the presence of the Director of Sericulture, especially his being properly attired in a dark suit with black tie and well-combed in the Court every time! When the plea describing the exploitation of reelers by the esoteric "towel" method, (the AG described it as a "Masonic ritual') came up, he asked the indulgence of the Court to let the Director demonstrate how it was done. The Justices agreed and so, I took my handkerchief and showed the Judges how it was done under it which fascinated the judges. The AG on his part, known for his leftist views, assured the Court that he would not go "left of Harold Laski" in his arguments which was also appreciated by the Court with sighs of relief as probably no Judge in India, not even Justice VR Krishna Iyer would quote Lenin or Trotsky!

The HC gave its verdict in a remarkably quick time of six months despite the delaying tactics of the merchants' advocates who had a conditional stay of no compulsion to come to the Silk Exchange. The Court held all the provisions for the functioning of the Silk Exchange as valid including the compulsory aspect. The only change the HC made was collection of fee of 2% each from buyers and sellers being reduced to 1% each. Meanwhile, the World Bank fixed the negotiations at Washington in March 1980. The negotiations at Washington went off without any hitch during the course of five days, from Monday to Friday as was usual for such projects. I attended it along with my Joint Director Mahadevappa who was a great help in preparing the project. Thus the historic Karnataka Sericulture Project for Rs 80 crores came through.

POLITICAL SEA CHANGE IN KARNATAKA AND THE EXIT OF DEVARAJ URS

However, things were changing very rapidly in the political scene of Karnataka. The Janata Party which had resoundingly defeated Mrs Gandhi's Congress(I) in 1977 was in turn totally rejected in the 1980 Parliament Elections. In their hubris, the Janata government headed by Morarji Desai as PM and Chaudhury Charan Singh as Home Minister had promptly arrested Mrs Gandhi for Emergency abuses which made her a martyr. By 1979 Sanjay Gandhi was the unchallenged *Il Duce* of Congress Party and he had selected Gundu Rao, who rose from humble beginning such as booking bus-tickets at bus stands on behalf of private bus owners which somehow eminently qualified him as the next CM of Karnataka in his master Sanjay Gandhi's judgment. Devaraj Urs was expelled and he started a new Party—*Congress-Urs* which lost heavily in the 1980 Parliamentary election and he started yet another party called *Karnataka Kranthi Ranga* which had a still-birth. His life ended as a Greek tragedy. After losing his party, chief ministership and even his friends, he became erratic and inexplicably came under the influence of a much younger officer of the Indian Foreign Service, a social butterfly, one Nirmala Jha *neé* Sundaram who had resigned from service and was hobnobbing with politicians. She became his inspirational adviser on politics and he described her as his "adopted daughter" much to the mortification of Chikkammanni Urs, his wife of fifty years. Deserted by his political friends, powerless and broken, he died in 1982 at the age of 67. When his body was taken from Bangalore to his native Hunsur in Mysore district, people from villages waited three deep on either side of the road throughout from Bangalore to his village Kallahally and, strangely, *clapped their hands when the cortege passed them.*

Understandably, Gundu Rao's ministry in 1980 had a strong Youth Congress stain though most of them had an unhealthy middle-age appearance because of indulgence and behaved like children due to congenital immaturity. In the January 1980 Parliamentary election Sanjay Gandhi, the architect of Emergency Family Planning, was also elected from the Amethi constituency (by even the people who were sterilized by him, such being the strength of India's 'vibrant' democracy!) and he became the unquestioned PM-in-Waiting. On his blessing, all kinds of upstarts and people without base and whose only strength was their loyalty and rootlessness, were packed in positions of power. The portfolio of Sericulture which was once held by Devaraj Urs the CM, was given to one Renuka, a former Dalit Lady Hostel Superintendent in her thirty's. But now that she was Cabinet Minister and dis-reputedly close to Gundu Rao, she started behaving like all immature people do.

The Moscow Olympics was taking place in August 1980 and her Personal Assistant, one Prasanna—a junior Karnataka Administrative Service Officer, telephoned me three months ahead of the Olympics saying, *Sir, the Minister is going to Moscow Olympics. Minister is asking how much Foreign Exchange the Director can arrange!* I pretended I did not understand and explained at length to him that foreign exchange for Ministers is sanctioned by the Ministry of External Affairs. But the thick-skinned Prasanna would not leave it and was more explicit, *That is official sir, but the Minister is asking how much the Director can personally arrange!* I told him curtly that the Director does not arrange any such thing and, for good measure, followed it by sending a D.O letter—for which I was remarkably renowned as the DO or Die DC—to the Chief Secretary Narasimha Rao, a mild-mannered thorough gentleman who was the son of former Mysore State Diwan Madhava Rao, that the Minister's PA had asked me to arrange foreign exchange as my personal contribution for her Moscow Olympics visit which I refused and, to rub salt, requested the matter to be brought to the notice of the Chief Minister. I learned later that the God's good CS did not know what to do with my letter and after a week of building courage, took it to the CM and read it over to him. Gundu Rao told him the Director must have mis-heard the PA and this the CS conveyed to me orally.

[It so happened that within one year, the Minister in her greed without caution collected 'baksheesh' for recommending a candidate for admission to a Medical College and when he was not selected, he insisted for refund which she was foolish enough to return by cheque which promptly bounced and when he complained the matter to the police, the upright DIG of CID, NB Bhat IPS, known for his integrity and boldness, filed a criminal prosecution against the Minister without even telling the CM, as a result of which she had to resign. Unfortunately, this was a little later after I left the Department on promotion and I did not have the pleasure to see her being taken to jail!]

Sanjay Gandhi died in one of Indian history's most ironically helpful helicopter crash on 23 June 1980 though, unfortunately, his trainer pilot also died. Gundu Rao ministry went into a paralytic shock for a week when no minister was available in Bangalore and everyone was in Delhi. On her return from Delhi, the Minister wanted my car to take the Karnataka quota of Sanjay Gandhi's ashes for immersion at *Tala Cauvery*, originating in Coorg district. As Director of Sericulture I had an old 1955 Dodge car which was a petrol-guzzler. It was otherwise a sturdy car and I got a diesel P-4 engine retro-fitted in it in a garage in Coimbatore. It was also refurbished and had become a comfortable car for long distance journeys. It was the pride of my driver Habib. Sanjay Gandhi's ashes were being spread in the length and breadth of the country, unjustly imitating Pandit Nehru's. What little of the ashes Gundu Rao could secure from Delhi, his favourite lady minister got after making an impressive bathetic tear-jerking *(Bathetic, from Greek Bathos !)*. Ministers have their own official cars and if it is a state occasion (immersion of a North Indian State MP's ashes was certainly not), the Deputy Secretary, Protocol could allot a high-powered car from government garage. In my unkind exhilaration I told the minister's PA, what has Sanjay Gandhi done to spread sericulture to deserve the Department car to take his ashes to spread in Talakavri 250 kms away? This sent the minister to another paroxysm and she promptly ran to Gundu Rao to complain but he could not take any notice, himself inconsolably weeping for his patron's ground level tragic acrobatics!

After Sanjay Gandhi's death, the political confidence of Gundu Rao weakened. He was becoming obliged to the MLAs as his *Sutradari* was no more and his self-confessed 'Drama Company' was in trouble. My batch became due for promotion to "super-time" scale posts. So, Jayakumar Anagol, the Principal Secretary to CM who was a seasoned "Development Administrator" in Irrigation and Agriculture, and my early mentor in Raichur district, decided that on promotion I should be posted as the Chairman and Administrator of the Command Area Development Authoity of the Upper Krishna Project covering Bijapur and Gulbarga which was the biggest Irrigation Project in the State and which was just then starting to store water. Concurrently I was also made the Divisional Commissioner of Gulbarga. Thus, within a few months of my eventful stint in Sericulture Department for four years and a successful negotiation of the historic first World Bank-assisted KSP, I got my promotion, back to Gulbarga district where the UKP was situated. I had the full satisfaction of bringing many structural changes in the Sericulture Department including its first big World Bank funded project. When I joined the Department in 1976 its annual Plan Budget was Rs.55 lakhs. When I left it in 1980 it had gone up to Rs.16 crores, thirty times higher, because of the sizeable project. It was not merely a quantum jump financially but also a qualitative change in sericulture. While my experience in the districts was Regulatory Administration, what I could do in Sericulture Department was Development Administration. I could do this only because of the support of CM Devaraj Urs, Chief Secretary GVK and Industry Secretary KSN and my untiring staff of Sericulture Department.

❖❖❖

CHAPTER 15

Back to Gulbarga—Return of the Native

Thus, in 1980 I went back again to Gulbarga which was becoming my second home. Altogether I have spent eight years of my service in field postings in Hyderabad-Karnataka. Work-wise, this was quite satisfying because there was no competition to get posted there and an officer who can be impartial and helpful to the poor was loved by the simple and rugged people of Gulbarga. Thus, I had a free hand to organize the irrigation development in the parched lands of Gulbarga-Bijapur as the Chairman and Administrator of the Command Area Development Authority of the Upper Krishna Project. It was the first time an IAS officer was posted as CADA Chairman as till then the post was held by a Chief Engineer. My concurrent posting as the Divisional Commissioner of Gulbarga Division also gave me a unique experience which very few IAS Officers ever had, in combining development and regulatory administration. In most sprawling princely states such as Hyderabad, Mysore and Baroda, to tighten East India Company's control, four or five districts were formed into a Division and its head was designated "Divisional Commissioner" who supervised the work of Deputy Commissioners. Due to the comparatively less developed communication facilities in the princely states, the Divisional Commissioner could *anticipate* the orders of the government and direct the Deputy Commissioners to act. Because of this tradition, Nizam's Hyderabad and the Wodeyars' Mysore (the two biggest princely states qualifying for 21 Gun Salute in recognition of their servile support) had the system of Resident Commissioner, the Divisional Commissioner and Deputy Commissioner. The residence of the Resident Commissioner of Mysore State in Bangalore became, after 1947, the Governor's residence, the *Raj Bhavan.*

The work of the Divisional Commissioner was essentially regulatory and supervisory while that of Administrator of CADA-UKP was developmental. There is often a misconstrued impression of dichotomy between Regulation and Development. In practice, Regulation without Development can degenerate to police state and

Development without Regulation becomes a capitalist oligarchy. All development activity should have an umpire to ensure misuse of freedom. Adam Smith's *laissez faire* requires a referee. A pragmatic mix of these two alone will ensure orderly development. Because of my position as Divisional Commissioner to supervise the district administration, I could easily get the cooperation of elected officials and all DCs and officers of all departments in the CADA work.

WATER USERS SOCIETIES, MANIBHAI DESAI AND SUBABUL

I visited Uruli Kanchan near Pune where Manibhai Desai, popularly the last Gandhian, was heading the Bharatiya Agro-Industries Foundation where graduates from the Institute of Rural Management, Anand, established by Verghese Kurien, the Milk Man of India, were doing excellent work in animal husbandry, of improving milk yield of cross-breed cows. Under the World Bank projects, the Training and Visit System of Daniel Benor had become the last word in Agriculture Extension. There was an intensive T&V system and exchange of views among Subject Matter Specialists and *Grama Sevaks* who would in turn advise farmers to take up 'Package of Practices'. But because of ingrained Indian *Varnadharma* psyche, the Grama *Sevaks* protested that they are not *'Sevaks'* (workers who were all *Shudras*) but Officers and so their designation was changed to Agricultural *Officers!* But, without any financial powers to make available credit to procure and practise improved methods, T&V System became just talk and came to mean *Tour and Vanish* System.

But the BAIF under Manibhai Desai's IRMA graduates was totally practical, with ideologically committed and rural-oriented young Extension Staff. I saw them wearing *Khakhi* clothes so that they would not quickly show dirt like white dress, had gum boots to enter fields unhesitatingly instead of chappals or shoes which makes the government extension worker reluctant to enter mud-field, drive sturdy motor-bikes to reach remote villages and saving time instead of depending upon public transport and generally commanding the confidence of the villagers. They were mostly doing extension work of artificial insemination from foreign cattle breeds. But they also knew all about agricultural crops. So, as CEO of CADA-UKP, I negotiated successfully with BAIF for deputation of ten IRMA graduates for extension work.

I found that, as in Tungabhadra Project area, in Gulbarga also the Andhra farmers had started purchasing lands, level the undulating land and grow paddy in violation of the legally notified cropping pattern. Most of the Contractors executing the canals and tunnel work in UKP were from Andhra Pradesh and they knew the alignment of the water courses and lands to be irrigated and the villages situated at the early reaches of the water Distributaries. In the coastal districts of Krishna, Godavari, Rajamundry, etc. the canals of Sir Arthur Cotton (1803-1899) had in their command two paddy crop lands costing over Rs 1 lakh per acre in 1980. On the other hand, land holdings in the hitherto dry, rain-fed taluks of Gulbarga coming under the UKP command area were large, the average being 10-12 acres. Gulbarga's dryland farmers were not accustomed to irrigation and some even had expressed fears of Malaria coming back with irrigation! Besides, they had to level their undulating land if water had to flow evenly in the land. The price of one acre of land in UKP area was hardly Rs 5,000 in 1980. So the coastal Andhra farmer would sell one acre of land in his Andhra village and would buy twenty acres in Shorapur, Shahpur or Jewargi taluks in Gulbarga district. The Andhra farmers were hardworking and knew the technique of preparing the land for paddy cultivation. While there was nothing illegal about the farmers from Andhra buying land in Karnataka, any one could nevertheless see the exploitation of the poor Gulbarga farmers who were indebted for generations and had seldom seen Rs 1,000 when they could get Rs 25,000 by selling five acres. So, as Divisional Commissioner who was the head of land administration, I had informally asked the Sub-Registrars of taluks who were in charge of registration of sale of land to go slow on registration of land-sale by raising many queries on instalment basis about the genuine identity of the Andhra purchasers of being agriculturists as only an agriculturist could buy agricultural land in Karnataka. Admittedly this was harassment but I had to balance between protecting the interest of the local poor farmers and the speculative practice of the more affluent Andhra landlords. Besides, they could only grow paddy and were not accustomed to the legally permitted light-irrigated crops like Sorghum, *Bajra*, sun flower, cotton or groundnut. The Sub-Registrars of the district followed my informal instructions because of the traditional status of the Divisional Commissioner. If I were only the Administrator of CADA this would not have been possible.

HOW TO CATCH ADULTERATORS OF MILK:

One incident would explain the complementary nature of Development and Regulation. With the help of BAIF and the IRMA Extension Staff whom we had employed, the milk production in Gulbarga and adjoining Bidar increased. Already under the Verghese Kurien model of Milk Marketing, many cooperative societies were established in Bidar and Gulbarga districts and milk became a marketable commodity and most of it flowed from rural to urban areas. Many critics said, in turn arrack flowed from urban to rural areas so that the protein-rich milk products like butter-milk disappeared from villages and arrack became available instead! Nothing, it would seem was an unmixed blessing. A "Mother Dairy" was established in Gulbarga town some years earlier with a daily capacity of 8,000 litres per day. My new office as Administrator of CADA was in a place called Bheemarayanagudi, about 25 kms south of Gulbarga on the State Highway to Bangalore and my office of Divisional Commissioner was in the traditional *Aiwan-e-Shahi*, the Nizam's lodge in Gulbarga. It was used partly as the VIP Circuit House and partly as Divisional Commissioner's office and residence. I stayed in my new house at Bheemarayanagudi and was shuttling between the two offices in thirty minutes. One day, when I was in Divisional Commissioner's office, a few workers of the Gulbarga Dairy met me and narrated about the corruption in the Dairy and how water was being added to the extent of 30% every day and the extra unaccounted 1,000 litres of adulterated milk was being sold daily at Rs.10 per litre to hotels and others and the amount being pocketed by the Manager, clerks and some union office bearers. The workers who met me were actually handling the Pasteurization plant and they said the union office bearers did not do any work but were all the time gossiping with the Manager and generally over-lording. I checked with my stenographer who was getting milk from the Dairy and he said the milk was alright. The workers explained that about 200 litres was the daily consumption in the *Aiwan-e-Shahi* colony where senior officials lived and unadulterated milk for government quarters around *Aiwan e Shahi*, built by GVK when he was the Divisional Commissioner there, was kept separately before adding water to the main tank. My PA lived in the *Aiwan-e-Shahi* quarters and so he and other officials got better, unadulterated milk. The adulterated milk was for the general public.

Under the Essential Commodities Act of 1955 many commodities including milk had been declared as 'essential commodity' and adulteration of it was a punishable offence. Government Dairy doing it certainly aggravated the offence. So, I asked the workers how the offenders could be caught. They told me the *modus operandi* of the water mixing. Every day around 6am water would be pumped into the main tank at the top floor and milk brought by farmers in cans would be collected throughout the day till 1 pm in a tank on the ground floor and after Pasteurization it would be pumped to the top tank with water, keeping aside a few cans of unadulterated milk for special customers! The workers told me that if I could come around 12 noon the next day and wait outside on the road without entering the Dairy, one of them would be standing at the balcony of the top floor and when sufficient milk was pumped from ground floor to the top tank with water, he would wave a white towel as signal. I could then enter with a reliable Food Inspector from DC's office with Lactometer and seize the adulterated milk from the top tank and get it tested on the spot. I agreed to this and they told me to keep this extremely confidential and not to tell any one. I informed the DC SV Ranganath IAS, who was a highly active and committed officer (he later on became Chief Secretary of Karnataka), and the Special DC Arvind Jhadav IAS (who also later in his turn became the CS), about the task. Next day the three of us along with the Food Assistant of DC went in an unmarked Ambassador car and waited on the road at a distance but within sight of the balcony of the Dairy. After about fifteen minutes, we saw some one waving a white cloth which was the agreed signal. We then barged in much to the shock of the Manager. The adulterated milk and also samples of unadulterated milk in cans still on the ground floor were seized. It was found that the milk was diluted to the extent of 25%. The Manager and his associates were arrested under the penal provisions of the Essential Commodities Act the same day. MISA had been repealed in 1977 and therefore they could not be sent to my favourite Bellary Resort!

The relationship between Development and Regulation would thus be obvious. In this case there was increasing availability of milk and there was the Milk Dairy to Pasteurize it and distribute to consumers. This increases the income of the farmers and the availability of protein to people. However, without regulation adulterated milk would make the dairy milk unpopular and the demand would go down which would ultimately affect supply by farmers and the government milk dairy would run in loss. Later, in 1990 when I was MD of Karnataka Power Corporation, I used to meet the Joint Secretary, Power in Sardar Patel Bhawan often. Once, in an expansive mood, he enlightened me (those were the days of Rebecca Mark of Enron of Texas lording it over Power Ministry), *Corruption is the Engine of Development!* Well, he was wrong. Corruption in India is ultimately funded by ordinary Indians. This is unlike corruption in Japan where its funding is recovered from export earning as the Japanese Income Tax rules allow adding "transaction cost" in their invoices. As to my Joint Secretary friend who was junior to me, well, understandably he became the Lieutenant Governor of the most important Union Territory in India! So, in India, corruption is certainly the engine for the individual development of many bureaucrats and their patrons!

KANCHI SHANKARACHARYA SNUBS THE PRESIDENT OF INDIA!

Another very interesting episode happened during my watch. The elderly Kanchi Shankaracharya decided to camp in Gulbarga district in the village Mahagaon of 5,000 population. It was 15 km north of Gulbarga on the highway to Bidar. The pontiff, as was his habit, stayed in the refurbished cattleshed of a local landlord, accompanied by the Junior Swamiji. Unlike most officers, I had not called on the Kanchi *Periyaval* (in Brahminised Tamil, 'noble soul'), the other *Periyar* (in pure Tamil, 'Eminent Person') being EV Ramaswamy Naicker, the atheist and iconoclast. Among the Hindu philosophies I was an admirer of the *Charvaka* school of Brihaspathi which said:

There is no other world other than this;
There is no heaven and no hell;
The realm of Shiva and like regions,
are fabricated by stupid imposters.
While life is yours, live joyously;
None can escape Death's searching eye:
When once this frame of ours they burn,
How shall it ever again return?

— *Sarvasiddhanta Samgraha, Verse 8*

Since my college days I had not been an admirer of Godmen, even of the few good Godmen among a plethora of charlatans. I had also read that because of the royal patronage by Emperor Ashoka, Buddhism and Jainism flourished for a time in India. But because of the renaissance of Hinduism along with the genocide of Buddhists and Jains by Adi Shankara in 8the century CE, both the protestant, reformist religions disappeared in the land of their birth. Writing about the ruthless activities of Sankaracharya, Swami Vivekananda observed:

"...such was the heart of Sankara that he burnt to death lots of the Buddhist monks after defeating them in the argument. What can you call such an action on Sankara's part except fanaticism?"

(Complete works of Swami Vivekananda, Vol.VII. p. 118, Calcutta, 1997)

I also recalled from my reading in college days of what Marx had said about Religion being the 'Opiate' of the masses. Actually, this is often incompletely quoted. Marx had actually said, *Religious suffering is, at one and the same time, the expression of real suffering and a protest against real suffering. Religion is the sigh of the oppressed creature, the heart of a heartless world, and the soul of soulless conditions. **It is the opium of the people.** [Part of the introduction to 'Critique of Hegel's Philosophy of Right', Marx, 1843]*

Because of my fascination to Marx's qualified criticism (like opium needed by a sick person in pain), I went to Mahagaon where Kanchi Sankaracharya was staying because of the impropriety of President Sanjiva Reddy. He was seeking a second term and on hearing that Kanchi Sankaracharya was camping in a Gulbarga village, he hurriedly issued a tour programme to visit Mahagaon where he had no official work. His only programme was to call on the Swamiji and seek his blessings for his re-election. He flew to Hyderabad by IAF aircraft and from there came to Mahagaon by helicopter. This was blatant misuse of office but none, no intellectuals, no opposition leaders, no media (without Emergency) protested against it because new norms of misbehaviour in high places were constantly being set to lower and lower bars. Being the President of India in office (and, not forgetting he issues the appointment orders of IAS officers), the DC Ranganath, SP, DIG and myself were expected to make reconnaissance missions and I had to go at least once to Mahagaon where no VIP helicopter had landed before. Having gone there, I made a courtesy call on the Swamiji. Besides, an elderly person staying in a cattle shed in the dusty Gulbarga (in contrast, the Mahatma stayed at the Birla House at Delhi the last five months of his life; he travelled by III Class but the entire compartment would be at his disposal and the 'Nightingale of India' Sarojini Naidu, *Bharat Kokila to the Mahatma,* exclaimed, *Oh Mahatma, the cost of keeping you poor!*), was indeed commendable. The Junior Swamiji told me that normally *Periyaval* does not receive visitors, excepting sometimes poor devotees coming from afar and certainly no VIPs. And then, the visitors had to sit outside a window of the cattle shed and the Swamji would speak briefly through the window bars from inside. I was speaking to the junior Swamiji in his native Tamil. Probably because of it, he said he would go and ask the Swamiji whether he could spare me a few minutes for us. Language is perhaps stronger than caste or even religion as Bangladesh showed. In the event, the Swamji indeed gave me a few minutes. He was a frail person with deep voice and obviously not in good health. After thanking him, I politely told him the President of India was coming to call on him and pay his respects in two days and the President would be grateful to spend about thirty minutes with the Swamji. He simply demurred and was non-committal.

When the President landed on a sweltering dusty day and we officials were the only persons to receive him as the Swamji through his Junior had made it explicit that there should not be any crowd at all near his cattle shed residence. What followed was really thrilling to me! Firstly, the President had to sit on his haunches outside the window of the cattle shed as no chair was allowed! The narrow raised platform adjacent to the main entrance of a house open to the street is called *Thinnai* in Tamil which was a must in South Indian villages and meant for passing travellers to take shelter without coming into the house. I stood two steps behind the awkwardly squatting President. There was no garlanding the Swamiji by the President as strictly told by the Junior Swamiji who went inside to inform the Swamiji. For about thirty minutes nothing happened and no sign of Swamjis, senior or junior. Then the elder Swamiji came to the window but he did not smile at the President nor even an eye-contact, in fact he was looking at the 'middle distance'! The President sought Swamiji's blessing but there was no visible reaction from him. This painful, surreal charade ended quickly when the Swamji abruptly stood up and left, the junior Swamji explaining that it was time for his *puja*. The President was totally humiliated by this treatment. But I thoroughly enjoyed it and my opinion of the Kanchi Swamiji went up by many notches as it was so nice of the old Swamiji to snub the erring President of India which few other Godmen in India would do.

BUT NT RAMA RAO GETS AUDIENCE, EVEN A SMILE FROM KANCHI SWAMIJI!

This was followed in a few months by a visit by the newly elected NT Rama Rao, the CM of Andhra Pradesh. NTR was a brilliant orator and lived upto his screen image. He was very much helped by the immature Rajiv Gandhi who was the AICC General Secretary. Once, after landing in Hyderabad's Begumpet airport he walked straight to the waiting helicopter to inspect the drought affected areas in Telengana, refusing to take the CM Anjaiah along with him. The CM and his entire Jumbo Cabinet of 60 waiting at the airport had arranged for a mega reception with drum-beat and girls dancing. Rajiv Gandhi went red at seeing this circus and pronounced Anjaiah a "buffoon" reducing him to tears which was duly reported by the media. NTR used this image of Anjaiah in tears and described it in his stentorian voice that Rajiv Gandhi did not insult Anjaiah but insulted the 6 crore Telugu people's *Atma Gowravam*—Self Respect. All that implied by the word *Atma Gowravam* became the central theme of NTR's Telugu Desam party's propaganda against the Congress in the 1983 Assembly election in which he trounced the Congress party which lost the state for the first time after independence. NTR was also treated by the Telugu people as Lord Rama and Krishna, the roles he played on the screen, and he also started dressing as Swami Vivekananda at home. Some also claimed that he wore sari for some hours at night before switching over to dhoti, to get the status of Lord Shiva's *Ardha-Nareeshwara!* Anyway, the first thing NTR did after winning the election in January 1983 was to make a trip to Gulbarga to pay respects to Kanchi Swamiji. He arrived at Gulbarga at 6am and he must have left Hyderabad at 2am which for him was normal hours. My batch mate UB Raghavendra Rao, a fine saintly person, was Secretary to CM and he had told me that NTR was usually ready for work at 3 am after a heavy breakfast with chicken and other delicacies and would start receiving the bleary-eyed Chief Secretary, DGP and other officers for discussions. I made it a point to receive NTR at Aiwan-e-Shahi as I had not seen him in person till then and I had admiration for the man who single-handedly defeated the Congress and Mrs Gandhi. Towering over me, he was profusely apologetic and in his best filmy style, told me I should not have come so early to meet him in what was his private visit. He was in his charming best and insisted on giving me tea and biscuits and very politely insisted I should go home. Later on, the SP told me that the Swamji chatted with NTR in Telugu for a half hour through the window! The Swamiji's selective *bonhomie* with an actor-CM and his snubbing the President of India was indeed intriguingly enjoyable. Some Swamjis could be admirably complicated!

IN GUNDU RAO'S REGIME, THE *SUBHEDAR* WAS LEFT ALONE TO PURSUE PUBLIC INTEREST!

In Nizam's government, the Divisional Commissioner was called *Subhedar* and his office in Aiwan-e-Shahi was named *Subhedari.* It is said that if the Mahatma is reborn in today's India, he will be saddened by all the *Himsa* going on and will promptly commit suicide and go back to his heavenly abode in great haste. But if Emperor Akbar or his Finance Minister Raja Todar Mal is reborn, they will be happy to find their Moghul Land Administration system is followed scrupulously to this day. Todar Mal had divided Akbar's empire into 8 Subhas (Provinces), sub-divided into 197 Sirkars (Districts) and further sub-divided to 3,367 Mahals (Small Taluks) or Parganas. Lands in Mahals were further sub-divided into Bighas, one Bigha being 3,600 *Ilahi Gaj* of about half acre (one Ilahi Gaj being equivalent to 41 fingers or 32 inches). One thirds of the produce of the farmer was collected as land revenue to the state. But, in a year of drought remission was made. But then, the real originator of India's land administration system was the unsung Sher Shah Suri who defeated Humayun and ruled most of North India briefly from 1538 to 1545. Raja Todar Mal was Suri's Revenue Officer first and after his death joined the court of Akbar. The *Sur* empire with its capital at *Sasaram* in today's Bihar, was divided into 47 *Sirkars* which were further sub-divided into *Parganas.* The head of Revenue and Finance administration was designated *Diwan-i-Wazarat* and the head of the Sirkar was *Shikdar.* Land was divided into three classifications according to yield. As famines were frequent, he created and maintained a Famine Relief Fund collecting 2½ seers of foodgrains from each *bigha.* He introduced silver coin of 178 grains and called it *Rupiya* which is even today the national currency in India, Pakistan, Nepal, Sri Lanka, Indonesia, Mauritius, Maldives, Seychelles, Bhutan and till some years ago, Afghanistan, Burma and many gulf countries. He had built the 2,500 km long *Badshai Sadak* (renamed Grand Trunk Road by the British) from Chittagong to Kabul. To mark the length of the road, Sher Shah Suri built *Kos Minar*—a milestone to mark every *kos,* each *kos* roughly equalling 1.8 km. He is truly unsung in Indian administration. It was his empire, from Kabul to Bengal, that Humayun won in 1555 after the death of Sher Shah and which Akbar inherited in 1556 when he was just 14 years old. Sher Shah Suri's only defect was his religious intolerance against Hindus. Otherwise it was he who built the Mughal Empire in India on the foundation of Babur.

After the death of Aurangazeb in 1707, the Viceroy of Mughal Empire in Hyderabad region, Asaf Jah I, became the ruler himself and, after 1757 Palashi battle, the British allowed the Asaf Jahi dynasty to rule Hyderabad as 'Client Prince'. Hyderabad was the largest and most prosperous among all the princely states. It covered 214,190 km^2 of territory and had a population of 16 million as per the 1941 census, of which a majority (85%) were Hindus. But, of the upper bureaucracy, 59 were Muslims, only 5 were Hindus and 38 were Europeans. The Nizam and his nobles, who were mostly Muslims, owned 40% of the total land in the state. The Hyderabad State continued the same land administration system and terminology as the Mughals. Thus, the Divisional Commissioner was continued to be called *Subhedar* by the people. After integration of Hyderabad State on 13 September 1948 in 'Operation Polo' executed by Major General Jayanto Nath Chaudhury and the last Nizam Mir Osman Ali Khan, the Asaf Jah VII, abdicated, Hyderabad was trifurcated and the predominantly Kannada-speaking districts joined Karnataka in the State Reorganization of 1956.

The Nizam was conferred with the titles, *His Exalted Highness,* and *"Faithful Ally of the British Government"* by the colonial British government for his collaborating role in the wars against Tipu Sultan of Mysore, and during the 'First War of Indian Independence' in 1857, becoming the only Indian prince to be given both these titles. *[Though, according to historian Romesh Chandra Majumdar, 1857 was neither the first as the Vellore*

Mutiny in the South was in 1806, nor 'Indian' because three-fourths of the British army which defeated the rebel Sepoys were Indians themselves, nor a War because it was confined to pockets in North India and rest of India did not rise, and not for independence because all that the rebels wanted was to restore the power of the Mughal Emperor!] The last Nizam Mir Osman Ali Khan was the fifth richest man in recorded history, with an estimated worth of US$210.8 billion adjusted for inflation. He was also well known for his miserliness! Most of all this I read sitting in my Aiwan e Shahi *Subhedari* office. I had a lot of time to read in Gulbarga, with remarkably brilliant DCs doing all the good work for which I took credit! I was singularly fortunate to have had the privilege of working with such fine DCs of world class calibre as SV Ranganath, Shantanu Consul, Vinay Kumar and Gokul Ram.

Living alone in Bheemarayanagudi's UKP Project-colony and left alone in the indifferent administration of Gundu Rao, I built a library and could read many of the books, all the time being paid full salary and without any political pinpricks! Gundu Rao was the CM, Narasimha Rau the CS and Jayakumar Anagol the Principal Secretary to CM. I was left to my own devices and I followed in the footsteps of good Nawabs of Nizam of bygone days! It was also in the Bheemarayanagudi colony in 1980 that I took to jogging 8 km a day, five days a week, at the age of 39. *[I am on my second round of the Equator! Equatorial distance of earth is 40,075 kms! But after turning 75, I only do brisk-walking. Modestly speaking, of course!]*

Moghul history overwhelmed me when my Urdu-knowing Sheristedar went on reading the *Firmans* of Nizam's government to me from the Guard File. While the Madras Province issued Government Orders (GO's) and the Bombay Government issued Government Resolutions (GR's), the Hyderabad government issued *Firmans* in which I found reference to the Geological Survey of Hyderabad edited by Leonard Munn who was known in Raichur district as *Savira Bhavigala Sardara* (Chief of a Thousand Wells.) Leonard Munn was the Chief Engineer in Nizam's government and still remembered by the people in Raichur-Gulbarga region because of his selfless service in providing safe drinking water and saving thousands of people from the dreaded Guinea Worm disease, *Dracunculiasis*, which is a parasitic infection by the Guinea worm. In Hyderabad-Karnataka region they had many large step wells. Since the feet come into contact with the water first, the fleas containing Guinea Worm larvae bite and the persons gets infected, apart from drinking that well water. In Gulbarga the disease was called *Naru* meaning 'thread' because the worm is thin and can be three feet long. The only remedy was to puncture the skin where the worm is seen and slowly roll it in a stick, which was the ancient 3,000 year old Egyptian remedy. The thread-worm can break while being rolled out and it would become septic and the person would die of gangrene. It was thus a horrible sight in the villages to see the infected persons, mostly women who usually fetch water from the step wells. Leonard Munn who headed the Geological Survey of Hyderabad and who was Special Officer of Well Sinking Department for seven years till his death in 1935 closed down step wells and constructed hexagonal shaped draw wells with three or four pulleys thus saving thousands of lives. He had constructed over 1,200 hexagonal shaped wells many of which were still in use in 1980's. He died in 1935 in Lingsugur, my old subdivision in 1967-1968 where his grave is situated behind AC's house, the old Captain's bungalow, and the Italian-polished pink granite stone was inscribed with:

[INSCRIPTION ON MUNN'S GRAVE AT LINGSUGUR, KARNATAKA]

Captain Leonard Munn
OBE (Mil.), Belgian Croix de Guerre
Younger son of the Rev. George Munn
Madresfield, Worcs.
Born 31 May 1878
Died at Lingsugur 21st October 1935
1909—1919 Mining Engineer
(with municipal survey)
H. E. H. the Nizam's Government
January 1916 to November 1919
Served during the Great War
in the Royal Engineers in France
April 1928 to October 1935 Director
Geological Survey and Special Officer
Well Sinking Department
During which period he and his staff
sank or remodelled more than 1200 wells
in the Famine Zone of this Raichur District
where his name is a household word
"Blessed is the man who passing
through the valley of weeping
make it a well" Psalm 84, 5-6

The self-less work of paragons like Leonard Munn (and Alexander Cunningham who established the Archaeological Society of India, who located and saved several Ashokan Edicts and James Princep who was the founder-editor of the Journal of Asiatic Society of Bengal and deciphered Kharoshti and Brahmi scripts—who were the real "Discoverers" of India) and countless others working their hearts and bodies out in a hot and dusty land thousands of miles away from their native land, sweating and suffering from tropical diseases and yet serving the poor and downtrodden and dying, not seeing their green and wet native England, made me meditate how insignificant my services were. Most educated Indians do not know the names of men like Leonard Munn as much as they know of Col. Reginald Edward Harry Dyer under whose illegal orders, at least 379 Indians were shot dead in Jallian Wallabagh, Amritsar on 13 April 1919 (I remember this date, because my DoB is also 13 April!) What is never mentioned is, the soldiers who opened fire were themselves Sikhs, Gorkhas, Pathans, Baluchis and Sindhis—all Indians who obeyed the illegal orders of an Englishman. There was not even the fig-leaf excuse of the Nazis that the Jews they were gassing were a different 'race'. These Indian soldiers of Dyer were killing their own countrymen. What could explain this?

THE HYDERABAD-KARNATAKA DEVELOPMENT COMMITTEE AND MY REPORT

Even three decades after the State Reorganization, the Gulbarga region of three districts were being referred to as "Hyderabad" Karnataka. This area was traditionally the most frequented by famine over centuries and in the integrated Karnataka State these districts were the most backward economically, socially, educationally and gender-equity wise. The only other kindred district was the bordering Bijapur which was "Bombay" Karnataka. The people of HK were bilingual in Urdu and Kannada and the elites were more at home in Urdu. Their orientation was towards Hyderabad which was closer than Bangalore. Reciprocally, the more mellifluous-Kannada speaking Old Mysore Southern districts considered the guttural Kannada of H-K Region as crude, not very civilized. One Southern Gowda-gentleman even told me, the Northern Lingayats came to the beautiful Mysore state as 'Rakshasas', the Avarnas according to Dr Manu! Even the pure-bred Lucknowi Muslims were horrified by the "Dhakkani" Urdu of Hyderabadis (e.g. Nakho Karo for 'Don't do!). At state level Government employment, the share of Hyderabad Karnataka was much less than proportionate to its population. Therefore, there was great discontent among the younger generation which was fanned by both by the Congress and the Janata Party. The politicians of H-K took their cue from the neighbouring Telengana where there was an agitation from 1969 for a separate State because of the discriminatory policies of the

AP government dominated by coastal area's economically powerful *Kamma* community. The PM had therefore constituted a Telengana Development Committee in 1969 which was to be the monitoring and watchdog body for Telengana's due share.

When I got my promotion and took charge in Gulbarga in 1980, there was already pressure on the government to form a H-K Development Committee as in Telengana. In Gundu Rao's ministry there were 5 ministers from Gulbarga region including the heavy weights Dharam Singh and Mallikarjun Kharge both from Gulbarga. Out of the 30 MLAs from the three districts 25 were from Congress. Because of their pressure, the government constituted a Hyderabad-Karnataka Development Committee with Dharm Singh, the Minister for Urban Development as its Chairman and Mallikarjuna Kharge as Vice-Chairman and I was appointed as its Secretary. All the 30 MLAs were members. In its first meeting I told the Committee that there cannot be an identity between the Telengana Development Committee and the HK Development Committee because the Telengana Committee was born due to a movement for a separate State which was unthinkable for Hyderabad Karnataka though there was some student agitation for a separate state. Without much natural and human resources such a separate HK State would be a disaster. The most the HK Committee could work for would be to prepare a plan of ten years during which the Gulbarga Division's (for convenience Bellary which was not part of Hyderabad Karnataka was also included in the jurisdiction of HK-Committee), economic and social infrastructure could be lifted to reach on par with State's *average* by special investment. This included health, education, public transport, roads, bridges, irrigation and electricity. This was agreed to. I got the data assistance of the Planning Department in preparing the HK-Development Plan which was completed in one year. The Hyderabad-Karnataka Development Plan prepared by me in its final version was presented to government in 1982. The one year I spent as Secretary of HK Development Committee in addition to my work as Chairman of UKP-CADA and Divisional Commissioner was highly educative to me though Planning was not new to me, having worked in the Planning Department for three years. It gave me the opportunity of working closely with MLAs and political leaders of different parties in the region and built my confidence level and self-assurance. It gave me the opportunity to know more about the backward regions of Telengana, North East and Vidharba which we had visited. We had also called on Mrs Gandhi in Delhi who gave us tea and sympathy but nothing else!

MY *"SUBHEDAR"* LETTER HEAD IN URDU AND GOVERNMENT'S REPRIMAND!

One of my last action in Gulbarga became controversial. Urdu with Persian roots used to be the Court Language in Hyderabad state till independence and most people spoke its corrupted version, *Dhakkani*. More than a third of Gulbarga city's population were Muslims and even the educated Hindus were more at home in Urdu. Many leaders, even Veerendra Patil, would lapse into his comfortable Urdu while speaking in public. Though I did not understand Urdu much, the very sound of it, its majestic intonation and elaborate floral protocol etiquette impressed me greatly. This was also because, my mother tongue Tamil is a strong and guttural language, unlike Kannada, Telugu or Malayalam which are melodious and mellifluous. Tamil for instance does not have the phonetic alphabets, *ba, ja, sha, ksha, ga, fa* and *ha*. Other South Indian languages have these mellifluous phonetics from Sanskrit, while Urdu had all the soft and hard sounds. Out of the total 44 *phonemes* (the smallest unit of sound in speech) in world languages, Urdu has 37. In my official letter head my name, designation and office address were written in only Kannada and English. Being in Gulbarga which was still being called "Hyderabad-Karnataka", and the elite being more refined in Urdu, I decided to add Urdu besides Kannada and English and got printed new letterhead pads showing my name in flowing Urdu calligraphy and my designation as *"Subhedar"*, by which the Divisional Commissioner was popularly called by the people and the address as *"Subhedari, Aiwan-e-Shai, Gulbarga"*. This delighted all the Urdu-knowing public including all advocates of Gulbarga. After all, Gulbarga was a place where Urdu *ghazals* were the weekly rage in the Municipal Gardens attracting huge crowds of all faiths. I found I was being treated with a new affection and politeness by everyone after seeing my new letterhead. However, within a month some kill-joy in the Secretariat saw my new *Subhedari* letterhead and was put up to the Revenue Commissioner and Chief Secretary and my explanation was called as to why I included Urdu in my official letter head without permission! I pointed with polite facetiousness that Urdu is one of the 22 official languages in India included in the 8th Schedule to the Constitution and, besides, in Gulbarga Division evidence was also taken in the Courts in Urdu. But the Government frowned upon my initiative but no action was taken against me as the Revenue Minister who hailed from Gulbarga liked my letterhead!

THE 1983 JANATA GOVERNMENT AND MY APPOINTMENT AS
SECRETARY TO CM

Elections to the State Assemblies of Karnataka and Andhra Pradesh were held in January 1983. In an upset result, thanks to Gundu Rao's maladministration, out of the total 224 seats in Karnataka, Congress could secure only 82, (but with 40% of votes polled) while the Janata Party led by Ramakrishna Hegde got 95 sets (with a lesser 33% of votes cast—Yes, this is possible in the bizarre *"First past post is winner"* democratic system which we are following blindly from the UK in contrast to the "50% + 1, run off" system of the French.) The BJP contesting seriously for the first time secured 18 seats with 8% of popular votes. Independents who were mostly rebel candidates of Congress Party, secured an astonishing 22 seats with 15% of votes. The two Communist Parties had secured 6 seats. However, Ramakrishna Hegde with less than a majority of his own Janata Party negotiated a post-election alliance by which the BJP, all the Independents and even the two Communist Parties pledged support to his government "from outside", that is, they will not have any ministerial berths but will support the government in the legislature. But Hegde was only a compromise candidate as the strong landed gentry communities of Okkaligas and Lingayats on the one hand and the chronic "party hopping, pre-existing condition", backward class leader Bangarappa on the other, fought for chief ministership. *[The latter was a staunch Socialist under the much-loved leader Shantaveri Gopala Gowda (both from Shimoga which was my first posting as DC & DM), then went over to Congress and then to Karnataka Congress Party, Karnataka Vikas Party, Janata Dal Secular, Karnataka Kranti Ranga, BJP and even Samajwadi Party…..one loses count! The only party he did not either join or admitted into was the Communist Party. He would put spinter Usein Bolt to shame. More about this fleet-footed political-athlete later.]*

Hegde was a smart *Havyaka* Brahmin from the highly literate coastal Karwar district and acceptable to most other contenders and he emerged as the compromise candidate which however was not acceptable to Bangarappa. Deve Gowda (who would later become Karnataka CM and also the accidental PM of India) was sent by Janata Party to pacify Bangarappa and accept being Deputy Chief Minister which he steadfastly refused, his stand being "CM or Nothing". In their Thai free-style wrestling the backward (class) leader who was a highly publicized (though poor) doubles shuttle-cock badminton player, tore Deve Gowda's *jibba* and did not even offer to replace it!

In Andhra Pradesh the result was still more astounding. Out of the total of 294 seats, the Telugu Desam Party led by NTR, a new-comer to politics and contesting elections for the first time, secured 202 seats with 46% of popular votes while the hitherto invincible Congress with Indira Gandhi and Rajiv Gandhi leading the party could get only 60 seats, though with a vote share of 34%. NTR became the first non-congress CM on 9 January 1983 immediately after which he had come to Gulbarga to seek the blessings of the Kanchi Seer which he received but the President of India did not as I have happily narrated! In Karnataka, Hegde became the CM on 8 January 1983 but the rationalist *Ajivika* and Epicurean sybarite did not visit Gulbarga to seek any Swamji's blessings nor did he make the usual temple visits which is a must for most newly elected leaders including most godless for public consumption! One week later, when I was in my Gulbarga office, a friend of mine who was junior to me by two years and who was scouting the corridors of Vidhana Soudha canvassing for Excise Commissioner's post (he succeeded!), excitedly telephoned me that I was being appointed as Secretary to CM in a day or two. I did not believe him, not because he was a Cretan sparse with truths but mainly because I had not known Hegde nor had worked under him in his various capacities earlier as cabinet Minister between 1962–71, nor was I DC of Karwar district where he hailed from. Frankly, I was not quite thrilled to work in the sensitive post of Secretary to CM leading a right of centre party. Besides, the post was perceived by bureaucrats as being a 'power centre' and I was in no way attracted to such controversial positions as I was more inclined to posts with regulatory and development tasks. About the CMs of Karnataka and their philosophies or lack of it, I will dwell long in a later chapter.

AN UNEXPECTED LAW AND ORDER PROBLEM IN BELLARY BEFORE I LEAVE GULBARGA TO JOIN AS SECRETARY TO CHIEF MINISTER

Three days before the order transferring me as Secretary to Chief Minister was issued, there was one unexpected grave law and order problem in Bellary. Gokulram, who as DC had to handle any law and order problem in the district had just left for his new job as Deputy Secretary to Chief Minister. So, at midnight the Home Secretary phoned and woke me up and informed there was rioting in Bellary because, allegedly a city Police Inspector had molested a Muslim girl. As the new DC had not yet joined, he asked me, having the experience in three districts, to reach Bellary at the earliest. So, I went to Bellary and found that the allegation was true. However, additional police force from other districts came and we imposed curfew in the city for two days and the situation was controlled without need to any firing. I got the Police Sub

Inspector to go on leave as his presence would incite the mobs. I stayed in Bellary for three days till normalcy returned during which the new CM, the Janata government was just fifteen days old, spoke to me and asked me to join duty at Bangalore early.

Driving back to Gulbarga, I ruminated over what had happened in Bellary and the way the police administration has evolved over time. The Police Department in India was established in 1843 by Sir Charles Napier on the model of the Royal Irish Constabulary. Ireland was part of England till 1919 and the RIC was a quasi-military organization with an Olive Green uniform, armed with Webley revolver and living in barracks. In England itself, Robert Peel as Home Secretary introduced the modern policing system both for Ireland and England. However, the Irish Constabulary differed markedly from the Metropolitan Police Force system for London at Scotland Yard in 1821. There was unrest and civil disobedience in Ireland because of the religious tax called *Tithe* imposed on the Catholic Church by the British. To control the unrest, the Royal Irish Constabulary had to use suppressive methods. There was no such unrest in the Protestant-majority England. Therefore, the policing system introduced by Sir Robert Peel in London was known as "policing with consent". The London policemen wore blue trousers with tail coat and a top hat just like civilians, carried only a short wooden truncheon, a pair of handcuffs and a whistle but no weapons and did not live in barracks. They had to walk in pairs every day 2.5 miles an hour for two hours (five miles a day) in daily patrol in their jurisdiction so that they would come to know personally all the inhabitants in their 'beat' area. Their duty was primarily to help and guide the residents and tourists including lighting the streets and fire-fighting. Their performance was assessed not by the number of arrests made but by the fall in crime rate. Because of this progressive attitude, Londoners loved their police and they were called "Bobbies" in honour of Sir Robert Peel. They worked seven days a week, with only five *un*paid holidays a year for which they received the grand sum of £1 a day. Their lives were strictly controlled: they were not allowed to vote in elections and required permission to get married and even to share a meal with a civilian. To allay the public's suspicion of being spied upon, officers were required to wear their uniforms both on and off duty. Thus the British 'Bobbies' patrolled the streets and kept the population safe from wrong-doers and helped children and senior citizens and lost tourists find their way back to the comfort of their hotels! They were people's friends.

But this did not happen in India. Charles Napier was sent to Sindh Province in 1843 and he followed the Irish Constabulary system which was designed to suppress Irish people and not the friendly "Bobby" system of London. The Great Mutiny of 1857 aggravated matters further. After the British Indian Army (it should be remembered that 80% of whom were Indians and only 20% including all the commanders were British and Europeans) had crushed the sepoys, killed innocent villagers, and burnt whole villages—all the Muslims of Delhi were evacuated—and India became British colony, the East India Company was abolished, and a Police Commission was appointed in 1859. This resulted in the India Police Act, 1861 followed by the Code of Criminal Procedure the same year and the Indian Penal Code of 1862 which are still the basis of criminal law in India today. The objective of all these legal provisions was to rule India as a part of the British Empire without dissent. There is no provision to treat the citizens as responsible persons whose cooperation is necessary to maintain law and order. These laws were extensively used to control and suppress the freedom movement which originated with Dadabhai Naoroji forming the East India Association in 1867 and Surendranath Banerjee founding the Indian National Association in 1876 followed by the Indian National Congress in Bombay in 1885 inspired by the retired ICS officer Allan Octavian Hume who was also a noted but not much publicized ornithologist and botanist. The unexplainable puzzle is why the Founding Fathers of Indian Constitution headed by the London School of Economics and Columbia University's liberal-educated Ambedkar did not adopt the progressive methods of basic and fundamental police work as in the Metropolitan Police Act of 1829 introduced by Sir Robert Peel the then Home Minister who went on to become the Prime Minister of England twice. Instead, India wrongly followed the imperial, Ruler-and-Ruled philosophy of Royal Irish Constabulary in the post-independence India. All the police reforms which have followed since 1947 only increased the facilities of police establishment such as increasing the number of policemen, weaponry, uniforms, better housing, communications, vehicles, etc, but never dealt with what should have been the change in behaviour of the constables who constitute 86% of the police force. No reforms on the pattern of London 'Bobby' system was introduced. The same Khaki uniform with two inch thick brown or black belt inspiring fear continues. No pair of policemen walk 5 miles a day in their allotted 'beat' area to get acquainted with the citizens which will also improve their health which even today the British Bobby does. Instead, in Karnataka they go in Hoysala Vans in the name of modernization, adding to their waistline. Also, unlike in other countries, the constables in India are not available for regular beat duty as they have other duties such as VIP traffic control of simply standing for hours at the VIPs' delayed motorcade route, orderly duties at the houses of senior officers as if they are domestic help, are deputed to work as "gunmen" and pilot-car duty with Ministers, protecting them from people, walking with processions, etc. The semi-militaristic Khaki colour of the uniform of Indian police has not changed in 150 years while the London Bobby's uniform visibly changed to blue with blue checked cap to merge with civilian dress, very different from the Irish Constabulary. The practices in pre-independence times such as detaining suspects in lockups for days without record, writing faulty First Information Reports, beating up persons on the sole of their feet to hide injury, meting out "aeroplane" treatment, etc. have not only not changed but have only intensified with the additional injustice of identifying themselves with the local politicians in power. With the democratic fragmentation of the multi-party system with the Westminster 'First Past the Post' candidate getting elected with even less than 20% of votes polled and the ballot paper having the size of a Sunday newspaper, MLAs suspected of defection being kidnapped and kept long in Resorts, etc., no reform appears on the horizon.

With these sombre thoughts I returned to Gulbarga from Bellary and handed over charge and proceeded immediately to Bangalore to assume my new charge as Secretary to the Chief Minister. My best moment in my second stint was when a sugar factory was for the time being established in Alland taluk in the cooperative sector, the farmers unanimously demanded that the Divisional Commissioner should be the Chief Promoter and the DC Ranganath be the Deputy Chief Promoter to collect share capital in contrast to the usual practice of having a political leader as Chief Promoter!

❖❖❖

CHAPTER 16

Secretary to Chief Minister

"These files make my clothes dirty, please find an alternative!"
– Ramakrishna Hegde

In an atmosphere of chaotic pell-mell headed by a minority government, I took charge as Secretary to CM. The former CM Gundu Rao had just been rejected in an avalanche, the Congress Party's tally falling from 149 to 82 in a total of 221 Assembly seats. The *Deccan Herald* published a cartoon on the front page without any comment showing a helicopter crashed on the ground and Gundu Rao sitting dazed with a question mark above his head, the implication being the CM's juvenile display of helicopter hops in the state causing his political crash. After Sanjay Gandhi's death Gundu Rao's 'drama company' also crashed. For administration he relied totally upon Chief Secretary Narasimha Rao. Though he was a fine gentleman, it was the Bureaucracy which had let down Gundu Rao by disregarding the problems of farmers. In 1981 about 18 tobacco farmers were killed in a *rasta roko* agitation on the National Highway No.4 at Nipani near Belgaum. In 1982, in a farmers agitation in Dharwad district against collection of Betterment Levy for irrigation, two were killed and scores were injured. These firings took place without the officials or ministers showing any willingness to have discussions with the farmers. In the Dharwad agitation, the DC had an unaccountably free hand to 'control' the situation and her response was to open fire on poor farmers and killing a few of them. There was a general conviction in rural area that the Gundu Rao government was anti-farmer and the Janata Party stalwarts, SR Bommai in Bombay Karnataka region, Deve Gowda in Old Mysore districts, Bangarappa in coastal and Malnad districts and Ramakrishna Hegde among the middle class—all forming a political *Kichadi*—consolidated this dissatisfaction into a default support for Janata in the 1983 assembly election. The

Congress Party lost even its traditional base of Dalits and Muslims. Out of 33 reserved seats for Scheduled Caste candidates in Karnataka, the Congress(I) won only nine as against 26 in the dissolved House. In Chitradurga district, where Muslims were a sizeable population, the Congress(I) bagged only two of the 11 seats. In Bangalore city, all the 15 seats contested were lost by the Congress(I); it had nine of them in the dissolved House. The Chikmagalur constituency, which returned Mrs Gandhi to the Lok Sabha in 1978 regardless of her collapse in the north a year earlier, this time voted so firmly against her party that only one of the seven Congress(I) candidates could win. Under the influence of Rajiv Gandhi's Doon School dummies—the twin evils Arun Nehru and Arun Singh, the party made blatant use of state intelligence services to a point of obsession, violating all norms of conduct. The DIG, Intelligence was directed by Gundu Rao and the Intelligence Bureau to scan the list of Congress(I) ticket-seekers and carry out a "Trend Analysis" of the constituencies. Most of the candidates predicted as winners by this IPS wizard lost miserably. The DIG was also said to be coaching Gundu Rao to play tennis apart from coordinating with a danseuse for whom the CM had great weakness! Obviously Gundu Rao could not play even half-court tennis and the gain of tennis was the loss for politics in Karnataka! As soon as the Janata party formed government in Karnataka, the DIG was bundled out pending a probe. When Hegde was sworn in, he declared that ministers would not use imported cars or helicopters, in a move clearly directed against the unpopular flamboyance of Gundu Rao.

Gokul Ram IAS, who was my deputy, was a very fine officer of spotless integrity and possessed an acute sense of right and wrong. He was a Dalit and an engineer. I was fortunate in having him to assist me. Post-1947, the Prime Minister's Office and the CM's Office in the States had gained the reputation of being Extra Constitutional Authority. MO Mathai was the Special Assistant to Pandit Nehru for 13 years from 1946 to 1959 and he was the first such Private Secretary to exercise improper bureaucratic power. His two books, *Reminiscences of Nehru Age* (1978) and *My Days With Nehru* (1979) became controversial and the first one was even banned in India. RK Dhawan was Private Secretary to Indira Gandhi from 1962 to 1984 all through in and out of PM's office and was the supreme example of an Extra Constitutional Authority. It was he who prepared the list of opposition leaders to be arrested in consultation with Om Mehta the Minister of State for Home and Sanjay Gandhi's side-kick on declaration of emergency. As a reward, RK Dhawan also became a member of Rajya Sabha twice, from 1990 to 1996 and from 2004 to 2010. These persons were merely bad stenographers. Their power was in becoming "gate-keepers" to their bosses. They were Personal Assistants who did every kind of work for their masters there being no dividing line between private and public work and reliable like eunuchs of Moghul time. On the other hand, there were ICS officers such as V Shankar and VP Menon (the latter was not ICS), to mention only two, who distinguished themselves in serving the country first while being loyal to their political masters. There is an amusing incident mentioned about VP Menon who rose from humble positions (incredibly, he had worked as a labourer in Kolar Gold Fields after running away from his home in Kerala) and ultimately became the right hand to not only Vallabbbhai Patel but even indispensable to British Viceroys Wavell, Linlithgow and Mountbatten:

[PIONEER, 21-1-2021]

' Nesamani Nadar, the Congress MP from Kanyakumari, stormed into VP Menon's guesthouse in Trivandrum and threatened him with dire consequences (for not helping him) when the bureaucrat was enjoying his sundowner. VP told him to get the hell out of his room. Nadar wrote a six-page complaint note to Patel, saying VP used the filthiest language in a drunken state. Patel asked young ICS officer V Shankar if VP drank alcohol. The embarrassed Shankar had to spill the beans. "Yes sir, VP occasionally enjoys a couple of drinks in the evening." Patel wanted to know what kind of drink. Shankar said, "VP prefers only Scotch." "Then Shankar, you must instruct all the top government officials to take scotch every evening. We can have more VPs to save our nation!," Patel said to him.'

In Karnataka, GVK was Secretary to Kengal Hanumanthiah, CM of Mysore but GVK's role was in development of state and he saw to it that the newly created important subject of Planning was kept with the CM and as his Secretary he became the Secretary, Planning which post he carried with him most of the time till he became Chief Secretary. Later, S Varadan was Secretary to Nijalingappa and JC Lynn in his long two innings as Secretary to Veerendra Patil and Devaraja Urs and Jayakumar Anagol was Secretary to Gundu Rao—all had concerned themselves with the interests of the state and did not promote their private interests abusing their proximity to CM.

The perceived power of the post of Secretary to CM is because of the time he spends with the CM. Government runs on File System. There are hundreds of files in various departments and inspite of the theory of Collective Responsibility of the Cabinet and the CM being only *Primus Inter Pares,* First Among Equals, the position of the CM in the state is unequalled, till he is toppled! Ministers and Secretaries to government look up to the CM and take orders. The all-important matter of allocation of portfolios among the ministers is with the CM who often consults his Secretary. Hence, the role of Secretary to CM also has become a *de facto* position of power. For this reason, Karnataka's CMs had a healthy tradition of having Secretaries to CM from outside their own caste and even from outside the state itself. S Varadan, JC Lynn, Jayakumar Anagol and myself did not belong to the major communities and some even non-Kannadigas and had no caste or community vested interest. That being the major qualification, the other "gate-keeper" function itself is most important but by itself does not contribute much to the government work except to the time-management of the CM. Therefore, to devoid myself of this gate-keeping distraction, first I selected an excellent officer, HFS Knight KAS, who was my very efficient and impartial Tahsildar of Bangalore South taluk when I was DC of Bangalore and who had by then been promoted. As soon as I took charge I got him appointed as Deputy Secretary in CM's office to be in charge of appointments of CM and protocol. Another officer I chose was Subhash Ghaste, KAS who was also my very efficient Tahsildar in Yadgir in Gulbarga district during the famine days. Ghaste was also a Dalit, a bachelor and an engineer. Scrupulously honest and meticulous, these are officers the like of whom one would not find even in any top private companies. The second source of CM's Secretary's perceived power is his role in effecting transfers and promotions of officers. While this is the bread and butter (and also jam!) to many MLAs, personnel matters were legally the domain of the Chief Secretary as he heads the Department of Personnel. Nevertheless, the pressure on CM for postings, promotions and transfers not only cannot be avoided, but over a period of time this has become a very important avenue of favour. Inspite of the Supreme Court monotonously directing that there should be a Civil Services Board to ensure objectivity in transfer and postings of civil service officers, especially the police officers, no state government in India has done this. Nor is the Supreme Court serious and hold in contempt the State Governments for such disregard. To reduce the undue time spent on transfer matters and avoid the role of vested interests, I devised a novelty. I got a young officer, Subhash Chandra Khuntia IAS, who was adept in the newly important computer knowledge to computerize the work as much as possible in CM's office. One advantage of being the Secretary to CM is, you could get any officer of your choice posted to your office. To start with, Subash Khuntia got the work-related information of gazetted officers computerized, such as their native place, where they have worked in the past ten years, even which MLA or politician is asking for his posting, etc. I also entrusted this matter of personnel postings to my ever-reliable and efficient Gokul Ram. It was amusing to see MLAs enquiring as to what happened to their request for posting of certain officers and Gokul Ram sadly telling them, *Look, the computer is saying he cannot be posted or transferred now to the place you have asked, what can we do!* Some times even the CM gave this explanation to adamant MLAs who had a healthy fear of computers! Ghaste and Subhash Khuntia helped Gokul Ram in tabulating the data and requests from MLAs for transfers. Between us we could divide and work as objectively as possible.

I also decided that I would not usurp the role of Secretaries to government. Whenever there was an important matter in which the discretion of the government was involved and the Secretary to the Department had recommended a certain course of action but the minister concerned over-ruled him which was not in public interest and in my opinion the Secretary was right, I would take the Secretary concerned with me to meet the CM personally to explain the matter. On all important matters, I made sure that the Secretary concerned met the CM personally and explained the issue. This also ensured that no Secretary to government felt they were being overshadowed by the Secretary to CM nor was there any impression that I was concentrating power in my position.

HOW NOT TO MAKE CM'S CLOTHES DIRTY!

One strange thing happened in the very first week of my starting the new job. During the office hours of 10 am to 6 pm the CM was very busy with visitors with no time to see files. Some of the files sent to the CM, even sent by the Chief Secretary, would be absurdly trivial and should have been disposed of at the level of Section Officer of that department. The hierarchy in the State Secretariat was: Assistant, Section Officer, Under Secretary, Deputy Secretary, Joint Secretary and Secretary. It was amusing to me who had worked as DC&DM for long, sending economic offenders to Bellary prison or exiling them, to see that when a government servant requires a reading glass *for the second time,* with a higher cost frame than the old rules restricted, the file had to go to the CS for permission even after the approval of the Government Minto Eye Hospital and the CS would choose to send the file for CM's approval as required by the Secretariat Manual! Thus the various types of files received from different departments daily, many of them inconsequential, would be about 5 standard boxes, each containing about 15 files. Most of them would be months or even years old, accumulating dust from various desks. I had to read all these files to know what each matter was, however trivial, before taking it to the CM and explaining it to him and get his orders. Every morning both Gokul Ram and I would go to meet the CM in the Air Force Guest House on the Sir CV Raman Road at one end of which was the Indian Institute of Science and on the same road CM's own house *KRITIKA*. Unlike his predecessors, Hegde chose to live in his own house. After his daily morning walk in the 371 acre, wooded campus of IISc, he would reach the Air Force Guest House around 8 am. He chose this place because entry to it was regulated by the Air Force Security and only those specifically pre-authorized by the CM would be allowed to enter which made the number of early morning visitors very rare.

Gokul and I would go at 8 am with our file boxes for about an hour of file-disposal. After three days, the CM told me it was impossible for him to handle such a large number of files every day because, firstly most of them were unimportant but, more importantly, his clothes were getting dirty by collecting the dirt from the file jackets! So he asked me to devise a system by which these files are not physically brought to him. I consulted my efficient deputies and thought about the problem for two days and evolved the "File Order Sheets System". Under this, I would read the file, then paraphrase the main issue for decision in a summary form for CM's decision—all in less than ten lines, give my own recommendation stating it is my own view and leave the last column with sufficient space for CM's written decision. Thus, in one page of an A-4 sheet two or three files could be summarized for CM's decision and a bunch of 20 files could be covered in 6 to 8 pages. On each page of the File Order Sheet, the first column would show the file number and department, the wider second column my paraphrased summary of the file matter below which my recommendation and the third column left blank for the CM to write his decision. This would meet the requirement of the CM provided I summarize faithfully all important aspects. The CM was immensely pleased with it now that his clothes would remain clean as he had to handle only the File Order Sheets in white paper in a clean folder and he need not touch the dusty files! Hegde was a speed reader like John F Kennedy and would not take more than ten minutes to read the summary of one bunch of 20 files in 8 pages and write his decisions. This he could do it at his own time, while travelling, having tea or breakfast and even while on the toilet for that matter! All that was needed was for me to be diligent in reading and faithfully summarizing and paraphrasing the content. After some persuasion, the CS agreed for the new system to be given a trial. In the event, the File Order Sheets system worked perfectly.

However, I made one exception for the files was the files sent by the Chief Secretary with his long notes. With his background in government of India's long file noting system, the CS would write notes running to many pages, examining thoroughly all aspects of the subject matter. Satishchandran used to come to office at 9 am and start dictating to one of his three PA's these long notes. So, when I took some of the files sent by him, the CM went through the long notes of the CS dutifully. The problem was the CS, as was common in GoI and also in his own careful style, would give for instance ten reasons why a certain course of action can be taken and also eleven reasons why such a course should be avoided! This is the traditional civil service methodology where the ideal civil servant points out the pros and cons of an issue thoroughly and leaves the decision to the minister. After reading some of the long notes of CS, running to five or six pages, Hegde exclaimed, *"I say, what is the CS trying to say, should this be done or not?"*. So all such files were also left for my summarizing for CM's decision and the CS got reconciled to it! The CM would agree to my recommendation or may not and say "No, I do not agree" on the Order portion and sometimes he would write "Please discuss" in which case I would take the file to him for discussion. This system speeded up the file disposal by CM greatly and no file sent to my office for CM's decision would be pending for more than a week. Of course, this increased my work enormously and every day I had to carry on an average three boxes of files home to read and to summarize them into the dictaphone (which practice I had continued from my Gulbarga DC days) so that the next day the File Order Sheets could be typed by my two stenographers. While reading the files exhaustively encroached a lot into my leisure time, it also gave me the insight how the hierarchy in the Secretariat treats a matter on the file. Mostly it would be a negative reaction as to why a request cannot be accepted as the rules do not provide for it, even when the rule is silent on it, yet the hierarchy upto the Secretary would take a negative attitude and reject a request which would otherwise have helped the person behind the file. What I found in most senior officers was that they did not want to differ with their subordinates and stick their necks out to help in even legitimate cases of less fortunate citizens where there was discretion. At the same time, in many cases, persons of their own class or caste would be helped even if their cases were less than justifiable!

DISTRICT ADMINISTRATION REVIEW BY THE CM

I had observed that Gundu Rao never had time to review the work done in the districts as he had left administration totally in the hands of bureaucracy. Even transfers which is lucrative to the MLAs was denied to them as Gundu Rao would simply tell them that for transfers they should meet the Chief Secretary, as CM's time was precious in learning tennis and admiring the performance of Manju Bharghavi eagerly arranged by his IPS Man Friday! So, Gokul Ram and I devised a method of finding CM's time for District Administration review. I arranged for the CM to visit each district and review in detail the implementation of various schemes and also help the district administration in any genuine difficulties they face. One day before the CM's review, Gokul Ram and I would be in the district and would review exhaustively the development schemes' implementation of each department with the officers and assess the achievements and deficit and the reasons for the lacunae including political interferences. I would then prepare brief paragraphs in bullet points which require CM's attention. These points were confidential and only two copies would be prepared, one for the CM and one to be retained with me. For getting the support from state level for the district level implementation, the Additional Chief Secretary MK Venkatesan was asked to attend the CM's review meeting. Though he had asked me for the copy of notes I had prepared from my earlier day's review, I made it a point that it was meant for only CM's eyes and did not give it. He had taken objection to it and complained to the CM. But the CM did not take him seriously. In fact nobody did as he was taken for a Court Jester! MKV had a penchant for incessant, continuous jokes or PJs—Poor Jokes. In the olden days kings used to have a Court *Vidhushak* whose duty it was to crack jokes and defuse the grave situation when the king becomes angry and about to cut off the head of some hapless courtier. MKV was the modern *Vidhushak* and all the meetings in which he would be present would be highly entertaining. He was also a shirker and inspite of being the Finance Secretary because of his seniority, he would simply disappear from his room, attending some Board meeting of a Public Sector Undertaking in many of which the Finance Secretary was a Director and demolish the snacks. All the hard work in the FD was done by his uncomplaining, diligent Joint Secretary Abhijit Sen Gupta IAS, who was also once my hardworking probationer when I was Gulbarga DC. MKV was also once the DC of Karwar district which was the native district of Hegde. So the CM knew his worth.

The CM's two hour reviews of districts exclusively with officers would be followed by a meeting of both officers and elected representatives. This proved to be very purposeful. We had at least two district reviews in a month. There were 19 districts. From these meetings, the CM came to know the problems in each district and could take remedial action promptly. The MLAs welcomed it because it gave them an opportunity to sit with the district officers and the CM together to discuss and take action on key matters. No MLA could complain that the CM was not visiting his district. It also gave me a ground level nuts and bolts knowledge of distrct problems.

DEPARTMENTS OF ENVIRONMENT, ECOLOGY AND SCIENCE & TECHNOLOGY

On the model of the Government of India, Karnataka also created two Departments of Environment & Ecology and of Science & Technology a few months before the 1983 State Assembly election. After forming the Janata government Hegde told me, as no minister understood these subjects and would even consider *infra dig* to hold the portfolio, he would keep these portfolios with himself in addition to Finance and as Secretary to CM I could be the Secretary to these new Departments. This was a great opportunity for me to learn new avenues far from the beaten track of the government. The landmark UN Conference on Environment had taken place in Stockholm in 1972 which was attended by 113 countries and India played an important role in it. I could foresee that Environment and Ecology would become vital subjects in the coming years. The Karnataka Pollution Control Board was established in 1974 to implement the Water Pollution Control Act of 1974 and Air Pollution Control Act in 1981. A serving Chief Engineer was appointed as Chairman of Pollution Control Board. As the Secretary of the Department I was an ex-officio member of the Board. The Act also gave powers to Government to issue mandatory directions to the PCB.

An interesting case came to my attention almost immediately. One day, the CM telephoned me that he was sending one SR Hiremath from Dharwad who had a complaint about water pollution in Tungabhadra river near the twin cities of Harihar-Davanagere which was the industrial hub of central Karnataka. Hiremath met me and he had a serious complaint. The Harihar Polyfibers was a major industry belonging to the Birla Group producing Viscose Staple Fibre from cellulose of wood. In the manufacturing process, the highly toxic Carbon Disulphide was used which should be recovered fully from effluent so that it will not pollute river-water. The PCB had prescribed control measures to the factory. These measures were energy-intensive and there was severe power cut in Karnataka. Since the factory was a continuous process industry, it had to install power generator using diesel to avoid interruptions. But, according to Hiremath, during power cuts, while the generator would supply power to the manufacturing process, there would be no power supply to the pollution control machinery resulting in the unrecovered Carbon Disulphide flowing into the river. Diesel energy was four times costlier than grid-supplied electricity and the management was saving on cost. If this was true, then the factory was clearly violating the provisions of the Water Pollution Control Act. The consequence of this was, fish downstream were dying and the villagers were also using the river water for drinking. This would therefore be a very serious offence. Hiremath was an engineer who had worked for over a decade in the United States, had married an American and had returned for good to Dharwad where he stayed and started a Voluntary Organization by name India Development Society and was doing rural development work.

It was clear from the papers he gave me that on many days the toxic level of Carbon Disulphide (CS_2) was much higher than the permissible level. He had been giving complaints to the Chairman of PCB but no action was taken. I therefore sent his letter to the Chairman to verify the complaint seriously and send me a report within a fortnight. I also asked Hiremath to file a complaint with the Assistant Commissioner & Sub-Divisional Magistrate of Davanagere under Section 145 of the Code of Criminal Procedure. This is a powerful but very little used section of Cr PC. The force of this section was, while its primary purpose was to deal with potential breach of peace because of disputes concerning any *land or water*, Macaulay's Law Commission had put it in such broad terms that it can very well be construed by the SDM that the risk to the livelihood of fishermen or the danger to the lives of villagers drinking the toxic water can create breach of the peace and if the SDM is so satisfied, he can immediately issue a *Conditional Order* restraining the persons from acting in that manner and ask them to appear before him to establish the facts. Most DMs and SDMs do not realize the utility of this Conditional Order which can be issued if there is just a *Prima Facie* case without waiting for recording evidence. I had used this section extensively as DM&DC to proceed against encroachers of public land. The British ruled India not with any great draconian law like MISA but just with Indian Penal Code of 1860, Police Act 1861 and Code of Criminal Procedure 1898. The Defence India Regulations Act came much later in 1915 during the World War I after the *Ghadar Conspiracy* inciting the British Indian Army soldiers to a mutiny.

So, I explained this section 145 of Cr PC to Hiremath and asked him to give a petition to the SDM. I also spoke to the SDM about the gravity of the problem if the river water is poisoned. Action was taken immediately both by the SDM and the PCB to bring sense to the factory management. Had I been only the Secretary of Environment and Ecology without being also the Secretary to CM, the government machinery may not have moved quick. After this incident, I also got CM's approval to nominate Hiremath as a member of the Pollution Control Board. This was in 1983 and subsequently he became a nationally well-known activist in environmental protection, his *pro bono* counsel being Prashant Bhushan. He would also become the prime mover in the Bellary Mining scam of Reddy Brothers—the Bellary Kings, in 2011 which brought down the BS Yeddyurappa government. About this much later.

OPERATION SEA BIRD PROJECT

One day, Admiral Stanley Dawson, Chief of Naval Staff of India was meeting the CM. Admiral Dawson was a native of Bangalore. The CM told me it was a confidential matter and only the Admiral would be in CM's chambers and no other officers from Navy or from State Government would attend, except myself to keep informal proceedings. He came to the point quick. During the India-Pakistan, Bangladesh War of December 1971 the Indian Navy had attacked Karachi and sank a Pakistan naval Destroyer and two Minesweepers. As a retaliation, three Pakistani submarines attacked Indian ships in Arabian sea and sank one Indian Naval destroyer. After this, GoI realized the importance of building up India's submarine fleet, in the Western sector. The Navy had decided to construct a modern Submarine 'Pen' which is like a sea-garage for protecting and repairing submarines. In such a Pen the submarines would directly sail from the sea into the bunker where they had rock cover as in a cave. For this, the Pen should be covered by solid rock on all sides with an easy deep sea entry from the sea. The Navy wanted to construct it on the Western coast of India. Bombay was too thickly populated and Goa was already having the Navy's biggest air base which also operated the Dabolim airport. So, the Navy finally selected the sparsely populated Karwar coast which had the best natural rock formation protruding into sea from which rock can be scooped out and a large submarine Pen could be constructed. While the Pen would be on the sea-coast, the Project, already code-named *Seabird,* would in its final phase employ about 2,000 sailors and have a township. As a native of Karnataka Admiral Dawson knew that 80% of Karwar district was forest. The Indian Forest (Conservation) Act 1980 had already been enacted under which no forest land can be used for any other purpose except with the prior approval of the Union government. But, since Project Seabird was for a defence purpose such permission could be quickly obtained. What the Admiral wanted from the CM was his tacit approval for allotting forest land and all cooperation from state government while executing the project. The sleepy Karwar district would also develop economically because of the project. I worried also about the maidens of Karwar with over a thousand sailors running amok but wisely kept quiet!

The CM readily expressed his willingness to help with forest land allotment. In a few days I went to Karwar with a Naval officer deputed from Goa and visited a few sites along with the Conservator of Forests as the Navy had already selected the rocky site on the coast for the proposed submarine Pen. About five fishermen's colonies would have to be shifted and alternative rehabilitation sites with wharfs for their fishing boats also had to be constructed. Thus the Project came through in a few months and made fast progress. Including its third, final phase to be completed by 2022, it would be the largest naval project east of Suez, costing about Rs 35,000 crores in 12,000 acres of land including 9,000 acres of forest land and the navy occupying 23 km of coast line. Ultimately, it would also have an airport with a 5,000 metre runway with civilian aircraft using it as an alternative airport to Goa which is just 95 km from Karwar. The Seabird Project, renamed as *INS Kadamba* would change the economy of the region. However, the project is still in progress.

MERCURY POISONING BY BALLARPUR INDUSTRIES LTD (BILT) IN BINAGA BAY AND CLOSURE OF THE CAUSTIC SODA PLANT OF BALLARPUR INDUSTRIES LTD.

The only major industry in Karwar district was the Caustic Soda plant of BILT which belonged to the Thapars Group. It was established near the picturesque Binaga Bay, about 4 km south of Karwar town due to the initiative of Hegde during his earlier stint as Finance Minister and he also belonged to that district. Due to the high water requirements of any chemical plant, the chemical factories all over the world are located near sea coast or lakes and rivers. Whenever the CM was away from Bangalore on political work, I used to visit Karwar to review the Seabird Project work. Binaga Bay was a secluded calm beach close to Karwar and I used to jog at Binaga Beach whenever I went to Karwar. One day when I returned to the Circuit House from the beach, the office bearers of Karwar Fishermen's Cooperative Society were waiting for me. They complained that in the Binaga Bay shoals of fish were dying and some fishermen had seen pieces of broken steel pipes floating within five kilometres from the coast. Since BILT factory was within a kilometre of the Binaga Bay, I enquired with its management as to the cause of broken pipes. They informed that when the factory was constructed in 1975 they were given permission by the PCB to lay a pipeline from the factory for a distance of 5km into the sea to let out the factory effluent, the reason being after that distance the effluent is taken away by the ocean current and will not return to the coast. But, unfortunately, a few days ago the pipe broke at the 4th kilometre and the factory was taking steps to repair the pipe which would take about a month. This was unconvincing and I also learnt that the National Institute of Oceanography (NIO) at Goa had been the consultants to the BILT for the disposal of effluents in the sea. So, I fixed an appointment with the Director of the NIO at Goa the next day and met him taking with me the DC&DM of Karwar. When I explained the problem, the NIO's experts informed that they have been studying the quality of sea water along Karwar coast and they have noticed the presence of Mercury for some time. When I mentioned about the broken pipes seen by the fishermen within their fishing limits, they said it was quite likely that due to corrosion the pipes disintegrated and the factory was supposed to replace the pipes once in five years. They however confirmed that BILT's effluents contain small quantities of Mercury which when accumulates in fish, can affect people who consume it. The Director told me about the *Minamata Disease* named after the Minamata Bay in Japan where a chemical factory was discharging Mercury Sulphate in its waste water into the sea over thirty years and people who consumed the fish had developed damage to the central nervous system resulting in numbness of limbs and also affecting vision, hearing and speech. He also told me that due to the harmful consequences of Mercury Sulphate, chemical industry world over do not dispose it off in water bodies but recover it within the factory itself as Mercury is also valuable.

After returning to Karwar from Goa, I asked the BILT to stop discharging its effluents in the sea but to treat it within the factory and recover the Mercury. The management demurred and said they would take it up with their head office. This is the usual ploy of any industry to buy time. So I called off their bluff and, in the presence of the fishermen and officers told them they can take their own time in taking up with their head office but the factory should stop discharging effluents immediately and since the effluents could not be stopped if the factory is operating, the management should close down its operation till the mercury-recovery process is complete. As soon as I returned to Bangalore I sent for the Chairman and Secretary of PCB and gave them the direction to close the factory if the management does not stop the effluent flow into the sea forthwith. The Secretary of the Board then took the order of the Board personally to BILT and with the help of DC closed the operations of the factory.

BILT was then a Birla Group company and its top people from Bombay reached Bangalore immediately and met the CM. I had meanwhile briefed the CM that in view of the gravity of the situation and the representation of the Fishermen who were a powerful body in Karwar and after consulting the NIO at Goa I had issued the directions to the Board. The CM agreed with it as public opinion was against BILT and fish from Binaga Bay was being sold every day in Karwar and even sent to Calcutta. The BILT management which was not taking any action till then, took immediate action when it was closed and within a fortnight had installed all machinery needed to treat the effluent within its premises and also to recover the valuable Mercury. This was another instance of the big Corporate sector treating environmental damage in a casual manner and taking it seriously only when pushed. It was remarkable that the CM did not admonish me for closing the factory in his own district without his permission but appreciated it which will not happen with any CM today.

DEPARTMENT OF SCIENCE AND TECHNOLOGY (DST)

Though the internationally famous Indian Institute of Science was in Bangalore since 1909, having been established by Jamsetji Tata with the 371 acres of land given by the Mysore Maharaja Krishnaraja Wodeyar IV, there was little interaction between the state government and the IISc. The Government of Karnataka had established a Department of Science and Technology (DST) in 1981 but there was no dialogue between the government and the IISc. The IISc and GoK had also constituted a Karnataka State Council for Science and Technology in 1975 with the CM as Chairman. But the previous CMs had little time to preside over its meetings. Within a few days of my assuming charge which was about a fortnight of Hegde's forming the government, Professor Amulya Reddy, a renowned Energy Scientist of IISc called on the CM when I was also present. The CM wanted to have close interaction with the IISc. As Secretary to the DST it became my pleasant duty to ensure CM's regular attendance in KSCST meetings and making the government departments aware of the programmes and applications of inventions in their schemes. Especially, the KSCST had a programme of popularizing smokeless rural cooking ovens which would utilize maximum heat energy of firewood used for cooking in villages and it would also greatly reduce the discomfort and vision damage to women by diverting the smoke above the roof by an earthen pipe and also reduce the quantity of wood burnt. Firewood consumption in rural area was one major factor of damage to forests in Karnataka. Professor Reddy had also established a subsidiary organization, Application of Science & Technology for Rural Advancement (ASTRA) which along with KSCST had evolved easily adaptable solar lights, rainwater harvesting, use of biofuel, popularizing mathematics among students, etc. In my twin capacity as Secretary to CM and Secretary of DST and Environment, I took up these application of scientific methods with the Deputy Commissioners who responded positively. This also made me come close to many Professors of IISc. I took particular interest in renewable energy matters which opened new avenues in my bureaucratic career in the coming years as I would explain in later chapters.

From the very busy but routine soul-killing, trouble-shooting work as CM's Secretary, the subjects of Environment, Ecology and Science & Technology was indeed a very welcome diversion. It was as Secretary of Ecology and Environment that I learned the fundamentals about Environment and Climate Change. As Secretary to CM I could buy books of general and specialized subjects and I created a small library in my own chambers. Fortunately, the very first book I read on Environment was Lester Brown's land mark, *The Twenty Ninth Day* (1978). Lester Brown was the world's leading environmental thinker, author and activist who founded the World Watch Institute in 1974 and later in 2001 The Global Watch Institute. He also explained, with energy shortages anticipated in the early eighties and a projected downturn in world oil production in the early nineties, the world must quickly shift to renewable energy resources. I was fortunate to know these seminal issues, away from the humdrum work as Secretary to CM though many bureaucrats were eager to exercise what they immaturely think "power" which is nothing more than influencing transfer and postings of officers, which has no substance. As per 1981 Census, Karnataka had a population of 5.5 crores, a little less than United Kingdom, Italy or the two Koreas put together. Yet in these countries (developing and developed) the post of Secretary of Science and Technology and Secretary of Ecology and Environment, each by itself, would be considered as of top rank. Yet there were no takers for this post here which showed our lopsided priorities. So, I was the beneficiary.

OPERATION BLUE STAR AND AN EPISODE IN BANGALORE

The early 1980's saw the rise of Jarnail Singh Bhindranwale in Punjab. He was the head of the orthodox Sikh religious school *Damdami Taksal*. In 1982 he moved to the Golden Temple complex and made it his headquarters. From inside the Temple complex, Bhindranwale led the insurgency campaign in Punjab. In June 1984 Operation Blue Star was carried out by the Indian Army to remove him from the buildings of the Harmandir Sahib in the Golden Temple Complex. Bhindranwale died in the assault in 1984 at the age of 37 and the temple complex was cleared of militants. The Operation Blue Star which took place for ten days had a casualty of 492 Sikh militants and civilians and 83 Indian army men. President Giani Zail Singh visited the temple premises after the operation and was shot at by a sniper from one of the buildings. The bullet only hit the arm of an army colonel accompanying the president.

The reason for my mentioning this is, the Operation Blue Star led to an unexpected episode in Bangalore. On one weekend the CM, who had hyper-tension, decided to take two days off with his family including his white Alsatian at the Nandi Hills near Bangalore. His instructions to me were, he should not be disturbed on any account, even by phone calls. Sunday was in any case his "total silence day". Using this opportunity, I had gone to Mangalore, in my capacity as Environment Secretary, to inspect the damage to the Mangroves along the coast of Mangalore due to sea erosion. After the visits on Saturday I was having dinner with DC Gautam Basu of 1970 batch IAS, who was also the daring Assistant Commissioner of Bangalore Rural Sub-division when I was DC of Bangalore. The DIG Revanasiddiah IPS, my batchmate, was also there. When we were having dinner, I received a phone call from Gokulram. For a person of unflappable temperament, Gokul was agitated. He told me the Chief Secretary had called him to his house and showed him a wireless message received from the Union Home Secretary. It said, Chiranjiv Singh of Karnataka cadre of 1969 batch had taken part two days earlier in a procession of Sikh citizens of Bangalore and went to the Raj Bhavan and submitted a Memorandum criticising the Prime Minister and the Operation Blue Star which was serious treason. Among the various demands in the Memorandum, one was that President Giani Zail Singh who as a Sikh had committed a sin in not preventing the attack on the sacred Amritsar Golden Temple and he should resign. The Wireless message had said further that Chiranjiv should be forthwith dismissed from service. Gokulram also told me that the CS was highly flustered and since he could not get the CM on the phone he wanted me to meet him but since I was away in Mangalore, he called Gokulram and gave him the file containing the draft dismissal order and asked him to immediately get me to Bangalore and take the file to the CM on Sunday and get his approval. I told him to calm down and I will reach Bangalore the next day after Gautam Basu's nice dinner which I did not want to miss halfway (and nothing like to have a good night's sleep on a happy stomach before taking major decisions) and both of us would go to Nandi Hills and meet the CM contrary to his instructions but respecting the wishes of CS.

I had time to think about this while driving from Mangalore to Bangalore. Chiranjiv was a very well-read, gentle officer. A polyglot and a linguist, well-versed in history and culture, he was once India's UNESCO representative at Paris. He was also a person of great integrity and deeply religious but not at all a person who could be remotely thought of capable of committing harm to anybody let alone treason. He also had a great sense of humour. Once, when he was Deputy Secretary to Devaraj Urs, there was a letter from the CM of UP which was totally in Hindi. Devaraj Urs did not know Hindi and so gave it to Chiranjv who found it to be of a routine nature. He prepared the reply fully in Kannada and the CM signed it in Kannada and it was sent to the CM of UP to his great puzzle what it was all about! Much earlier, when he was AC&SDM of Tarikere Sub-division in Chikmagalur district, his DC, two years senior to him and who was well-grounded in feudal habits and was harsh against farmers. Being sensitive, Chiranjiv had not carried out DC's orders against the farmers. The low brow DC wrote to Chiranjiv an angry letter that orders of superiors must be carried out by subordinates without questioning. To this, the scholarly Chiranjiv wrote back, that an officer—even a junior officer—must exercise his reason to distinguish between right and wrong and, for good measure, went on to add, *"The last man who blindly obeyed orders is still languishing in Spandau prison!"* He was of course referring to Nazi Germany's Armaments Minister Albert Speer who at the Nuremberg Trial claimed that he was only "obeying orders" but who was nevertheless sentenced to 20 years of solitary imprisonment at the Spandau prison in Berlin though the Soviet Union insisted upon his death sentence. Innocent of a liberal education, the unlettered DC, his favourite book being his Bank Pass Book and Hotel Menus for intensive reading, was puzzled—(*Ye Panda Kanda Kya Cheez?*) and had no idea what this Spandau was. Fortunately, the rustic DC decided that the Sardarji AC must have gone crazy and left him alone! This was the Chiranjiv, an officer and gentleman. Of modest means and frugal habits, a sudden dismissal without pension would ruin Chiranjiv and his family with small children. It would be an act of injustice to take such an extreme step against a person of his calibre and character. The problem I found with very efficient and very senior officers such as the CS, Satishchandran was, compassion did not contaminate their purity of reason. They were moulded on self protective, Survival of the Fittest objectivity and they also believed that in government work injustice is inevitable, even justified. To the CS it was just a file of legal issue and the logical decision was to follow hierarchical instructions from the Home Ministry. Any attempt to protect the junior officer in a sedition case could land the loyal CS himself in trouble. So, I reasoned that, against the recommendation of the CS I should somehow persuade the CM to protect Chiranjiv.

The next day Gokulram and myself set out for Nandi Hills contrary to CM's instructions not to disturb him. On the way I discussed with Gokulram what could be done. He agreed with me that Chiranjiv must be saved. When we reached the Horticulture Department's Guest House at Nandi Hills where once Mahatma Gandhi had stayed, the CM was in a good mood, having a nice weekend. When I showed him the file, after reading the note of CS, he was worried. He too knew Chiranjiv as a soft-spoken officer and one who could speak and write chaste Kannada. The CM asked me what to do with the long note the CS had written and the Home Ministry's instructions for dismissal. Only a few days earlier a Sardarji IFS officer, Mr Mann, serving in Europe was dismissed for sedition because of issuing a statement condemning Operation Blue Star. So, as rehearsed, I described the good qualities of Chiranjiv, both as officer and a person, with all of which the CM agreed. Then I played my trump card, referring to the IB report from the wireless message: *There was a prayer meeting at the Sikh Gurudhwara opposite the Ulsoor lake in the morning after which they decided to go in a procession and give a memorandum to the Governor. About a hundred of them started from the Gurudhwara. They reached the Raj Bhavan and the Governor agreed to receive them. In Sikh tradition whenever there is a grave situation, 'Five Beloved Men' should come forward to sacrifice themselves. Since this was an important occasion and since Chiranjiv was a senior IAS officer, he was asked to be one of the Panch Pyaras to submit the Memorandum to the Governor.* Then, our conversation went like this:

CM: "Look at the Memorandum. It says the President Giani Zail Singh should resign in shame. Aren't you IAS fellows appointed by the President? And he is asking the President to resign? He appointed him."

Self: But sir, the point is timing;

CM: What timing?

Self: The procession reached Raj Bhavan at 1130. A little later the Memorandum was submitted to the Governor by the Panch Pyaras including Chiranjiv;

CM: Yes, so?

Self: Sir, the Memorandum was given to the Governor at 12 noon. How can you hold a good Sardarji responsible for what he does at 12 noon?

That really did it! The CM had a hearty laugh. No doubt it was a racist joke on my part but if it could save a good officer, why not? I knew the CM would enjoy a good joke. He certainly was not a racist, far from it. His sons-in-law were, one a Sindhi and another a Tamilian. Nor was I a racist. I was a great admirer of Jaspal Singh Bhatti who according to me was the greatest comedian of India ever and unfortunately he died at the unjust age of 57. When the mirth was over, CM asked, *The Union Home Secretary has asked the CS to sack him and the CS has agreed, so what can be done?*

I suggested an Enquiry Officer could be appointed to go over the facts as there was nothing on record except a wireless message which may not be factually correct and it was necessary to give an opportunity to the officer to hear his side as was normally done in government. Gokulram suggested TP Issar, who was Additional Chief Secretary, could be appointed as EO to give a report within fifteen days. TP Issar was from Punjab and a very fine, impartial person with a great sense of flowing humour who would not do injustice to anyone. He would also later become Chief Secretary. The CM readily agreed and wrote his decision in his own handwriting on the file. As anticipated, Issar exonerated Chiranjiv giving him the benefit of doubt. Thus ended an otherwise ticklish problem. Gokulram and I felt happy that we could do our little bit for a good officer inspite of the Home Ministry and CS.

THE ASSASINATION OF MRS.INDIRA GANDHI AND HEGDE'S REACTION

On 31 October 1984 I was in my office. The CM had gone to London for a week for treatment of his persistent stomach ulcer problem which he thought was a "gift" from Mrs Gandhi during his incarceration in prison during Emergency. I got a call from the DGP Garudachar at 1130. He said exitedly that Mrs Gandhi was shot and she had received 17 bullet wounds and had been taken to the hospital. He also said that though there was no confirmation of her death, no one could survive seventeen bullets. I contacted the CM at London where it was early morning. When I told him the news, he said he was already seeing it on BBC news. I had hurriedly drafted a 10-line condolence containing the usual praise for Mrs Gandhi and sorrow at her death and read it over the phone which the CM listened to carefully. But his reaction surprised me. He said, *'No, the emphasis should be, She was the daughter of a great leader Pandit Nehru and she had the opportunity to be the Prime Minister for over a decade.'* There was to be no praise for her and just one line of formal condolence for her death. He himself dictated the four line message to me. He had not forgiven her for giving him stomach ulcer in prison!

I LEAVE CM'S OFFICE AFTER THREE YEARS

Soon after there was a Parliamentary election in December 1984 in which the Rajiv Gandhi-led Congress secured a landslide victory of 404 seats out of 514 in the Lok Sabha and 49% of the total votes. Indian democracy is always praised for the great 'maturity' of its masses for making right choices in elections. Nothing can be farther from the truth. Lubricated with money, TV sets, sarees, dhoties, Ambur Dum-Biriyani, etc., emotional, caste and community appeals decide the voting behaviour. Thus, Rajiv Gandhi who had no experience whatsoever of holding a public office and had only a humdrum pilot's experience was catapulted into Prime Ministership and elected by the people in a sympathy wave, much to the chagrin of Pranab Mukherjee. In the then Janata stronghold of Karnataka also the Congress secured 24 out of 28 Parliamentary seats. Losing little time, the Congress Party demanded imposition of President's rule in Karnataka and to hold Assembly elections claiming the ruling Janata Party had lost the confidence of the people. Hegde also expected this would happen and was preparing to resign. However, surprisingly, when Hegde called on the new PM Rajiv Gandhi, he said that there was no need for President's rule or for him to resign as in any case the elections to the Assembly was due in March 1985. Tactically this gave time to the Janata Party to plan a strategy to contest the election. Even Hegde thought Janata would not come to power in the background of the sympathy wave. This was clear from what I observed in a meeting of the CM with Prannoy Roy in January 1985. The CM was in Delhi for ministerial meetings and I had also gone with him. He wanted an opinion survey and Janata Party's election strategy for the impending Karnataka Assembly elections. So he had asked Prannoy Roy who was just then becoming famous for his team of psephologists and election surveys. Roy came to the CM's suite in Karnataka Bhavan. The CM explained to him the major issues to be covered in the survey. He agreed and when the CM asked him about the fees for the survey, Roy said hesitantly it would cost Rs.10 lakhs (which was a big amount in 1985) and also requested haltingly, since they were establishing themselves just then, he would be thankful if he could get half the fees upfront and the balance after the survey. Hegde completely floored him by saying he would arrange to pay the entire fee upfront. He also smiled at Roy and said, with politicians he should always ask for the full advance as one could never be sure what would happen after the elections! Even the unflappable Prannoy blushed. When I came out, I found an acolyte of Khodays from Bangalore. Obviously he was waiting to pay for the survey in full!

The Karnataka election results in March 1985 took everyone by surprise. On the counting day, the CM had fixed a cabinet meeting so that all the ministers could be present and whatever decision had to be taken in the event of losing the election, could be an immediate joint decision. In fact, he was expecting a defeat. As the progress in counting was streaming in, it was clear within two hours that Janata Party was leading in over 125 seats. Everyone left the cabinet room to their constituencies to celebrate their victory. The Janata Party won 139 seats and the Congress only 65 out of a total of 224 seats. The fickle-mindedness of the voters, not the 'maturity', was evident because the death of Mrs Gandhi four months earlier was old news as sympathy wave does not last long! People demand exciting news every fortnight! On the other hand, the Janata Party had not also harmed farmers or any section of population as Gundu Rao regime did. The next day the CM called me and asked me whether the swearing in could be done with only the CM. I told him though it was done once in Tamil Nadu with only MGR as CM, there was some litigation about it, and it is safer to have one or two closest colleagues to be sworn in as the Constitution requires a "Council of Ministers", which requires at least two and preferably three. Especially in view of the Governor being AN Bannerjee, a retired IAS Officer and loyalist of Mrs Gandhi who had lowered the national flag in Raj Bhavan on just learning of the shooting of Mrs Gandhi even though her death was officially announced only in the evening, following the Moghul protocol! So, ultimately SR Bommai and Deve Gowda the Lingayat and Okkaliga stalwarts from Northern and Southern Karnataka respectively were to be sworn in. Hegde did not want the customary Raj Bhavan to be the venue for swearing in and wanted it to be a "Peoples Function" where a large crowd without the Raj Bhavan entry restrictions could attend, like in Kanteerava stadium. But I suggested the obvious place would be the majestic portals of Vidhana Soudha in front of which over ten thousand persons could gather upto the High Court. The CM liked this idea and agreed. But the Governor raised some objections regarding the deviation from established procedure and also the security question. These were duly answered and thus for the first time the swearing in ceremony was held on the wide top steps of Vidhana Soudha's Roman-Dravidian facade and the vast boulevard upto the High Court building was full of people.

From then on it became customary to hold the swearing-in in front of Vidhana Soudha.

However, I found a distinct difference in Hegde's functioning in his second term from 1985. With a comfortable majority of 139 Janata MLAs compared with his 1983 Ministry with only 95 Janata MLAs when he had to make tight-rope walking with the 18 BJP MLAs and some of the 22 Independents who were giving support "from outside", increasingly he started spending more time in Delhi on political work, image building and developed ambition for central leadership. Even in Bangalore he was spending more time with editors of Delhi-based media such as *India Today, Sunday* and *Outlook*. While his treatment of Gokulram and me continued to be as affectionate as ever, I could detect his slight contemptuous reference to his hitherto close associates like Bommai who was Minister of Industries and Deve Gowda who was PWD Minister. The usual morning file discussions at the Air Force Guest House with us continued but I found he was spending more and more time with the DIG Intelligence Mallurkar who was a fine, self-effacing, soft spoken IPS officer, always whispering to the CM out of my hearing.

I was already completing three years as Secretary to CM. I found that the post of Member-Secretary and CEO of the Central Silk Board whose headquarters had recently been shifted to Bangalore from Bombay, was falling vacant. Because of my background in sericulture as Director in Karnataka which was the major silk state in India, I was sure I would be the most suitable officer to the post. Besides, its headquarters was in Bangalore with all-India jurisdiction. I was already 'empanelled' for Joint Secretary rank in Government of India three years earlier. So I told Satishchandran about my desire for the central deputation. He agreed with me that it is necessary for every IAS officer to work in central deputation and I would be most suitable to the Central Silk Board job and he would send my name to the Department of Personnel. But he also told me that being Secretary to CM, I should first get it cleared with the CM who should agree for my release. This was delicate but I had to broach the subject and when I did, the CM was quite surprised. *Why do you want desert me,* was his response! I told him that was the last thing I would do but in the IAS we had to work in the central government at Joint Secretary level for at least five years if we have to be considered for further senior positions and the post of CEO of Silk Board was ideal for me. With my background in sericulture I could do a lot for Karnataka also. He said he would think about it. At my request, Satishchandran was good enough to speak on my behalf. After a few days the CM asked me whom would I recommend to succeed me. I told him it is CM's choice. After a few moments he asked, *What about Sankaranarayanan?* This surprised me. He was just about five years junior to the Chief Secretary and since the CS would be retiring soon, the new CS would be uncomfortable to have a very senior person as Secretary to CM. With almost same seniority, for all practical purposes the new CS would be a second-fiddle to the CM's Secretary if the latter was also a very senior person. It was necessary not to undermine the authority of the CS in any manner. So I explained these reasons and my reservations to the CM. He agreed and asked, then who? So I told him the general criteria followed in Karnataka that the Secretary to CM should not be of the same caste as the CM and it would be helpful if he is not even a native of Karnataka and not an officer close in seniority to the CS to make him uncomfortable. I then suggested two names: My batch mate A Ravindra who was mild-mannered and a person with an academic bent of mind and of high integrity. His parents were from Andhra Pradesh and of Naidu community though he himself was a Bangalorean. Besides, he had also worked in CM's native Karwar district and also as DC of famine prone Kolar district. However, I found the CM was not highly thrilled with my suggestion. He was still inclined towards Sankaranarayanan. I again pointed out to the tradition in Karnataka of having a comparatively junior person as CM's Secretary so that there would be no conflict between the CS and the CM's Secretary and in any event, the Chief Secretary's position should not be overshadowed and the CM's Secretary should not become an extra-constitutional authority as it had become in Northern states. Ultimately he saw the merit in my argument and chose the name of Gopal Reddy which was the second name I had suggested as he was from AP. As Additional Secretary in Finance Department Gopal Reddy used to meet the CM many times as the CM was also holding the Finance portfolio. He was one year junior to me and was a Dalit (adding 'Reddy' was the time-honoured futile attempt to move up in the caste hierarchy!) and Karnataka had never had a Dalit as Secretary to CM. It would be a good gesture, especially when the CM belongs to higher caste. So he qualified on all counts and he was appointed to succeed me. I was thus posted as Member-Secretary and CEO of the Central Silk Board.

A RECAPITULATION OF MY WORK AS SECRETARY TO CM

In retrospect, my work as Secretary to CM did not have any significant substance to it, except for my experience as Secretary of Environment and Science & Technology. But this is not the perception of other members of the IAS. The Principal Secretary to the CM or Special Assistant or Private Secretary to a Union Minister is a greatly coveted post. It is a typical *Brahmanical* attitude of Indians of the Priest being in the *Sanctum Sanctorum* of the Deity or the *Katib* (scribe) to be always with the Ottomon Caliph, copied by the Moghuls. Proximity to Power had become an end in itself and there were officers who would do anything to get into these positions. Later, one officer of much-acknowledged dishonesty had fallen at the feet of a Lingayat Swamiji to whose *Mutt* the later CM also belonged, be posted as Principal Secretary to CM which post he obviously construed as being the Principal *Fixer* or the *Kapo* of concentration camps! Many of them become extra-constitutional authorities and also become graft-kings. About these characters later, enthusiastically!

Much more satisfying to me was my experience as Secretary of the Environment & Ecology Department and of Science and Technology. It gave me the unique opportunity to come into contact with the scientists of the Indian Institute of Science and learn many of the expanding avenues of science and technology, such as Renewable Energy. But proximity to the CM also gave me the opportunity to learn how political leaders work. As politicians go, Ramakrishna Hegde was exceptional in being an intellectual (*he* would correct my English and not the other way round), charismatic and acceptable to all castes inspite of being a Brahmin. He was suave, absolutely secular, a sybarite, an Epicurean and a connoisseur of all things beautiful! I could also observe how even the best of politicians are also not spotless. Corruption in political leaders is only a matter of degree. Traditionally, Excise Contractors were the source of funds for political parties in Karnataka. In turn, they could violate various provisions of law and the Excise Department officials would even close their Nelson's one eye. When the budget for Irrigation increased manifold, another avenue of Contractors was added. It was well-known in early 1970s, even Devaraj Urs had arranged with Excise and Irrigation contractors a monthly 'stipend' of Rs.10,000 to each ruling party MLA which would be equivalent to Rs 3 lakhs per month in 2020. This practice was continued in all subsequent ministries as 'pre-existing disease'! On the whole, the experience of being Secretary to CM was a valuable learning experience for me.

❖❖❖

CHAPTER 17

My Second Stint in Silk—Central Silk Board and Learning from China

"I have not told the half of what I saw"—*The last words of Marco Polo, who made the Silk Road famous*

PREPARATION OF A NATIONAL SERICULTURE PROJECT WITH WORLD BANK FUNDING BY THE CENTRAL SILK BOARD

Mulberry silk which is the internationally traded silk, is produced in just 20 districts out of the 800 or so districts in India, mainly in Karnataka. Therefore, the scope for developing sericulture on a national scale was enormous. As my mentor GVK had remarked, *'In government, only your capacity will be your limitation'*. With this conviction I launched myself into my new job as CEO and Member-Secretary of CSB. The advantage in an independent Board under the Ministry of Textiles away from Delhi was that you are left alone most of the time and you have the freedom to plan and execute new schemes. I was with the CSB for four years from 1986 to 1990. When I joined, the CSB was a small organization with about 1,200 employees, half of them scientists, spread all over India. The annual budget of CSB was just Rs 4 crores most of which going to salaries. I had the advantage of having conceived and prepared the Karnataka Sericulture Project the final expenditure of which was Rs 128 crores.

While there was legitimate criticism that most of the WB-funded projects came with strings attached in the form of 'Conditionalities' such as choosing from international contracting firms and consultants, policy issues such as emphasis on privatization, recovery of cost and no subsidy to the poor, etc, I found that in sericulture and in KSP there was no big contracts and therefore all civil contracts were awarded on NCB—Nationally Competitive Bids with only Indian contractors bidding and not on ICB—Internationally Competitive Bids which was a must as in the case of Hydro-Electric Projects, Steel Plants, National Highways, etc. The average size of mulberry farm in Karnataka was just 2 acres. Besides, sericulture had the advantage of employing more women than men as rearing silkworms is an in-door activity, highly labour intensive, employing Muslims and Dalits especially in reeling, a cycle of five to six rearings in a year so that cashflow is during the whole year. It transfers income from the silk-consuming rich to the cocoon and yarn-producing poor, environmentally benign as mulberry consumes less than half of water as cotton, sugarcane or paddy and drought-resistant, highly export-oriented as developed countries do not produce silk while their demand for silk is high—all these factors worked in favour of the Karnataka Sericulture Project. It was therefore a pro-poor, pro-developing country, pro-environment, gender-benign and pro export-oriented project and not in conflict with the interests of rich countries—whom Anthropologist-Ecologist Jared Diamond describes in his *The World Until Yesterday* (2013) as WEIRD countries—*Western, Educated, Industrialized, Rich, Democracies.*

With the experience of KSP, from day one I set about preparing a National Sericulture Project with World Bank funding. The main advantage of getting external funding was, one can prepare a project with Rs 30 in hand as Rs 70 is given as loan which is repayable in twenty years at low service charge. I was fortunate in getting Dr Raje Urs, a scientist who had undergone a course in the Indian Institute of Management in Project Preparation. I organized a small team for preparation of the Project covering the CSB with all its Research Institutions and also the traditional states of Jammu & Kashmir, West Bengal, Andhra Pradesh and Tamil Nadu where sericulture was practised and also included Karnataka which after the first KSP was implemented, had not prepared a follow-up project after my departure. My guidance to the Project Team was not to bother with the cost aspect in the beginning as funds could be found always for a good project, but to include all the important components for sericulture development and primarily CSB's requirement for R and D. As for the five states, I wrote to the respective Directors to prepare a project outline suited to their requirements. For CSB, it was mainly to strengthen R & D such as procuring scientific equipment, creating a germplasm bank for improved varieties of mulberry, facilities for evolving better varieties of silkworms suited to India's climatic conditions, construction of a few modern grainages to produce improved Bivoltine silkworm eggs, extension centres to test new varieties of mulberry and silkworms in the field, testing house for raw silk as in Yokohama in Japan and recruitment and training in India and Japan of scientists and technical staff to implement such a project. Fortunately, by this time I had an excellent Secretary of Textiles in RL Misra, a senior officer of Rajasthan cadre who was open to all development work. Since other states in India did not have whatever infrastructure Karnataka was having, it was necessary for the CSB to take up development in new states. He totally agreed to support such a CSB Project.

It took almost six months to prepare a respectable Project Proposal. When I showed it to Misra, he was impressed by the technical and economic content of it. The Project cost came to Rs 180 crores (Rs 900 crores in 2020) in a period of five years. He thought it was a rather ambitious project for the Textiles Ministry but after reading through it felt that it should be posed to the World Bank through the Department of Economic Affairs which was the 'nodal' department for external funding. However, he agreed to my request I may informally show the Project Proposal to any World Bank representative who may happen to visit India in connection with some other project to which he agreed as he was also obviously excited about the project.

The World Bank missions keep on visiting India once in six months. It so happened that within about two months a senior officer, Mr Abdul Haji of the Agro-Industries Division of India Department of WB was visiting India. I got in touch with him and requested for a meeting. He promptly agreed as the WB considered the earlier Karnataka Project as highly successful. So, I arranged for a dinner meeting with him and three of his mission members in Hotel Ashok in Delhi. We met at the Afghan Room of Hotel Ashok with Abdul Haji, the Loan Officer of India Department of WB, an Agricultural Expert and an Economist. Abdul Haji was from Tanzania and was of Indian origin, settled in Washington. He was a Chartered Accountant by training and so had a good figure sense. I had earlier given copies of NSP proposal at the Hotel Taj Mansingh where the mission members were staying.

When I started to explain the project proposal, to my surprise Abdul Haji said, *Mr.Balu, we have gone through your NSP document and it looks to be a good proposal, but there is one problem with it.* So, I braced myself anticipating their remark that it was too big a project for sericulture sector and said defensively, *We can try to clip it in some aspects and reduce the size.* Then I got my shock when he said, *No, no, we do not want you to reduce it. On the contrary, can you increase the size of the NSP to about Rs 500 crores from Rs 180 crores proposed?* This was so unexpected as normally a banker would try to scale down the demand of a borrower and not increase it. Abdul Haji was a pleasant person and he explained to me the reason for his remark which might appear strange to me. India was the biggest borrower from the WB at about US$ 2 billion earmarked for the next year, followed by Brazil, Indonesia and some other Latin American countries. In 1986 China was not borrowing from WB. Most of the Projects which the India Department of WB was then examining were Hydro-Electric and Irrigation projects, each costing more than Rs 2,000 crores but since recently had run into some difficult environment problems of submersion of forest land. So, the WB would be interested in an environment-friendly project such as the NSP which had the added advantage of being drought resistant and favouring women's employment. The current WB Chairman considered both environment and gender issues very important, Abdul Haji said. I agreed I would be able to enhance the scope of the NSP and would require about two months to modify the proposal. He agreed and the rest of the evening ended pleasantly.

It was now my turn to be worried. I realized that this was a great opportunity to prepare a larger project both in content and geographical spread. So, my team and I worked hard to identify suitable areas in the states of UP, Bihar, Orissa, Madhya Pradesh, Maharashtra, Himachal Pradesh, North Eastern States and also in Kerala, in addition to the traditional five states. In fact, hilly areas with 1,000mm rainfall like Idukki in Kerala, Dehra Dun in UP, the entire North East, North Bengal, the whole of Himachal Pradesh were all ideal for mulberry plantations. The difficulty was not growing mulberry but extension and training of farmers in rearing of silkworms, supply of silkworm eggs and marketing of cocoons which the farmers produce and immediate conversion into silk yarn. The fact that in 1780s, Tippu Sultan introduced the entirely new sericulture industry in Mysore all the way from Bengal by just organizing training and giving royal support which made the distant Mysore State the near-monopoly producer of silk in India was proof enough that, after two centuries and with more modern facilities, it can be done in rest of India.

So, within two months we prepared the revised NSP covering eight new states. When I showed it to RL Misra, he was aghast how the desert people of Rajasthan would take to it, he being from Rajasthan or UP with its caste-rigours. When I pointed out to him how sericulture was introduced in the warm South India and how Tea and Coffee were introduced in India from China and Arabia and that silkworms can thrive where mulberry plant or even mulberry trees as in J & K, Uzbekistan, Azerbaizan, etc. can grow luxuriantly, he finally lent his support to the revised Rs 500 crore NSP. When I contacted Abdul Haji at Washington and informed we are ready with a revised bigger project he asked me whether I and my assistant Dr Raje Urs who did the detailed calculations, can come over to Washington for ten working days and clarify all issues to the different experts and the Loan Officer who was the key person, to avoid delay in the Bank's organizing one more Mission to come to India to make a 'Project Reconnaissance' visit. I informed him he would have to speak to Secretary, Textiles as such a visit by us had to be approved by the Ministry. Abdul Haji lost no time and within a week the Secretary, Textiles phoned me that he has received the request and has authorized a two weeks' visit for me and Dr Raje Urs to go to Washington and explain the NSP to WB.

All this was done without Secretary, Textiles seeking any approval of the Department of Economic Affairs as preparing a draft project and activities related to it were within his powers and the DEA comes into the picture only when the project has to be officially included in what was called the "Pipe Line" of projects to be posed to the WB by the DEA. But in the Moghul culture that prevails in Delhi bureaucracy, the DEA firmly believed that any contact with the WB was the domain of DEA and no intrusion would be allowed into its 'kingdom'. So, when the Director (who was below the Secretary, Additional Secretary and Joint Secretary in hierarchy) in the DEA came to know about our proposed visit to Washington, she hit the roof and tried to block our visit to Washington. But the Secretary, Textiles stood his ground and politely informed the Secretary, DEA that such a project would be in national interest and would also help to meet the DEA's targets. So, Raje Urs and I went to Washington and explained the revised NSP. When I tried to explain the geographical spread of the project area to be covered, the locations were not comprehensible to the WB team. So Abdul Haji took all of us to the "Map Room" of the WB. I was astonished to find very detailed maps of every State of India in 1: 25,000 scale maps including what the Survey of India classified as DSM—Defence Series Maps. When I had tried to obtain such maps from the Survey of India office at Bangalore, I had to get special permission from the Ministries of Home Affairs and Defence as these were of 'restricted' circulation! And yet, I saw them wall-mounted in the Map Room of WB in enlarged detail. I was sure the WB and IMF (which was just across the 'H' Street, and both WB and IMF are connected by an underground tunnel), had better satellite maps from NASA than the Survey of India! Our discussions went off well. and our visit ended successfully.

After my return I briefed the Secretary, Textiles who was happy to send it to the DEA for posing it to the World Bank. Just like the Karnataka Project was sold before it was officially posed to the World Bank, the bigger NSP was also viewed favourably before the DEA sent it to the WB! This was sufficient proof that even in highly bureaucratic bodies such as the GoI and the WB, if care is taken to establish informal contacts and if the project is intrinsically sound, it can move very fast.

The World Bank is an organization dominated by the United States and its other G-7 members namely, UK, Japan, Germany, France, Italy and Canada. But the US has the single biggest voting power with about 16%. India has just about 3%. Unlike the UN General Assembly where one country has one vote, the WB and IMF follow the principle of "one dollar, one vote". The WB also had a reputation of reflecting US foreign policy in WB lending. The very first loan of the WB in 1946 for $ 250 million to France was approved only after France agreed to the condition of the US that the French Communist Party's Coalition members in its post war government were dropped! From then on, the WB loans had many "conditionalities" imposed by the US and its allies who controlled 40% of votes. Thus, in 1972 when Chile's Socialist government of Salvador Allende nationalized the US-dominated Copper Mines, the US instigated the WB to suspend the loans already sanctioned to Chile and allowed the resumption only after the CIA-inspired 'suicide' of the democratically elected President Allende in 1973 by General Augusto Pinochet after which he imposed a brutal military dictatorship and still got the WB assistance. In 1955, the huge WB loan negotiated by Egypt for its Aswan Dam was cancelled under the Anglo-US influence when President Gamal Abdel Nasser nationalized the Suez Canal Company in 1956. Similarly, till 1975 South Vietnamese government under military rule received WB loans due to US support but when the US fled in 1975 and United Vietnam came under Communist rule, the WB cancelled the loan. So much for the Anglo-Saxon version of Democracy, Human Rights, fair-play etc.! But, India had no such problem as, according to World Bank, India was too big to be bullied, and a good borrower who never defaulted loan repayment and always used the loan for the intended purpose unlike some African and South American countries which used part of the WB loans for constructing swimming pools for their Presidents!

The NSP project of Rs.500 crores at the then exchange rate of Rs 13 was about $ 380 million of which the loan was about $ 270 million. After the formal appraisal of the project by the WB which took about six months, finally negotiations were fixed in early 1990 in Washington. I found that the bureaucracy in the WB was a worthy rival to India as every project had to go through five stages of different coloured Cover Reports namely, White, Orange, Yellow, Red and Green besides a Peer Review! Everything went off well and at the concluding day's dinner,

Abdul Haji informed that this NSP Project was the biggest single agricultural project funded in India by the WB till then.

ON THE FOOTSTEPS OF MARCO POLO—MY VISITS TO CHINA AND OTHER COUNTRIES ON THE 'SILK ROAD'

Working in the Central Silk Board, I have travelled in China twice and also many of the Central Asian Republics such as Azerbaizan, Uzbekistan and visited the famous Silk Road Cities Samarkhand and Firghana, the birthplace of Babur. Silk and porcelain were the oldest luxury products used by the aristocracy world over and the 'Silk Road' from China to Europe was the first International Trade Route made popular by Marco Polo of Venice. China is the home of silk as was a long list of inventions such as Tea, Gunpowder, Compass, Fireworks, Printing, Irrigation, Porcelain, Kite, Matches, Bamboo Bridges, Flying Toys, Double Hulled Ship, Elite Civil Service by competitive examination, use of human waste as Organic Manure, Noodles, Chopsticks, Acupuncture and so on. Being a rare product involving a laborious process, silk accounts for only 0.2% of the total world fibre production after Polyester, Cotton and Wool. Therefore, it will always remain a luxury product. Silk was the fashion for the aristocracy in Europe and rest of the world. Before the Second World War Japan's trade surplus mainly came from export of women's silk stockings to the United States from which they imported machinery and technology from the West, industrialized and also became a military power. But, after 1949 China regained its position as world's largest producer of silk because of its labour intensiveness and export earnings. Currently, China produces over 85% of the World's silk. India is a poor second and the quality of Indian silk is also the lowest with not a single kilogram of its silk yarn usable in modern foreign looms as India's handlooms. Other small producers are Brazil, Thailand, Uzbekistan, Azerbaizan and Vietnam. Once the home of silk in Indian sub-continent, it totally disappeared from today's Bangladesh. There is a small production of low grade multi-voltine silk in Malda district of West Bengal with the legacy of the old Gaur Kingdom. It thrived mainly in the five old Mysore districts because of the state patronage starting with Tipu Sultan and it also took root in the adjoining areas such as Anantapur in AP and Dharmapuri in Tamil Nadu.

Inspite of becoming the workshop of the world China, unlike Japan and South Korea, has nurtured its traditional, labour-intensive sericulture industry so that currently China has a near-monopoly in the production of good quality of raw silk yarn. Even India imports from

China one-fourths of its mulberry raw silk for its power looms besides smuggled silk through Nepal and Bangladesh. Indian silk export and local consumption is only the silk cloth woven mostly in handlooms. There are no silk handlooms in other countries except a few in Thailand and Malaysia. Only in India handloom silk is still important, protected by government subsidy to Silk Cooperatives which, again, is mostly siphoned off by political leaders, controlling the handloom organizations.

There is an important aspect of agriculture I learnt in China which India should consider seriously. Though China has the world's third largest land mass after Russia and Canada, its net arable land is only 357 million acres while India's net cultivated land is 403 million acres. Only 12% of land mass is cultivable in China (the rest being deserts and hills) while it is about 60% in India. To ensure food security, China has a rigorous policy of having a 'Red Line' of 300 million acres for grains below which it should not fall. Over centuries, China has been using human waste as farm yard manure, supplemented by chemical fertilizers, due to which China produces about 500 million tons of foodgrains while with a larger area India's grain production has been hovering below 300 million tons. While silk yarn is the final product of sericulture, in China its by-product of excreta of silkworms during its four weeks of leaf consumption, which is also protein-rich, is dumped into fish ponds as feed for fish. China cannot afford to waste any land and therefore mulberry is planted even on the bunds of rice fields. In India it is estimated that bunds in fields account for 6% of total land which is not used. Indian railways have huge lands on either side of the rail tracks and public roads and canals have acquired land as 'borrow pits' which, being at lower level collect rainwater, but which are now left fallow whereas in China all lands are planted upto the brim of roads and railways. Even a simple matter as use of human excreta in fields which is common in all South East and East Asian countries, is taboo in India and no agricultural expert has the courage to seriously advocate it. Even with fast urbanization, 40% of China's population is still rural and therefore to find rural employment China has steadfastly nurtured its labour-intensive sericulture over the decades which also transfers income from richer to poorer families as silk is consumed mainly by the rich. In India rural population still accounts for 70% and there is all the more reason to develop sericulture. Yet sericulture is practised in only a small area. India has about 850 districts and 5,500 taluks. But India's 70% of mulberry silk production is from only 23 taluks of five districts of Karnataka's 174 taluks in 30 districts. The scope for expanding silk production in India and in Karnataka itself is immense. India's population would exceed China's at 1.5 billion before 2030 and the growing upper middle class (though only 10% of population in our skewed economic development) would consume more silk as silk sari would never be replaced by western gowns in India unlike in China, Korea and Japan and silk is also traditionally a must for Indian religious customs of birth, weddings and even funerals.

WHAT I LEARNED IN CHINA

I visited China in 1989 and in 1990 and travelled extensively for three weeks each time in the rural areas apart from the even then glittering cities of Shanghai, Beijing, Guangzhou and Hangzhou. I headed a three-member team of CSB in a Science and Technology Exchange programme. While the Chinese Government offered to arrange travel by China Airlines, I requested for travel by train so that I could observe rural life better. From the air all countries look the same and airports are all monotonously modern. But when you travel by train you meet different people and see the countryside close at hand and learn. So, from Hong Kong to Guangzhou to Shanghai and Beijing, I travelled entirely by train which in 1990 (and even now) is the main means of transport to most Chinese. In 2020 China has 65% of World's High Speed Trains criss-crossing the country. But in 1990 the trains were low-speed and all painted green and there were two Classes, the Hard and the Soft, the soft having cushions and a head lamp like the First-AC compartments in India. The trains were very long with three dining compartments, at each end and in the middle. The whole train was connected by a vestibule so that passengers could walk throughout. The dining compartments were busy throughout day and night as I found the Chinese were in the habit of eating a lot and all the time. The Chinese Department of Sericulture had given us one interpreter who spoke tolerable English and another technical person knowing some English to help him. Our Soft Class Cabin had four berths and the three of us from CSB and the interpreter stayed together in one cabin and the Chinese Technical expert in another.

One evening, I heard some commotion from the next cabin and I asked our interpreter what was it about. He went out to enquire and came back and said, it was a quarrel between two villagers because one called the other *"Fertilizer Face"*. Seeing my puzzle, he explained that in Chinese the word for Fertilizer and human excreta was the same! In another small town, we were staying in a government guest house which was just like the Circuit Houses in India. We were to visit another village to see silkworm rearing and the breakfast was to be the at the usual 5am.

When I complained 5am was too early to have breakfast, they made a concession and said, *OK, you have it at 5.30!* When we were finishing the rice-gruel and catfish breakfast (they do not have the ten breakfast variety as we have in South India*)*, there was some commotion outside. The driver of the van was also with us having his breakfast. Both in China and Japan the driver eats along with the host and guests unlike in India where we practice cultural, caste, religious and class *apartheid* scrupulously. The driver went out and came back and said something excitedly to our Technical Expert and both of them went out. To my query, our interpreter told me that the small child of the guest house caretaker was bitten by a dog and had to be taken to the hospital in our van. He also said that it was the only child of the caretaker. When I asked whether the one-child norm applies strictly to rural areas also, he said that while the government is not strict about it in rural areas, still most rural couples also have only one child. When I asked him how about the risk of child mortality, he said it is virtually unknown and that even the dog bite we saw was very unusual as there were very few dogs in China! In fact, only the earlier evening when we were reaching the guest house from the railway station, a dog ran across our van and the driver had said, *"there goes our dinner"* only half in jest!

I visited a few villages around Hangzhou to see how the Chinese farmers practice sericulture. Like India, China was also a land of villages with about 9 lakh villages in 1949 (by 2020 it came down to 5 lakhs) compared to about 580,000 Revenue villages in India. The big difference between India in 1947 and China in 1949 was, India came unscathed from the Second World War while Chinese economy was shattered by Japanese occupation, the Nanjing massacre in which officially 250,000 civilians were massacred by Japanese army and the civil war after 1945 between Mao's Peoples Liberation Army and Chiang Kai Shek's Kuo Min Tang forces which had destroyed most of the infrastructure. But, unlike India, China has been one unified country since the time of Emperor Qin (221- 206 BCE) and subsequent Han (202 BCE- 220 CE) dynasty established a centralized empire, which remained as one country throughout history inspite of the invasion and rule by Kublai Khan and later by the Japanese occupation from 1931. The word "China" comes from the Romanized spelling of Qin, which is pronounced "Ch'in," while the Chinese refer to themselves as "the people of Han."

The major divergence between the two different paths to development and political organization between India and China started even before the communist revolution in China, at the time of the Long March of 9,000 kms by Mao and his Red Army from Jianxi in the South to Shanxi in the North West, escaping the KMT army. When entering a village, the Communist cadre and soldiers would tie up the leading landlords of the village and would ask the assembled villagers to describe all the atrocities committed by the landlords. Reluctantly, some old tenant would start which then would become a torrent. This was known as the 'Speak Bitterness Meetings' *(suku fuchou—Speaking Bitterness and Seeking Vengence)*, which was an effective psychological method of consolidating the collective anger of people. Their objective was to create group solidarity among the poor peasants to make them participate in Land Reforms and as an important step of politicization of the peasants. It successfully turned suppressed anger of trauma and suffering into a surfaced revenge by collective consciousness and cut across the Confucian values of loyalty and submission. At the end of the meeting, the PLA would publicly execute the landlords by shooting them to demonstrate that the once powerful landlords could be obliterated by the Chinese Communist Party. It occurred to me that such a violent social revolution had not taken place in India at any time by the 'depressed castes' against the upper castes or by the landless against landlords.

I first visited China just after the Tiananmen Square agitation of June 1989 and China's relentless economic growth was visible. The Deputy Director of Sericulture who took me around Hangzhou villages was a well-educated lady officer. She informed me that her college education was interrupted in 1970 because of the Cultural Revolution campaign by Chairman Mao to cleanse China's administration of "Elitism and capitalist infiltration". Her college was closed and the lecturers were sent to communes to work in the fields to learn the dignity of labour. Some of the actions of the mostly teen-age Red Guards were amusing. For instance, she told me that in Hangzhou which was a beautiful all-green, lake town with wide roads, the Red Guards changed the traffic rules to make RED for GO because Red is a noble colour of revolution and progress and GREEN for STOP. When this caused utter chaos and a large number of accidents, they reverted to the old system! The Red Guards were constantly displaying the Little Red Book of Mao's Thoughts. Later, when I visited Shanghai I also bought a copy of Mao's Thoughts in English translation and the blue Mao Jacket. (Incidentally, the *'The Thoughts of Mao'* in Chinese is the largest printed book in the world and the Holy Bible in all languages the second and, surprisingly, the Communist Manifesto the third.) The blue tunic of Mao Jacket, blue pants, blue cap and canvas shoe was the uniform of the entire country from leaders to peasants. The Little Red Book was quite interesting as it contained Mao's views on many matters such as, *Learn from the Masses before teaching them* and *Build on the Weak.* The sight of all farmers, both men and women, wearing blue tunic, cap and shoes was quite impressive to me who was accustomed to see farmers in my districts wearing torn clothes and going barefoot. One reason was, in the temperate climate of China all have to cover their bodies fully.

The Deputy Director who took me to the sericulture villages also introduced to me a 'Barefoot Doctor' (*chìjiǎo yīshēng*) who happened to be visiting the same village when I was there. She explained to me that the term 'bare foot' had a special significance in Chinese history. Traditionally, the peasants did not wear any footwear as they had to work in muddy paddy fields and the term 'barefoot' came to be derogatory akin to poor "country cousins" in English and *sans culottes—* 'Without Breeches' in French for commoners. Mao deliberately chose this term in 1965 when young farmers from villages (both men and women) who had passed secondary school examination were chosen and given 6 months training in hospitals in identifying and diagnosing common diseases and administering vaccinations and traditional acupuncture and advise preventive and hygienic practices. Mao had set a target of one barefoot doctor for every 1,000 persons and by 1980 there were close to one million such 'Barefoot' doctors. As they were living in the villages and doing part time farming, there was trust between them and the villagers. They referred patients with major complaints to bigger hospitals. It was a successful Rural Health Programme and in 1978 the WHO in its Alma Ata (Kazakhstan) Declaration recommended it to all developing countries. In 1985 when China became more prosperous and with many doctors qualified in Western Medicine, the barefoot doctors were given opportunty to join medical schools and get proper training and become Village Doctors. Due to the Barefoot doctor system, and the availability of better food and higher protein content in pork, fish and vegetables and extensive bicycling, the general health of the Chinese improved greatly. This is reflected, not in the least, in the number of Olympic medals China gets, next only to the US.

I visited a local primary school and saw the children to be very healthy and lively. The head-mistress explained to me the principle in education policy which teachers followed thus: The Communist government from 1949 followed the principle of *"Building on the Weak"* which meant, the teacher should concentrate on the poorly performing students so that the *average* for the class can be lifted up. This was in contrast to many countries such as Japan, South Korea and even India was following namely, encouraging the smarter children more so that they can perform highly in examination and the reputation of the school would go up. The Chinese leaders' view was, the smart children would perform better in any case and it is the weakest who require the attention of the teacher. This was reflected in their entire education system till 1990s when they concentrated in improving the primary school system both in attendance and quality without starting too many higher education and specialized educational institutions. I felt that China built a strong foundation while India went for a specialized super-structure for the benefit of upper middle class and the rich with a weak foundation.

I continued my train journey from the lake city of Hangzhou to the biggest, old city of Shanghai which was the Textile capital of China. Shanghai and Hong Kong were the earliest maritime cities the West came into contact with in China. Unlike India, China was never colonized by the West. Even after the West won three Opium Wars by 1856, the Chinese Emperor as advised by his powerful Mandarin civil servants, allowed the Western powers to trade only in the specified 80 Port Cities and five Leased Territories including Hong Kong. This is unlike India where the Moghul Emperor Jahangir allowed the European East India Companies to extend their activities to the interior of the country and allowing them taking sides with Princely States, one against the other.

The Silk Road travelled by Marco Polo from Venice to Dadu (today's Beijing) which was a camel route, was made safe by Genghiz Khan's grandson Kublai Khan, who was China's only foreign ruler and his Yuan dynasty ruled China till 1368. After that only Japan invaded China in 1930s. After Vasco da Gama's discovery of sea route via Cape of Good Hope to India in 1498, in early 17th Century the four East India Companies of the Dutch, Portuguese, French and the British came to South East Asia with their state-supported Mercantilist imperialist trade (*'with a Bible on one hand and a Sword on the other, to save the heathens and a divine justification for pillage'!),* in search of spices, silk, gemstones, tea, porcelain and saltpetre for explosives. Of these, China produced everything except spices which was produced by India and the Indonesian Archipelago. However, successive Chinese Emperors (as also the Emperor of Japan) did not allow the Europeans to penetrate into the interior country to carry on trading and proselytization. The European traders were confined to major ports such as Shanghai, Hong Kong and Canton (Guangzhou). However, in an important sense, it was India which contributed to the fall of China to Western domination. After the Moghul Emperor Jahangir gave permission in 1612 to Sir Thomas Roe, the Ambassador sent by King James I of England to India for trading without paying customs duties, the East India Company, popularly known as John Company established its "Factories" (Warehouses) in 23 towns in India including Surat, Madras, Bombay and Calcutta. In China, in 1757—the same year as the Battle of Palashi when Clive virtually established the British Empire in India—the Qing dynasty Emperor of China, on the advice of his Mandarin Scholar-Bureaucrats of the Imperial Service, issued a decree making all the ports in China except Canton out of bounds for the foreign Companies. In Canton 13 places were earmarked for the East India Companies to bring their goods and export Chinese goods. This was called the Canton System. But, for a long time, the foreigners were confined to their ships at the Canton port and small *Sampans* had to bring the imported goods from the ships to Canton city and, for exporting, local Chinese merchants had to be engaged to take Chinese goods to the waiting ships. Even when the foreigners were allowed to physically come to the permitted 13 warehouses they could stay only for six months in Canton and could not travel beyond Canton town.

The John Company was the first to take drastic steps to bring China under its domination. Opium was in demand by Chinese aristocrats and the rich. So, the Company organized cultivation of *Poppy* in Bengal Province (today's West Bengal, Bangladesh, Bihar, eastern UP and Odisha—their combined population in 2018 being 401 million, the third biggest 'country' in the world after China and India!) by its compulsory cultivation by farmers licenced by the Company and monopoly procurement of the latex from poppy flowers to produce opium. To increase the cultivation of Poppy, the Company which had the *'Dhiwani'* in Bengal imposed a 50% tax on paddy cultivation which reduced the availability of rice resulting in the Great Bengal Famine of 1770 in which an estimated 10 million people died of starvation. *[This atrocity would be repeated in 1943 when 4 million Indians died of starvation because of the decision of the 'War Hero' Winston Churchill to divert food-grain ships to Europe. ('Churchill's Secret War', by Madhusree Mukerjee, 2010.) He would have qualified as a War Criminal according to the 1949 Geneva Convention.]*

Surprisingly, the justification for the First Opium War (there were three Opium Wars) in 1858 ending in the Treaty of Tianjin under which China had to agree to 23 more concessions, including war reparation of 300 tons of silver, the principle of 'Extra-Territoriality' namely, non-application of Chinese laws to foreign companies and merchants but only their own foreign laws in Chinese territory, freedom for Western Missionaries to propagate Christianity in China and the full legalization of sale of opium throughout China! All this was justified by Britain and its allies USA, France, Holland and Russia on the principle of Free Trade and Open Market even attributing it to Adam Smith's *Laissez Faire* doctrine. On this precedent, Colombia today, if it had the military power, should export narcotics to the USA and Europe! Sardar KM Panikkar's *'Asia and Western Dominance'* (1953) admirably analyses the history of how England and other European countries treated Asian countries and the double standards they followed in their own countries and in Asia.

I visited a silk weaving factory in Shanghai. The factories in China were huge. The Managing Director described it 'middle size' with 20,000 workers and situated in about 25 acres. There were 8,000 silk looms (in contrast, the Govt. Silk Weaving Factory in Mysore had 150 looms.) Earlier, in Hangzhou I had visited Reeling Filatures which were also very large. These were all having "automatic reeling" which means the thickness of the yarn is maintained to a uniform 20/22 denier (that is, 9,000 meters of yarn has a weight of 20 to 22 grams) by a device called Denier Controller while in Karnataka the reeler manually feeds a uniform number of about 10 cocoons continuously to maintain the standard thickness of the yarn which is not a 100% accurate method to obtain uniform thickness. As a result, China produces about 143,000 tons of 2A quality of raw silk yarn annually while India is a distant second with about 13,000 tons of the last 'H' grade yarn which can be used only in Indian handlooms. Though the silk filatures in China were fitted with automatic machines, there were still a large number of workers, especially women, to sort the cocoons into batches of uniform sizes and the labour discipline was exemplary with one supervisor for every 20 workers continuously walking up and down the aisle behind the workers.

I found a similar workers discipline in the silk weaving factory in Shanghai. Silk looms were not fully made automatic, not as fast as in polyester air looms and therefore there was one worker, usually a woman, for each loom. The MD took me around the looms on which fine silk fabrics were being woven. While he was explaining, I noticed that the lady worker's eyes never left the loom and never once did she glance in our direction even though darkish Indians were very rare visitors. Another thing I noticed was, as the MD and I were walking along on the aisles of the factory, no worker followed us as in India where a small delegation of workers would follow the MD with 'instant' petitions! I also found each worker was having a bowl of rice and fish close to her loom and some of them were also eating while working. When I asked, does it not affect production or quality the MD said, on the contrary it improves production because the worker need not walk three times to the canteen in a shift of 8 hours by which one hour was saved. Allowing her to bring her bowl to her loom saves her the walk and the time for the factory. Wages were on piece-rate and subject to quality standards. There were three canteens within the factory premises which also I visited. Alcoholic drinks were not served but there was ample sticky rice, fish and vegetables and the ubiquitous hot tea in flasks which was free. The Chinese tea is not like anything we have in India but tea leaves in permanently hot water without any milk or sugar and therefore very healthy. In the hotel room there was a big tea flask. When we were coming out of the factory, I also noticed that the loudspeaker was constantly blaring something. I asked the MD what was being said. He explained that the announcement was the names of the workers who had produced less than the standard minimum the earlier day. He said this was very effective because in Chinese tradition one's name being announced in public for being laggard amounts to loss of face which was quite a humiliation and such workers would increase their production next day to avoid being announced on the public loudspeaker.

Being the textile centre, I bought a Mao Jacket used by all Chinese from leaders to farmers for ¥ 100, about Rs 800 then. In Chinese it was called *Zhongshan* jacket which was originally popularized by Sun Yat Sen who is still considered as the Father of the Nation. China became a Republic when the last Emperor of Qing dynasty abdicated in 1912 in the anti-monarchical revolution by Sun Yat Sen. His uniform, *Zhongshan,* later came to be called the Mao jacket. Till the 1950s cotton was the main fabric in China. But later polyester and polyester-cotton mix cloth became the norm. In India there was tight control for import and licensing of polymers for indigenous production of Polyester fibre which was first developed by DuPont in the US who produced the Terylene and Dacron which came to be described the Miracle Fiber as the clothes made of Terylene did not require ironing for 58 days, it was claimed. Because of manufacturing restrictions in India, firms like Reliance of Dhirubhai Ambani, the Birlas and the Bombay Dyeing became big industrial houses by manipulating state machinery with Licence-Permit Raj for importing polymers and restrictions on production of the polyester fibre and cloth. But China became the largest producer of man-made fibres and durable cloth and Shanghai was its Textile capital by 1980's.

INDIAN AND CHINESE ATTITUDES

The Chinese values throughout its 2,500 years history was influenced by the teachings of *Kong Fuzhi* meaning Master Kong, his Latinized name being "Confucius" coined in the late 16th century by the early Portuguese Jesuit missionaries. He lived in the 6th century BCE.

His teachings were moral principles consisting of the "five bonds"—relations between ruler and subject, father and son, husband and wife, older and younger brother, friend and friend. The first four "bonds" are hierarchical; the fifth deals with relations between equals. These values are secular and Max Weber called them "inner-worldly" while most other religions were preaching about "other-worldliness" of sins, redemption, heaven and hell. The ideal was the Confucian gentleman, who looked down on the false comforts of religion and faced life with an attitude of stoicism. Confucius also created the notion of the "mandate of heaven": The Emperor has his "mandate", the basis of his legitimacy only if he rules in accordance with the moral rules governing relations between him and his subjects. If he does not so rule justly, the "mandate of heaven" will be withdrawn, his rule becomes illegitimate and his subjects have a valid reason to disobey or even overthrow him. Once, when the stables were burnt down, on returning from court, Confucius said, *"Was anyone hurt?"* He did not ask about the damage. He did not attach much importance to property damage as he did about the health of people. When a disciple asked: "Is there any one word that could guide a person throughout life?" the Master replied: "How about 'reciprocity'! Never impose on others what you would not choose for yourself." He considered the idea and action of reciprocity more important than action done out of self-interest.

Confucius did not believe in the concept of "democracy", which was an Athenian concept unknown in ancient China as also in India. He expressed fears that the masses lacked the intellect to make decisions for themselves, and that, in his view, since not everyone is created equal, not everyone has a right of self-government. In substance, Confucius taught about the importance of the family and social harmony, loyalty to Emperor, filial loyalty to elders in the family and loyalty to peers rather than about God or an otherworldly source of spiritual values. The core of Confucianism was humanistic and rested upon the belief that human beings are fundamentally good, and teachable, improvable, and perfectible through personal and communal endeavour, especially self-cultivation and self-creation. It does not advocate knowledge of *sutras* and ritual purity, iron-clad caste system, inequality by birth, untouchability, pollution, purification by donating cows to Brahmins, *karma*, a son to ensure heaven, etc. It favours direct understanding through meditation and interaction with an accomplished teacher. It follows from the Buddha's *Sorrowful Three Visions—Old Age, Illness and Death* and the role of Monks to help people in such crises. In ancient China Buddhist monks had a virtual monopoly in the conducting of funerals. This was because, if a loved person had just died, he would like to hear a Buddhist Monk's consoling words rather than the Confucian prescriptions on proper relations between the dead and the living!

Mao died in 1976 at the age of 83 and Zou Enlai a few months before. With the death of Mao Cultural Revolution was reversed and Deng rose to power. With that Confucius was also resurrected. In other words, Mao died but Confucius lived. Since then China has established Confucius Institutes all over the world on the model of Portugal's Instituto Camões, Britain's British Council, France's Alliance Française, Italy's Società Dante Alighieri, Spain's Instituto Cervantes and Germany's Goethe-Institut. There are nearly 1,000 Confucius Institutes in 150 countries including 90 in the USA and 4 in India even. Surprisingly, India with its rich cultural heritage has not created any such institution. Probably no country will buy the idea of caste from us! Shrewdly, China did not include Party propaganda material but confined to teaching Confucian thoughts and learning of Chinese language in their 1,200 class rooms through which about 9 million students have passed through. Surprisingly, China hosts the second largest number of foreign students, a little more than 5 lakhs which is growing at 11% annually, while USA is the most popular destination for foreign students with 1.2 million. There are even over 30,000 Indian students in China. Strategically, China had named it Confucius Institute instead of China Institute let alone Mao Institute! There was another political reason for the resurrection of Confucius. After Deng's economic liberalization from 1980, the Communist Party and bureaucracy became increasingly corrupt which led to the Tiananmen Square Protests set off by the death of pro-reform Communist general secretary Hu Yaobang in April 1989, in which about 3,000, mostly students, died. Also, slowly but steadily China's real GDP started growing at 8% annually because of which many persons were becoming rich using unscrupulous means. Hence, the need for resurrecting Confucius who had said that people must lead a virtuous life within their means and must be loyal to their family elders and to the Emperor, was obvious, while Mao was inciting young people to rebel. But the Chinese Communist Party did not give up Mao either after economic progress. In fact Deng, the architect of New Economic Policy had famously said, *'Mao was 70% right and 30% wrong!'* In a typical Chinese method of Harmony and Synthesis, Mao's teachings were also intensified along with Confucian Values of Loyalty. So, since 1990 China is an amalgam of both Confucianism and Maoism, taking the common elements of both.

During my CSB tenure, I also travelled in Vietnam, Thailand, Malaysia, Bangladesh, Uzbekistan, Azerbaizan, Russia, France, Italy, Germany, Holland, Greece and UK, all relating to silk. I had the rare opportunity of observing not just sericulture in these countries but also their culture and history. In fact, the revival of Belt and Road Initiative of Xi Jinping with a mind-boggling estimated investment of US$ 8 trillion in infrastructure projects in 142 countries by 2040 is bound to replace the US as the dominant economic power and its influence over World financial institutions.

I LEAVE CSB AFTER FOUR FRUITFUL YEARS

Soon after my negotiating the National Sericulture Project in 1990 I left the Central Silk Board. But, before I left the CSB there was one more significant task I was successful at. Though the CSB's headquarters was at Bombay till 1967, one year before I joined CSB in 1985 there were rumblings that it may be shifted either to Delhi or, intriguingly to Patna! While the other Commodity Boards for Coffee, Tea, Tobacco, Rubber, etc. had their own established own buildings housing their headquarters offices, the CSB was functioning from a rented building in Mahatma Gandhi Road in Bangalore. In Government March is a crucial month, being the end of the financial year, when the budget allocations for each department will have to be spent and the unspent amount will 'lapse'. For a statutory, autonomous organization like the CSB this will not apply as it was not a 'department' but an 'attached office' to the Ministry. Every Ministry in Government of India has an Internal Finance Adviser and Krishnamurthy of Indian Audit & Accounts Service, from Tamil Nadu who was settled in Delhi was the IFA for Textiles Ministry and I had become friendly with him. So, I ascertained from him in early March that in the other wings of Textile Ministry such as Handlooms, Handicrafts, Fashion Technology, Special Programmes for Bihar and UP, etc., there was unspent funds of about Rs 2.5 crores. I worked on Krishnamurthy that if that amount is given to the CSB instead of being allowed to lapse to no one's advantage, I could use it for construction of a suitable building which will benefit CSB in Bangalore as we had already secured 9 acres of land from the Bangalore Development Authority on the Bangalore-Hosur National Highway which was just about eight kilometres from MG Road. Krishnamurthy was sympathetic to my idea but told me that the Planning Commission also should agree as both Handicrafts and Handlooms were important sectors nationally and diverting funds from them may attract political criticism. The Adviser in the Planning Commission dealing with Textiles was RS Rao who was from Karnataka but settled in Delhi. Following the methodology of GVK of meeting different officers in different departments and keeping them in good humour, I used to meet Rao in Planning Commission whenever I had gone to Delhi and I had good relations with him. Also, I had met the Member of Planning

Commission dealing with Textiles, Abid Hussain IAS of Andhra Pradesh cadre who was fifteen years senior to me. I found him to be a delightful person. He knew about the big World Bank funded National Sericulture Project and I had earlier invited him to visit Bangalore and Mysore to see the various advantages of sericulture and he came to Bangalore and was duly impressed. This also helped. So, I met RS Rao and persuaded him to recommend to Abid Hussain that if there is any fund getting lapsed within the Departments of Textile Ministry, it can be transferred to the CSB. Long story short, CSB received Rs 2.5 crore from the Ministry by the middle of March which had no precedent.

Rail India Technical & Economic Services (RITES), a government company, was good enough to prepare a plan and estimate within two weeks and on 29th of March I deposited an amount of Rs 3 crores, including Rs 50 lakhs of CSB's own funds with the RITES for the construction of the CSB's Headquarters. Thus, my initiative in getting the additional funds ensured the continuance of the CSB in Bangalore once and for all. The "Silk Board" building became a land mark for Bangalore, especially in traffic bulletins it was always referred as 'Traffic jam at Silk Board Junction'! In the 9 acres of land not only the CSB headquarters and the Silk Technological Institute but also some hostel facilities for trainees and staff quarters were built. So, I can legitimately take pride in taking action to ensure the retention of CSB in Bangalore because of my getting support from Abid Hussain, RS Rao and Krihnamurthy the IFA of Textiles Ministry and RL Misra, Textile Secretary.

A footnote: When the grand new CSB-building complex was completed in two years by RITES and inaugurated, the Member-Secretary of CSB, an IAS officer of Karnataka cadre, junior to me and who succeeded me, 'forgot' to send me an invitation to attend the function though I was very much in Bangalore! Many scientists of CSB told me that in meetings he used to criticize the National Sericulture Project as being lopsided and inadequate, which I was instrumental to get through as the first and only time in CSB's history! I can never forget the Indian Ambassador Avatar Singh's pithy statement, 'Two Japanese means One Plus One. Two Indians mean One Minus One!'

❖❖❖

CHAPTER 18

The Fall from Grace:
A Kaleidoscope of Chief Ministers of Karnataka

After 1956, Karnataka had 20 Chief Ministers in 64 years with an average tenure of three years by each CM. Excluding the comparatively long tenure of 16 years of Nijalingappa and Devaraj Urs (8 years each), the average tenure of 18 CMs is just 2½ years. Besides Nijalingappa and Devaraj Urs only SM Krishna and Siddaramaiah were CMs for five years each and the other 16 were CMs for less than 2½ years. This is in contrast to the neighbouring Tamil Nadu which from 1956 to 2020 had just 7 CMs in 64 years giving an average of nine years each. Of these seven CMs, Karunanidhi was CM for 20 years in four terms and Jayalilitha for 14 years and MG Ramachandran for 10 years and Kamaraj for 9 years. Interestingly, after 1967 for 53 years in a row it is the two Dravidian parties of DMK and AIADMK which have been in power without interruption. The other important point is, apart from the comparative stable government for sustained long periods, after 1967 whichever of the two Dravidian parties was in power, they had supported the ruling party in the centre getting them benefits of sharing power in return. Karunadhi could even insist on specific lucrative portfolios to his party such as Transport for TN Baalu and Telecommunications to Andimuthu Raja. In contrast, most of the time the ruling party in Karnataka was in opposition to the ruling party in the centre denying central support.

VEERENDRA PATIL—A GENTLEMAN, BUT A STAUNCH LINGAYAT

When I reported as IAS probationer at Bangalore from the Academy at Mussoorie in 1966, it was Nijalingappa who was the CM. His Secretary S Varadan, more than ten years my senior, took us to the CM's chambers for a pep-talk. I found him to be a jolly, roly-poly 65-year old smiling Buddha who indulged in polite conversation with each of us. But CMs are consummate actors. He was a wily politician belonging to Lingayat community from Davanagere district. After the retirement of Kamaraj as the Congress President, in the power struggle between Indira Gandhi and the right-wing Syndicate, Nijalingappa was made the

Congress President. He relinquished his Chief Ministership and his protégé, the 44-year old Veerendra Patil was made the CM in preference to BD Jatti, also a veteran Lingayat leader from Bijapur who would later become the Vice President of India. It was during my first posting as Assistant Commissioner & Sub Divisional Magistrate of Lingsugur in 1968 that I came across Verendra Patil. As mentioned, I had attached the tractors of his cabinet minister, Basavarajeswari, a Lingayat and his great supporter but the CM did not transfer me. Heeding to the advice of Chief Secretary Naryanaswamy that it would send a wrong message to the civil service, I was sent for a one-month's training course to the National Institute of Community Development to cool things down. I am narrating this again because such a benign treatment of a junior bureaucrat by the CM is unthinkable today when very senior officers are shunted out by the CM on trivial, motivated, personal complaints of MLAs. Not only in my case but in general Veerendra Patil's reputation was that he was very careful not to do any injustice to any officer. This might have been also due to the tradition in Nizam's Hyderabad administration where officers were highly respected.

The next time I came into contact with Veerendra Patil was when I was appointed as the DC and DM of Gulbarga in 1972 to deal with the acute famine situation. He was in opposition then, having lost power to Devaraj Urs. As the famine intensified there were many occasions when Veerendra Patil would lead delegations to my office with many demands. On all these occasions, he would be very polite, extending due deference to the office of the DC&DM and not having the air of a former CM and Opposition Leader. One particular instance is worth mentioning. When the local Congress MP, Dharma Rao Afzalpurkar had died, I had to conduct the by-election which was happening at the end of a series of five Assembly by-elections in the State which the Congress had lost. Therefore it was a highly prestigious contest for both Devaraj Urs and Veerendra Patil and Gulbarga being the native place of the latter, it was fought bitterly. Yet, he behaved as a responsible Opposition Leader and did not indulge in petty politics and violence to garner support for his candidate. Congress won handsomely because of relief works, I flattered myself, but it was mainly due to the *Gharibi Hatao* slogan, though empty, of Mrs Gandhi.

The next time I had come in close contact with Veerendra Patil was when he was Chief Minister and also the ex-officio Chairman of the Karnataka Power Corporation. After his first stint as CM from 1968-1971, he became CM again in 1989 when Congress won in Karnataka State with 178 seats out of 224 due to Janata Party misrule, while

Congress lost in the centre with only 197 MPs out of 525 seats and VP Singh became the PM replacing Rajiv Gandhi. I was then working in Delhi as Joint Secretary in the Ministry of Textiles, after my 4-year stint in the Central Silk Board. In his very first visit to Delhi to call on VP Singh the PM, Veerendra Patil invited all the IAS and IPS officers from Karnataka cadre working in Delhi for a dinner in the Karnataka Bhavan. PP Prabhu who was one year senior to me was the newly appointed Secretary to CM holding concurrently his erstwhile post as Managing Director of the Karnataka Power Corporation. Prabhu was an ebullient, cheerful officer always smiling and busy. The first words he would utter when he came to your room would be, *I have no time, I have to leave now!* He was also Veerendra Patil's Private Secretary when he was Minister for Shipping and Surface Transport earlier and he would be very open and even blunt with the Minister. I knew of one instance. Gundu Rao in Karnataka as CM was no admirer of Veerendra Patil. Because of his bull-in-the-China-shop manners Gundu Rao's stock with the national press was quite low. So, to boost his image, his Coorgi friend and benefactor FM ('Field Marshal') Khan—*Father Mother Khan* to Gundu Rao—had arranged a sumptuous Mysore breakfast for MJ Akbar, the Editor of the then popular *Sunday* magazine at the government Kumara Krupa guest house. The impetuous Gundu Rao boasted to Akbar that he was so popular with the Congress High Command that it would take him only "22 hours" to get rid of Veerendra Patil from state politics. When Akbar wondered whether it was "24 hours?" Gundu Rao re-affirmed, *No, only 22 hours!* When this was duly reported in *Sunday,* Veerendra Patil was angry and asked Prabhu to draft a rejoinder. But Prabhu firmly told his minister to ignore it totally so that people would correctly understand the worth of Gundu Rao and the minister. Verendra Patil followed Prabhu's advice and in retrospect it was the correct decision.

The dinner of Veerendra Patil as CM with Delhi-based Karnataka cadre officers was Prabhu's idea. It was very well-attended. Since Veerendra Patil had known me well, he took me aside along with Prabhu and asked me whether I would like to come back to Karnataka. I told him I still had about three months tenure left in Delhi but would not mind to return prematurely. He asked Prabhu to put up a letter from him to the PM. Accordingly, the letter was sent and he also followed it up with a phone call to VP Singh. Thus the order for my repatriation to the State was issued within a week and I returned to Bangalore. Prabhu told me there was the post of MD, Karnataka Power Corporation immediately available which he was still holding as additional charge. I also knew that the KPC was a unique government company which was formed when GVK was Development Commissioner and I was his Deputy when the distribution of electricity by the Karnataka Electricity Board was separated from generation to be exclusively done by the new KPC which no other state had done. GVK's reason was, generation required large investment with bank loans while the Balance Sheets of State Electricity Boards were showing large accumulated losses, making borrowing from nationalized Banks even with State Guarantee difficult for them. On the other hand, if only generation is done by a separate company, that company could sell the generated energy to the KEB on a Cost-plus basis which would make the KPC a financially viable company with net profit and with its good Balance Sheet banks would give loans readily. The KPC was formed in 1970 by the initiative of GVK when Veerendra Patil was the CM in his first term and Ramakrishna Hegde was his Finance Minister. (Nurtured by Nijalingappa, the two used to be called *Lava-Kusha* in Karnataka administration.) PR Nayak who was eleven years senior to me and working in New York as the Director of Indian Investment Centre, was brought back by GVK to form the KPC and he was the founder-MD of KPC in its first five formative years. With his far-reaching vision he had organized the KPC as an ideal infrastructure-building corporation. He saw to it that the CM was the ex-officio Chairman of KPC so that no small time politician would head it nor would there be any scope for political interference with the MD from MLAs. It was a government company unlike any and engaged in a crucial infra-structure building work in a power-scarce economy. Stalwarts like Varadan and AMR Moses were its MDs before Prabhu. In 1989 it had an installed capacity of 3,500 MW of Power. So, I was happy to head KPC. It was an exciting job with a huge investment of about Rs 900 crores with the Yen loan from the Overseas Economic Cooperation Fund of Japan in constructing the third and fourth units of the Raichur Thermal Electric Plant with 440 MW. I was quite flattered in being asked, for the first and last time, to choose my posting! At all other times, I would learn of my posting from the 'Official Notifications' column in the newspaper!

I received full cooperation from the CM as Chairman in managing the KPC. I would mention one important episode. For all his progressive administration, favouritism in appointment of Lingayats was the Achilles Heel of Veerendra Patil. It is the curse of Karnataka administration that in 67 years from 1952 to 2019 Karnataka had Chief Ministers from Lingayat community for 25 years and Okkaliga CMs for 15 years the only significant breaks being the 8 years of Devaraj Urs rule, 7 years of Brahmin rule by Gundu Rao and Ramakrishna Hegde and 5 years of Siddarmaiah who was from Kuruba community. Whenever the two major community CMs were at the helm, their community officers had a clear edge in postings. But, with the merit oriented tradition established by PR Nayak, KPC was free of communal politics within the organization. But during my stint in 1990 there came a test to it. The Finance Director of KPC was an important post as any file you touch there would be for not less than a Rs 100 crore contract. So, it was always an Accountant General from Centre on deputation to KPC as its Finance Director. In early 1990 the then Finance Director, one Acharya, an upright Accountant General was retiring and I was in search of a good AG to replace him. I called on the Comptroller & Auditor General of India CG Somiah, who was from Coorg, and requested him for posting an AG with commercial audit background as Finance Director to the KPC. He was good enough to promise he will help. However, there was a Chief Accountant in KPC, one Aradhya who was from the upper crust of Lingayat community and he had decided that he should be the Finance Director breaking the tradition of having an AG on deputation. The only problem was, his hands were greasy. Acharya the retiring Finance Director had told me that as the Committee Chairman of Employees' Provident Fund, Aradhya had invested all the considerable Employees' Provident Fund in just one branch of Syndicate Bank. There was also an audit para against him in the AG's Report and I had even initiated a Departmental Enquiry into it. Inspite of this, Aradhya was able to mobilize the support of 15 Lingayat MLAs of all parties who had gone in a delegation to Veerendra Patil recommending Aradhya. Even a Swamiji of a famous Lingayat Mutt, who had no business to intervene in temporal matters, had sponsored his name! The god-fearing Acharya was horrified by the effrontery of his subordinate and the political support he could manage but there was nothing he could do.

I first explained the seriousness of the matter to Prabhu who as my predecessor had also known about Aradhya. He agreed with me but said what could he do when 15 Lingayat MLAs and a Swamiji to boot also put pressure on the CM. So I asked him could I brief the CM? He told me to try my luck. So, I went to see the CM and was surprised to find him reading newspaper in his office without any visitors which was of the rarest of rare sights. I had seen Devaraj Urs having some 60-70 people in his chambers, 10 in his ante-room and even 4 or 5 in his toilet! It was indeed strange for any CM to be free of favour-seekers. But that was Veerendra Patil, especially in his second term when he did not encourage MLAs to come to him for favours and would ask them to go and see the concerned departmental ministers. He also had a very strict, orthodox, old-school Finance Minister in Rajasekhara Murthy who was even senior to Veerendra Patil and a very important Lingayat Leader from Mysore who would not hesitate to tell any MLA to behave. I had met him a few times regarding KPC's OECF loan proposal and was greatly impressed by his ethical approach. But, even he supported Aradhya. So, I explained to the CM in great detail the tradition in KPC and the background and reputation of Aradhya. Above all, when KPC was negotiating a large loan from Japan, the role of Finance Director was crucial and the Japanese have a great respect for senior bureaucrats, especially from central government such as Accountant General being on the Board of KPC. *[I even explained to him, much to his amusement, the practice in Japanese Corporations called "Amakudari" (Descent from Heaven), the induction of retired bureaucrats as Directors on their Boards as goodwill bridge between Government and Industry.)* Above all, I informed the CM, I had initiated a departmental enquiry against Aradhya and it would be highly embarrassing to have the object of enquiry being the Finance Director of the company. The CM heard me silently for over half hour. Then he finally said cryptically, *OK, if that is the case we can get another AG from Government of India*. I told him that I had already met the CAG informally and he was likely to send the name of Mrs Anasuya Basu IA&AS who was the wife of Gautam Basu IAS of Karnataka cadre who had worked with me in Bangalore district and we could approve it. He agreed but requested me to wait for the announcement of her posting to KPC till the end of the Assembly session for two weeks so that after that the MLAs would be away from Bangalore and they would not come in a group and pester him about Aradhya. This was indeed very objective of Veerendra Patil in the background of a large number of his community MLAs and a highly earth-bound, even sub-soil, Swamiji sponsoring Aradhya. Such a thing would not happen under any other CM. The crestfallen Aradhya became the butt of KPC employees' joke when the new Finance Director took charge.

There was one more episode during the period I was MD of KPC and Veerendra Patil its Chairman in which I was involved. This was during the rise of Naxalite movement in India after its suppression since the 1970s. After it was launched in Naxalbari in West Bengal in 1967, Mrs Gandhi's government passed the Unlawful Activities (Prevention) Act in 1969 and it was used ruthlessly by the Indian Army in that state during the President's rule in 1970-1971. It was termed "Operation Steeplechase" and implemented by Lt General JFR Jacob and Union Home Secretary Govind Narain with instructions "there should be no publicity and no records" and Jacob's request to give the orders in writing was also denied by Sam Manekshaw. Hundreds of young college students were killed and terms such as "Police Encounters", "Shot while

Escaping" became common in police vernacular and about 20,000
Naxalite cadres, leaders and suspects were imprisoned. However, the
suppression in West Bengal gave rise to the movement going
underground and dispersed in many states and a "Red Corridor" of over
100 districts out of the then 320 districts of India, from Purnea in Bihar-
Nepal border to Kannanur in Kerala were in that Corridor. In
Karnataka, two taluks namely, Chincholi in Gulbarga bordering
Telengana and Pavagada in Tumkar district also bordering AP were
identified as places with intensifying Naxalite activities. So, one day the
CM sent for me and I found the Chief Secretary, DGP and the Home
Secretary with him. There was also a DIG who was introduced to me as
heading a Task Force for control of Naxalitism in Karnataka. The Home
Secretary explained that Chincholi being the remotest taluk bordering
Telengana in the State (which I already knew as DC of Gulbarga, and it
was also the native taluk of Veerendra Patil), the Naxal cadres were
active in the big and remotest area of Konchavaram Panchayat.
Similarly, in Tumkur district which was bordering Bangalore district, the
Telugu speaking pocket of Pavagada which was like a 'land island'
surrounded on all sides by Ananthapur district of Andhra Pradesh was
also active with Naxalaties. The CM told me he wanted me to go to
these two places and give a factual report and what measures should be
taken to bring the rebellious people into mainstream.

I was a little baffled because firstly, as MD of KPC I had nothing to
do with the Naxalite problem and secondly I would be treading on the
toes of the district administration. I expressed these to the CM but he
said that the Chief Secretary had already spoken to the DC and SP
concerned and they would extend all cooperation to me. When I further
raised a doubt, instead of a bureaucrat would not an elder politician
acceptable to all parties and local people be more appropriate to report
on the situation, the CM said that since I knew Gulbarga well and also
Tumkur-Anantapur districts because of my stint in Sericulture, I was
chosen in consultation with the Chief Secretary. The CS
Sankaranarayanan told me that my visit would of course be treated as
confidential and I should keep away from the Press and said I should
attend to this work immediately. I told him that I would make two visits
and that I would not require any police assistance as that would be a red
rag. I knew Konchavaram well from my three years as the 'Famine DC'
of Gulbarga. Thus I went to Konchawaram. The Panchayat Chairman
and members had arranged a meeting in the Town Panchayat Office. To
my delight I found the Chairman and some members who had known
me from my DC days were still there and they were happy to receive me.
I had a very frank discussion with them. From my long discussion with

them and other villagers, the village teacher and some Lambani workers for two days I had a good idea of what was happening.

This is what I learnt from them: Though Gulbarga district was arid, the Konchavaram area had a forest with a surprising 40% canopy. In the rainforests of Amazon and Malaysia where sunlight does not reach the forest floor, the canopy is 100%. Konchavaram area which was the eastern-most portion of the district protruding into Telengana had an annual normal rainfall of about 900mm just like Bangalore which explained the growth of about 30,000 acres of semi-deciduous forest and the construction of Chandrampalli Dam which again increased the ground water level. There were 1,500 landless families who were cultivating small pieces of land which was officially forest land. There were also 10 Lambani *thandas* (hamlets) which were dependent upon the forest produce and small animals like wild pigs and rabbits. The forest had hyenas, Indian wolf and even panthers. They told me, since recently the forest department officials had increased harassment of the landless people living in forest and the Lambanis collecting forest produce such as honey, fallen tree-branches and hunting small animals. While the minimum wage notified for agricultural labour was Rs 8 per day, the actual payment was just Rs 5 for men and Rs 3 for women. The practice of *'Sambala'* which was bonded labour of young boys on annual payment of 5 bags of jowar from Ugadi to Ugadi and a pair of new clothes was very common. There were also complaints that young Lambani girls many of whom had features of their Afghan-Rajasthani origin, were being harassed by officials. Because of this rampant exploitation, both by landlords and government officials for the past one year, some educated youth from Hyderabad and also from the Sharana Basavesvara College of Gulbarga had been visiting Konchavaram and educating them of their rights and organizing them against government though there has been no violence yet. After spending two days in Konchavaram and another day in Gulbarga for discussions with Revenue, Police, Forest, Labour and Social Welfare Departments, I got a good idea of the "Naxalite Problem" of Konchavaram and returned to Bangalore.

My next visit was to Pavagaga to reach which I had to go through the historic Lepakshi town and Anantapur in Andhra Pradesh by road. I found the exploitation here was worse with matching resistance and violence. Many of the Panchayat members and youth told me of one Muthyal Naik who was from the neighbouring Madaksira taluk in Anantapur district of AP who was organizing the landless agriculture labour to boycott the landlords who were not paying the minimum wages. Just a few days ago, during early hours, a group of people all wearing white dress from head to toe to make identification difficult, had forcibly entered the house of the biggest landlord belonging to Reddy community and compelled him at gun point to pay the arrears of minimum wages to the labourers. Mr Reddy the landlord told me that Muthyal Naik had led the group of about 30 persons and he had a pistol with him. The local police had registered a case against 30 persons even though the landlord could not identify any of them except Muthyal Naik. The most interesting thing I noted was that here also the agricultural labourers belonged to Lambani community, classified as SC in Karnataka.

In my report to the Chief Secretary I highlighted that there was a basic problem of exploitation of landless labour by the landlords and in Konchavaram especially by the Forest Department officials and unless that was stopped and minimum wages were paid as per law, the problem will only worsen. The Police Department under instructions of Special DIG who had just recently returned from a central government training course in Hyderabad to handle Naxalitism, was treating it just as a doctrinaire terrorist problem learned in his recent training course and was for intensifying arrests and using the Unlawful Activities (Prevention) Act liberally which would only further aggravate the problem and cause violence. The solution lay in stopping the Law and Order approach and instead to make the Labour Inspectors implement the Minimum Wages Act scrupulously and to regularize the cultivation of small pieces of forest land for decades by the landless as permitted by the Forest Act and also to permit the forest dwellers to continue to take away the minor forest products as 'usufructs' as long as trees were not cut. Besides, cases should be filed against the officials for molesting Lambani girls. Above all, the schemes under the Social Welfare Department for SC/ST persons and by other departments should be implemented vigorously with special instructions to the DCs of the two districts to strictly supervise them, besides withdrawing criminal cases against the agricultural workers.

My main recommendation that cases against the labourers should be withdrawn and the district administration should stop treating it as a Naxalite Law and Order problem was not taken kindly by the Home Department. But Veerendra Patil being a native from Chincholi, knew intimately the Konchawaram area (the Chandrampalli Dam Project was due to his initiative) and some of the landlords who were exploiting the agricultural labourers were personally known to him and were also his supporters. After hearing me at length and realizing the common factors between Konchawaram and Pavagada, he agreed with me and asked the

Home Secretary to prepare a Cabinet Note to implement my recommendations and also a special scheme to assist the agricultural labour. It was remarkable that the CM took a pro-labour view while the prevailing mood in the central and state governments in India was to have a law and order approach to control the Red Corridor expansion. This was in dire contrast to the police firings during the Gundu Rao Government during 1980-1984 on the advice of the Home Secretary and implemented by a trigger-happy DC which brought down the Congress government in Karnataka in March 1985 and enabling Janata Party to come to power.

It was also in Veerendra Patil's short 10-months rule as CM that two senior IAS officers of Secretary's rank and one senior medical doctor of Director of Health rank working in the Bangalore City Corporation were proceeded against on charges of corruption and suspended after the then Vigilance Commission raided their houses and the CM did not interfere even though one of the IAS officers was from his own community. Only, they were rescued by Veerendra Patil's successor Bangarappa who brought in an obliging DGP to the Investigation Wing of Vigilance Commission who filed a "B" Report (meaning, Investigation does not prove charges) before the High Court and they went scot-free. One reinstated IAS officer was made Chief Secretary by a later CM. After retirement he formally joined the Congress Party, contested Parliamentary elections and lost, thankfully! *(Otherwise, he would surely have become a Minister!)* This was the administrative skill of *lumpen*-leaders like Bangarappa, JH Patil and even the suave SM Krishna! Such progress speaks volumes of the difference in quality of the CMs and also how corrupt IAS officers can make their version of Pilgrim's Progress under corrupt or imbecile CMs. More of these CMs and their favourite officers and how they degraded administration are explained with relish in later sections.

DEVARAJ URS
A Unique Greek Tragedy of Karnataka

The second CM whom I have worked under for many years was Devaraj Urs. He was a staunch follower of Indira Gandhi and in the 1972 Karnataka Assembly elections the Congress (I) trounced the Congress (Organization) with 165 MLAs to Congress (O)'s 24 MLAs in the 216 members Assembly, the polling being 62% of which Congress (I) secured twice as much votes as the Congress(O). Urs became the Chief Minister of the State which he held for 8 years till the muscleman and ex-disciple Gundu Rao toppled him. It was during Urs' regime that I was appointed the as DC and DM of Shimoga, Gulbarga, Bangalore and Director of Sericulture. I had opportunity to meet him on official work many times. It was Urs, belonging to a small community of mostly former employees of the Maharaja of Mysore, who tried the bold experiment of breaking the stranglehold of political power of the economically strong Lingayat and Okkaliga communities in Karnataka by making the backward castes (OBC), SC/STs and Muslim candidates contest in a large number of constituencies who became MLAs for the first time. For instance, in Veerendra Patil's native place of Chincholi constituency (from which he himself did not contest because of the portends), one unknown Devendrappa Ghalappa Jamadar belonging to Boatman-Fisherman-*Kabbaliga* community defeated the Lingayat candidate of Congress (O) who was a relative of Patil in a straight fight by over 10,000 votes. As a reward, he was made a Minister of State over many seniors though he was a first time MLA. *[An interesting aftermath: The very next year, in 1973 when I was DC of Gulbarga, Jamadar and his friend Shivanna belonging to SC, who was also elected for the first time from the neighbouring Raichur district and made a Minister, were found in a drunken state riding a cycle-rickshaw at 2 am returning from a house of ill repute in Gulbarga to the Aiwan-e-Shahi guest house where they were staying. When the constable at the gate did not recognize the happily singing, unsteady cycle-rickshaw riders and stopped them, they quarrelled with him and the constable arrested both of them! This made great news in the next day's local rag paper 'Kranti'! Such was the calibre of some of the young ministers of Devaraj Urs in Karnataka!]*

I met Devaraj Urs for the first time in 1972 as DC of Shimoga when he came to visit the district. In one year, I was transferred to Gulbarga to handle the bad 1973 'Marathwada Famine' and communal disturbance situation. I was DC in Gulbarga for three years and I received full support from the CM who had sent his Finance Minister, the Cambridge-educated MY Ghorpade to Gulbarga for one week to assess the famine situation and to check whether I was exaggerating the demand for relief funds. MYG and Urs gave me *carte blanche* to take all action I deemed fit and incur expenditure much to the horror of the righteous Finance Secretary Satishchandran.

Devaraj Urs was the first and only CM who successfully implemented a strategy to bring down the political dominance of Lingayats and Okkaligas and simultaneously bring up the Dalits, Other Backward Castes (OBCs) and Muslims. Though the Caste-wise Census has been blocked from being made public, the Venkatawamy

Commission (1986) which surveyed 92% of all households in Karnataka arrived at the following caste composition:

1.	Lingayats	17%
2.	Okkaligas	12%
3.	SCs	17%
4.	STs	7%
5.	Muslims	13%
6.	Kurubas	7%
7.	Other OBCs	21%
8.	Brahmins	3%
9.	Christians	3%
		100

It was interesting to note that the two dominant Lingayat and Okkaliga communities together accounted for less than one-thirds of the population and the other OBCs, dalits and Muslims were almost two-thirds. The strategy of Urs was to bring the latter together politically. Mysore State has a long history of protecting the interests of Dalits and Backward Castes. The Dalits were called 'Depressed Castes' in Mysore state before 1947. As early as 1918 the Maharaja's Government appointed Judge Sir Leslie Miller, ICS to enquire into the representation of non-Brahmins in State Administration which recommended 50% reservation in higher level posts and 75% reservation in the next levels of government posts to non-Brahmins. It is seldom publicized that the great administrator and visionary, M Visveswaraya who was Diwan of Mysore resigned in protest on the ground that sacrificing merit in selection of government servants would destroy the quality of public administration! Sir Leslie Miller said in his Report:

"Efficiency, however, is not to be measured solely or even mainly by academic qualification and it will not be denied that there are many important branches of administration in which other qualities such as sympathy, honesty of purpose, energy and common sense go as far to make an efficient officer as literary superiority. For the fact cannot be ignored that an officer in the exercise of his duty, making appointments and promotions, finds it easier to see the virtues of his own community than those of others." (Miller:1919. p 12)

To the credit of the Maharaja's government, it implemented Miller's recommendations which led the major communities to organize in 1928 communal riots when Sir Mirza Ismail was the Diwan, which broke the non-Brahmin movement. Later, under the Government of Mysore Act 1940, the government reserved 30 seats to Depressed Classes, 30 for minorities and the balance 250 to general candidates in the Mysore Representative Assembly. The Brahmins opposed the reservation to Dalits in 1940 on the ground that *it will lead to only two dominant groups in civil services, the Brahmins and the Depressed Castes* (Omvedt: 1994: p 269).

Having lived under the Mysore Maharaja's rule, when Urs came to power he tried to transfer political power to Dalits and Backward classes from the dominant communities. In the 1972 Assembly elections, for the 216 seats, 133 candidates from SC/STs, OBCs and Muslims were given tickets and 92 of them won. In total, the Congress under Urs secured 165 seats. It was due to Urs that the share of Lingayat and Okkaligas who had 60% of MLAs in the 1967 Assembly was brought down to 49% in 1972. Out of the top five senior ministers in his cabinet, not one was from the two dominant communities. His most ardent supporter was the Dalit firebrand Basavalingappa who as Municipal Administration minister, was the first in India to stop the practice of manual scavenging in Karnataka. Widespread land reforms making the tenant the owner of the land, abolishing the practice of bonded labour, release of mortgaged articles of poor people with money lenders at unlawful rates of interest, building shelters for homeless, distribution of house sites to the siteless poor people, establishing the Electronic City at the outskirts of the then Bangalore city—were some of his major achievements.

Mrs Gandhi lost the 1977 Parliamentary elections miserably when her party won only 153 seats out of 543 Parliamentary seats. Karnataka, however, elected 26 Congress-I MPs out of 28 seats which was mainly due to the restraint of Devaraj Urs in not using force in family planning sterilizations unlike in the North and also the progressive policies such as land reforms which were grouped under the Twenty Point Programme. Devaraj Urs became the unquestioned leader of the Congress in Karnataka. However, Sanjay Gandhi became the Extra-Constitutional Authority to whom all other Congress leaders became subservient. Although he had not been elected, nor held any office, Sanjay began bullying Cabinet ministers, senior civil serants and police officers. While some Cabinet ministers resigned in protest, Sanjay appointed their successors. In one famous example, the urbane Inder Kumar Gujral resigned from the Ministry of Information and Broadcasting when Sanjay attempted to direct the affairs of his ministry. Gujral reportedly rebuked Sanjay and refused to take orders from an unelected person. He was replaced by Vidya Charan Shukla, a Sanjay Gandhi acolyte. In another incident, after popular Bollywood singer Kishore Kumar refused to sing at a function of the Indian Youth Congress, his songs were banned on All India Radio. Whenever Sanjay Gandhi visited state capitals the Congress leaders thronged at the airport ingratiating themselves. The Congress CMs were all watched by his *lumpen* followers whether they were "airport going CMs" with Urs being the prominent disobedient CM. The instance of Narayan Dutt Tiwari, the CM of Uttar Pradesh carrying the slippers of Sanjay Gandhi when the latter was climbing on to an elephant, much to the embarrassment of the pachyderm, made into the tabloids. Thus, Urs came under the Black List of Sanjay Gandhi who had by then selected his 'shadow CMs' in every state and in Karnataka it was the highly un-lettered Gundu Rao. The hold of Sanjay Gandhi on Mrs Gandhi was inexplicable though there were some 'explanations' such as, he was the one fully in the know of where Congress had kept its treasure chest and when Sanjay Gandhi's new Pitts S-2A plane completed its second somersault on the ground and he died instantly and when Mrs Gandhi on reaching the accident spot, the first thing she had allegedly asked was, *Where is his watch?* It was speculated to be a customized watch which had recorded cash details! Mrs Gandhi relied upon Sanjay Gandhi and she began distancing herself from Devaraj Urs. This was also the time when Urs began developing all-India ambitions himself and even started to learn Hindi!

Devaraj Urs left Mrs Gandhi's camp in 1979 and started his own regional Congress (Urs) faction. But, in 1980 Mrs Gandhi was swept back to power with 353 out of 540 seats in Parliament. Politically Urs was wiped out. Gundu Rao, who was once the protégé of Urs when the former was said to be canvassing passengers for a commission for mufussil buses at Kushalnagar bus stand in Coorg in yester years, became in January 1980, the "Youngest CM" of Karnataka as he proudly proclaimed. He taunted his former mentor a "paper leader". Devaraj Urs died a broken person on 6 June 1982 at the age of 67. He even started another party called *Karnataka Kranti Ranga* before his death. His last years after 1979 were of confused uncertainty. One episodic disgrace, which never found its way to the press, was about his "adopted daughter". One lady officer from the Indian Foreign Service who had married an IAS officer of Tamil Nadu cadre, left the IFS and metamorphosed into a political-butterfly. Suddenly she appeared to have emerged as an 'Adviser-cum-*Adopted Daughter*' to the hapless Urs which job-title was rather mischievous if not down-right naughty. After the defeat of Mrs Gandhi in the 1977 Parliamentary election, Urs became increasingly erratic. He made his son-in-law MD Nataraj an MLC who formed the "Indira Brigade" officially described as the Gestapo-like organization to protect Indira Gandhi and his second in command was the hitman MP Jayaraj who started a magazine titled "*Gharibi Hatao*"! This was the muscle-power which Urs established. He also increasingly depended upon the Excise Contractors for funding. If the Excise Contractor HR Basavaraj wanted a meeting with the CM, it was Urs who rushed to the house of Basavaraj and not the other way round! Basavaraj was nominated to Rajya Sabha by Urs in 1978 as Excise Contractors are traditionally considered venerable 'Elders' in Karnataka! It was widely believed that while Urs did not enrich himself, he 'institutionalized' corruption in the state by making the Excise Contractors give a monthly retainer of Rs 10,000 to Congress MLAs though this may look a pittance today. But all that did not help because he did not pay tribute to the Heir Apparent *Dauphin* Sanjay Gandhi as Gundu Rao and his coterie did. Urs was removed from Congress Party in 1979 and resigned as CM in January 1980. After the indignity of his fall from grace, Urs disintegrated and died in June 1982, a fallen idol and a broken man rivalling the heroes of great Greek Tragedies.

His body was taken from Bangalore to his native village Kallahalli in Hunsur taluk in Mysore district. Throughout the entire distance of 185 kms which took five hours for the slow moving cortege to traverse, people stood on both sides of the road. They also did one strange thing—*they clapped hands when his body passed them.* Clapped? Why? Incredibly but most understandably, it was the most unorthodox, spontaneous expression of the masses to appreciate what he did for them. His life was the classical Greek Tragedy of the mighty Titan Prometheus who gifted Fire to the people for which he was punished eternally by Zeus the Greek King of Gods. Only in the case of Urs, it was the Indian Goddess who was considered to be the reincarnation of Mother Kali who destroyed him. There is a saying in Kannada, *"Sharanara Savannu Maranadalli Kaanu (See the saint in his death)".* Millions lining up and clapping on his last journey was proof enough of what people of Karnataka thought of him. A contrast, however indecorous, for the record: Sanjay Gandhi crashed his plane on 23 June 1980 near Safdar Jang airport in Delhi and it took eight surgeons four hours to stitch up his mutilated body. [Vinod Mehta *"The Sanjay Story"*, 2015 Harper Collins Publishers India.] On 31 October 1984, two of Mrs Gandhi's bodyguards, Satwant Singh and Beant Singh, shot her with their service weapons in the garden of the Prime Minister's residence. The post-mortem examination conducted by a team of doctors headed by Dr. Tirath Das Dogra showed that she sustained as many as 30 bullet wounds, from two sources: a Sterling submachine gun and a pistol. The assailants had fired 31 bullets at her, of which 30 had hit; 23 had passed through her body while 7 were trapped inside her. No one clapped in her last journey. Gundu Rao once told the Sunday magazine when the editor asked him about the rising criticism within his party against his style of functioning, that he does not bother because Congress is a Drama Company and the *Sutradari* was in Delhi and as long as she asked him to perform he would perform and nobody could do anything to him. Only when the *Sutradari* tells "stop" the drama would be over! In January 1983, he single-handedly lost the congress power by securing just 82 seats out of 224 in the State Legislative Assembly. He died, officially, of Leukemia in London on 22 August 1993, aged 57. He was ailing for months and no one outside the family was even allowed to visit him and his body, it was said, was not even brought to India and there were speculations about the nature of his terminal illness and secrecy surrounding it. The point being made is, Devaraj Urs received a standing ovation from the people of Karnataka for five hours all the way from Bangalore to his village Kallahalli, millions standing on both sides of the road. Nothing can be more illustrative of the saying: *"Sharanara Savannu Maranadalli Kaanu (See the saint in his death)"*.

After the death of Devaraj Urs, Karnataka politics resumed its interrupted power culture by the two dominant communities. In retrospect and hindsight, Urs had under-estimated the image of Mrs Gandhi among the masses of India. Once the evil sterilization programme of Sanjay Gandhi was stopped, Chaudhury Charan Singh's devastating 1977 election slogan *'Indira Hatao, Indriya Bachao'* lost its sting and Mrs.Gandhi's more durable slogan *Garibhi Hatao* resumed its hold. In fact even Sanjay Gandhi won from Amethi in UP with a margin of 128,000 votes while Mrs Gandhi had a winning margin of 173,000 against Rajmata Vijaya Rajey Scindia in Rae Bareilly. This time people had changed their minds and voted *en masse* for the real Rajmata! One is reminded of the scathing poem of Poet Nissar Ahmed of Karnataka, *Kurigalu Saar, Kurigalu! (Sheep Sir, Sheep!)* The functioning of the 'World's Largest Democracy' can by explained by just two words: SLOGANS for SHEEP! There is no substance here.

After Gundu Rao's losing the 1983 Karnataka Assembly elections, bringing Janata Party to power with the "support from outside" by the BJP, there was yet another Assembly election in 1984 after the assassination of Mrs Gandhi in October 1984 which brought Rajiv Gandhi to power with an unprecedented 414 seats out of 541 Lok Sabha seats. The Janata Party headed by Ramakrishna Hegde won the Assembly elections in March 1985 with a comfortable Janata majority (the 'sympathy factor' forgotten by amnesiac masses) and it was business as usual with the dominant communities wielding political power. While in the Urs-led 1978 Assembly elections, the number of Lingayat, Okkaliga, Muslim and OBC MLAs were 53, 47, 17 and 45 respectively, the power shifted in the 1983 elections with the same communities having 65, 54, 2 and 36 MLAs respectively. In other words, the two Major communities' MLAs strength increased from 100 to 119 while that of Muslims and OBCs went down from 62 to 38. The efforts of Devaraj to bring up the Dalits, Backward Castes and Minorities were in vain. He became a nobody and a non-person (or post-person) the moment he fell out with Mrs Gandhi in 1980. From 1988 till 2019 in 31 years, the CMs in Karnataka for 11 years were Okkaligas and for 11 years Lingayats. Karnataka never had a Dalit or Muslim as CM inspite of they having a share of 37% of the population while it had Brahmin CMs for nearly 8 years, having a population share of just 3%. The grip of the two major communities in Karnataka's democracy is iron-clad and the brief interregnum of Devaraj Urs' Backward castes' power reform was only an astounding aberration. The French saying is, *"plus ça change, plus c'est la même chose"*—"the more things change, the more they stay the same."

RAMA RAO GUNDURAO
"Who Wants To Stop Matka? Everybody Wants Matka!"

When I was Divisional Commissioner Gundu Rao once came to Bellary to review the 20 Point Programme. Jayakumar Anagol, the Philosopher-DC under whom I was honed in my first posting as Assistant Commissioner, was the Secretary to CM and he had also accompanied the CM. I had gone early to the Circuit House where they were staying to brief the CM on the various problems of the district as the DC was away on leave. The problem of "Matka" gambling was then acute in Bellary. This was a gambling of betting on two numbers started before independence when the New York Cotton Exchange would inform the Bombay Cotton Exchange the opening and closing numbers of cotton prices. After independence, it just became a simple method of taking two pieces of paper containing *Jodi* (pair) numbers between 00 and 99— say, for example 24 and 70—from an earthen pot, hence the name *Matka,* by a neutral patron which would be communicated by the brokers of the Matka King Rattan Khatri from Bombay to all over India. Those few who guessed the Jodi numbers correctly would make a fortune which they would collect from the agents. In this there was absolutely no cheating or delay and the Mutka gambling worked as a well-oiled perfect mechanism with everyone's trust. Even though Matka was illegal and Rattan Khatri was detained under MISA during the Emergency, after his release Matka became virulent. In Bellary district, the winning numbers would be written on the back of KSRTC buses so that it would be known very quickly all over the district.

As many people including farmers were getting addicted to Matka, I told the CM that the police should take stringent steps to arrest the organizers who were said to be in Youth Congress and the police was reluctant to act against them. While Anagol, though his priority was agricultural development and not so much the regulatory role of government, nevertheless wholeheartedly agreed and told the CM that he should ask the DGP to instruct all the SPs to take action. But, surprisingly, the CM yawned and told me, *"Mr Balu, who is against Matka, everybody supports it!"* He only confirmed what everyone in Bellary knew, that the Youth Congress *Baba-log* who were the *Hitlerjugend* (Hitler Youth) in India under Sanjay Gandhi who were running the organized crime in the district. That was not all and the day was just beginning. The CM was to go for breakfast to the house of Bhaskar Naidu MLA, a very prominent citizen of Bellary, after which he was to conduct the review of the district 20 Point Programme in DC's office at 11 to be followed by a press meet at 12 and then leave for Bangalore by helicopter at 3 pm to reach Bangalore well before sunset. Anagol and I decided to wait at the DC's office for the CM to arrive from his breakfast. He did not till 1130 while the meeting was to have started at 11. The SP spoke on the wireless and informed me that the CM was delayed at Naidu's house. I was more worried about the CM's Press Meet scheduled at 12 and if he was late for it, there would be heavy criticism by the press. Then, the Tahsildar who was close to Naidu, obviously appointed by him, took me aside and whispered to me that the CM was having drinks at Naidu's house and it does not look like he is coming to any meeting soon. Naidu was known to be a connoisseur of different kinds of fine spirits though, it was said, he himself was a teetotaller. He was a good host and a great supporter of CM. Gundu Rao was known to like his liquor. In fact all the CMs of Karnataka were great worshippers of Bachhus except perhaps Deve Gowda who wisely confined to healthy *Majjige* (butter-milk). The favourite of Devaraj Urs was Royal Salute whiskey and JH Patel's was Napoleon XO (Extra Old) brandy. Johny Walker Black Label was the favourite of Ramakrishna Hegde. Quite early Gundu Rao appeared to have got liver problem because of excessive drinking and wrong advice was given by his oafish confidantes that Champagne was good for the liver. His company being less than half-educated, no one told him that though Champagne had only about 12% alcohol by volume like red and white wine, the bubbles in Champagne which is CO_2 make the alcohol to be absorbed much more quickly by the liver which is why people who drink champagne get drunk very quickly and for this reason it is generally restricted to introductory toast. Now, Bhasker Naidu being a great connoisseur of wines, had obviously a good stock of Champagne which Gundu Rao was helping himself. By 11 he was drunk, according to the Tahsildar. But it was not yet over. The Press meet was important. So, Anagol and I went to Naidu's house and the CM slurred to us that the Press meet can be cancelled and he would go directly to his helicopter at 3 pm. Ultimately it was a big job for the poor SP to navigate the CM in an *impromptu* contraption of two wheelchairs put face to face (at one quintal Gundu Rao did justice to his name) safely without much public attention. When I told the Press that the CM had suddenly taken ill and was too indisposed to have a press meet, they just sniggered. The Karnataka press was inimical to him. When Gundu Rao finally lost the Assembly Elections in 1983, the *Deccan Herald* published a cartoon without any caption the picture of a helicopter having crashed on the ground and a dazed Gundu Rao sitting next to it with a question mark above his head in place of a halo.

To say that Gundu Rao was hardly CM material would be a gross understatment. In 1960, at the age of 23, he became the President of the Town Municipal Council of his native Kushalnagar in Kodagu district. He was the TMC President for ten years. With his bisoneque physique, he was a regular wrestler and thus came to the notice of Devaraj Urs who was also a wrestler! My first experience with him was when I was Director of Sericulture. When Urs was still in power in 1979 I had succeeded in getting a legislation to create a regulated market for raw silk yarn where all the producers from Dalit and Muslim communities and the purchasers of about 200 merchants of Vysya community Settys and Marwaris representing master-weavers of Varanasi in UP would have to buy and sell at the Silk Exchange. To bring transparency in buying and selling the expenive silk yarn costing Rs 3,000 per kilogram, I had prepared a draft legislation and it had an easy passage in the Legislative Assembly. However, the silk merchants went to the High Court but did not get a stay and the case was going on when Urs was toppled and Gundu Rao took over.

The Sericulture Minister, Runuka Rajendran was a Youth Congress Women's Wing leader and was erstwhile Superintendent of a SC Girls Hostel in Kolar. Her husband Rajendran was my District Information Officer in Bangalore when I was DC & DM there and, for some reason, he was terribly afraid to meet me. Since Gundu Rao had made her a cabinet minister for talents he found in her, she thought she had arrived. The Summer Olympics of 1980 was to be held in Moscow in July 1980 and she was selected by Gundu Rao to attend it at government cost. She expected me to fund her shopping which I not only refused but put it in writing to the Chief Secretary. He showed it to Gundu Rao who came to her rescue and said the Director must have heard wrongly!

Renuka came to sad existential end by her own corruption. She had collected a bribe to recommend a medical college seat to a candidate (in Gundu Rao's time a large number of private Medical Colleges were permitted; it was said that it was easy to start a medical college in Karnataka than to get admission in one!) and when the candidate did not get the seat, his parents demanded refund from the minister who, in her hubris and inexperience, gave a rubber cheque which promptly bounced. The parents filed a police complaint and the upright DIG of Corps of Detectives, NB Bhat IPS arrested her on return from Kashmir where she was holidaying and took her from airport to jail by the shortest route and she had to resign.

NB Bhat was an IPS Officer two years senior to me and was of immaculate discipline and spotless integrity and his clarification to Gundu Rao that any Sub-Inspector of a Police Station could arrest any person for a serious cognizable offence under the Cr.PC and IPC and no prior permission of government was needed could not be understood by Gundu Rao. He did not want Bhat anywhere in the State and told the Chief Secretary that he should be posted to the farthest place, like Assam. When the CS enlightened him that Karnataka CM could not transfer him to Assam and it could be done only by the Union Home Ministry, he asked the CS to go to Delhi and get it done. Narasimha Rao was a mild-mannered gentleman of Old-Mysore. And that was precisely the problem. In an administrator you do not require a saint. You require a headmaster who can encourage good deeds and punish bad behaviour. Most good officers when they reach top position such as Chief Secretary, lose all testoterone and look forward to peaceful retirement and an uneventful sterile life. Worse, they lose the sense of right and wrong and even obey illegal and unethical orders in the name of Neutrality and Discipline of Civil Servants. It goes back to the basic principle of Nuremberg trial that illegal orders should not be obeyed. Civil servants become invertebrates with no courage to defend the right and the just. They cannot stand up and can only crawl as George Fernandes once remarked.

So, the CS camped in Delhi for a week and pleaded for the immediate central deputation of Bhat even though he had not asked for it according to procedure and what was worse, that he be posted to North East specifically. Even though Gundu Rao's guardian angel was not alive to help in flesh, Indira Gandhi had a soft corner to Gundu Rao who, along with Field Marshall Khan had protected her from stone throwing by covering her with Coorg's country made durable bamboo umbrellas when she was travelling in Kodagu in her wilderness years between 1977 and 1980. This had a lasting impression on her (in Delhi's continuing Moghul culture, unquestioned loyalty is the only criterion) and as the PM was the Minister of Department of Personnel, she instructed the Secretary DoP accordingly. So, the CS returned to Bangalore with Bhat's posting orders to Guwahati much to the delight of Gundu Rao after ascertaining where this Guwahati place was! This was the most ungentlemanly act done by a gentleman CS of Karnataka. Bhat resigned and started legal practice (he was an LL.M) defending government servants in service matters in the High Court and continues to be a roaring success as there is no dearth of civil servants' grievances.

What I have been narrating may show Gundu Rao as a blustering bull in Chinashop, failed wrestler, the gain of wresting being the loss of politics, but there were other aspects to him also. Because he never cultivated the media, he was always painted as a bad CM by the press even though the Press was predominantly from upper caste. But he was basically a realist who knew his limitations. On the advice of Narasimha Rao, whom he venerated, Gundu Rao took Jayakumar Anagol as his Secretary. A Jain and agnostic, Anagol had a high ethical sense and mature views. On his advice, Gundu Rao started getting up at 4 am and reading files to understand administrative matters. He totally stopped the interference of MLAs in transfers of officers. In this, he was the one and only CM who did that. Whenever an MLA approached him for an officer's transfer, he would curtly tell him to go and see the Chief Secretary. Nor did he arrange stipends to MLAs as even Urs had done. He totally relied upon Bureaucracy to administer the state and decided that he would take charge of only matters political which meant pleasing Delhi. He once gave an interview to Suman Dubey of *India Today* in which he gave frank expression to his philosophy which is worth producing *in extenso* as an example of his administrative acumen and maturity: *[Gundu Rao's grammar was corrected by Dubey]*

Q. How would you assess your first eight months in Karnataka?

A.   *There was no discipline in the administration. And in every stage there used to be interference, either by political persons or by middlemen, and relations. What is the remedy for this? Only, you should be very strict in all matters. Someone should start to give a clean administration. Why do people have to come to the Secretariat every day? Because they know that unless they go and meet the concerned clerk, their file will not be passed. For the last few years this sort of tendency has developed. And unless the local MLA speaks the work will not be done. Unless a person can meet the minister the work will not be done. To meet the minister we should go through somebody. So I must wipe out this. So far I have succeeded 70 per cent. Within this month I will succeed in the remaining 50 per cent (?!) also. From November 1st I will give a very very efficient, clean government.*

Q. You mean people are not bothered about economic development?

A. Not the ordinary man in the street. It is only some intellectuals who are bothered about economic development. People are not bothered about those big-big factories. People are bothered about their day to day work: it should go on smoothly. When they approach the Tahsildar, the Deputy Commissioner, their work should be done without any difficulties.

Q. Everyone says you are here because of Mrs Gandhi. Shouldn't you build an independent base?

A. I am here because of my party. My party is here because of Mrs Gandhi at the moment.

Q. Shouldn't you as chief minister want to have your own independent strength?

A. Independent strength is party strength. Individual strength doesn't count in a democracy. That is what Devraj Urs did. He should not have thought that the individual is more important than the party. Party is much more important.

Q. But Mrs Gandhi is an individual...

A. Party is under Mrs Gandhi's leadership. Leadership is necessary, a strong leader, an accepted leader. Unless the commander-in-chief is strong, the army is useless even though it may be a 10,000 army. But a strong leadership with 2,000 in the army can defeat a 10,000 army because there is no leader.

Q. But shouldn't the majority within the party decide, like the majority within the country decides?

A. Yes. Majority means again discipline. Discipline means a leader. Under a leader everything will be there. In the Assembly, the majority party will get everything passed through. But there is discipline. So without a leader the party can't function. A strong party is necessary. At the same time a strong party can be there only if there is a strong leader. Otherwise there will be no party, there will be no democracy.

Q. But you can't separate the two, can you?

A. Yes you can. When there is kingship, there is no kinship. Aurangzeb put his own father behind bars and ruled.

Q. How do you see the future?

A. She is the only hope. If Mrs Gandhi goes, as far as things stand today, there will be chaos in the country. Because, she is the acceptable leader today right from Kashmir to Cape-Comorin. At least, the majority of people have faith in her so they look to her. For the time being, we can say she is the saviour of democracy in India.

[And so on and on and on...]

"File Clearance" was a fetish with Gundu Rao. He got the strong notion that all the mal-administration in government was due to files being kept pending for long periods. So every three months he started a campaign that all files pending for more than one year in each department must be disposed off. When he found the corridors of Vidhana Soudha thronged by file-chasing brokers, he ordered the closure of all gates to Vidhana Soudha and Multi Storied Building (extended Secretariat) between 1030 and 1700 during the "File Disposal Week" every two months! Even MLAs were not allowed to enter during that week without the permission of Gundu Rao! So, the unbeatable Bureaucracy closed all files more than one year old *and promptly reopened new files on the same subject to get one more year's currency!* The tragedy of Gundu Rao was, the bureaucracy on which he totally relied upon for administration, completely failed him. If only GVK was the CS when Gundu Rao was in power, the State might have achieved many milestones. As it happened with weak administrative leadership, the administration bumped from one scandal to another. Because of bureaucratic rigidity, sticking to dry rules and not justice and in not talking to farmers, Gundu Rao's period also saw the birth of the farmer's movement, which culminated in the formation of "Karnataka Rajya Raitha Sangha" by MD Nanjundaswamy. It all began when it was decided to collect betterment levy on irrigated lands in 1980. In July 1981 the farmers in Navalgund, Nargund and Gadag in Dharwad district began staging hunger strike in front the Tahshildars' offices demanding the abolition of Betterment Levy and Water Tax and also demanding immediate compensation for lands acquired for irrigation canals. The government did not ask the DC to have discussions and pacify the agitating farmers. Instead, it was treated as a law and order problem. With a trigger-happy DC, the movement reacted violently and in the ensuing police firing two persons were killed at Nargund and

Navalgund. The stir spread to other areas of North Karnataka and violence and firing took place in Koppal, Shiggali, Saundatti, Dudda Nipani and other places. Scores of farmers were killed by police firing. In October 1982 a massive rally was organized by the farmers in Bangalore and the Raitha Sangha demanded the government to constitute a judicial committee to enquire into the police firing on farmers. According to a report in Prajavani (21 July, 1989), Gundu Rao's rule saw the death of 143 farmers in police action.

When Rajiv Gandhi became the PM after the death of Mrs Gandhi, Gundu Rao was humiliated by being refused to contest elections. Though he did become a Member of Parliament in 1989, his health deteriorated and he died in 1993, aged 56 in London by leukemia, officially. Rajiv Gandhi was himself assassinated in 1991 in Sriperumpudur near Madras by a suicide bomber of Liberation Tigers of Tamil Ealam. Mrs Gandhi, Sanjay Gandhi, Rajiv Gandhi, Gundu Rao, Bangarappa, JH Patel—had all exercised powers in their time. But, when they died *Nobody Clapped*. That Royal Salute of the people was reserved for the King of Hearts from Kallahalli village.

❖❖❖

sarekoppabangarappa
[he deserves only small font and lower case!]

The Golden Age of Corruption in Karnataka

"Bribe is my Birthright; Corruption is Destiny".
—*Karnataka's 'Goldfather'*

When I was DC of Shimoga there were three young Socialist Party MLAs out of nine. These three were, Kagodu Thimmappa, Konandur Lingappa and Sarekoppa Bangarappa, followers of Shantaveri Gopala Gowda, the dedicated Socialist Party leader who had devoted his life to the poor and landless. Being an advocate of Shimoga bar, Bangarappa used to appear in my court while also being an MLA, on behalf of farmers in land title matters. He would always seek adjournments, some times by sending a letter by post. The DC&DM exercises quasi-judicial powers under different laws and is the District Magistrate under the Code of Criminal Procedure, IPC, Police Act, etc. There is court protocol to be observed and the DC has a Court Room with a Dais covered by red cloth in the front. Certain dress code has to be observed by both the DC in the Courtroom and also by the advocates and the public. One was, I always wore a suit and tie while hearing cases though not the black gown which was prescribed only for the judiciary. The advocates however wore black gowns or suits and had to 'pray' for adjournments in person and not by letter. When posted to Shimoga, I had called on the District Judge Rudrayya a veteran, who told me that generally he would give three adjournments of two weeks each time unless the case is a complicated one. I had followed his advice.

I had a lot of respect for Bangarppa to start with as he was appearing *pro bono* for farmers. However, I found that amidst his political work he was not at all prepared to argue his cases and was simply asking for adjournments. After two months I gently told him I could not give adjournments as a matter of routine and would issue orders on merits if he does not argue his cases. This sobered him up. It so happened that I developed a problem with the district minister Badri Narayana Iyengar who was a Brahmin and the Education Minister in the cabinet. The problem was: The government had allotted 20 acres of irrigated land in a different taluk to the family of the Minister as their land was submerged under the Sharavathy dam. But the allotted land was under unauthorized cultivation of dalit farmers for a long time and under the Land RevenueAct, they were entitled for its grant to them. So I put them in possession. This had offended the Minister who was otherwise a good person. At this time, there was a severe famine and communal disturbance in Gulbarga. So, I was transferred to Gulbarga and the DC, Gulbarga was posted to Shimoga in my place. The same day evening there was a public meeting in Shimoga's famous Shivappa Naika Circle in which Bangarappa, Kagodu Thimmappa, Konandur Lingappa—the three socialist Musketeers and the Shimoga Municipal President Jyoti Rao spoke against the DC's transfer and demanded its cancellation. The street meeting at the circle went on for two more days and it came in the newspapers. I handed over charge the very next day after getting a call from the Chief Secretary RJ Rebello who said my transfer had nothing to do with political pressure and I proceeded to Gulbarga. The reason why I am repeating this is, I came to the scrutiny of the Socialist MLAs of Shimoga including Bangarappa in 1972 itself and it was not as if he did not know me as he later pretended when he became CM. In fact, he had made fiery public speeches for three days for my retention as DC in Shimoga.

However, if ever there was a champion to outrun Usain Bolt, in running from one party to another, it was Bangarappa. His Political Migration was: From 1967 to 1976 he was a Lohia Socialist. From 1977 to 1983 Congress-I and Minister under both Urs and Gundu Rao. In 1983 he started Karnataka Kranti Ranga and hobnobbed with Janata Party. When Janata Party—KKR combo became the biggest group in the 1983 Assembly elections, he wanted to be the CM but the smooth-as-silk Ramakrishna Hegde outmaneured his crude rival and was made the CM and Deve Gowda was sent to Bangarappa's house to persuade him to accept Deputy CM's post. But Bangarappa would hear none of it (his motto being "CM or Nothig") and in fact wanted to give a resounding overhead badminton smash on the *'Mannina Maga'* of Hassan and in the ensuing free-style wrestling, poor Deve Gowda's *jibba* was torn to rags! Again, he joined the Congress in 1985. From 1990 to 1992 he was made the CM by Rajiv Gandhi from Bangalore's HAL airport in a casual press interaction. Because of scandals he was removed in 1992 and he started Karnataka Congress Party. In 1998 he started the Karnataka Vikas Party. In 1999 he again joined Congress. In 2004 he joined BJP. In 2005 he resigned from BJP and joined Samajawadi Party. Again in 2009 he joined Congress. In 2010 he joined Janata Dal-Secular. Much weakened of constant running, his health then deteriorated and he could not join or start any other party and he died in December 2011. He was duly acknowledged as the Turncoat *par excellence* and should find a pride of place in the Guinness Book. (The origin of the term *Turncoat* is, in the English Civil War during the 17th century, the siege of Corfe Castle was won by Oliver Cromwell's soldiers when they *turned their coats inside out* to match the colors of the Royal army!) Bangarappa's coat was turned inside out so many times, that he had to keep many sets ready as they were all getting worn out by constant turning! He should have been also advised to keep a few new jibbas ready to compensate his adversaries whose jibbas he was in the habit of tearing!

Bangarappa belonged to the Idiga community concentrated in Karnataka's coastal Dakshina Kannada district and Shimoga and in Kerala where they were known as *Ezhavas*. The saintly, reformist Narayana Guru who established the *Sree Narayana Dharma Paribalana Yogam*, also belonged to this *Avarna* or outcast *Ezhavas* proscribed by the Brahmins of Kerala. Most of them were engaged in toddy tapping. Many of the liquor barons in Karnataka belonged to this community whose black money was legendary. As a result, even though in Karnataka they constituted only 2.5% of the population, in the 1985 Assembly elections 11 MLAs were elected from Idiga community making them the single largest group among the OBC MLAs. Because of the concentration of the community in Malnad and coastal area and their money power and sterling loyalty for Bangarappa, he won elections seven times from 1967 to 1998 when he finally lost to BJP's Ayyanur Manjunath in the

Parliamentary elections. Till then he was praised as *Solillada Sardar*— Leader of No Defeat. However, his success made him think he was invincible. After Shimoga, I had an encounter with him in 1980 when he was Revenue Minister in Gundu Rao's cabinet. It was my last days as Director of Sericulture and there was a Starred Question in the Assembly about sericulture. As the Sericulture Minister Renuka Rajendran was state guest in Parappana Agrahara for issuing rubber-cheques, Bangarappa was entrusted to answer the question. For starred questions there would be unexpected "supplementary questions" by any member and I had to brief him in his chambers. Though he had known me quite well in Shimoga and had given fiery speeches for my retention, yet when I met him as Revenue Minister he displayed acute amnesia and I also did not tell him about my Shimoga past. But, after some time, with a crooked smile (he had by then developed a paralytic problem and had crooked lips, matching his thoughts), and looking askance, he asked me, *Were you not in Shimoga?* I returned his smile but said nothing! I am good in my own insulting ways! I was highly fortunate in never having to meet him again in person.

My second experience with him came in 1990 when he was made the CM by the Congress President Rajiv Gandhi, the 'Hope of the Nation' as the huge illegal hoarding put up by Congress party across the road outside the HAL Airport said, when he dismissed Veerendra Patil who had suffered a mild stroke and informed the Press that Bangarappa would be the next CM. Karnataka was a placid state where the civil servants do not change positions with a new CM, unlike in UP or Bihar. Even the Secretary to CM used to continue with the new CM. But not when Bangarappa became the CM. He took guidance from his supporting Liquor Barons and some officers who were close to the Liquor Lobby. Sankaranarayanan, an upright officer was the CS. Veerendra Patil had selected him as CS in preference to NK Prabhakar Rao who was Excise Commissioner once and close to the Liquor Lobby. The first thing Bangarappa did was to appoint Prabhakar Rao as CS and to suspend Sankaranarayanan for speaking to the Press. In no other state would an honest Chief Secretary be suspended by a new CM. He also made a whole lot of changes in all the senior positions. I was MD of the huge Karnataka Power Corporation for just a year. Since the CM was the ex-officio Chairman of KPC (where any file would be for a contract of not less than Rs 100 crores), as soon as Bangarappa became CM, I sought to meet him as a courtesy for the Chairman but was told by his new Joint Secretary to CM, a junior Lingayat officer promoted from the Karnataka Administrative Service, that the CM was extremely busy. The next day I saw from the "Official Postings" column in the Deccan

Herald that I was one in the long list of 25 officers who was transferred. My new posting was as CMD of Mysore Sugar Company which post was held by a good officer though some twelve years junior to me. An engineer of CM's choice was appointed as MD of KPC. Similarly, the Karnataka Electricity Board, a key-post in the energy starved state was held by BR Prabhakara, two years senior to me and who was just a few months old in that job, was replaced by another engineer, a doyen of corruption. Prabhakara was posted as CMD of Mysore Acetate & Chemicals Co which was even smaller than Mysore Sugar Company to which I was posted.

This was the first time in Karnataka's administrative history a clear message was sent to the bureaucracy that officers of proven corruption were in high demand. While all the CMs of Karnataka had been dependent upon the Excise and PWD contractors in varying degrees to fund elections, including Devaraj Urs, Veerendra Patil and Ramakrishna Hegde, they had nevertheless given comparatively clean administration. But Bangarappa's innovation was democratic decentralization of corruption in which every department was given a target and many IAS officers treated it as an honour to be chosen to strengthen the hands of the CM! There is a saying in Kannada, *A person extracting honey, will he not lick his elbow?* These mercenary IAS officers of Bangarappa's choice certainly licked, and how! Very small amounts were collected which even brought down the reputation of corruption standards! For instance, Bangarappa allegedly received Rs 10 lakh (Yes, just Rs 10 lakhs) for sanctioning the PC Dental College although Bangalore University was not in favour of another Dental college as there were more dental colleges in the city than teeth in the human mouth. Students were admitted far in excess of university norms and the High Court held it invalid. Those who were off-loaded filed cases in the Court. A CM of a big state of 21-Gun Salutes in British times receiving Rs 10 lakhs? Even a lowly Village Panchayat Vice-President would be ashamed by the fallen standards set by Bangarappa!

After Rajiv Gandhi was assassinated in May 1991 there was no dynastic authority to control the few remaining Congress CMs which gave a free hand to Bangarappa who ran amok in ruining Karnataka. He appointed a junior IAS officer as Chief Secretary superseding three senior officers of integrity, Christopher Lynn, Cecil Noronha and BR Prabhakara. Bangarappa's choice was of fish-catcher origin who was earlier, unsurprisingly, the Excise Commissioner and in 1990 when Veerendra Patil was the CM, his house and houses of two other IAS officers and a Joint Director of Health in the Bangalore City Corporation were raided by the Vigilance Commissioner. However, in 1991 when Bangarappa came to power he brought in a new DGP in the Vigilance Commission who obligingly filed "B" Reports for insufficient evidence for investigation before the court and the cases were buried. The IAS officer whose administrative conquests could be compared to only that of the great Macedonian Emperor, was appointed as Additional Chief Secretary, Finance Dept and later as Chief Secretary. The most unique innovation was, while being CS, he also held charge of Finance Department and also was Chairman of State Finance Corpn, Chairman of BDA and Chairman of Mysore Sales International Ltd, a Government company which was in charge of all marketing of liquor in Karnataka!

But, the most blatant case of robbing the state exchequer jointly by the ACS cum Finance Commissioner-cum-Chief Secretary and the CM Bangarappa was the celebrated case of Classik Computer Systems in 1991-1992 when the ACS-FC-CS approved the purchase of 100 Apple Macintosh computers without tender at an exorbitant price of Rs 5.27 lakhs each from one unknown broker, Gokul Krishna and paid a 30% advance of Rs 1.58 crores and the CBI filed the charge sheet before the High Court. Parallel to this CBI case, there was a Writ Petition by the Opposition Leader MC Nanaiah, MLC, that the contract given to Classik Computers without open tender was mala fide and the High Court held the contract invalid and the appeal filed by the dealer was also dismissed. *The computers were never delivered and the advance given was never returned by him. Later a suit to recover the advance filed before the High Court was not pursued by the government in 2003 when SM Krishna was the CM! About him a little later! Karnataka and Bihar are not very different! But this has not happened even in Bihar!*

Inspite of all this, the CBI case before the High Court fell through when the ACS-FC was made the Chief Secretary by Bangarappa in 1992, superseding four officers senior to him. The new Bangarappa-*pyari* CS prepared a cabinet note to approve the purchase of these 100 Apple Computers and the Cabinet approved it! It was this approval by the cabinet which the HC relied upon by saying that the purchase was a "collective decision" and the thieving duo of CM and CS alone could not be paired out for corruption! The HC decision in the parallel case filed by MC Nanaiah the Opposition Leader declaring the contract illegal was just ignored by the same HC, by a different bench, in the CBI case on the strange ground that the duo were not the accused in that case and the only issue there was the legality of the contract! Mysterious are the ways of God and Courts! Arriving at Truth as in the Continental

Inquisitorial System is not the objective in India's Anglo-Saxon Adversarial system. The Rule of Law in India is, *Show me the Man, I will show you the Rule.* A village accountant caught receiving a bribe of Rs.5,000 or a Health Inspector showing a favour for Rs.10,000 to a hotelier would be sent to jail, but not the Chief Secretry and Chief Minister swindling the state of Rs 5 crores. In the cabinet meetings held on 3-7-1992 and 20-8-1992, the decision to purchase the 100 Apple Computers from Classik Computers was unanimously approved by the cabinet including Aswatha Reddy, the PWD Minister, Veerappa Moily the Minister for Education and Parliamentary Affairs (he would later succeed Bangarappa as CM! Still later he would head the Second Administrative Reforms Commission in 2005—one can imagine what *deforms* these leaders can give!), Chikke Gowda, Agriculture Minister (my former Minister and *bête noire* in Bangalore district) and Mallikarjuna Kharge who had all deposed before the Court and swore that the cabinet decision was unanimous! So much for 'collective responsibility' in public embezzlement. *Quis custodiet ipsos custodes?*— Who will guard the guardians, Roman poet Juvenal asked in his *Satires* and became a basic question in Roman law. But not in India if leaders are involved.

Bangarappa was removed as CM in November 1992 by the untiring efforts of Veerappa Moily playing piped *apasvara* music to PV Narasimha Rao and was rewarded to be Chief Minister. Bangarappa's invincible Chief Secretary also retired with full pension. (For people of such calibre, pension is not needed as they can pay royalty to government!) Immediately, he joined the Congress Party, won the election from Bangalore, India being a vibrant democracy with herd-immunity and was also made a cabinet minister in the ministry of suave SM Krishna in 2000! He also became the President of the City Unit of the Congress Party. Later, he was made Chairman of the Karnataka Pollution Control Board for two years with cabinet rank till 2004 and after that he was President of the YMCA till 2008. However, scandals were his inseparable shadow. The 30 July 2009 issue of Mid-Day.com reported that after his term as YMCA President ended in March 2008, the new management filed a complaint with Ulsoor Gate Police Station, Bangalore to the effect that 15 acres of land belonging to YMCA near Kumbalagod, on the outskirts of Bangalore, was sold to Gopalan Enterprises, a land developer and promoter of shopping malls. The complaint narrated that the President had sold property worth about Rs 15 crore to Gopalan Enterprises, but made the deal appear worth only Rs 9.3 crore. Shreedharan, partner, Gopalan Enterprises, was allegedly a close friend of the former Chief Secretary turned cabinet Minister. The same Mid-day.com in its issue dated 4 May 2009 published a report quoting Saratchandra the then Chairman of the Pollution Control Board that sofa sets, cots and tables, worth Rs 5 lakh, belonging to the KSPCB which should have been returned to the Board after his two-year term as chairman ended in 2004 but were still with the former Chairman and ex CS and Cabinet Minister! The Pollution Control Board had provided him with furniture, a car and three security guards, as the Chairman's post was notified equal in rank to that of a cabinet minister! However, the furniture continued to remain at the ex-Chairman's house. The report also gave the details of what he had kept back in his home, thus: 2 sofa sets, 2 centre tables, a TV unit, a shoe rack, 2 dining tables, 2 double cots, a side table, 2 showcases, a cupboard, 3 'suspenders', a Melamine table top kit, a drawer kit, a wooden dining table and a low back stool!

I am giving this matter a long treatment to raise a basic question about the psychology of corruption by even senior IAS officers, who become Chief Secretaries, and amass wealth sufficient for seven generations. Why do officers who have earned crores of rupees stoop so low and steal small things? Shoe rack? Cupboard? Low Back Stool? After all, how much are these worth—a few thousand rupees? To my knowledge there has been no sociological or psychological study of corruption in civil service. One can understand big time corruption of nation-robbers and Political Leaders stealing public funds and keeping it in off-shore accounts in Panama, StKitts, Cayman Island, British Virgin Islands, Mauritius and 87 such Black Money Havens as analysed by Nicholas Shaxson in *Treasure Islands: Tax Havens and the Men who Stole the World (2011)*. But Dining table, Double Cot, TV set? One reason may be, persons who were deprived of small comforts early in life as children due to poverty cannot, when they reach higher positions in life, help grabbing whatever is available so that unconsciously greed becomes a Pre-existing Condition in their sub-conscious or a second nature bordering on Kleptomania or Anxiety Disorder, not being able to differentiate between small and big things! The mental turmoil of a deprived child fighting with six siblings for hand-me-down shirts and shorts always two sizes too big can be visualized and which may make one understand an officer's craving for gifts varying from Armani or a *desi* Rs 1 lakh worth Raymond Woollen suit, a car, a refrigerator, an apartment, down to a side table, a stool or a tea-poy. One of the items mentioned in the FIR against Bangarappa's *sans culottes* Chief Secretary was a set of two deep sea fishing motor boats probably reminiscent of childhood memories of the family's country fishing boat without engine. Otherwise why should a Chief Secretary working in Bangalore aspire for mechanized deep sea fishing boats in Kerala coast?

The earliest philosophical doctrine on human behaviour coming from the time of Aristotle is *Tabula Rasa,* which in Latin means "Clean Slate", that is, when we are born we are in a state of Clean Slate, that nothing is written on the mind. All knowledge, all behaviour, all uniqueness, all weirdness—are *Acquired* after birth. Everything is 'Nurture and not Nature'. *No one is Born anything, Everyone Becomes.* Except for certain hereditary diseases encoded in genes, everything else is acquired experience. So, a corrupt person is corrupt because of his upbringing, his early deprivations and to a significant extent because of the lack of ethical values he inculcates by imitation. Not the least is the fearlessness that the system will not punish him and if caught, the court will acquit if an expensive advocate is employed and, if punished, the property stolen will not be confiscated. Corruption's sacredness is guaranteed in India. Most philosophers and psycho-analysts have said that Selfishness is a stronger trait than Altruism which rare altruism is also more due to taboos and fear of rules for living in civilized society, the only exception being selfless, instinctive maternal love which is common to all—humans, birds, reptiles and fish, necessary for the evolutionary reason of preservation of the species. Or simply, the ex-Chief Secretary and the Chief Minister shnunned ethics and consiciously chose wrong from right. Only punishment or fear of it could have prevented them. But our legal system connives at corruption, especially in high places.

Bangarappa and his Chief Secretary had a symbiotic relationship. Though mercifully Bangarappa's rule of Karnataka state was only for two years from October 1990 to November 1992, it was a water-shed era and had an evil impact on bureaucracy for all time to come. This was the first time when corruption was organized as state policy and corrupt officers were chosen as heads of departments, Secretaries to Government and also as Chief Secretary. In another instance, within weeks of Bangarappa replacing Veerendra Patil as CM, he appointed one Murthy, an engineer of Karnataka Electricity Board as its Chairman. Usually, senior IAS officers were posted as KEB Chairmen. This same Chief Engineer, when Veerendra Patil was made CM in 1989, had called on him and ingratiated himself by suggesting that if he is made Chairman he could collect funds for election! According to Prabhu who was the Secretary to CM, Veerendra Patil asked Murthy how would he collect such large sums to which he replied that the KEB purchases large quantities of transformers as about 15,000 burn out each year due to surges besides cement pillars, aluminium wires and other materials from many contractors throughout the year and he could collect 25% from them! A disgusted Veerendra Patil just asked him to leave. This same gentleman was appointed as Chairman of KEB within a month of Bangarappa assuming power and BR Prabhakara who was a senior officer of high integrity and who was Chairman of KEB for just a few months, was transferred to a junior post as CMD of Mysore Acetate and Chemicals at Mandya. How much Murthy collected and how much he passed on to Bangarappa is not known but the empirical estimate in KEB was 50-50! Both Prabhkara who was senior to me by two years (and who, incidentally was also the batchmate and senior to Bangarappa's favourite manservant and chosen Chief Secretary) and I as MD of KPC were transferred the same day, along with about 25 other senior officers in addition to the suspension of Sankaranarayanan the honest CS. Such was the administration of Sarekoppa Bangarappa!

I took charge at Mandya from a nice officer many years junior to me. Though I was upset for a week because I had spent less than a year in KPC and had many plans to take up new renewable energy projects, I recovered soon as Sugar industry was entirely new to me and it was an opportunity to learn. Mysore Sugar Company's office was in Bangalore while the sugar factory with its distillery was in Mandya, about 95 km and two hours by train. So I bought the monthly railway season ticket for Rs 415 and commuted three days a week. I had 4 hours of undisturbed time when I travelled in the AC Chair Car which time I used to read (which would be difficult in the bumpy car ride on the winding road) the standard 1100-page *Cane Sugar Handbook* by James Chen to understand the technical nature of processing sugar from sugar cane to crystal sugar. I had the additional advantage of observing the working of the machines—from boiler to the crushing of sugarcane to the evaporator in the mill to the bagging of crystal sugar—every time I visited the sugar factory. I also understood the practices and malpractices in the liquor industry as the Mysore Sugar Factory had one of the oldest distilleries in the South, established in 1936. Mysore Sugar used to export its famous rum to the middle eastern countries and was also a supplier to the Indian Army and Navy. So, for the annual renewal of the contract I went to Bombay to the Naval headquarters to get a higher quota and called on the Rear Admiral in charge of the procurement. He was very nice to me but wondered why the IAS CMD himself had come for a routine matter and I could have sent the Chief Engineer for the usual terms of supply. I later understood that "usual terms" meant a bribe of Rs 20 lakhs which I refused to pay much to the grief of my Chief Engineer! Understandably, Mysore Sugar Company did not get the renewal and the entire contract went to Khodays' Hercules XXX rum. However, I learned the sugar and liquor industry during the one year I spent in Mysore Sugar. This stood me in good stead as even 30 years after my Mysore Sugars posting and two decades after my retirement, I am still continuing as the Nominee Director of Indian Renewable Energy Development Agency of the Government of India in three of the biggest sugar factories in Karnataka which received IREDA's loans. As MG Pimputkar who was our Director in the National Academy of Administration where my 1965 batch was the first to be trained by him used to say, *"Every job in government is important unless declared otherwise and it is the officer who makes the job, not the job that makes the officer."* GVK, my mentor, had said the same too, *Your capacity will be your limitation.*

In the old Mysore State, there was a delightful term, *Mamool,* to describe a small appreciative gift for work done. This was not the big time bribe and it was not demanded and the work would have been done with or without *mamool* too with some delay. It was what the PWD contractor routinely gave graciously to the Assistant Engineer for passing his bill or the farmer gave the Village Accountant for entering his name in the land records on the death of his father, usually 10% of the monetary value of the benefit. It was like the 'tip' one gives to the server who was quick in serving the meal in a restaurant. It was not even counted by the receiver as it was understood it would be a token amount in appreciation. Indeed, *'Mamool'* literally meant 'Usual, Customary, Normal, Routine'. Neither the giver nor the receiver considered it serious or a bribe. It was considered a courtesy in the genteel manners of Maharaja's government! But Bangarappa and his Man Friday the Chief Secretary had travelled far downhill from the *'Mamool'* system. While the previous CMs confined themselves to essentially two sectors namely, the Excise, PWD and Irrigation Contractors with significant 25 % kickback, Bangarappa and his *Sancho Panza* scientifically believed in Theory of Elasticity in Economics by which collection of a small percent, but from a large number of persons makes the total bribes received much higher, that is, the *Elasticity of Bribe* is more than 1 even if each bribe is small. It is the same as, if the price of a product falls by say 10% but the total demand for it goes up by more than 10%, then the total revenue is higher than what was before. For instance, the amount collected from Classik Computer deal was just Rs 1.5 crore, which was picayune even to a Municipal Vice President, let alone the CM of a big state. But many such small amounts make the total quantum high. The Bangarappa administration, aided and abetted by his chosen mercenary officers, made bribery the 'no worries' New Norm. Together, they made corruption 'cheap'.

Corruption among the top bureaucracy is measured in a Scale of 1 to 10, one being incorruptible and ten being incorrigible. Some 30%

would be close to 1 while another 30% would be close to 10 and the balance 40% would be hovering around 5. If this middle ground people sitting on the fence finds that corrupt officers get political patronage and courts let the few even if prosecuted, go free on technical grounds and in many cases the corrupt officers against whom *prima facie* case exists are not even given prior sanction for prosecution by the government under the antequated British era provision of section 197 of the Code of Criminal Procedure, and in any case the collected bribe is not confiscated even if found guilty, the fence-sitting officers also join the corrupt and the whole system becomes a pillage.

There was a time when there were Chief Ministers like Dr BC Roy in West Bengal, BG Kher in Bombay State, Rajaji and Kamaraj in Tamil Nadu and Chief Secretaries in Karnataka itself such as PVR Rao, GVK Rao, RA Naik, TR Satishchandran and JC Lynn. From those Olympian heights to the nadirs of abyss of Bangarappa administration, both in politics and bureaucracy, the fall from grace was indeed fathomless. While in earlier days it was the cream of milk that rose to the top, in Bangarappa's reign it was the scum of the sewer which rose to the top of the gutter along with him. However, unlike the case of Gundu Rao, when Bangarappa died there were mourners. All his admirers came down from the coconut trees and wept for their Sardar!

MY LUCKY BREAK FROM SAREKOPPA BANGARAPPA'S REGIME

While I had the good opportunity of learning the Sugar Industry when I was posted to a junior position as CEO of Mysore Sugar Company in 1990, I also had a series of lucky breaks of getting out of the increasingly decadent Karnataka administration. When I was in the Central Silk Board for five years, my name was suggested by the Textile Ministry to the Commonwealth Secretariat as a Consultant for Sericulture to African countries. It materialized in 1991 and I was asked to lead a team of experts to Zambia to prepare a Pilot Project of Sericulture and to implement it as a Demonstration Project. Inspite of the opposition of my successor to the CSB who was also from the Karnataka cadre and junior to me, obviously because he himself wanted to lead the team, the Ministry of Textiles stuck to me. I selected three of my former diligent officers from the CSB and went to Lusaka. This was my first visit to Africa.

Zambia and Zimbabwe, separated by the mighty Zambezi river, were together earlier as Rhodesia named after the British Imperialist Cecil Rhodes who established the British South African Company which like the British East India Company had virtually ruled many of the

African countries. Zambia is a copper-rich country of about 2 crores population in a territory four times bigger than Karnataka. Zambia became independent from Britain in 1962 with an elected President Kenneth Kaunda who was a great admirer of Mahatma Gandhi. The great waterfall across Zambezi was "discovered" by the Scottish explorer David Livingstone in 1864 and was named Victoria Falls though it was known for thousands of years as *"Mosi-o-Tunya"* or "thundering smoke" in the local Lozi dialect. Lusaka the capital at 4,100 feet above sea level, was more comfortable than Bangalore and had a population of less than two million with wide roads and gardens. Surprisingly, Kenneth Kaunda, its first President since 1964 handed over power in 1991 to a young trade union leader, Frederick Chiluba in a clean election and the latter secured 74% of the popular vote. I was in Zambia when the election took place.

My task was to introduce Sericulture as a demonstration project for the rural development of Zambia as its economy was in dire straits because of depending unduly on export of copper ore the price of which had fallen drastically from 1980s. Lusaka was a beautiful city and I stayed in a nice little hotel by name Ridgeway which was close to the Indian High Commission and our contact Ministry of Industries of Zambia on the Cairo Road. There indeed was a Cape Town to Cairo Road and also a railway line by the same name. I learnt later that both were in good only in patches. My first visit of one month was for Activity Planning to be followed later by an Implementation Phase lasting five months. Though in CSB I had done three small consultancy assignments for FAO in preparing Reports for which they gave me US$ 5,000 and two visits on behalf of Swiss Development Cooperation to Vietnam in 1987 and Bangladesh in 1988 each for a duration of one month, this Commonwealth assignment to Zambia (which also included brief visits to Zimbabwe and Uganda) was hard work of travelling in rural Africa and I received a good fee by Indian standards. The Consultancy fee was £ 300 a day plus £ 100 for board and lodge. I had selected the comfortable, yet economical Ridgeway Hotel and with some bargaining for the long term stay for the four of us, the management agreed to charge us just £ 40 per night after a hefty discount. So I could manage my entire expenditure well within the daily allowance, keeping the fee of £ 300/day as saving. The Commonwealth Secretariat gave half the total fee in advance and the balance in two instalments. As it was rather risky to take the cheque to the crime-ridden Lusaka I had obtained Reserve Bank of India permission to deposit my fees with the branch of Canara Bank in London. This proved to be an unexpected bonanza to me. Though my stay in Lusaka was only for 6 months, it was spaced in nine months in 1992 and I received the last payment after submitting my final report which was in 1993. The RBI had allowed me to keep my London account open till the end of 1993. The £ which was worth Rs 27 when I started my work in Lusaka in 1991, appreciated to Rs 46 due to devaluation of Indian rupee by the Narasimha Rao-Manmohan Singh government in 1991 following their Liberalization—Privatization—Globalization (LPG!) model of development and the rupee further depreciated by over 70% by end of 1993. So, when I closed my London account by end of 1993 I received over Rs 30 lakhs in India which was over 25 times my annual salary in the IAS.

I am giving these tawdry details for a reason. This consultancy and the others which followed created a lot of jealousy in some of my seniors and peers for no fault of mine as these assignments came my way without my approaching anyone. Jealousy can be the root of most of the Seven Biblical Sins namely, Pride, Greed, Lust, Envy, Gluttony, Wrath and Sloth. It is also proof that an officer who learns well his job can be recognized by international organizations for assignments. More on these internal jealousies and bureaucratic victimizations later as it is a prime mover in Karnataka apart from the caste factor. Having the financial and lodging problems sorted out, I plunged right earnest into the work at hand. Mr Kaumba, the Director of Small Industries Development Organization, put me in touch with a white farming company, the Zambezi Ranching and Cropping Ltd, at Mazabooka about 30 kms from Lusaka for implementing the project. Accustomed to farmers in Karnataka typically growing less than five acres of mulberry, I was stunned by the 12,000 acres manicured Zambezi farm. Its British expatriate Managing Director told me that it was only a mid-size farm and the biggest were of 20,000 acres range and the smallest about 1,500 acres. He took me around the farm which was growing mainly Maize because the staple food in Zambia was the *Kshima* which was a thick maize porridge taken with a stew of either beef or vegetables, much like the *Ragi* ball and stew in Karnataka. Besides Maize and excellent vegetables, the farm grew many varieties of roses and tulips which were exported to Holland. With mechanization for maize, the farm had no problem for labour for growing roses and was employing about a hundred workers, mostly women. So, when I told him to plant mulberry cuttings, which we had imported from Bangalore, in *two acres* he laughed and said what kind of crop is mulberry to be grown in just two acres! So, I showed him the 30min. documentary film on sericulture I had taken with me explaining different aspects of sericulture with labour intensity, which fascinated him. So, a two-acre plot was selected and the cuttings were planted and provided with irrigation and fertilizers which would grow into a good garden in four months. An existing building was selected for rearing silkworms and rearing trays and stands were made along with bamboo spiral chandrikes for silkworms to spin the cocoons. Thus I prepared the Detailed Project Report with the help of my team members in one month and I went back to the Commonwealth Secretaariat, London to discuss the project. It was approved.

I and my team returned to Zambia after three months to implement the project. We stayed in the same comfortable Ridgeway Hotel for a longer stay. My team members stayed in the Zambezi Farm itself to supervise the work effectively. The Financial Controller of the Farm was Ramakrishnan, a Chartered Accountant from Madras which helped our task greatly. I found a sizeable Indian community in Lusaka. I went to the Indian High Commission to get the previous week's Indian newspapers. I found most of the Indian community lived within a few gated communities exclusively of Indians with barbed-wire fencing and gun-toting security men. I had also visited the University of Zambia. One of the common underlying sentiment of the local elite, often strongly articulated, was that the Indian community inspite of being very important and visible in trade and commerce (half of the telephone directory consisted of 'Patels'), did not mingle with the Zambians as equals! Mixed marriages were unheard of. The Tatas had a big presence in Zambia and owned the five-star *Taj Pamodzi* hotel in Lusaka which we visited every Sunday for its fabulous Indian buffet lunch. The Group CEO of Tatas, Raman Dhawan, was good enough to arrange for our visit to the majestic Victoria Falls.

Our project made good progress as the mulberry had grown luxuriantly. I had arranged for the import of silkworm eggs from Bangalore and the rearing of silkworms went well. However, a catastrophe almost destroyed our silkworms. Christmas was a big occasion in Zambia with a week-long government holiday from Christmas Eve to New Year and people would be absent from work for two weeks. Our silkworms were to reach the stage of spinning of cocoons by end of December 1991. But Dr Iyengar, our Agronomist, found to his horror that all his ten workers who were cutting the mulberry leaves, feeding the silkworms and cleaning the rearing trays four times a day had all simply disappeared on 20 December which week was the most crucial time in our batch of rearing which was in the final stage. Our Chartered Accountant friend, Ramakrishnan informed that this is common in all offices both in government and private corporations and the employees would simply go away for a fortnight and would return to work around tenth of January! I also found that funerals were great occasions in Zambia when many would disappear for ten days attending the funeral functions in the village. At that time AIDS was raging in Zambia and Sub-Saharan Africa, including South Africa, which was the world capital of AIDS. One Zambian University Professor amusingly told me, much to my horror, that after the funeral of the man who died of AIDS, his close male relatives would have sex with the widow which was the Zambian way of comforting the widow! No doubt, Zambia had very high death rate from AIDS and the general hospital road was known as One-Way-Traffic! The High Commissioner Balakrishnan had warned me earlier never to go to any government hospital or even private nursing homes in any emergency but to contact him so that he could send me to the High Commission's accredited doctor. In the event, with the workers missing, my team of Iyengar, Ghosh and Srinivasan had to stay in the rearing house for one whole week including nights, rearing the silkworms, with myself occasionally helping them! It could be well-said that we really earned our consultancy fees the hard way! The silkworms survived and spun the cocoons and Ghosh reeled them in his machines into silk yarn. But it also taught me that the Zambian labour was perhaps one of the most irresponsible, in the world.

I used to go jogging every morning from my hotel to the Independence Avenue which was a beautiful boulevard with big flowering trees and very few buildings, at the end of which was the huge and elegant Presidential Palace called State House which was the residence of Kenneth Kaunda. He was known as KK and was President for 27 years from 1964 to 1991, having established his one-party rule of United National Independence Party in 1973. The Director of SIDO, Kaumba told me an interesting story. Though KK was a staunch Presbyterian, he had an *Indian Guru* by name Swami Chandrasekhar who was given a suite of rooms in the Presidential State House for meditation, yoga and guiding KK! Some of the staff in the High Commission also confirmed this to me saying, KK did not do anything without consulting the Swamiji. Under the autocratic rule of KK assisted by the Swamiji, Zambian economy duly teetered with Zambian *Kwacha* depreciating over 90% in just one year (my hotel tariff was always quoted and paid in US dollars so that the hotel would not lose) and corruption was sky-rocketing and after 3 days of violent rioting in Lusaka, KK announced Parliament elections to be held in August 1991. KK's United Natonal Independent Party was opposed by a new party, the *Movement for Multi-party Democracy (MMD)* launched by the young Trade Union leader Dr Frederick Chiluba who was just 48. I was in Lusaka during those weeks and it was a marvel that it was a peaceful, totally rig-free election compared to the election rigging in other African countries such as Mobutu's neighbouring Democratic Republic of Congo (renamed Zaire) who declared that he is "neither left nor right, nor even centre!" and Idi Amin of Uganda earlier who had declared that he had defeated the British and added "CBE" to his title for "Conqueror of the British Empire". (Radio Uganda every time announced his entire title: "His Excellency President for Life, Field Marshal Alhaji Dr Idi Amin Dada, VC, DSO, MC, CBE!) Inspite of the undemocratic atmosphere in Africa, Zambia held clean elections in 1991 and Chiluba won a landslide victory with 74% of popular votes and his MMD party with young college-educated youth formed the government. Kaunda retired gracefully and his Godman Swami Chandrasekhar settled in England. *[It also struck me that the 'Invisible Export' that we learn in Economics, is enormous in the case of India, from the services of 'godmen' (and god-women) such as Dhirendra Brahmachari (India's Rasputin in Mrs.Gandhi's regime), Chandraswami, Sathya Sai Baba, Acharya Rajneesh, Sri Sri Ravishankar (US Congressman Joseph Crawley nominated him for Nobel Prize!), Anandmayi Ma, Radhe Maa, Sant Rampal, Baba Ramdev, Swami Sadachari, Swami Nithyananda (he is absconding after a rape case in Bangalore was filed against him, owns an island 'Kailaasa' near the coast of Ecuador and there is a Red Corner Notice by Interpol against him!), Gurmeet Ram Raheem Singh Insaan, Asa Ram Bapu—the list is endless, and many of them are in jail! But the Godmen who are outside, blessing their bhaktas outnumber the jailbirds by at least 100 to 1!]*

But, within a short period the press started writing about the corruption of President Chiluba and his extravagance in Armani suits and customized elevator shoes—he had 11 trunks of custom made suits and 110 'elevator shoes' of 3 inches lift, as he was just 5 ft tall! An apocryphal story started circulating in Lusaka about Chiluba government: In the first cabinet meeting in 1991 Chiluba outlined to his colleagues the need to take up popular programmes to provide rural employment, development of agriculture, subsidized *Kshima* supply, cheaper national Beer (!), etc. But his London-educated finance minister Kasonde told him that the treasury was empty and as much as US$ 1 billion was spirited away by Kaunda and kept in his Numbered Account in a Swiss Bank in Zurich. So, the cabinet decided that the President himself should go to Zurich and arrange for the remittance back of the illegally deposited funds to Zambia. So Chiluba goes to Zurich and arrives at the Bank and the Chairman and all the Directors of the Bank receive him at the entrance and take him to the Board room. There, Chiluba was polite in explaining the dire financial straits of Zambia and the gross immorality of KK siphoning away the state funds to a numbered account in the Swiss Bank and how it would be only very correct for the Bank to remit the deposit back to Zambia. To this the Bank Chairman equally politely replies that Swiss Banks work strictly under Swiss Banking Laws which prohibit revealing the details of the numbered account nor could the Bank empty any account and remit funds to Zambia without the account holder's instructions. Then Chiluba changes tactics and tells the Chairman and Directors sternly that if the right thing as he asks for in Zambia's interest was not done, his government would be constrained to break diplomatic relations with Switzerland. To this the Chairman sorrowfully replies that it would be greatly unfortunate to Switzerland but then, as a small Bank, what can he do and he has to follow rules and therefore his bank could not help the good President. At this, Chiluba gets very angry, opens his brief case, takes a pistol, points it at the Bank Chairman and says, *If you do not agree to reveal the numbered account so that the money could be drawn and sent to Zambia, I am going to shoot you!* There is a stunned silence for a minute. And then the Bank Chairman stands up, places his right hand on his left chest and says, *Your Excellency, as a loyal employee of the Bank, I am very sorry I cannot reveal the numbered account because of the Banking Secrecy Laws to which I have taken loyal oath and if I have to lay down my life, so be it, I am ready to die for my Bank.* So saying, he sang the official anthem of the Bank (not the Swiss National Anthem!), and told Chiluba, *Your Excellency, I am now ready to die for my Bank, you can shoot me,* and bared his chest! Chiluba was stunned and blurts out, *What, you will even die for your banking secrecy laws!* There was total silence in the Board room for some moments. Then, Chiluba smiled, put the pistol down and said, *Now I am convinced you will protect the secrecy of the numbered account. Look, I have brought a million dollars, please open a Numbered Account for me!* It was also true that after a few years Chiluba was prosecuted and even convicted for corruption but was acquitted on appeal! Zambia also follows the Anglo Saxon Adversarial System of Justice, just like India where corrupt politicians go scot-free.

For a civil servant like me frowning at the corruption in India, my African experience was like thunderbolt. I also found a lot of crime in Lusaka. The important Director of Mines of Zambia was a South Indian by name Subramani having a British Passport who spelt his name in a prosperous style as 'S Money' which greatly impressed Zambians! He invited me to his house for dinner. He picked me up in his British Land Rover and after dinner dropped me at my hotel. Next day when I phoned him to thank, he told me his car which he had parked inside his compound instead of in the garage due to late hour, was completely stripped and only a skeleton was standing on rims! Zambia did not make even toy cars and the spare parts for cars were hard to come by. I also learnt from my SIDO Director Kaumba that when we travel by car the driver should always be sitting in the car as no car can be left unattended during even day time for a few minutes on the busy Cairo Road where SIDO was located, because a professional gang would strip away any unguarded car in minutes.

Our project ended successfully. And I was candid in my report. I explained that the climate and soil conditions of Zambia were most suitable for sericulture but the real limitation was labour. I found that only women were sincere workers in Zambia. Men did not work attentively and most of the time they were drunk or simply absent. The social custom of walking away from work for days together without permission for attending festivals, weddings and funerals would destroy rearing of silkworms which was a highly labour-intensive and disciplined activity with strict time-table for rearing. Therefore, labour-discipline, preferably training women, was essential to the success of sericulture in Zambia. After discussing all issues with my team I prepared the candid report and gave it to Dr Amako, a Nigerian and Project Director in London. He told me that he will have to send the draft report to the concerned Secretary of Zambian government and my critical observation about labour discipline might not be a cheerful thing for the Secretary to read. There was a discussion in the Africa Division of the Commonwealth Secretariat taken by a senior officer Keith Maddison, Adviser to Industrial Development Unit and I gave a detailed presentation of what we had done in Zambia and our experience and for any further bigger project of assistance, the crux of the labour problem should be addressed. Keith Maddison was British and he and others appreciated the Project report and thus I left London with a sense of accomplishment.

I had the opportunity to visit Uganda and Zimbabwe also in 1991 where I met many Indians and Africans. Most of the Indians were either in business or Chartered Accountants in companies. It was striking that most top companies and Banks in Africa employ Indian Chartered Accountants. Surprisingly all the Indians expressed the opinion that independent Africa with over 50 countries (then) had no future. They said, excepting a few countries like Botswana, Namibia and Ghana corruption was rampant everywhere and in many countries military *coup d'état* had taken place. The military dictator of Uganda Idi Amin Dada (whose nickname was 'machete') did not believe in wasting food and was said to *eat* his enemies after killing them! One trader in Harare told me in 1991 that 'Zambia is gone, Zimbabwe is going!' Inspite of charismatic leaders such as Kwame Nkrumah of Ghana, Julius Nyerere of Tanzania, Patrice Lumumba of Congo, Jomo Kenyatta of Kenya and Nelson Mandela himself who had just been released from his 27 year imprisonment in 1990, African countries failed to provide stable governments and many of them have become Failed States. Of the nine countries informally ranked as Failed States in the world, excepting Afghanistan the rest are in Africa, riven by tribal wars. What is Caste in India, it is Tribe in Africa which fragments African society. Corruption was rampant in Zambia, Zimbabwe and Uganda and India may be catching up with them.

MY FOUR YEAR ASSIGNMENT
WITH INTERNATIONAL ENERGY INITIATIVE

Soon after I returned from Zambia in 1991 I got a 4-year assignment in an International NGO, to my great relief of escape from the corrupt administration of Bangarappa and his mercenary officers ruling at the top. The background was: When I was appointed as Secretary to CM, Hegde in 1983, he had asked me to be the Secretary of the newly created Departments of Science & Technology and Environment & Ecology. In these two departments I came in close contact with Professor Amulya Reddy who was the Secretary of the Karnataka State Council of Science and Technology. He also headed a group of scientists within IISc known as Application of Science and Technology for Rural Advancement (ASTRA). I worked closely with KSCST and ASTRA and helped in propagating schemes such as smokeless rural household ovens using less firewood to reduce its consumption and mitigate eye distress of women from smoke circulating inside the kitchen, improved un-burnt hollow bricks for building construction, introducing energy efficiency methods to reduce electricity consumption, etc. After three years as Secretary to CM and Secretary DST and EE, I had left for the central government post of CEO of the Central Silk Board in 1986. Hegde stepped down as CM in 1988 after the telephone tapping scandal involving his cabinet colleagues was exposed by Dr Subramaniam Swamy. Bangarappa was CM for two years from 1990 to 1992. During this period when I was working as CMD of the Mysore Sugar Company, I had gone to Zambia on a Commonwealth Secretariat consultancy for six months.

A few weeks after I returned from Zambia, Professor Amulya Reddy of IISc met me in 1992 and complained about the contempt of Bangarappa and his CS and that after Hegde's departure the subsequent CMs never attended the KSCST meetings nor did the Secretaries to the

CM visit the KSCST in IISc even once. But the reason why he met me was different. After the Rio de Janeiro conference of Earth Summit in 1992, 'Sustainable Development' became the watchword for development and energy consumption without contributing to global warming and renewable energy sources such as solar, wind, biomass and energy efficiency had become very important. A group of scientists headed by Professor José Goldemberg who was Rector of Saò Paulo University and later Minister for Science & Technology and Education in the Federal Government of Brazil and who played a leading part in organizing and conducting the Rio Conference and a few other Environment and Energy scientists from Norway, Sweden, the USA and UK were establishing an international NGO with the name, International Energy Initiative (IEI) to promote energy efficiency measures in developing countries. The Swedish International Development Agency (SIDA), the Norwegian Agency for Development Cooperation (NORAD) and the Rockefeller Foundation of the USA had agreed to fund the IEI. It would have three offices, in South America, Africa and Asia with a small administrative office in New York. Professor José Goldemberg was the Chairman of IEI and he also would head the Sao Paulo office as its President, Professor Amulya Reddy would be the President for Asia and another Expert from Zimbabwe would head the Africa office at Harare in Zimbabwe. Thus, Professor Amulya had to establish the Asia office within three months. Much to my surprise he asked me whether I would agree to be the Director, Asia Region of the IEI in view of my background and experience and being compatible with the twin cultures of Scientists and Bureaucracy. He further said that my remuneration would be on par with UN scale though, being an NGO, it would not carry pension benefit or diplomatic status. The initial contract would be for four years. My responsibilities as Director, Asia of IEI would be to establish the office first and to organize the main activity of advocacy and creating awareness among governments in Asia to adopt energy efficiency measures and the IEI could also fund Pilot and Demonstration projects.

As it was a great opportunity for me to get away from a corrupt administration and, more importantly, to pursue the exciting avenue of renewable energy and environment, I readily agreed to his offer. He told me he was inclined to establish the Asia office in Geneva which had many UN institutions and both of us could go there and reconnoitre the feasibility of establishing the IEI-Asia office there. So we went to Geneva for a week when Professor José Goldemberg also came there. However, I found that the rent for even a two-room commercial apartment of about 600 ft^2 in Geneva was not less than US$ 30,000 a year besides everything else being very expensive as many international organizations were functioning from Geneva. So I suggested that from all points of view—both Prof.Amulya and myself being in Bangalore and the IISc and my contacts were mostly in Bangalore and India being the important country after China in energy consumption—it was advisable to establish the Asian office of IEI at Bangalore itself, especially when we could get a decent independent house for office at 10% of the rent in Geneva and would have more funds for projects, organizing conferences, etc. Both José Goldemberg and Amulya Reddy agreed and thus the IEI-Asia office came to be established in Bangalore. I selected an independent two-floor house in Benson Town, ten minutes from my house, at a monthly rent of Rs 25,000, less than 10% of Geneva rent. I was also fortunate in getting on deputation a highly competent officer, Dr Gladys Sumithra who was Director of Planning in Karnataka government and who had specialized in energy matters, to be deputed to IEI, besides a competent accountant, Nagaraj, from my former Karnataka Power Corporation, a Researcher from IISc, Ms Antoinette and another Research Assistant from KSCST. Thus with this skeleton staff of four and one attender, the IEI started functioning with myself as Director, Asia attending office every day except when I was travelling and Prof. Amulya attending whenever he was in Bangalore.

My work involved contacting state governments in India and other Asian countries, conducting Workshops, printing information on renewable energy, meeting senior officers, Energy Companies and the like in the line of Advocacy and Action. I was a constant visitor to the Ministry of Non-Conventional Energy Sources (MNES as it then was till it was re-named Ministry of New Energy Sources). During my time with IEI, I conducted conferences in Singapore, Dhaka, Khatmandu and Geneva besides at Bangalore and most state capitals in India. One of the highly successful programmes was a two-day workshop in Bangalore on Co-generation in Sugar Factories. With my background in the Mysore Sugar Company during which time I was also the Chairman of the South India Sugar Manufacturers' Association (SISMA) and a member of the Indian Sugar Mills Association (ISMA), I organized a two-day conference at Windsor Manor Hotel in Bangalore on installing Cogeneration in sugar factories so that electricity can be generated along with production of sugar. About 30 sugar factories had attended the Conference and many of them came forward to install cogeneration. The IEI funded 50% of the cost of preparing the Detailed Project Report. Once the DPR is prepared, it becomes easy for the sugar factory to approach the financial institutions to fund the Cogeneration project.

Because of my initiative in Cogeneration, the IREDA appointed me as its Nominee Director in sugar factories to which IREDA had given loans for cogeneration. In fact, even after thirty years since my IEI work, I continue to be a Director in many sugar factories, even after my retirement. All these sugar factories, once they had repaid the loan to IREDA, have insisted on my continuing to be on their Board even though IREDA no longer has any representation on their Boards as its loans have been repaid. *[What Bangarappa and his flunkeys contemptuously thought as a 'punishment posting', turned out to be a blessing to me.]* After this, the International Energy Agency invited me to conduct a Seminar in Geneva on Cogeneration in Sugar Factories! Altogether, it was a very rewarding experience for me in the IEI. I had time to read and meet many scientists, Ministers of various states in India and abroad, conducting seminars and meetings, visiting many countries apart from the financial benefit and staying in Bangalore and walking to my office in just ten minutes! Importantly, I learned to use internet and computer programmes as IEI was an international organization with no clerkdom and paper files. This job built my confidence greatly as I had no subordinates as in government and had to do many things by myself including getting the then precious landline phone connection!

After the completion of the initial four years I wanted to continue in the IEI. However, the Establishment Officer in the Department of Personnel who is the Controlling Officer for IAS Officers in the Government of India was, to my woe, one Narasimhan just one year senior to me from Gujarat cadre. He was a Palakkad Brahmin and was inexplicably greatly cut up that I had done my central deputation in the Central Silk Board in Bangalore and, on top of it, was also doing international deputation at Bangalore drawing UN scale of pay and conducting international seminars and hobnobbing with academicians and energy scientists and travelling footloose to many countries. He was so visibly upset when he had gone through my service history in my file that he would not even give me an appointment to meet him. I had to approach PP Prabhu his batchmate from Karnataka and my friend whom I had succeeded in the Karnataka Power Corporation and who was by then the Additional Secretary in Commerce Ministry in Delhi when I was in the IEI. Prabhu telephoned Narasimhan who grudgingly agreed to meet me. But he made me wait in Delhi's hot June in the corridor of North Block building for one hour and when I was finally ushered into his AC room, he dismissed me in two minutes curtly saying that the services of senior officers like me are needed in India and since I had already done my foreign deputation for four years I should forthwith return to Karnataka administration and that he was issuing orders immediately. I realized, though somewhat on a racist line, that he was a typical mind-constipated Palakkad Brahmin who was resentful of the good times of a *Shudra*, who had unjustly managed to get into the IAS, and therefore would not hesitate to exercise his 'power' over politically unsponsored low-caste officers. There is this type of officers who would either catch your throat, and if that was not possible, catch your feet! Narasimhan obviously belonged to this category as otherwise there was no need for him to be mean towards me, even when he was not showing me any favour. Had I gone to Ramakrishna Hegde and made him telephone Margaret Alva, also from Karnataka and well known to Hegde, who was the Minister of State for the Department of Personnel under whom Narasimhan worked and if she had telephoned him, Narasimhan would have given me tea and even cake and agreed to my extension! But I had not done it because of my lofty principle of not approaching politicians for my personal benefit. I also remembered the treatment meted out to me by the Chief Accountant in Tube Investments, Madras who was also a Palakkad Brahmin when I worked there for three years before getting through the IAS examination in 1965. He did not even congratulate me for becoming an IAS officer which was big thing in Tamil Nadu and especially among Palakkad Brahmins! It may not be entirely unjustified to think that even though there is a large number of Brahmin intellectuals and fine examples of altruism along with the two-thousand years of the Brahmin's self-serving, pollution-invented, oppressive caste history, in the case of Palakkad Brahmins, however, there is something of a peculiar, extra-mean streak as in the case of a Cobra among snakes. (One of the rather harsh slogans of EeVeRa Periyar was, *If you see a Parpan (for Brahmin, in Tamil) and a snake, spare the snake!* The general derision of most Delhi-ites for *Tam-Brahms* (Tamil-Brahmins) actually refers to Palakkad Brahmins as the ignorant Northerners cannot differentiate between one South Indian Brahmin from another, indeed one South Indian from another, all being painted with the same tarbrush as *Madrasis*. More about Palakkad Brahmins later as it is an interesting sociological and psychological phenomenon though with some inevitable racist flavour and kernel, especially for me who was at the receiving end of their hostility.

I therefore took leave of IEI after four years of a rewarding experience and returned to the state. JH Patel was the CM and an officer of his caste, the same officer whose house was raided for disproportionate assets during Veerendra Patil's regime and whose successor Bangarappa buried the investigation by getting an obliging DGP Officer to file a 'B" Report, had become the all-powerful Secretary to CM (getting the post after strongly catching the feet of a Lingayat

Swamiji like a *Udu*—a lizard of Komodo family, it was widely said!) and even the Chief Secretary was mortally scared of him. So, after Narasimhan wanted the services of a 'senior officer' like me desperately for state administration, I was posted as the Administrator to the Bangalore City Corporation as stop-gap arrangement till the election to the BCC took place! But I lasted there just for one month only!

MY FINAL STINT WITH GOVERNMENT OF INDIA

So, I reverted to Karnataka in 1996 from my fine job as Director, Asia of the International Energy Iniatitive. I spent three weeks in Bangalore in my new job as Administrator which was like Mayor-in-Council as there was no elected body for Bangalore City Corporation. Just two weeks earlier, Deve Gowda had become the "Accidental Prime Minister" of India. The 1996 Parliamentary elections gave a hung verdict. The BJP emerged as the single largest party bagging 161 seats while Congress won 140, the Janata Dal 46 and the Left front 44 and regional parties 100 seats. After the first BJP government under Atal Bihari Vajpayee was pulled down in just 16 days after 'Revolutionary Leader' Jayalalithaa (two 'a'**s** to avoid the unlucky odd number, in a former rationalist Dravidian Party of EeVeRa!) withdrew support. With the Congress supporting a non-BJP government, fourteen parties (only) formed a coalition government with Fodder King Lalu Prasad emerging as king-maker. Their first three choices were VP Singh, Jyoti Basu and Moopanar of Tamil Nadu and all declined. It was said apocryphally that in sheer desperation Lalu Prasad told his Bihari body-guards, *'Arey kooch Ghadda (donkey) lao, kuch Goda (horse) Lao'* and his minions went to search and landing in Karnataka Bhavan and shouted *"Kuch Gadda ya Goda Hai?),* and one person knowing only railway station Hindi answered, *I am Gowda, Hajir Hai,* and so they bundled poor, unwilling, Deve Gowda to their master's presence as it sounded like the South Indian version of *Goda!* In his hotchpotch ministry, Deve gowda made Ibrahim from Karnataka as cabinet minister for civil aviation (that season he was in Janata-U) and RL Jalappa, a former Revenue Minister in Karnataka, as Minister of State for Textiles. Immediately after taking oath, Jalappa snached the swearing-in invitation from his neighbour and wrote his resignation on its blank side and gave to Deve Gowda, creating a Guinness record for the shortest ministership anywhere, ever. He was objecting to the elevation of a junior foot-loose Ibrahim as cabinet minister while he, a senior and firm-footed minister in Karnataka since 1989 (he was earier a follower of Devaraj Urs and later since 1992 Janata Dal's Ramakrishna Hegde), was given a junior status. The PM had to hurriedly elevate him as cabinet minister for Textiles ministry. Jalappa was from the silk powerloom town of Doddaballapur in Bangalore Rural district and even before my working as Director of Sericulture he had known me as the DC&DM of Bangalore in 1975-1976 during Emergency when I had detained under MISA the Vice President of the District Cooperative Central Bank, for malpractices when Jalappa was the President of the DCC Bank and he had congratulated me in person for taking action against his erring VP who was his rival but, most probably for sparing him! Jalappa learned that the National Textile Corporation, which had come into existence with the marathon Textile Strike in Mumbai by the trade union firebrand Datta Samanth since 1981 which had crippled the textile mills, came directly under him. Mrs Gandhi had nationalized 125 sick textile mills, all from the private sector including a few belonging to Tatas like the Indu Mills and Tata Mills in Bombay

The NTC Mills were a big headache to the government. Due to the concentration of textile mills in central Bombay around Shivaji Park the area was known as *Girangaon* (Mill Village). In 1982 the uncompromising Dattatreya Samant leading an independent militant union, organized the Great Mill Strike of Bombay with over 2 lakh workers striking. The strike officially never ended. All the mills were closed. To curb the influence of Datta Samant (he was detained under MISA during the Emergency), Mrs Gandhi nationalized sick mills by forming the NTC in 1968 itself. In 1996, the NTC had 119 mills with over 100 of them remaining closed and paying idle wages to over a lakh workers. (This was for *not working*, because if the Mills had worked, the loss would have have been greater than the idle wages, such was the economics of public enterprises under Mrs Gandhi's *Gharibi Hatao!)* But, the NTC mills also had over 1,300 acres of land, housing the closed mills and in Bombay itself it had about 500 acres. This was very valuable land and even in 1996 valued at Rs 5,500 Cr. and there was a proposal to revive some of NTC's closed mills in the country by selling the lands in Bombay, Ahmedabad and Bangalore. The real estate Mafia of Bombay was very active in the land sale transactions of mill lands. In fact, just two years earlier, in 1994 Sunit Khatau, the owner of Khatau Mills who was trying to sell his mill land and relocate the mill, was murdered in his Mercedes car on way to his mill in a *Supari* (Contract) killing. Some of the celebrity names I heard of the land Mafia trying to get a hand in the mill lands were: Karim Lala, said to be the founder of Indian Mafia, Haji Mastan, the doyen of smuggling who was detained during the Emergency in 1975 in Bangalore, his able apprentice Dawood Ibrahim, founder of D-Company who became the biggest fugitive gangster who master-minded the 1993 bombings in Bombay and ranked No.3 in Forbes' World's Top 11 criminals list, Abu Salem, a disciple of Dawood Ibrahim and a real estate agent, Varadarajan Mudaliar, known as "Vardha" the Lord of Dharavi Slum, who was highly respected by Bal Thackeray, 'Bada' Rajan, an 'officer' of D-Company, 'Chhota' Rajan who took over the gang of his senior Rajan after the latter's murder and who became a great rival of Dawood Ibrahim, Tiger Memon, Chhota Shakeel—and their followers. The story of Bombay's underworld gangsters from 1960s through the phases of smuggling, exhortation, kidnapping, supporting political parties, film financing and subsequently in real estate is unrivalled in global crime story. Al Capone of Chicago's illegal breweries who was ultimately imprisoned for a minor tax evasion, of all crimes, would be blushing in envy in his grave at the crimes and prosperity of Bombay's underworld!

This was the murky world of Bombay Mafia and Politicians I came into when I took over as the CMD of NTC Holding Company which was planning to sell its vast land to rehabilitate about 30 mills. The IB had obviously warned the government about the land Mafia involvement in Bombay mill lands. So, the new PM Deve Gowda who was a God-fearing South Indian and a great follower of the Srirangam temple in Tiruchi in Tamil Nadu, and a loyalist of 'Rajguru' Dwarakanath, the famous astrologer of Bangalore who had many VIP clients, cautioned Jalappa about the danger of land Mafia which had an eye for NTC lands. The NTC was a huge Public Sector Undertaking with over Rs 20,000 crore share capital and having a Holding Company at the apex and nine subsidiaries in Bombay South, Bombay North, Delhi, Kanpur, Calcutta, Bangalore, Ahmedabad, Coimbatore and Pondicherry having in all 119 mills under them. Only the Coimbatore subsidiary was working without cash loss. The wage bill which the Holding Company had to remit to the subsidiaries for idle labour of over 100.000 was a stupendous Rs 20 crores monthly. Since 1994 there was no Managing Director to the NTC Holding Company whose headquarters was Delhi. Normally, no Additional Secretary level post in Delhi is left unfilled as many officers from UP, Bihar, Haryana, Punjab and MP would be dying to get a Delhi posting while South Indians would generally consider Delhi as rather less civilized and avoid. But because of the troubles NTC was facing, there was no taker for the job. Frightened by the scandals NTC would create (Dutta Samanth would himself be gunned down in 1997 by the 'supari' of Chhota Rajan), Deve Gowda warned Jalappa to be careful about the land sale of NTC and get a reliable Karnataka officer as CMD. So, Jalappa remembered me as the DC&DM of Bangalore and suggested my name to the PM. Deve Gowda had known me as Secretary to Ramakrishna Hegde when he was Minister of PWD in 1985-1988. Firstly, he brought an engineer as the Secretary to PWD which was a departure from the past when an IAS officer was always the Secretary. He also took his departmental files directly to the CM instead of routing it through the Chief Secretary or Secretary to CM. Hegde was also slightly scared of him and so he would send me to discuss with him some administrative matters. So, for some reason Deve Gowda liked me and used to telephone me when he wanted a third opinion, first opinon his and second opinion also his!

DEVE GOWDA AS KARNATAKA CM AND THE VASUDEVAN INCIDENT

Because of the lack-lustre rule of Congress Party's Veerappa Moily for two years (like his mentor Narasimha Rao, Moily never could never take any decision—'Not taking a decision is also a decision; given time a problem solves itself'!), in the 1994 Assembly elections, the JD(S) secured 115 seats, the BJP 40 and the Congress just 34 seats and Deve Gowda became CM. Despite the general impression in the media of his being rather rustic (he was referred to as 'Mannina Maga'—son of the soil, which title he relished and in fact much later he even sympathized with the fugitive Vijay Mallya and supported his case because Mallya was also a Mannina Maga!), I found him to be quite affectionate towards Officers. One instance was noteworthy when he became CM. Vasudevan was the Secretary for Urban Development having supervision of the Bangalore City Corporation. He was an excellent officer of unimpeachable integrity and very impartial. He was three years junior to me. In the Corporation there was the usual dispute of seniority between two Executive Engineers, the junior being a Dalit. The latter Dhananjaya had moved the Supreme Court which had blandly said without being specific that his rights had to be protected. After that, in the same matter, the High Court had given a ruling that he was not eligible to be made Chief Engineer, above his senior. The Urban Development Department issued an order appointing the senior as Chief Engineer in the City Corporation and Dhananjaya as Superintending Engineer after vetting the draft order with the Law Department and also the Advocate General Santhosh Hegde. Against this, Dhananjaya went to the Supreme Court again and pleaded that there was a 'Contempt of Court' by the Secretary, Urban Development in not protecting his rights and that he should be made the Chief Engineer. Though in litigation of service matters this was a routine matter, the SC in this case took an extremely serious but contestible view and issued a contempt notice to Vasudevan. Deve Gowda took no risk and appointed the renowned counsel Fali Nariman to defend Vasudevan. Contempt of court cases against senior officers are common. I have myself been issued with such contempt notices by the High Court many a time. In all those cases, whatever is the merit of the case (and very often the Court would be short on facts and would be only concerned with why its orders, irrespective of whether right or wrong, was not obeyed), the officer is always advised by the Advocate General to appear in person before the Chief Justice and to submit a pitiable affidavit profusely apologizing for his gross error and grovel abjectly with flowing tears if possible, for mercy. Added to this, I had always appeared before the Court appropriately attired in a three-piece suit with black tie and black shoes even if it was sizzling summer! This would invariably tickle the vanity of their Lordships, the suited officer cringing before them as a common criminal and so, being mollified, the officer would be let off with a frowned warning! However, in this case, Fali Nariman, because of his legal eminence, after pleading for forgiveness for the apologetic contemner, also pleaded unnecessarily on the facts (a grave mistake), that the High Court of Karnataka had said Dhananjaya was not eligible to be promoted and that the order was drafted by the Advocate General himself etc., much to the annoyance of their Lordships, who themselves are usually a little scared of Nariman. This was also because Nariman was always legally right and his fees for one appearance was more than six months' salary of the Judges! Nariman had asked the AG, Santhosh Hegde himself to be present in the court so that he could point out to the CJI the presence of the AG to corroborate on the preparation of the government order as the AG himself had vetted the draft order. But it so happened that the AG, though he was in the SC premises, at that precise moment had gone to another court hall. Added to this, the main error was Vasudevan was not present himself in the court hall in full regalia as he was told that both AG and Fali Nariman would handle the case in the courthall. When their Lordships found that the contemner was not present before the court in sackcloth, ashes and in tears and the AG was also not present, the Judge's fury knew no bounds and he pronounced an imprisonment of one month to Vasudevan. Immediately a review petition for mercy was filed by Fali Nariman before which was heard on the eighth day by the Court and duly rejected. Meanwhile there were some bizarre developments. Another senior Dalit officer, Swatantar Rao, a good soul and one year junior to Vasudeven, his good friend, took to his head to fly to Delhi and called on the Judge at his residence (both the Judge and Swantantar Rao were Dalits and Vasudevan a Brahmin, and Swatantar Rao had produced a film on the life of Baba Saheb Ambedkar though no theatre would screen it, let alone secure any award!), and at the breakfast given to him by the Judge—the Judge had known Swatantar Rao well enough to give breakfast—and the good Rao pleaded for mercy for Vasudevan! Though this was legally inexcusable and a clear case of contempt by itself, the Judge only demurred and sent him away without even giving him coffee! The same bizarre act was also said to have been done by CM Deve Gowda himself when he also met the Judge, though he was not offered any breakfast! Deve Gowda then met the President of India, Shankar Dayal Sharma and pleaded for a Presidential Pardon which however, did not materialise as Congress was in power in Delhi and Deve Gowda was Janata! (Besides, the President of secular India was quite tired, having just returned from doing his *Urulu Sèvè*—bodily roll penance in Tirupati Devasthanam!)

The matter was hotly discussed in the state Legislative Assembly when even the opposition took government to task for not protecting honest officers. A heart-broken Deve Gowda told the Assembly all that he had done, even considering asking Vasudevan to stay in government guest house *Bala Brooie* and declare it "Prison" by a notification in the gazette! But this could not be done because the alert Supreme Court had designated two judges from Karnataka High Court as watchdog (or watchmen) to supervise on a daily basis leaving their pendency of cases and see that Vasudevan indeed physically spent one month in Prison! Deve Gowda was even considering to instruct the DGP not to arrest Vasudevan and see what SC would do! But he was advised by the AG that this would be a humongous first instance of a constitutional breakdown for which the state government could even be dismissed. Chastised, Deve Gowda spoke for hours in the Assembly and finally said, *"Is this country governed according to the Constitution? Do we want the country to go to chaos by sending an honest IAS officer to jail? If those supposed to uphold the rule of law do not discharge their duties, God alone can save this country."* So saying, he shed two more buckets of tears and had to be carried out of the House by the Marshals.

The IAS Officers Association of Karnataka which, though meek as a lamb, was provoked to call an Executive Committee meeting to discuss the Vasudevan matter. I was in IEI at Bangalore and was also a member of the EC. I and a few junior members of the EC urged for a protest at the Gandhi Statue on Mahatma Gandhi Road which was negatived by the President of the IAS Association who was to be the next Chief Secretary in a few months. Obviously he did not want to jeopardise his chances of becoming the CS! Inspite of this, some of us Young Turks informed by phone as many officers as possible for a protest before the Gandhi statue that Sunday from 10 am to 6 pm. Altogether 75 officers, almost wholly junior officers, came to the Protest though none of the senior officers turned up and I was the senior-most for that honour. None of my batchmates nor my seniors came to the protest because they knew that the Intelligence Bureau would send their constable in clearly identifiable plainclothes to note down the names of the protesting officers and send it to the Home Ministry. I realized that many officers had become biological miracles losing backbones and were trying to prove the reverse of Darwinian Theory namely, life started with single cells, and as amoeba and gradually fish crawled to the land, developed vertabra and the ape stood up and ever since man walked tall. But these senior IAS officers had lost their vertebrae and would crawl back to the sea if it avoids the least risk. Even senior officers from Bengal, the state once known for its intellectuals and revolutionaries, developed frost-bite very quickly and stayed behind locked doors! Once George Fernandes when he was Industry Minister in the first Janata Ministry in 1977 remarked that when all he wanted was the IAS officers to bend a little, they simply crawled! This was understandable because none of the seniors dared to go against the government and endanger their promotions and the chance of becoming Chief Secretary on a later date even though every one of us knew how unjust it was to imprison Vasudevan. To most officers career and capturing and holding chairs like Shivaji's *Udu* holding on to the fort wall is the only ideology and would sacrifice honour at the first smell of danger. Self interest and self-preservation are the primary motives of most IAS officers. However, one remarkable exception was Adhip Choudhury IAS of 1967 batch and another, the Secretary of the Indian Forest Service Association, Laxman IFS, who came and sat with us till sunset in solidarity with us. It was a shame many IAS officers, who would of course later become Chief Secretaries, did not have the elementary decency shown by a sister service.

The rumour in Bangalore was, and Bangalore is one place where facts faithfully follow all rumours, that the senior Judge whom Swatantar Rao had met and had breakfast with, was having his house in Bangalore being constructed by Dhananjaya! Often, facts can be stranger than fiction. But, Bangalore is a place where site-bite is more poisonous than snake-bite and every file on site allotment you put your hand in, you will find a cobra! More of this a little later when I deal with my post-retirement job of five years to identify and recover Encroached Public Land, where I came across 84 judges of High Court and Supreme Court committed impropriety in becoming members of a Cooperative Housing Society and got allotted house-sites which even the High Court held they were not eligible to. They got sites from the State Judicial Employees

Cooperative Housing Society while HC and SC Judges are not "employees" of state government but appointed under the Constitution.

I am dwelling long on this Vasudevan episode only to show that, contrary to the adverse public image of Deve Gowda created by the high-caste dominant Indian print and electronic media (for instance, he was always shown as dozing in meetings and on waking, spoke bad English!), he was more humane than even supreme court judges. When Vasudevan had to be kept in the Bangalore Central Jail under the unprecedented, argus-eyed watch of two High Court Judges, Deve Gowda had instructed the DIG-Prisons to meet Vasudevan every day forenoon and keep him engaged in conversation so that he would not suffer from depression as he was not willing to meet even his family members. When he was released, he was given a lighter posting as Secretary for Housing. Just before he was sent to prison, some of us from the IAS Officers Association met Deve Gowda in a small delegation at the government guest house *Balabrooie*. As the frightened senior officers had declined to come, I had to explain to the CM Deve Gowda that the Association members would be sitting on the steps of Mahatma Gandhi statue to protest the Supreme Court order. Deve Gowda was visibly quite sad though this time he did not shed any more tears but only asked me, what good will it do? But I could see that he was somewhat relieved that the Association was at least protesting.

MY RISKY ASSIGNMENT WITH NATIONAL TEXTILE CORPORATION

I had not met Deve Gowda after that. But he had obviously remembered me from my days as Secretary to Ramakrishna Hegde and when Jalappa, his new Textile Minister, told him about the risk of handling sale of NTC lands and that the post of CMD of NTC Holding Company was vacant and he wanted a reliable officer, Deve Gowda suggested my name. Jalappa was quite happy to have me at the NTC. So, the PM instructed the cabinet secretary TSR Subramaniam, who was earlier the Textile Secretary when I was in the Central Silk Board and who also had known me, to have me appointed as CMD of NTC Holding Company immediately. The Appointments Committee of the Cabinet met at short notice and approved my appointment. All this was done within three days without my knowing and one evening I received a call from Jalappa followed by a call from TSR to leave Bangalore the next day and join duty at Delhi. I was taken by surprise and told TSR that the state government will have to release me according to procedure, etc. He said the PM had already spoken to JH Patel who had become CM and the issue of notification, etc. are only formalities I need not bother with.

I was *persona non grata* with the top bureaucracy of Karnataka when I had just returned from my IEI assignment for the simple reason that I had the audacity of doing my central deputation and 'foreign assignment' in Bangalore itself, just as Narashimhan, the Establishment Officer in Delhi had felt. Though I had known JH Patel when he was Industry Minister in Ramakrishna Hegde ministry, and he was also from Shimoga where I was DC, I did not meet JHPatel and proceeded the next day to Delhi on a cold evening and took charge of the dreaded, 'untouchable' post of CMD of NTC Holding Company. Jalappa was extremely nice to me. Within a week he took me to Bombay to meet the CM Manohar Joshi who headed the first Shivsena-BJP alliance in Maharashtra. Though the Central government was a non-BJP government, Joshi was all milk and honey towards Jalappa. He said he very much welcomed the plan of NTC to sell the lands of its closed mills in Bombay provided a part of the lands is given to the state government which would be used for housing the poor, mostly the ex-mill workers. Later, when I had discussions with the Secretary to CM, Bonghirwar and the Secretary, Urban Development, the proposal of the state was, out of the 500 acres of NTC land, one-thirds should be transferred to the Brihan Mumbhai Corporation for public purposes, another one-thirds to the state government for housing, both free of cost and the remaining land can be retained by NTC for sale. This was not acceptable to NTC as in our internal discussions in the Textiles Ministry we had found that NTC would require 75% of the land to be sold to raise funds for renovation of viable mills and only 25% could be allotted to the state government for its purposes at a reasonable price. Since NTC was a government company we could not be asked directly for a kick-back. But that did not prevent Maharashtra from dropping dark hints that it could agree to NTC's proposals provided some 'donation of land' was made! This of course was not acceptable to NTC.

Since NTC had about 500 acres of land spread over in about 15 mills in Central Bombay, I met the renowned architect Charles Correa at his modest office in Mumbai and gave him details of NTC lands in Mumbai and requested him whether he could prepare a comprehensive 'green plan' for the mill lands. Within a month he prepared an excellent plan of consolidating together the fragmented mill lands by exchanging some vacant government land and prepared a proposal of having segments of consolidated large areas of 50 to 100 acres which could be the large parks of Bombay. Though Bombay could not have the likes of the 850-acre Central Park of New York in one place, it could still have parks of 50 to 100 acres each in Central Bombay with NTC lands. These NTC parks would each be much bigger than the Shivaji Park which was less than 30 acres though it was long converted into a *'maidan'* instead of a park where Sachin Tendulkar's learning cricket was folklore. I gave the Charles Correa plan to the Urban Development Secretary of Maharashtra for approval which would benefit the city. Though I had met the CM Manohar Joshi three times after that, nothing came out of the Charles Correa plan as the pull of real estate Mafia was very strong with the government. Deve Gowda government lasted just eleven months when he resigned as PM in April 1997 when the left parties withdrew support and Inder Kumar Gujral became the PM.

I could not be posted as Secretary in Central government as I was not empanelled for that rank on the ground that my Annual Confidential Reports for the past five years were not available— for the years I was on deputation with the International Energy Initiative. The procedure in the Government for selecting officers to the post of Secretary was that the Appointment Committee of the Cabinet should "empanel" the officer on the basis of, ostensibly, five years ACRs. This was not always followed and there were cases where at the intervention of the Prime Minister an officer could still be appointed as Secretary. I had not approached Deve Gowda regarding my case. But I did make a compromise and that was meeting senior officers about my service problems provided the senior officer was an officer of integrity. TR Satishchandran who had retired ten years ago in 1987 was taken by Deve Gowda as Principal Secretary to PM in 1996 as soon as he became PM. So, I met him in his South Block office and requested him that even though my ACRs for the past five years were not available because the international NGO had no practice of writing such ACRs and my case was unique and the first such case of deputation to an international NGO and my ACRs prior to that were impeccable and on that basis whether the ACC could consider my case. He was sympathetic as he knew my work well. However, within a few days Deve Gowda had to resign, the government fell, Satishchandran left and nothing was done in my case. Jalappa also resigned immediately. Thus I returned to Bangalore where JH Patel was the CM for one year already, succeeding Deve Gowda. Thus ended my unsatisfying sojourn with NTC.

❖❖❖

J H PATEL "THE 11-7 CM"

Karnataka's First Eleven—7, Bottle N'babe, External Only CM

Race to the bottom

I was appointed as the Principal Secretary of Revenue Department when I returned from Delhi. In the earlier Mysore state the Revenue Commissioner was next only to the Chief Secretary but over time it was down-graded (with great short-sight—short-sight because Land is limited and it is one asset which appreciates in value while others *depreciate* and Land-Real Estate-Corruption are symbiotic) and became one of the Principal Secretaries to government though land matters were still very important and Deputy Commissioners of Districts came under supervision of Revenue Department. My fight with the CM's office started immediately. The very first file that came to me from the CM's office through the Revenue Minister was a typical scam. The Revenue Minister was. Ramesh Jigajinagi whom I had known well in Hegde's first Janata Dal government in 1983. He was from Bijapur district and was a Dalit. He was earlier working in the Police Department from which he resigned and contested under Janata Dal ticket and won. Hegde made him a Minister of State for Home Guards and Prisons when he was just thirty years. Jigajinagi was a very gentle and soft-spoken person and I was embarrassed when he always addressed me as Balu*ji*! He was a loyal follower of Hegde till the latter's demise in 2004 and had followed him even when he had started a still-born party, *the Rashtriya Nav Nirman Vedike* after he was expelled from Janata Dal by Deve Gowda, and also later when Hegde started another non-starter, the *Lok Shakti*. JH Patel was also a follower of Hegde and Jigajinagi was made the Revenue Minister by him in 1996. He was very happy when I was posted as the Revenue Secretary, still addressing me as *Baluji!* But all that did not stop him to be a party to a land-grab which I noticed in the very first file I received.

It was for allotment of 7,600 sft of land for Rs.70,000 from the residence compound of the DC&DM of Belgaum to the Deputy Chairman of Legislative Council. The district of Belgaum was formed by the British East India Company in 1836. Since then there was a Collector and his official residence was in a five acre land full of trees. In British times the District Collector's bungalow was always a city land mark amidst acres of land. One acre equalled 40 Guntas and one Gunta was 1,089 sq. feet. In the 17th century when England passed the inglorious Inclosure Acts making the Lords of Manors owners of most of the Commons, denying its use to the landless, accurate measurement of lands was needed. Hence, the British mathematician, clergyman and astronomer Edmund Gunter determined the imperial system of land measurement as one acre equals 10 Gunter's Chain, one Chain squared being 22 yards x 22 yards equalling 484 square yards and 10 Chains measuring one acre of 4,840 sq. yards. The cricket pitch was determined as 1 chain or 22 yards in length by Gunter which it still remains. In Madras Province the emaciated local village workers found it easier to cut Gunter's steel chain into half and carry 11 yards of Chain and therefore the half Chain came to be called a *'Gunta'* in Kannada in honour of Gunter. So, 40 Guntas was 11 yards by 11 yards x 40 making one acre. Thus one Gunta is 121 square yards which is equal to 1089 square feet (121*9), one acre being equal to 43,560 feet² (4,840*9). The generous DC of Belgaum recommended allotment of 7 Guntas equalling 7,623 sft of land from his own residence compound to Deputy Chairman of Karnataka Legislative Council at a price of Rs 70,000 at Rs 9 per sft. Now, I found the whole transaction extremely amusing besides being illegal. Amusing, because the DC was a Lingayat officer promoted to the IAS, the land-allottee Mamani the Deputy Chairman of the Legislative Council was an influential Lingayat leader from Saundatti taluk of Belgaum district, the Chief Minister's *Swamiji's feet-grabbing Secretary* (I am never tired of repeating this!) who engineered the transaction was a Lingayat IAS Officer (Special Recruit, not writing all the papers as the direct recruitment officers) and of course the CM was also a Lingayat. The Minister Jigajinigi was no doubt a good Dalit but he depended upon the support of the influential Lingayat community for getting elected from a Lingayat dominated Belgaum district. This was the reason he had forwarded the file to the CM's Secretary in the first place. Only, I as the new Revenue Secretary was the fly in the ointment though, having spent a major part of my postings in Gulbarga division which was also a stronghold of Lingayat community, I should have, in all fairness, qualified as an *honourary* Lingayat!

I decided I would kill this brazen attempt to steal government land from DC bungalow compound. *[This is like imagining the Governor allotting a 75ft * 100ft site from Raj Bhavan's Rose Garden to JH Patel!]* The Land Grant Rules said that if a person has been given a site by government anywhere in the state once, no further site can be given to the same person. I was sure that any politician of Karnataka worth his black money would have got a site from the BDA by using various short-cuts including "G" sites discretionary quota misused by all CMs. So I spoke to the Commissioner of BDA, Lakshmi Venkatachalam, an upright IAS officer of 1978 batch (and who would later become a Vice-President of Asian Development Bank), and requested her to check whether the Deputy Chairman Mamani had ever been given a site in

Bangalore by the BDA. She was very quick and informed me the next day that he was indeed allotted a site in Bangalore long ago! I asked her to send the information in writing which she did. When the BDA reply was on its way, I sent the file back to the CM's office through the Revenue Minister pointing out the violation of Land Grant Rules namely, (a) that the availability of site should be first published on the notice board of the Belgaum Tahsildar office and applications should be invited, (b) the first choice of site allotment should be to siteless persons belonging to SC/STs, (c) only if no SC/ST person from Belgaum town applies, other applications can be considered, (d) then SC/ST applicants from outside Belgaum town should first be considered, (e) if there is no SC/ST applicant also from outside Belgaum, only then siteless persons from other sections can be considered, provided their annual income was less than Rs 60,000. If government (which includes the BDA) had allotted site to a person already, he cannot be given another site by government anywhere in the State. Besides, the market value of land in the high end area of DC's bungalow was Rs 950 per square feet in 1998 according to the Guidance Value of the Registration Department at which rate, one Gunta of 1,089 square feet would cost Rs.10.34 lakhs and 7 guntas being proposed would therefore cost Rs 72.4 lakhs and the proposed Rs 70,000 was mala-fide exercise of power by the DC and the government. Also, the entire proposal was built up in just fifteen days time from the Taluk Office of Belgaum to the Secretariat at Bangalore which smacked of alarmingly indecent haste and extreme nepotism. With these remarks I sent the file up. It came back from CM's office after ten days with a lame note that the price may be fixed at Rs 10 lakhs for the entire 7 guntas of land! By this time I had with me the letter from the BDA that a site was already allotted to him earlier in Bangalore. It would therefore be blatantly illegal to allot any more government land at whatever price to the Deputy Chairman. So, I sent the file to the Law Department seeking its opinion knowing fully well that it can only point out the illegality.

In the event, the CM's office could not give the land to the favoured applicant during my tenure. The reason why I am narrating this episode in detail is to show how lawless and decadent senior IAS officers and public servants such as Ministers and Legislators can become greedy and attempt without any qualm to grab public property and how imbecile CMs can be abettors. In this case, it was firstly criminal on the part of the Belgaum DC to propose a chunk of land from his own residence which had been existing since 1836. He was sacrificing public land to benefit a rich political leader, illegally disregarding the first claim of SC/ST persons. Historically, all the residences of District Collectors in India have large extent of land when the institution of DC&DM was created over two centuries ago in 1776 when land was plenty in those small towns which have now become urban sprawl. In fact, in my first posting as DC & DM of Shimoga district, my official residence had over ten acres of land from which, on one side, land was given to construct a row of twenty quarters for officers. I had then given the remaining vacant land surrounding the DC's residence to the Horticulture Department to plant fruit trees on condition that as and when they yield fruits, the department should auction them and at no time they could part with the land for any other purpose. This ensured a lung space to Shimoga city and kept it away from the prying eyes of greedy politicians and bureaucrats. But when lawbreakers become lawmakers and witless imbecile jelly rise to become senior officers and criminals themselves, theft of public property becomes the norm. But if a Secretary to government has a backbone, he can still prevent such loot.

THE MAL-ADMINISTRATION OF J H PATEL
An Amalgam of Abdicator and a Vidhushak

JH Patel was elected to the Parliament in 1967 on a Socialist Party ticket. His family owned most of the land in Kariganur village in Channagiri taluk which was in Shimoga district then. He became famous by being the first MP to speak in Kannada in the Parliament. He was detained during the Emergency along with Ramakrishna Hegde, SR Bommai, Deve Gowda, PGR Sindhia and others. He won the Karnataka Assembly elections in 1983 and became Industries Minister in the cabinet headed by Hegde. It was my first contact with JH Patel in my capacity as Secretary to CM. In the pecking order he was just after SR Bommai and Deve Gowda. He wanted a particular 'politico' officer as Director of Industries.

Inspite of his handling politics smoothly which had made Hegde the first non-congress CM (and the second Brahmin but the antipode of Gundu Rao) in 1983, in Hedgde's second term as CM in 1985 (I left my job as his Secretary by middle of 1985 for the CSB), there were series of scandals such as the "Arrack Bottling Case" favouring some 18 *benami* persons to benefit close political allies and his son in law, and the Supreme Court passed strictures against him in 1987. The second major scandal was tapping the phones of his own cabinet ministers including Deve Gowda which was leaked out and publicized by the gadfly of Indian politics, Dr Subramanian Swamy in 1988. Hegde resigned and SR Bommai became the CM for less than a year and in the 1989 Assembly Elections, Congress Party came to power. Though the

Congress Party had a brute majority of 178 MLAs in a house of 223 and Janata Dal was reduced to just two dozen, soon scandals created by Bangarappa plagued the government and in 1994 Congress lost power winning only 34 seats to Janata Dal's 115 and BJP securing 40. In Karnataka people do not consciously choose a party to rule them, but instead throw out the ruling party because of scandalous misrule euphemistically called 'Incumbency Factor' by experts. People have the great democratic choice of voting for Crook A, Crook B or Crook C which is very different from a dictatorial system where they have the choice of selecting only Crook A! Therefore democracy is superior! The great litterateur Shivarama Karanth, who was a Gnanapith Award Winner, lost the 1971 election from Uttara Kannada district Lok Sabha constituency saving his deposit narrowly. He came Number 3! Elections are won by mob, muscle, caste and money power and decent and honest candidates have no chance. Intellectuals have now invented the term 'Majoritarianism' to describe pejoratively the mob rule. Soon, we will hear the old Greek term *Ochlocracy!*

Deve Gowda became the CM of Karnataka in 1994 and JH Patel the Deputy CM. When Deve Gowda became the 'Accidental PM'—in 1996 JH Patel stepped in as CM, as Karnataka mostly has an Odd-Even-Odd cycle of Lingayat-Okkaliga succession with some Brahmin—Backward Class aberrations thrown in like Gundu Rao, Hegde, Bangarappa or Veerappa Moily! JH Patel had a jumbo cabinet of 45 ministers—one of every three MLAs becoming a minister—and the rest 70 appointed as Chairmen of some 60-odd State Corporations and Boards and the few left-outs sulking! This is another anomalous position in Karnataka. The Chairpersons of Government Corporations are not the CEOs but only fix the date of the Board meeting, preside over them and demolish sumptuous snacks. But the malleable CEOs of PSUs and Boards are so servile that they abdicate their powers and the Chairmen illegally exercise powers they do not have and collect their bribes. Hence, the scramble for Chairman posts if they do not get ministerial berths and these posts are given 'cabinet rank' which means constitutionally nothing except flying the national flag on their cars.

MEANING OF "11—SEVEN CM, BNB, EO" EXPLAINED!

In the United States and in some other countries such as Japan there are 7-ELEVEN shops with trade mark bright Red-White-Green stripes painted. These small shops sell snacks like donuts, sandwiches, coffee and soft drinks from 7 am in the morning till 11 pm in the night for the convenience of people when most other shops are closed. However, JH

Patel as CM was a remarkable anti-thesis of 7-ELEVEN because he could only work with great difficulty from *11 am* to *7 pm*! The civil servants in Bangalore have a predisposition to drop everything when the temperature rises above 30°C and run to Bangalore Club for a draft beer! But the CM of Karnataka would drop everything, regardless of the temperature, and run for his sun-downer at 6.30pm. His favourite drink was *Napoleon VSOP* (Very Superior Old Pale) brandy which his chosen, obliging *Sancho Panza* Director of Industries kept a steady supply of since the time when JH Patel became Industry Minister first. While *Napoleon* was from good French grapes and healthy in moderation, the only problem was Patel would polish off three quarters of the 750ml bottle before falling unconscious, like the accident-prone Mughal Emperor Humayun who was reputed to drink 14 glasses of wine, fall unconscious and get up after six hours and start the next 14 glasses-cum-falling routine. So, Patel's first 'B' in the honorific 'BnB' was for *'Bottle'*, the other 'B' in 'BnB' denotes *Babe* which weakness he was enthusiastically confessing to and which his lady MLA supporters and admirers were thrilled about and even bragged. After all, no other CM in India was so truthful to publicly admit his amorous life! They proudly held him as the great Krishna Leela practitioner.

He once gave a long interview to *India Today* (31-12-1996) published under the title: *Karnataka CM Patel's Admission of His Fondness for 'Women and Wine' Provokes Public Outcry*, went on to say: *Whisky after sundown. And women. If that doesn't sound like the stuff politicians are supposed to be made of, there is another major point of divergence from those of his ilk— Patel's candour. The chief minister freely acknowledges his weakness for the bottle and the fairer sex. Patel's boyhood friend, writer UR Ananthamurthy was quoted as saying, "I wish he'd be more disciplined in his personal life".* The chief minister, for his part, was unrepentant and said *" I am not answerable to anybody other than my wife. Only she has to forgive me."*

He had a knack of saying politically incorrect things. There was a protest against a beauty contest in Bangalore. When protesters battled the police over the Miss World contest in Bangalore, his response was typically *Patilian: "Those who want to show will show. Those who want to see will see."* When well-known Kannada writers joined the protests, he taunted them for being *"too old to see and appreciate the good things in life".* And later he had this to say about protests by women's groups: *"Only the ugly ones are protesting. All the pretty ones are telling me they support the beauty contest."* When he recommended a woman for nomination to the state Legislative Council, a senior minister questioned her relationship with the chief minister and a rather heavily hurt Patel's response was, *"Why should I need her when I have the most fashionable models to choose from?"* An important JD MLA Vaijanath Patil from Gulbarga put it, *"Patel is a majawadi (pleasure seeker), and not a samajwadi (socialist)."* He added, *"When we hand over a memorandum, he simply hands it over to Gunman Thimme Gowda."* As a result, "arrogant" officers are ruling the roost, other MLAs said. In the first year of his office, he had visited only 8 of the then 19 districts. This is to be contrasted with the tight schedule of Ramakrishna Hegde who had held a review meeting in every district sending me one day earlier to find out the problems in each district. Early in his tenure, Patel had said that, unlike his predecessors, he could not set a hectic schedule for himself. *"My ministers will do that,"* he said. But, though there were 45 of them, few were known to be diligent. According to the secretariat staff, less than half of them turned up for work.

There was an interesting episode of his Caligula problem in the Karnataka Bhavan in Delhi when I was the Resident Commissioner there. Within a year of my tenure as Principal Secretary of Revenue Department, due to the untimely demise of an Additional Chief Secretary one year senior to me, there was a reshuffle and promotions to the top posts. I was promoted. But, even though I was the obvious choice for the important non-political post of Development Commissioner and Agricultural Production Commissioner because of my stint, as DC, Divisional Commissioner & CADA Chairman, Director of Sericulture, Secretary to CM, international experience, etc., all of which made me the most eligible person to be appointed as the Development Commissioner of the State—and I would have followed in the footsteps of my mentor GVK—yet inspite of all this, I was kicked upstairs and shunted out to Delhi to be the under-employed, glorified, sinecure Hotel Manager of Karnataka Bhavan of the State government, which was what the high-sounding 'Resident Commissioner' of Karnataka Bhavan actually meant, even the name sounding like that of a Udupi Vegetarian hotel! A small cabal of officers headed by the CM's Principal Secretary who was known as the Principal Fixer exercising power in the name of 11—7 Patel who was otherwise engaged in BnB (EO)— Bottle and Babe, External Only (incidentally EO stood for 'External Only' as one wiseacre MLA who knew his marbles and onions put it, after one bottle of brandy you are in 'super-slow motion' as in 'action replay' and can only indulge in 'Externalities'!) had wanted me out of Bangalore as a lesson for others for not toeing their line. Crude and coarse as they were, their attitude was, 'Either you are with me or against me'. They also wanted to demonstrate their Power. Essentially, they could not forgive me for not paying obeisance to them, for having done my Central and international deputation, all in Bangalore and rubbing it with UN scale of pay. Jealousy—like anger, fear, hunger, libido, lust and greed—can be a great motivating factor, both for constructive but mostly for destructive purposes. To my fault, I was too proud to pay Court to these pygmies as I thought, nay I knew, I had much to be proud about compared to them. The leader of them reputedly had fallen at the feet of a Lingayat Swamiji to be posted as the Principal Fixer to the CM, and the Swamiji being absolutely extra-temporal, obliged. It was said there was tough competition between the *Sancho Panza* supplier of *Napoleon* and this aspiring Lingayat-leader officer, to become Secretary to CM. But unfortunately, the Sancho Panza was from outside the state and he could not garner the support of any Swamiji, so he lost the race! In Karnataka the Swamijis and most political leaders have symbiotic relations because many leaders allegedly keep their black money with these Swamijis as it was safe with these Godmen and the God-fearing Income Tax officers do not raid *Mutts*. The Chief Vizier himself was scared of the Principal Fixer and would adopt the proverbial simian's *See no Eveil, Hear no Evil, Speak no Evil.*

So, without bothering to call on the CM and disregarding the bureaucrat-junta, I proceeded to Delhi and took charge as RC of Karnataka Bhavan. I had an efficient deputy in Balkishan Das Negi, IAS who was from Himachal Pradesh and very familiar with Delhi. I also had another illustrious IAS Officer by name Jesu Das Seelam who was earlier DC of Mandya district when I was CMD of Mysore Sugar Co. He was an indescribably efficient Dalit officer. He was exceptional because he was also politically high octane and would later take Voluntary Retirement and become an MP from Andhra Pradesh and Union Minister of State for Finance! As my deputy, he too was extremely helpful to me. Within a few weeks of my taking charge as RC, JH Patel made his first visit to Delhi. Excepting Congress CMs when Congress was also in power in Dehi and Hegde, who had all-India ambitions, the Janata Dal CMs abhorred visiting Delhi. Tamil Nadu's Muthuvel Karunanidhi who was CM for 20 years was said to have visited Delhi only three times in his entire tenure. The protocol in KB was, whenever the CM came to Delhi, the RC would receive him in the airport. So, I went to receive JH Patel when he landed around 5 pm one day. Like all CMs of Karnataka he was very polite and nice. From the airport to KB it used to take about 40 minutes. Somehow the topic came to Socialism. JH Patel was earlier in Socialist Party and was never in Congress unlike Hegde or Deve Gowda. So I talked to him about Lenin's *State and Revolution,* of how the State is a tool to oppress one class even in a democratic republic. JH Patel got quite excited and recalled his early days when he first read Lenin and how when he was detained during emergency he again read the book in the prison. This was quite an experience for me for the image I had of him.

But then all intellectual pursuit ended for Patel at 7pm. This was like *Dr Jekyll* and *Mr Hyde*. During day time JH Patel was jovial, witty and even mildly rational. But, come 7 pm he would become an entirely changed person with bipolar disorder. In Karnataka Bhavan-*Cauvery*, there was a separate suite with a small attached kitchen for the CM on the third floor, away from prying eyes. The Karnataka Bhavan was a highly indisciplined organization. RCs stay only for six months and it was like a short-term Parking Lot and typically the RC never takes the job seriously spending a few months as a prelude to go on central deputation or, on completion of central tenure, some time to wind up their affairs in Delhi. The most influential persons in the KB were therefore, shockingly, the Clerks and 'Room Boys'. Clerks knowing Hindi became close to the Ministers because the Karnataka Ministers, not knowing beyond 'railway station' Hindi, require assistance in visiting central government ministries. When MPs from Karnataka became even central ministers, they usually took a Personal Assistant from Karnataka Bhavan. Therefore, many of KB clerks become very smart and also very close to ministers to the extent their houses also got raided in sympathy by CBI along with their bosses whenever the central government changed! The 'Room Boys' who were only of the rank of peons had a special source of strength. Unlike Banglaore, in Delhi it is a lot of botheration to buy liquor. There were not many Liquor shops in Delhi and the licenced few were run by Delhi Tourism Development Corporation in shabby premises by shabby staff in still more shabbier surroundings compared to the glossy ambience of wine shops in Bangalore. Many days a week they would also be closed. So, the Room Boys of KB were stockpiling liquor and selling at premium to persons staying in KB like first of every month, festivals, procession-days, etc. So, the Room Boys would stock hard liquor in generous quantity and sell to legislators and guest. There used to be late night orgies in KB. To bring some discipline I had given notice to the Room Boys, at the peril of disciplinary action, prohibing sale of liquor to guests and banned drinking in the rooms beyond 9 pm as the KB Mess would open at 8.30pm and close at 10pm. Naturally this was resented by Room Boys and also by many MLAs and Ministers. It so happened that one night one of the Room Boys, himself in an inebriated condition, went out around midnight to bring some ice for a group of partying MLAs in KB-2-*Krishna*, walking distance from *Cauvery*. The KB-2 had a full-size glass door and when the swaying Room Boy returned with two ice-buckets, and asked the person on the other side of the door to open, that person would not oblige. In his sloshed state, the room boy did not realize that he was talking to his own reflection. When he found the other fellow was mimicking him, the room boy got angry and hit the other person. Naturally the person on the other side also hit him simultaneously. In this surreal battle the glass-door broke and inflicted its own revenge on the room boy's face and arms! Another drunken colleague of his could not locate the entry gate of Karnataka Bhavan I in his divine confusion and went by mistake into the Tamil Nadu Illam just opposite KB-1 and insisted on entering. The Security staff of Tamil Nadu Illam promptly put him in their 'Lock up' room (being a semi-independent State, Tamil Nadu had brought its own policemen!) and next day morning when the bombed-out 'boy' slurred his identity, Seelam, my very efficient Deputy RC had to go and rescue him! I made the KB Manager file a police complaint against both Room Boys for drunken, disorderly behaviour and damage to public property and also simultaneously ordered a departmental enquiry appointing the Additional RC, BKD Negi as the Enquiry Officer. When the enquiry was completed and charges were proved, I dismissed both from service with future bar of government employment while the criminal cases continued. But they went on appeal to the Chief Secretary as provided in the Civil Service Rules and I learned much later when I was no longer the RC that they were reinstated as Room Boys at the intervention of a cabinet minister in SM Krishna's government, who was also the main financier for the Congress party and the shadow Chief Minister! Such was the power of KB Room Boys compared to Resident Commissioner and the wondrous backbone-missing Chief Secretaries!

The problem of drinking was therefore serious in Karnataka Bhavan. So, when the 11-7 Patel had come to Delhi the first time when I was RC, there was an interesting episode. A Pimp-cum-Cabinet Minister, a faded Kannada actor of yester-years, was Patel's shadow wherever he went. Having come from the glamourous film-field he was in touch with many 'extras' and his main portfolio was to be the *major dōmō* for CM's salacious routine and this extended to Delhi also. After reaching KB from the airport I asked the CM whether he wants to meet any central minister the next day. He said he had no plans and so I took leave of him. The Joint Secretary to CM invariably accompanied the CM as the Principal Fixer had no capacity to discuss anything intelligible with Delhi bureaucracy or leaders and in any case no Delhi man would give any money to him! His forte was his caste matters and making money in Bangalore. But the JS was a sober person and not privy to the CM's debaucheries. What I learnt next day from my Deputy RC Seelam, who had adroitly used Room Boys to spy on MLAs,

Ministers and especially the CM, was this: the 11-7CM, his constant Cabinet-cohort and two selected MLAs had made steady progress with drinking well into the night in the CM's suite with their *femmes de la nuit*, when one MLA got aggressive and complained to 11-7 that the RC had banned drinking in the rooms of KB beyond 9 pm which would include CM's suite also. This was certainly not good news and the *major domo* was worried. He wanted to know the details and one of the renegade Room Boys serving CM's suite-converted-bordello explained rather colourfully the restrictions the RC had imposed on drinking and action for violation. This made the *major domo* very angry and he told the CM, *"Buddhi (*a respectful term a menial uses to his master or a poor tenant to his landlord in Old Mysore State*), You have to teach a lesson to this RC, you should transfer him tomorrow itself."* The fairly sloshed 11-7*Buddhi* was in extreme laboured, feeble, slow-motion Krishna Leela attempts on his *femme* and, annoyed, could pay little attention to him. So, the *major domo* raised his voice and took the CM's half-empty Napoleon, shook it and explained to him the gravity of the situation. When the CM realized that his Napoleon himself was in danger of being captured, he became alarmed and asked what can be done. The two agitated MLAs said the RC should be summoned to CM's suite at once and a dressing down should be administered for such high-handedness. My official residence was within the same compound of the KB. 11-7 was skeptical and told the agitated audience that the RC, if he comes there now, may probably start giving a lecture on Trotsky, vaguely recalling the talk on Lenin from the airport. Meanwhile the CM's *femme de la nuit* was bored (she could not understand why her patrons were bad-mouthing RC which was an OK whiskey as far as she knew!), and became restless, pulling at the *jibba* sleeves of 11-7.) Anxious to return to his ultra-slow-motion activities, 11-7 suggested to get his JS, who was more knowledgeable in grave administrative matters such as on hand, to the suite and seek his advice. So, a Room Boy was despatched to JS's comfortable room 202 on second floor and he was woken up and brought somewhat groggy himself before the CM. But when he quickly assessed the situation, he very strongly advised against calling the RC to the scene at this devil's hour because, he said, even during daytime the RC was reputedly unpredictable and there was no telling what he would do now as he had recently got two Room Boys even arrested for supplying liquor after 9 pm. So, he firmly advised that the RC could be asked in the morning about the liquor-supply, preferably after breakfast. This wise advice was readily accepted by 11-7 and thus was avoided a potentially IPC situation. Next day everyone forgot about interviewing the RC. New Day, New Dawn.

After a few weeks, there was the annual Planning Commission discussions in Yojana Bhavan to decide the Annual Plan size of Karnataka for the next year. The Karnataka team headed by the CM along with Chief Secretary, Planning Secretary and Finance Secretary landed in KB. After a preliminary meeting of officers in KB the earlier evening, it was decided the CS, the Finance and Planning Secretaries and I would meet the CM next day morning at 9am to brief him for the 11am meeting at Yojana Bhavan, though the JS was highly skeptical about any likelihood of a 9am meeting with 11-7. However, next day morning at 8.50am we trooped to CM's suite but were informed that the CM was still in bed! The JS was strongly advised to go in and wake him up as Karnataka's next year's budget depends upon the CM persuading Deputy Chairman Jaswant Singh to agree to Karnataka's plan size. So, we went in after 15 minutes and found the CM in his pyjamas on his bed in a semi-recumbent position. We sat around the bed and the CS explained in his 30/70-Kannada-English the intricacies. I did not think the CM understood anything from the briefing except a vague feeling that the state did not have enough tax revenue to finance its plan. It was already 10am and it took about 30 minutes to reach Yojana Bhavan from KB-1 and another ten minutes to reach the meeting hall and settle down and the CM was still in pyjamas! So he told us to go in advance to the meeting and he would join by 11. So we left. The Deputy Chairman Jaswant Singh was a gentleman and being an ex-army man, was punctual. The CM joined after one hour. The Deputy Chairman was quite polite about it instead of cutting another Rs 100 crores for being unpunctual. When he asked the CM for his remarks, JHPatel went on a tirade against the central policies and the state's helplessness in finding resources in an unfair financial power sharing between centre and states, which were all totally irrelevant to the agenda for the meeting.

Such was the administration of Karnataka under JH Patel. Actually, apart from the prurience of the CM there was no contribution by him to the administration as it was all left to the small gang of his caste, half-educated bureaucrats sponsored by an earthern Swamiji and a whilom actor. In Kannada 'Bangara' means Gold. Thus, Bangarappa's reign of two years was known as the Golden Age of Corruption though of less than 12 karats. The 11-7's regime could be described as the Aluminium Age as any gross illegality was made malleable and legal by his chosen Kapo. The Krishna Leela, BnB-External Only(EO), 11-7 did not have time for administration of the state which was hijacked by this cabal. It was not as if other CMs of Karnataka were paragons of virtue. There were many l'amour stories about Kengal Hanumanthiah who was the CM for four years till 1956. But he was also a hard task master and he personally supervised the construction of Vidhana Soudha and had even controversially employed prisoners from the Central Jail for quick completion. He had appointed the sterling GVK as his Secretary. Gundu Rao was allegedly infatuated with the dance-star of *Shankarabharanam* movie and when the Venus Circus tent went in flames in 1981 killing over 92 persons, mostly children, Gundu Rao was said to be enjoying her performance! Ramakrishna Hegde's playboy life style was well known from his early days. He used to give exclusive *tete-e-tete* interviews at his residence to female cub reporters and they would be floored when he poured pale Darjeeling tea in bone-thin China, wearing his ankle length blue velvet Japanese *Yukata* telling stories in his husky voice through his thick, sensuous lips and the dreamy lady-reporters would swoon and write about him lyrically. He was highly impressed by Protima Bedi and granted 10 acres of government land in Hessarghatta near Bangalore where she established the *Nrityagram*. Later, he took the renowned danseuse Pratibha Prahlad thirty five years younger to him as his *amante*. They had twin sons and she shifted to Delhi. But, Kengal Hanumanthiah and Hegde were good administrators while 11-7 abdicated administration to his *Kapo* and he lived for his 7 pm meeting with Napoleon and daily dose of touchy-feelies!

In theory, in a Democracy people elect a party and the party elects its leader in the legislature to form the government and rule the state for the good of the people. The primary duty of the Chief Minister is therefore to administer the state. If he has no time or capacity to attend to administration, he has no reason to continue as CM. In the case of JH Patel, his lewd profligacies became his main function and administration was handed over to his *Kapo*. And his extra-curricular activities were not in the nature of reading, writing or travelling and the like. It was just drinking and debauchery. The head of the government need not be saints morally. There are innumerable examples where leaders have built nations while not leading a conventionally moral life. The unique example is Kemal Pasha Mustafa of Turkey. The 600-year old strong Ottoman Empire became progressively decadent and after the first World War became like the Moghul Empire after the death of Aurangazeb (1707). Kemal Pasha Mustafa, heading the Turkish Army deposed the last puppet emperor and made Turkey a Republic in 1923. From the day he became the President in 1923, he started changing Turkey politically, economically, socially and culturally. Tsar Nicholas I of Russia had described Ottoman Turkey as 'A Very, Very Sick Man of Europe'. Kemal Pasha ruled Turkey only for 15 years, from 1923 to 1938 when he died due to excssive drinking, smoking and womanizing, all prohibited by Islam. But in that period he transformed Turkey. He converted the 600 or so *Madrasas* into schools where science must be taught. As a key to change the Arabic orthodox Islamic cultural mindset of Turkey, he formed a 9 Member Scholars Commission to change the Arabic script of Turkish to Latin script. The Commission said it would require five years to complete such an exercise. Kemal Pasha told them to compete it in three months and locked them up in a palace till they completed the task. They ultimately did it in six months in 1928. Notable among the revolutionary changes he brought were: abolition of the Caliphate; abolition of Sharia Courts and Madrasas and introduction of civil and criminal codes adopting the Swiss and Italian law; free and compulsory primary education to both boys and girls; passing a "Hat Law" by which Turkish men should not wear the cylindrical, Ottoman Red Fez Cap with a black tuft resting on the side; no *burqa, hijab or niqaab* for women; giving voting rights to both men and women and the right to women to get elected to Parliament much before many European countries; adoption of metric system of measurements; adoption of Gregorian Calendar; changing weekend holiday to Sunday instead of Friday; constitutionally making the Turkish Armed Forces and Judiciary the guarantor of *laïcité*—secularism as in France after the 1789 Revolution when complete separation of religion from government affairs was written into the Constitution of the First Republic; abolition of *Ulema* system of issuing *Fatwas*; shifted the capital to the more central Ankara; outlawed Polygamy; established the National Railways and the first Turkish National Bank; agricultural land reforms and promotion of industries; he changed the status of Hagia Sophia into a Museum which was constructed in 537 CE as a holy cathedral and converted into a Mosque in 1453 with Ottomon conquest of Istanbul; [*The present Presdent Recep Tayyip Erdoğan has in 2020 changed it back to a mosque.]* He changed the political, economic and social system of Turkey totally in 15 years by "Europeonizing" Turkey from a medieval, decadent monarchic system. For this, the Turkish people revered him and named him *Ataturk*—the Father of Turkey. Indeed no one in history deserved the title more.

For all his greatness, Kemal Pasha's personal life was debauched and licentious. He was given to heavy drinking and smoking, both of which are prohibited in Islam and he was a compulsive womanizer. He was married to a Paris-educated Turkish lady but the marriage lasted for only two years since she objected to his profligate lifestyle and divorced him. They had no children though Kemal Pasha adopted nine children, mostly orphans. He did not occupy the traditional, sprawling *Topkapi* palace where the Ottoman Emperors resided but lived in the smaller *Dolmabahçe Palace* where he died of cirrhosis of liver in 1938 at the age of 57. No other leader of a nation had ever achieved so much in so few, fifteen years. Inspite of his licentious life-style he did splendid duty to his country selflessly. His funeral procession was two miles long with the entire population of Istanbul joining. [One needs to repeat, *"Sharanara Savannu Maranadalli Kaanu—See the saint in his death"]* Of course, to talk of Kemal Pasha Ataturk and the 11-7 Jayadevappa Halappa Patel in the same breath is crashing from the sublime to the ridiculous. There was no redeeming feature in Patel's chief ministership of 3 years in Karnataka, his Bacchanalian orgies taking his toll on his health. In *Hamlet,* Marcellus the guard observing the debauchery going on inside the Elsinore Castle tells Horatio the scholar, *Something is Rotten in the State of Denmark!* He would have fainted had he seen the daily depravities in Patel's bordello. His frank admission of his libertine life-style and politically incorrect, vulgar, sexist, misogynist comments were lapped up by a titillation-starved media as Churchillian wit! His frank admission of his *'Krishna Leela'* in his inappropriately named residence *Punya* were praised for transparency! The greatest tragedy in the annals of Karnataka was the destruction of a comparatively virtuous bureaucracy and creating a venal, corrupt gang of officers headed by the Chief Secretary himself selected by Bangarappa superseding honest officers and continued by Patel. Honest and efficient officers were sidelined, even punished as in the case of Sankaranarayanan who was the only Chief Secretary in the country to be suspended whimsically. While every crime in Bangarappa's regime was committed with his initiative, full knowledge and approval, this was however not the case with JH Patel. Along with venality, corruption and community favour and clannism, added to all this was the total neglect of CM's attention to administration and, instead, domination by CM's personal Principal *Kapo* with a scared Chief Vizier only conducting endless, meaningless, purposeless meetings and taking inconsequential decisions which nobody bothered about implementing and wasting everybody's time. All this was because 11-7CM had no time or inclination to administration and yet his party continued him as CM!

Caligula was the third emperor of Rome. JH Patel was the third Janata-non-Congress CM after the first Janata CM Hegde. Because of his mis-rule Caligula was assassinated by his Praetorian guards, stabbed thirty times. But in India, though there is plenty of misrule, leaders do not end up assassinated, Mrs.Gandhi being an exception who inevitably reaped the harvest from nurturing Bhindranwale. But Karnataka being a mild state, the helpless people use the elections to vote-out the mis-ruling party. They do not vote for a party, *they vote against a party.* Frankly, JH Patel was no Caligula. He was merely the Chief *Vidhushak-Tenaliraman* combo of the Janata Darbar feebly attempting Casanova tricks! So, in the ensuing Assembly elections in October 1999, the JD(U) of JH Patel lost miserably. It secured just 18 out of the 224 seats and its vote share was just 14%. JH Patel himself lost his seat from his native Channagiri, being number 3 in the race after the BJP-supported Independent and the Congress candidates. He barely got a little above one-sixth of votes polled and just escaped forfeiting his deposit. Thanks to the maladministration of JH Patel, the undeserving Congress was the gratuitous, default beneficiary securing a whopping 132 seats out of 224 and a vote share of 41%. The BJP was second with 44 seats and 21% of the vote share portending its coming of age in the state. Patel was already in failing health, frequently staying in Jindal Naturecure Institute near Bangalore (which charged Rs 12,000 per day for a 'Deluxe Hut' paid by his excise *'Yajaman'*) and died of liver disease in December 2000 at the Manipal Hospital. He was 70. The only praise his obituary writers could agree upon was that he was a great wit, mistaking his sexist *bon mots* and buffoonery for humour. He was just a joker. *Of course Nobody Clapped!*

AN ASSIGNMENT IN NEPAL

While being shunted as Inn-keeper of Karnataka Bhavan in 1998, instead of swatting flies in the KB, I went to the UNDP Office and re-acquinted with the Nepal Desk Officer. As a result, I did one more UNDP assignment in Nepal. I had been to Nepal once before in 1996 at the request of the UNDP for preparing a pilot project on sericulture. So, in 1999 the UNDP again asked me whether I can spend two months in Nepal to get the project implemented. I agreed and thus I landed again in Kathmandu which is the highly congested capital with a population of about 25 lakh people and a temperate climate and high rainfall. The Director of UNDP, Nepal was now a German and he informed me that I would be assisted by a Country Counterpart for the project. He was one Dr Shrestha, about 35 years of age and was teaching Economics in the University. He was a pleasant, chatty person and new to sericulture as there was no sericulture except a little weaving of imported Chinese silk yarn in Nepal. But there was a Silk Association of Nepal (SAN) whose chairperson was an ebullient Mrs Margaret Shah, a Briton married to a Nepali industrialist owning a distillery in Kathmandu. She was highly knowledgeable and enthusiastic about sericulture. Being classified as Hardship Assignment because of the need to visit remote villages, it was a well paid consultancy with a fee of US$ 500 per day and a *per diem* of $ 100. [*I am repeating these tawdry money matters as guidance to increase the general knowledge of my honest younger colleagues who can prosper by legitimate means! With concentration on whatever posting one gets and with some initiative, honest officers can enjoy their work and also earn legitimately what corrupt officers earn illegally! So, young officers need not be sold out on Faustian bargain and can still take heart from my experience.]*

It was an adventurous experience to establish the project, travelling in rural areas. To give an example, Dr Shrestha and I had to visit a few villages close to the famous Chitwan National Park which was in the Terai region bordering India, about 250 km from Kathmandu. We left early morning in a Cessna Turboprop which took only 40 minutes to reach Chitwan. From there we travelled by a sedan for about an hour and then switched to a 5-gear Mitsubishi van for 20 kms. When the road ended in a narrow footpath, we got on the pillion of four motor-bikes waiting for us which took us to a river bank. The river was three feet deep and the motor-bikes had to be left behind. Four sturdy buffaloes were waiting and each of us got on to the back of the buffaloes and I held on tightly to the rider! In this manner I reached the village in the evening after travelling in all five modes of transport, from medieval to modern, for about 8 hours. The return journey after three days had to be done in the reverse order. Between villages the travel was always by motorbikes and buffaloes! This was a great experience. I was 58 years. I was physically fit as I have been a jogger since my fortieth year.

I completed my Final Project Report for implementation and met the Director of UNDP before submission. While the Director during my previous visit was a friendly British lady, this time the Director was a German and was of a different disposition with traces of latent Nazi mannerism. He frankly told me that nothing could be implemented in Nepal by government officials and UNDP would have to rely upon NGOs. I found that Nepal, with a population of 2.5 crores and ranking 160th in per capita income globally, had as many as 40,000 NGOs of which nearly 2,000 were international NGOs, mostly in Kathmandu. So, I agreed with him that the Sericulture Project could be implemented with the close involvement of NGOs apart from government support. However, I did not mention that SAN and its Chairperson Maggie Shah, who was British, should have an important role because I strongly suspected that this German Director probably thought the Second World War was not yet over! Besides, I had to get my final instalment of consultancy fee on acceptance of my Project Report by the Director! Fotunately, I had a *coup de grace*. I remembered my meetings with the German aid agency GiZ (it has a foot-long unpronounceble title having all the 27 German alphabets!) in Bhikaji Cama place in New Delhi on renewable energy matters. I had also seen a GiZ office in Kathmandu. So I told the Director that the GiZ could be involved closely with the Nepal Sericulture Project as it was the most efficient aid agency! This brightened him immensely and he immediately ordered his secretary to bring black tea and also produced from his cupboard his personal supply of the Leibniz cream biscuits! Later, I learned the Director seldom shared his biscuits with any one! My appointment with him, though scheduled for 7 minutes with Germanic precision, however extended to half hour and I found I had scored with him and my consultancy fee was safe! Thus ended my last consultancy assignment very successfully and I returned to Delhi to continue with my job of Resident Commissioner and Glorified Hotel Manager of Karnataka Bhavan.

❖❖❖

CHAPTER 19

Somanahalli Mallaiah Krishna

A Very Smooth Exterior !

Within a month of my returning to Delhi from Nepal, the elections to Karnataka Assembly took place in October 1999. There is no charismatic leader in Karnataka. Reputed men of letters like Shivarama Karanth and honest persons cannot get elected on their own. Due to the disgraceful, Caligula rule, in the 1999 Assembly elections, JH Patel and his JD(S) were summarily rejected by the people with JD(S) securing just 18 seats while the BJP got 44 seats and the residual Congress got 132 seats in default. SMK got his chance to be the CM, finally. It was not as if SMK was brilliant and beloved leader. People's revulsion of Patel's bawdy administration was so overwhelming than their love for Congress. More than half of the voters who went for voting just wanted to get rid of JD-U. People, whom the Poet Nissar Ahmad lamented as *Kurigalu Sar, Kurigalu* ('Sheep Sir, Sheep'), nevertheless just reject the ruling party to get rid of it rather than choose a dazzling opposition party because of the latter's sterling qualities.

The tragedy in Karnataka's *Mock-Democracy* is, every government mis-rules and the people vote out the ruling crook party and elect another crook party in the next election and after its misrule, elects again the earlier crook party in a vicious circle of helpless democracy! If in this fake Democracy, no party gets a majority of seats, no matter, resort can be taken to *'Resort Democracy'*—a patented Karnataka invention which all democratic and constitutional institutions, including the Judiciary, and all 'intellectuals' have come to accept as the new norm! It started with Ramakrishna Hegde when he rescued NTR whose Telugu Desam MLAs were precariously kept in Hyderabad's Hotel Viceroy and Hegde arranged safe transport of two busloads of them to Hotel Dasaprakash in Mysore for a week! Hegde's much publicized *Value-based Politics* was more a *'Politics-based Value!'* Since Dasapakrash does not serve non-vegetarian or liquor, after 1985 the kidnapped MLAs are luxuriously kept in Resorts !

Within a month I was transferred to Bangalore as Additional Chief Secretary in charge of Public Works Department and Housing. Dharam Singh from Gulbarga was the minister for PWD and Kamarul Islam of Muslim League, also from Gulbarga, was the Minister for Housing. I learned that the original proposal was I should be the ACS for PWD and Irrigation Departments as I had the previous experience as Chairman and Administrator of Upper Krishna Project. But the minister for Irrigation was HK Patil from Dharwad district with whom I had not worked at any time but, more importantly, the Irrigation Engineers were mortally alarmed at the prospect of my supervising their work. So, in the last moment Housing replaced Irrigation. The PWD Engineers were also crestfallen to having me in their domain but Dharam Singh stood firm in having me. Kamrul Islam was a budding leader of the Muslim League in Gulbarga when I was DC&DM there and I had the pleasure of detaining him under MISA along with other riff-raffs for inciting communal violence during the Ganesh Chaturthi. His reservations were brushed aside and I became ACS for PWD and Housing by end of 1999.

I had fifteen months to retire when I took charge as ACS when SMK was CM. Actually, I was most suited for the post of ACS and Development Commissioner for Agricultural Production in view of my experience. But, an officer who was sceptical of the difference between a ton and a quintal (1 qtl = 100kg; 1 ton = 1,000kg = 10 qtl) and closer to the Chief Vizier was therefore posted as Development Commissioner in public interest! SMK was obviously cautioned about my being in the *KD* List and it was only because Dharam Singh knew me well that I was made ACS for PWD with Housing added. Otherwise I would have continued as Hotel Manager of Karnataka Bhavan in Delhi. There were two projects to be immediately attended to during my tenure. The important one was the Rs 2,500 crore project for improvement of 2,000 km of state highways to be posed for World Bank loan. The second was, as soon as SMK took over as CM, he had announced his plan to construct a *'Vikasa Soudha'*, a replica of Vidhana Souda by its side, by demolishing some 100-years old buildings housing the Government Press, the Directorate of Industries, etc. He had already proposed a budget provision of Rs. 100 crores before any detailed plan and estimate was even prepared. The PWD was thrilled of its cut in a new Rs 100-crore show-piece. But, on my part, I urged that bureaucracy was already bloated with an excess of about 30% staff and they do not require any new addition to the Secretariat. Employees Associations and MLAs never allow retrenchment of staff. The larger the bureaucracy the larger the number of transfers and the higher the opportunity to collect "transaction fee" by the MLAs. I pointed out that since computerization, out-sourcing and task-based contract appointments have become common in all countries, the need for recruiting more and more government servants should come down and with it also the need for their office accommodation.

I suggested that, in this background there was no need to construct a new Vikasa Soudha. Besides, the new building would be asymmetrical because the main Vidhana Soudha covered an area of 60 acres while the land available for Vikasa Soudha was only 7½ acres on the south of Vidhana Soudha. To be symmetrical there should be a similar building on the north side also as otherwise, it would look like a cow and its lone calf together. The North-side land was occupied by the rose garden of Raj Bhavan (which was the Residency constructed in 1840 by Sir Mark Cubbon when he was Resident of Mysore State) and no one dared to ask the Governor to part with the Rose Garden as this would cause head injury to the Governor hitting the 50-foot ceiling of Raj Bhavan! But the decision was already taken by SMK to construct Vikasa Soudha. Obviously the contractor was also selected before the plan and estimate which I did not know!

At this time there came a letter of invitation from the Minister for Public Works of Malaysia, Mr Samy Vellu addressed to his Karnataka counterpart Dharam Singh, inviting him to visit Malaysia with a view to promote cooperation between Malaysia and Karnataka in construction of various projects. Malaysia is a small country with a population of 32 million, about half of Karnataka's, but endowed with rich natural resources of petroleum, palm oil, rubber, tin, pepper and timber. Malaysia had constructed the world's then tallest building, the Petronas Twin Towers, 1,500 feet high and 88 storeys tall. It had also started constructing a new Capital city, the *Putra Jaya* and an Information Technology city, *Cyber Jaya* and a huge international airport. However, due to the high speculative activities and banks indiscriminately funding risky real estate activities, the economies of many South East Asian countries—the Asian Tigers and Cubs, notably Thailand, Indonesia, Malaysia, Taiwan and South Korea were greatly affected in what came to be called the 1997-Financial Crisis. This caused the construction companies of Malaysia incurring huge losses and they were making intense attempts to get contracts abroad, especially in other Asian countries like India. Though many of their projects in Malaysia were stalled, it had the technical expertise and machinery which was idle and they were attempting opportunities abroad. Hence, Minister Samy Vellu's warm invitation to Dharam Singh. I told him plainly that Karnataka must follow the "best practices" of the world, in calling for

ICBs—Internationally Competitive Bids and once the bid was accepted, no "negotiations" with any other bidders and that we could not have any "agreement" with Malaysia and choose just one contractor to execute the works without open tenders. However, since Malaysia had the world class technical expertise to execute big infrastructure projects, Karnataka could enter into a Memorandum of Understanding to use its expertise in planning and training Karnataka engineers in modern methods.

So, at my instance, Dharam Singh thanked Samy Vellu and accepted his invitation. He wanted me to accompany him and also to take a civil Chief Engineer as part of the team. However, I told him that the Rs 2,500 crores, 2,000km Karnataka State Highways Improvements Project with World Bank assistance was under final stages of preparation and the main agency to implement it should be the newly formed Karnataka Road Development Corporation and therefore, Karnataka would benefit more if its Managing Director could be in the team. Its MD was a direct recruit IAS Officer known to me when I was the CEO of the Central Silk Board and I was instrumental in getting him posted as the Director of Silk Export Promotion Council with headquarters in Bombay and had also given one of the two apartments of CSB's guest house in the accommodation-scarce city as his quarters. He was an engineer himself and very hardworking. It would be immensely helpful for the K-SHIP if he could observe and learn from the Malaysian projects. The Minister agreed to replace the Chief Engineer with the MD of KRDC and we went to Kuala Lumpur for a week.

Samy Vellu was all charm and was delighted when I spoke to him in Tamil, which was his mother tongue too. About 7% of Malaysians were of Tamil origin. T Ananda Krishnan ('TAK') the second richest man in Malaysia worth US$ 9 billion was a Tamilian. He was said to be the brain behind the Petronas Towers completed in 1999 at a cost of US$ 1.6 billion and was later duly involved in financial scandals including the Aircel money laundering case in India investigated by the CBI. He was close to the PM Mahathir Mohammad and Samy Vellu who was minister for public works for over two decades and was considered to be the right-hand man of the PM who was in power since 1981. The officers of Malaysian Public Works Department—*Jabatan Kerja Raya* Malaysia— 'JKR', along with some leading construction companies took us around their projects. We also visited *Putra Jaya,* the new government city and *Cyber Jaya,* the IT City which were under construction. Though many of the works were making slow progress, the scale of their projects was mind boggling. They were following all the modern methods, their engineers having been trained in Australia. The buildings in *Putra Jaya* especially impressed me greatly. Their architecture was not just copying the skyline of Western cities but a blending of traditional Malaysian structures which were actually South Indian temple architecture with a blend of the Western. It was the Dravidian architecture of buildings like the Vidhana Soudha in Bangalore. Both Malaysia and Indonesia, before the advent of Islam in 13-14th century, were steeped in Buddhist and Shaivite culture. Malaysia was described in Tamil literature as *Malai-ooru,* (Hill Country) which became *Mala-yur,* then *Malayu* and finally *Malaya.* 10th century King Raja Raja Cholan helped a Sri Vijaya king of South East Asia to build the *Chudamani Buddha Vihara* at Nagapattinam port on the eastern coast of Tamil Nadu. *[It was destroyed in 1867 by the Portuguese Jesuits to construct a Church, in their Rescue and Civilize mission for the heathens!]* Thus the ties between Malaya and South India were ancient. I dwelt at some length on this history to Samy Vellu's delight. In the MoU which was signed in the presence of the formidable High Commissioner of India to Malaysia Mrs Veena Sikri which I had drafted, I had included, apart from the generalities and without compromising transparency of contracts system, a specific highway from Mysore to Mercara in Coorg which would be surveyed by Malaysia and with part-loan assistance from Malaysia could be taken up after floating tenders. Thus the visit ended successfully. I made a mental note to include the Malaysian companies which were building *Putra Jaya* to bid when we invited ICB tenders for the *Vikasa Soudha* (avoidable but already decided as necessary by SMK) in Bangalore and Dharam Singh agreed with me. *[His popularity among politicians and bureaucrats was due to his genetic incapacity to never disagree with anybody on any matter which sterling quality ultimately made him the CM of Karnataka in 2004 by the Congress High Command after SMK was dumped at Deve Gowda's insistence to support Congress!]*

But what happened after we returned to Bangalore was entirely different. I learned that a Pune-based firm was influencing the government for the contract. The problem with Dharam Singh was, he was what one would call *The Adorable Yes Man* because he did not have any convictions on public interest to say 'No' even to manifestly illegal things to persons whom he suspected to be even remotely powerful. So, when he was told that the contract had to be given to a Pune firm, Dharam Singh simply agreed despite the coaching he had received from me about the procedure of Internationally Competitive Bids. I still gave a Power Point presentation to the cabinet about the construction of Vidhana Soudha in the 1950s with a built of up area of 505,000 square feet in an area of 60 acres using even prisoners from the Central Jail to save cost and how even the then construction cost of Rs 1.5 crore caused complaints of corruption which ultimately brought down the ministry of Kengal Hanumanthiah in 1956. I also explained that if the decision was to construct the *Vikasa Soudha*, it was necessary to have a global competition of architects for the best design and then to float ICBs. But these were of course not agreed to by SMK who had only a silver tongue and laminated exterior.

The PWD in India is a great stumbling block for any new ideas of architecture or economic construction. In government, each department is an empire and the PWD is one of the oldest and the most corrupt as Rajaji had said. The Karnataka PWD has a peculiar rule for bidding of any work being open to only those contractors who are "registered" with it. The world's most competent construction companies do not even know about Karnataka's projects and they are certainly not registered with it. So they cannot bid. And then, the PWD swears by "Divisional Schedule of Rates—DSR" which is usually an archaic table of materials and labour to be used, the quantity for each type of work and the rates for it. Conveniently, the DSR is not updated annually. Since Housing was also in my jurisdiction, I had tried to make the PWD follow the designs of the famous Architect Laurie Baker. I had visited his unorthodox house on a rock donated by the local church in Thiruvananthapuram in 1990 when I was in the Central Silk Board, for constructing cost-effective, environment-friendly and climate-compatible buildings for rearing silkworms and grainages. I had also seen the four storey Centre for Development Studies of Prof KN Raj at Ulloor at the outskirts of Thiruvananthapuram entirely built in an unconventional manner, using locally available strong laterite stones and not following the Western Steel-Cement-Concrete model of the PWD. But the Karnataka PWD Technical Committee vetoed my proposal that the materials used by Laurie Baker are not in the DSR and therefore it cannot be approved!

The corruption in government contracts arises because of not following the "best practices" which are common and accepted all over the world and even in India in projects funded by external financial institutions such as the World Bank and ADB who insist on following such practices. These practices are well-known. Firstly, before a project is approved there should be a Detailed Project Report prepared by a reputed Consultant selected on the basis of competitive bids. The DPR is then published and the criteria for offering the tender called Pre-Qualification of Tenderers is prepared by the same consultants. This is to avoid nepotism and incompetent "registered" crony-*benami*-firms and relatives of bureaucrats and politicians getting the contract. Once the

Qualified tenderers are short-listed by a committee headed by an expert from outside the government such as the Indian Institute of Science or the Indian Institute of Management, the actual tender document is prepared by the DPR consultant and it is published for Internationally Competitive Bids and the bidders are required to submit their bids in two parts namely, the Technical Tender and the Financial Tender. The Technical Tender gives all the technical information of how the tenderer would implement the work stage by stage and the Financial Tender would specify the cost of each component and the total cost of the work. The same Experts Committee with an outside Expert heading it, first opens the Technical Tenders and after scrutinizing them, ranks them. Only after this, the Financial Tenders are opened and the committee ranks them and correlates them to the Technical Tenders. The best technically qualified tender may not be the least-cost(L-1) financial tender. It is also not necessary that the lowest-cost tender must be accepted. The best technical tender with the appropriate financial cost, unless it is exorbitantly high according to the committee, is accepted. It is then sent to the Chief Secretary for approval. At this stage no "negotiations" are permitted. Currently, the PWD invariably enters into "negotiations" with the next lower L-2, L-3, L-4 tenderers whose financial tender are progressively costlier and asks them whether they can reduce their cost to match the level of L-1 which is the lowest. All corruption starts here because even an L-4 tenderer could agree to bring down his cost to the level of the least-cost L-1 by deliberately sacrificing the quality of work, the ostensibly saved cost being shared by the contractor, officials and politicians. This is not possible under the externally aided projects as the best technical tenderer is given the contract. Besides, once the work is started by the successful tenderer, quality control is entrusted to an outside agency selected on the basis of competitive bidding which may be ICB or LCB (Locally Competitive Bids Indian contractors.) If the Quality Control Agency certifies that the work done is according to the DPR specifications, only then the bill is passed for payment. If the contractor does the work ahead of time limit, he is given a bonus and if he delays, a penalty is imposed. This practice is unheard of in the PWD projects without external funding. In fact, currently there is incentive to both the contractor and the PWD in delaying the execution of work. The longer the delay, the higher the cost because of inflation and the officers would falsely certify that the delay is not due to the fault of the contractor and the higher cost is justified due to price increase and the higher, extra payment is shared between the two. The ostensibly 'reduced cost' is thus illusory as the actual cost is increased while delaying execution. Contacts being given at DSR+100%

is common in Karnataka. Quality control is done by the PWD itself and even defective work is certified for payment as there is no independent agency involved to check quality. The reason why the National Highways do not have potholes but the BBMP roads have moon-craters, is precisely because the defective works are certified as correctly done by the engineers of BBMP. It is always a puzzle to me why the superior Courts in India while hearing innumerable cases of aggrieved parties in civil contracts, have not insisted upon government to adhere to the best practices enumerated above which would prevent the monumental corruption in government spending. The inescapable conclusion is, the Judiciary in India is not as keen in protecting public interest and public property as it is in protecting private interest and private property.

I pointed out all these matters to Dharam Singh and SMK and suggested that as the cabinet had already decided on the *Vikasa Soudha*, ICBs should be invited and quality control should be by an outside agency. The Cabinet rejected all these Best Practices prevailing in other countries and entrusted the work to the PWD. The ACS post is only ostensibly supervisory and it is not legally mandatory for the Secretary to put up the files to the ACS. Tenders were called from contractors only registered with the Karnataka PWD which included all the favourites of the PWD and also relatives with *benami* contractors. Fortunately, there was the reputed firm Larsen & Toubro, Bangalore which was already registered with the PWD. The lowest tender for Rs.76 crores was by L & T and a higher tender was by a Pune-based firm, the favourite of government. In the usual manner, the Committee headed by the Secretary, PWD who was a Chief Engineer, called the Pune contractor for "negotiations" as to whether they can match the L & T offer. He naturally agreed and the contract was awarded by the cabinet to the Pune firm whose reputation was nowhere near that of L & T. But what transpired was, ultimately the actual delayed final project cost when completed in 2004, ended at Rs.150 crores after the cost-overrun and time over-run were certified by the PWD as justifiable! Much later, a monstrous Rs 500 crore *Suvarna Vidhana Soudha* at Belgaum was constructed in 2012 and the contract was given to the same Pune firm. Though its original PWD estimate was Rs 230cr, there was an engineered delay of two years with the objective of increasing the cost to Rs 500 crores. No publicly-tendered agency prepared the DPR, no ICB was invited, no external quality control agency was chosen to certify the work and all this for a building which would be used for one month in a year to hold the Legislature session. The specious excuse given was, the dangerous claim by Maharashtra that Belgaum belongs to it would be effectively repudiated by a great building! As for Vikasa Soudha, It was a pity that the Fulbright scholar did not realize that the construction of magnificent Red Fort and Taj Mahal did not ensure the permanence of Mughal rule. Even a half-bright leader would have known that monuments do not save empires. SMK lost his chief ministership in May 2004, nine months *before* inaugurating *Vikasa Soudha*. Earlier, Kengal Hanumanthiah had lost his chief ministership in 1956 and he could not occupy the Vidhana Soudha which he built. So, a new superstition for any CM should be, *Do Not Start any New Big Building Project!*

The other bigger project of Karnataka State Highways Improvement Project, on the other hand, went according to the procedure established by the Best Practices because of World Bank's insistence. By the time I took over as ACS the preparation of the DPR by a UK Consultant firm was already in final stage. The project covered improvement of about 2,000 km of existing state highways and construction of 1,500 km of almost entirely new highways at a total estimated cost of about Rs 2,500 crores of which 70% was a soft loan from the World Bank to the Government of India. Three-fourths of this loan was channelled by the GoI to the State by way of Plan Assistance which again was 70% central loan and 30% grant. The 25% of the world bank assistance which the GoI does not pass on to Karnataka (and other better administered states in their projects) would be kept by the GoI to assist North Eastern states and 'laggard' states such as UP and Bihar in the interest of regional equity but actually a subsidy for inefficiency and corruption. The advantages in seeking external assistance for a physical infrastructure project like Roads are firstly, if the state has an initial resource of Rs 30 of its own, it can implement a sizeable project of Rs 100. Secondly, efficiency factors such as ICB, LCB, impartial selection process of contractors, Quality Control of work by an independent agency and annual review of progress of work by World Bank team enables mid-course correction if needed. Also, for every one tree which had to be cleared for the widening of the highway, four trees had to be planted as 'compensatory afforestation' by the Forest department the cost of which was included in the project. The officer of the World Bank who was in charge of the K-SHIP-1 was a young engineer, Mr Yang of Chinese origin. He was highly knowledgeable and very urbane. We got along well.

As a result, though Karnataka was late-comer to prepare Highways Project behind many states such as Rajasthan, Tamil Nadu and Kerala, we finished the preparation of the project first and got internal approvals at Karnataka and Central government levels ahead of other states. The most radical pre-condition of the World Bank was that the selection of contractors on the basis of ICBs was final without any further negotiations with any contractor and the award of the contracts does not require the approval of the cabinet but the approval of a Committee headed by the Chief Secretary was enough. This was different from the PWD procedure that any award of work costing more than Rs.1 crore (in 2000) had to be approved by the cabinet. However, the World Bank was firm on this issue and it insisted that this was a pre-condition for the approval of loan. This was to avoid political interference to influence award of contracts and the ultimate award of work was purely on merit based on established procedure of best practices. In fact, this was also the main reason why BIMARU states such as Bihar do not prepare such infrastructure projects. In Tamil Nadu, whose Highways Department I had visited to know the practices they were following, I learned that any file involving more than Rs 1 crore had to be personally approved by *Amma*, not even by the cabinet! Karnataka had to agree to the World Bank's condition as otherwise there was no project funding. Thus the K-SHIP-1 was prepared in final form and a team from Karnataka and a representative of the Department of Economic Affairs of the Union Finance Ministry had to go to Washington for negotiations. I had earlier prevailed over Dharam Singh that the project implementation agency for K-SHIP-1 should be the KRDC under its able MD. It was therefore decided that for K-SHIP-1 negotiations myself and the MD of KRDC would go to Washington with the representative of DEA from Delhi.

The World Bank fixed the date for loan negotiation in March 2001 and I was retiring in April. The MD of KRDC and I had made all the arrangements of booking the hotel in Washington and we had got our visas and tickets. However, just a week before our departure there was a totally unexpected hitch. One morning, the Secretary to CM telephoned me to say that the Chief Secretary had sent a note to CM that as there was another World Bank project for Ways and Means Funding to Karnataka which was likely to be finalized in May 2001 for which the Finance Secretary and Chief Secretary were to go to Washington, and therefore they could themselves negotiate the K-SHIP-1 project also in May and therefore the March discussion of K-SHIP can be cancelled. This was totally strange and I was surprised that the CS had sent such a proposal without even discussing it with me. So, I told Dharam Singh what was happening. He told SMK that K-SHIP was an important project for the state and it cannot be jeopardised by postponing the negotiations. Surprisingly for all his image of a highly educated person and experienced administrator having worked both at the centre and the state and a Fulbright Scholar to boot SMK, allgedly could not decide what to do. It was said that he consulted Jayaram Ramesh who was an "intellectual" guide and, more importantly, close to Sonia Gandhi and he advised SMK firmly not to meddle with the negotiations fixed by the World Bank and in any case any change in dates would have to be agreed to by the World Bank and the DEA in Delhi being the borrowing body, it cannot be cancelled unilaterally by Karnataka. The childish act of the CS surprised me which I could attribute only to jealousy, ignorance and showing-off who was boss. In some people, as age advances, instead of maturity going up, it is meanness which races up. I could never understand the pettiness of the CS behind such a behaviour. Perhaps, like ambition induces over-stepping, power overcomes fair-play. Small people reaching higher positions through sheer biological accidents and 'Ovarian Lottery' cannot be broad-minded because of their upbringing.

In the event, I and my team went to Washington on schedule. The negotiations with WB went off without any hitch. The Project Officer of the WB, Yang, was quite happy that the negotiations ended well without any modification to the draft we had prepared. The World Bank normally fixes the negotiations for five days from Monday to Friday. As we had finished our negotiations by Thursday, the next day we were free. Yang invited me for a lunch at the Washington Yacht Club. He knew that I was retiring the next month. As he would be in charge of the project in the World Bank for two more years, he asked me whether I could persuade the government to head the KRDC to guide the project implementation for two years. I told him the PWD Minister was then the Chairman of KRDC and in India it is quite common that the government could any time appoint a politician denied of ministership as Chairman. We discussed it for some time and he suggested that if I could be appointed as the full time Executive Vice-Chairman of KRDC, I could associate with the implementation apart from the Managing Director who was the Chief Executive Officer. I told him I would propose it to my minister after returning to Bangalore.

The day I returned to Bangalore, the CM addressed a Press conference announcing proudly that he had sent a team headed by me for the successful negotiations of the Rs 2,500 crore Highways Project and how it would improve the roads in the state between district headquarters. The irony did not escape me. This was the same person who had doubts about our team going to Washington for negotiations at the intervention of the Chief Secretary. When everything ended well, he took credit for it! I checked the legal provisions of the Company Law for the appointment of an Executive Vice-Chairman in addition to the Managing Director and the Chairman who only chaired the Board meetings with no executive powers. I found that there were many PSUs where there were even Executive Chairmen, Executive Vice-Chairmen and even more than one Managing Director heading individual departments as in Steel Authority of India. I discussed it with Dharam Singh and he asked me why could I not be the Chairman myself. I told him it is better the Minister continues as Chairman so that support at cabinet level will be easy. He agreed and told me to send him a note so that he could get CM's approval. A few days later, the Principal Secretary to CM met me and asked me whether I had anything else in mind than just associating myself with KRDC as Executive Vice-Chairman, after retiring. I told him I do not have any other proposal and my only interest was to be somewhat busy with useful work after retiring. Accordingly, the order was issued just a few days before my retirement and a day later I joined KRDC as Executive VC.

But this lasted hardly for a month as it turned out. I was stripped of the "Executive" from the Vice-President designation so that I could not attend office except when there would be a Board meeting. I learned from Dharam Singh that the MD of KRDC had met the CS and both of them decided that I need not be given any executive powers. So, the CS wrote a long note and took it personally to CM and explained to him that under the Company's Act there cannot be an Executive VP in addition to the Managing Director. This was manifestly false as there can be even more than one MD in a company under the law. But then I was not an Okkaliga and therefore the CM could not care less and he obviously had not relished my objections for a Vikasa Soudha. More importantly, I had retired and was of no use to the CM while the CS had one more year to go and SMK need not displease the CS for a non-Okkaliga. Such was the administrative acumen of the head of administration. Only then it struck me that I had not realized that the MD of KRDC was a Palakkad Brahmin! Even though this was a racist sentiment, I could not help notice that persons of this denomination have been my Nemesis in my otherwise pleasant working years.

The Secretary to CM informed me about the file stripping me of executive powers at the instance of the MD of KRDC and the CS personally taking the file to CM and getting his approval. This CS was the same officer whom I had helped, when I was Secretary to Hegde, to get a posting to Delhi. I had only helped my colleagues in my career and the act of this officer showing off 'power' and ticking me off was not *kosher*. I did not bother to clarify the legal position either to the PWD Minister or to the CM. But I felt bad that the MD of KRDC whom in 1990 I had helped in getting a posting as CEO of the Silk Export

Promotion Council at Bombay and arranged for him one of the two apartments of the CSB's Guest House as his quarters in the house-scarce Bombay and later in 1999 prevailed over the PWD minister that he as MD of KRDC be included in the team going to Malaysia in place of the engineer Secretary of the PWD and later made him and the KRDC as the implementing agency of the world-bank funded K-SHIP Project, all at my own initiative, would stab me in the back and conspire with the CS, who suffered amnesia of my help in Delhi posting, to humiliate me. Dharam Singh told me, *Look, you had supported the MD throughout and see now what he has done to you.* But I explained to myself that the leopard cannot change its spots, a canine cannot straighten its tail and a Palakkad Brahmin cannot but be amoral. I know this was racist thinking on my part. But is that as clear as black and white? Is there a tiny little kernal of truth that when people are historically insecure, the survival instinct will harden into ruthless selfishness in the persecuted minority groups of people such as the Jews and Gypsies in Europe, Armenians and Kurds in Turkey, Zoroastrians in Persia—all of whom were small minorities suffering discrimination and had to be closely knit and be cold-blooded and cut throats to survive amidst a hostile society. It is relevant to recall the reaction of even the enlightened Dewan Visvesvaraya, not even from Palakkad, when the Mysore Maharaja's government appointed the Leslie Miller Committee in 1918 to enquire into the representation of non-Brahmins in State administration and it recommended 25% reservation for non-Brahmins and Depressed Classes, in protest Visvesvaraya resigned.

Surprisingly, after more than 70 years of independence, while the percentage of Brahmin population in India is about 5%, its representation in various branches of government is as follows: IAS Officers 72%; IPS Officers 61%; Radio & TV 83%; CBI, Customs & Central Excise 72%; Loksabha 48%; Rajyasabha 36%; Governors/L.G 50%; Secretary to Governor/ Lieutenant Governor 54%; Union government Secretaries 53%; Chief Secretaries to State governments 54%; Private Secretaries to Ministers 70%; JS/ Additional Secretaries 62%; Vice Chancellors to Universities 51%; Supreme Court Judges 65%; High Court Judges/ Addl. Judges 50%; Ambassadors 41%; Chief Executive of Public Undertakings: (i) Central 57%; (ii) State 82%.

"We Palakkad Brahmins make good cooks, crooks and civil servants", former Chief Election Commissioner T.N Seshan had once said. Actually, Palakkad Brahmins community have indeed produced many brilliant men and women. A sociological study of 130 PB families by the Bharatiyar University, Coimbatore showed that there were 36 IAS

officers from that group. At one time the IA&AS Service (the Indian Audit and Accounts Service) was known as *Indian Aiyars and Ayyangars Service*. Though Palakkad Brahmins were only about half per cent of Kerala's population, they had produced many famous musicians, actors and writers. Historically, some Brahmins from Kumbakonam, Madurai and Tiruchy of Tamil Nadu had migrated across the border to Palakkad through the Walayar Gap in Western Ghats after Allauddin Khilji's general Mallik Gafoor sacked Madurai in early 14th century (and took away the sacred diamond nose ring and other treasures but he did not destroy the *Angayarkanni [Meenakshi]* temple because he was a Gujarati Hindu himself who was castrated by his merchant-boss in his youth for having a liaison with his daughter after which he ran away and became a boatswain to an Arab ship owner from which position he rose to be a general to Alaudin Khalji.) But Kerala's native Namboodiri Brahmins did not allow the Palakkad Brahmins equal status and most of them had to take up other avocations such as cooks to Namboodiris, musicians, astrologers and even traders. The hostility from the Namboodiris obviously made the 1.75 lakh Tamil Brahmins of Palakkad work hard and fight for survival as a group in their 165 *Agraharams*—which were neat exclusive enclaves. They speak a peculiar mixture of Tamil and Malayalam known as *Manipravalam*. They are considered extremely clever even by *Kumbakonam's* Tamil Brahmins who themselves are renowned for their razor-sharp practices. In fact, the place name of *Kumbakonam* came to mean chicanery in Tamil, like being called a *Cretan* in Greece.

Anyway, despite their brilliance or because of it, which is understandable objectively, I was at the receiving end of the joint plot of the Palakkad Brahmin MD of KRDC and the amnesiac, malefic, CS. I did not meet the PWD Minister or CM to restore my position as I was too proud to do it. I was not in need of any job for monetary benefit. Having led an extremely busy and eventful 36 years of official life I was looking forward to a transitional, tapering, semi-active life to do something useful and keep my time usefully occupied. Most active persons who retire after having worked in busy, senior positions in government, age remarkably quick after retirement, suddenly becoming fully grey, puzzled, morose, getting depressed and even getting Alzheimers and Parkinsons, not keeping themselves busy mentally and physically. I had seen a fine person like TR Satishchandran who was Chief Secretary for four years and after getting an extension also, suffered Alzheimers after retirement. This was not my problem. I had intense reading habits (I had just during one of my visits to the US purchased the complete 11 volume set of *Story of Civilization* by Ariel and

Will Durant which would take me years to read besides my 40 km jog per week regimen. Long ago I had convinced myself that life is a card game and you are dealt with genes on which you have no control (CRISPR gene-editing is being developed only since 2020), but how you play it—carefully, carelessly, wisely, foolishly, with principles or without and pay the price or reward for whatever choices you make—are all upto you. There is this concept of 'Considered Life'. If as an agnostic you have a strong philosophy and convictions, just like the deep religious convictions of many good believers, and act while meeting any situation subjecting it to the litmus test of your beliefs, then it is a 'Considered' and *Examined* life. It is like a paper where a boundary is drawn. Many live a blank life without marking any such boundary. I tell my wife, we are not Rich but we are Sufficient, unlike many of my IAS colleagues who have become Rich but not Sufficient.

Back to SMK. His lacklustre administration was in shambles with Dr.Rajkumar kidnapped by Veerappan. He made it worse by appointing a junior officer as Chief Secretary. The senior most person was from Mysore and of proven capability and impeccable integrity who was also a direct recruit. His only drawback was, he was a good and honest Mysore Brahmin without any political clout. But such persons were not the need of the hour for SMK and so the Fulbright scholar superseded him and appointed the junior-most person in that batch who was not even a regular recruit. More importantly, this was the same officer whom the 11-7-JHPatel had chosen as his Principal Fixer and, not to forget, whose house was raided when Veerendra Patil was CM in 1989 and Bangarappa made the DG of Vigilance Commission file 'B' Report dropping the investigation. His greatest merit was he was a Lingayat and supported by MLAs and a temporal, soil-level Swamiji! This was supposedly a Machiavellian act by appointing a person of the other dominant caste to enlist the support of Lingayat community ! But none of it helped the collapse of SMK's government.

The misrule of SMK in Karnataka for five years resulted in the BJP emerging as the largest party in the Assembly in 2004. In the May 2004 Assembly elections, Congress secured only 65 seats (down from 132 in 1999), while the BJP got 79 and Deve Gowda's JD(S) 58. This was the first time the BJP became the biggest party in the Assembly. For the first time the Lingayat community in Hyderabad and Bombay Karnataka, traditionally the fortress of Congress, overwhelmingly voted for BJP (inspite of SMK's delusory Machiavellian maneuvre of superseding a senior, honest, Brahmin officer and bringing in a tainted Lingayat junior) while the Okkaligas in the eight 'Old-Mysore' districts voted as customarily for JD (S) and SMK's Congress, with its Muslim-SC-OBC vote bank split among the three parties, crashed on no-man's land. Unlike the other South Indian States of Kerala, Tamil Nadu and Andhra Pradesh, Karnataka elections are caste and community dominated and the only ideology is caste and cash, also called 'Cash and Carry'. The only leader who tried to break the Lingayat-Okkaliga *udu*-grip was Devaraj Urs who brought the Backward Castes to political power but after him, the historical pattern of caste domination and obscurantist normalcy has resumed.

SMK's ham-handed style of administration, which he flattered himself was modern, totally misfired and it was Deve Gowda and BS Yeddyurappa who consolidated their caste votes while others' votes got split among all the three parties. SC/STs and other minorities became the NPA—non-performing asset of Congress. But, totally disregarding all principles, the Congress offered an unholy alliance to JD (S) and both formed an unnatural cohabitation, but Deve Gowda exacted his price by getting SMK exiled as Governor of Maharashtra! It is an irony that much later SMK resigned from Congress to join the BJP. But it was said, Amit Shah, without receiving him, went away to the farthest Manipur and SMK was left high and dry, what is called Run-Out in cricket when you leave your crease in a haste without ascertaining the other end can be reached! He had to cool his heels before given entry! These "leaders" have a highly inflated opinion about their importance without realizing that their only followers are their musclemen as long as they are paid. Even Devaraj Urs made that mistake of being wiped out when he formed his own party. In Karnataka, Congress itself has became its own nuisance and BJP did not require SMK's nuisance-value defection. He was already a dead-duck, spent force and a disaster. In the 2018 Assembly election, the JDS swept all the seats in SMK's Mandya district.

❖❖❖

CHAPTER 20

You Only Live Twice
The Second, More Rewarding, After Retirement

After being back-stabbed by my Palakkad Brahmin colleague and an amnesiac CS, I was finally free from government. Most busy and honest officers accustomed to a 9 to 5 life, feel lost after retirement. It becomes a change of life, like a male menopause. There is a great title song by Nancy Sinatra in the James Bond movie with music by John Barr which starts as *You Only Live Twice....One Life for Yourself. And One for Your Dreams'.* In my case, this came to be true. Within two weeks I received a call from Dr Bhaktavatsalam, the MD of Indian Renewable Energy Development Agency of the Ministry of New Energy Sources in Delhi. The International Energy Agency, Paris had approached IREDA to conduct an International Congress on Renewable Energy of the 120 member countries, for the first time in India in 2003. He asked me, would I agree to be the whole-time Executive Vice-President of the ICORE till it was conducted in Bangalore? The Chairman of Tata Solar Power, Arun Vohra, would be the Honorary Chairman and it may take about eighteen months to organize the Congress in Bangalore. Thus, when one door closed another opened. I readily agreed as it would keep me busy for two years in my favourite subject. Ultimately we conducted the ICORE in January 2004 for five days at Hotel Ashok which was attended by 280 delegates including 120 from abroad. We had collected Rs.65 lakhs in donations and after expenditure of Rs.31 lakhs, I gave a cheque for Rs.34 lakhs to the Solar Energy Society of India which was the biggest cheque it had ever received. Understandably, I did not invite SMK to the prestigious ICORE-2004 but instead, I got the Governor to inaugurate!

A few days after ICORE, Jalappa, the former Revenue Minister in Karnataka and a protégé of Devaraj Urs and who was my former Textile Minister when I was the CMD of the National Textile Corporation, New Delhi contacted me. He had formed the Sri Devaraj Urs Educational Trust which was managing a medical college, a 1,050-bed hospital, a Nursing School, Nursing Training Institute, an Engineering

College and an International School. He asked me whether I can meet him as he could not personally come since he was over seventy five and had a severe Glaucoma problem and required some one even to read aloud the daily newspaper to him. When I met him he informed that his Committee of Trustees were all liquor people without much education (Jalappa belonged to Idiga community.) He wanted his Trust to become a self-governing Deemed Autonomous University with professional management to manage all its existing institutions. As a first step, he wanted me to help him to attain the status of a Deemed University by following the procedural requirements. At that time there were only two Deemed Universities in Karnataka, the LES (originally, *Lingayat* Education Society which became *Liberal* Education Society and then back to *Lingayat* replacing *Liberal,* reflecting the politically changed caste identity in Karnataka after Urs), and the other being Sathya Sai Baba DU. I demurred that after retirement I was enjoying my freedom to read, write and travel UNESCO-heritage sites. He told me to help him at least for one year and I need to visit his institutions in Kolar only one or two days a week, select my own team and get approvals from the Government of India for the DU. I told him I would think about it. He requested me to first see for myself the institutions before I took a decision. So, he himself took me next day to the Medical College and other institutions which were near Kolar, about 65 km from Bangalore. His Trust had over fifty acres of land at Kolar town in which a 1,050-bed hospital had come up with all modern facilities including MRI, a dormitory for relatives of poor patients to stay upto one week, a medical college with administrative building in the style of Vidhana Soudha, well equipped hostels for boys and girls, a garden and a guest house. The Nursing School had half the students from rural areas of Karnataka and the other half from outside, mainly Kerala. The International School and Engineering College were at Doddaballapur and had about 50 acres with all facilities including computers, hostels, gym and nutritious food. There were Principals for each of these institutions who were all well-qualified. There were also Air-conditioned buses of the Trust to bring those staff members staying in Bangalore. Traveling back, I frankly told him (Jalappa was a no-nonsense person) that while his institutions had every facility to achieve the status of a DU, I had a problem of associating myself with the medical and engineering colleges which were charging 'capitation fees', a source of black money. He assured me that the admissions come once a year and it would be entirely managed by the Secretary of the Trust who was his brother in law and I would in no way be dealing with admissions to the colleges under the Trust. My role would be limited to only fulfilling the requirements to become a Deemed University.

Thus I joined Jalappa's Trust for one year to keep myself busy and also because of this new opportunity to know about educational institutions as I had never worked in Education Department before. As a first step, I got a consultant to establish the procedure to get the ISO Certificate for the Trust institutions which status it got within six months. I made several visits to Delhi to meet the Union Education and Health Secretaries. As the Trust had all infrastructure and was in a rural area, everything made good progress and in one year it was granted the status of a Deemed University.

Though I was kept away from admissions and donations, I could not help noticing many flagrant irregularities in these private institutions. The main problem was, the Chairman of the Medical Council of India Dr Ketan Desai was an alpha scoundrel, incomparably corrupt and ruthless who had doctors, administrators and politicians in his deep pockets. Already his house was raided by the Income Tax Department and cases were going on. All the private medical colleges were beholden to him because it was the MCI which would grant recognition to the Colleges and also fix the number of seats for intake of students every year. Besides, MCI inspected the medical colleges annually to assess the teaching and medical facilities. In private medical colleges, after reservation, certain number of seats were called "Management Seats" which can be sold by them. This was the bread, butter, jam and the very life of the managements. The going donation even in 2004 was not less than Rs 1 crore for the management seats and if the applicant was from abroad such as Iran or Nigeria as some of them were, the price was as high as Rs 3 crores. While the Supreme Court had technically prohibited collection of donation, the managements adopted a simple and crude method to overcome the ban. Every medical college management also has many separate Private Charitable Trusts managed by the close relatives and friends of the management. The parents of the management seat student would be asked to donate to that Charitable Trust even by cheque if they so wished in which case the donation would be higher than if it was in cash, and a receipt would also be given. Government and the Courts knew about it but no one plugged the loophole. This was because each medical college surrendered upto ten management seats to the CM and even to the judges. The market price of the seats was an average Rs 2 crores per seat.

Finally, Ketan Desai was caught red-handed receiving a bribe of Rs 2 crore to grant recognition to a medical college. But that did not deter him from even becoming the Chairman of the World Medical Council headquartered in Paris. Such was the octopus-grip of Ketan Desai even globally. He was the Godfather of the Doctors' Mafia which the Medical Council of India had become since 1996 when he became its President. He was the master-crook among doctors globally perhaps of all time and the 'Noble Profession' ought to be ashamed of nurturing him for over two decades. Finally, the government had to bring in a legislation in 2019 to abolish the MCI and constituting a National Medical Commission whose members and chairman would be nominated by the Union government and not elected by doctors' organizations. The health care in India, like much else, is in shambles. There are about 600 Medical Colleges & *Research Institutes* in India (it is almost mandatory to add 'Research' to their title though a study found that about 60% of them had never published a single Research paper in any medical journal). There were about 8 lakh qualified doctors in India and also an estimated 7 lakh fakes and quacks killing people in the name of practising medicine. About 74,000 Indian doctors had migrated to the US and 45,000 to the UK. Interestingly, one of the most surprising medical statistics I found was that the tiny country of Cuba, suffering from the economic blockade of the US for seventy years, led the world in medical care and it had 8 doctors per 1,000 population, while the US and UK have about 6 per 1,000 population and India has 0.9 per 1,000 and China 2 per 1,000.

Another very common blatant practice all the medical colleges, including government medical colleges, was regarding the annual "inspection" by the MCI. The dates of inspection would be known in advance. Besides lavishly wining and dining the MCI-members (besides a brief case), the management would temporarily get doctors with PhD qualification from other medical colleges as all the Heads of Departments in a medical college should have such qualification for continued recognition. Doctors with such qualification available in other medical colleges would be "rented" for about 15 days immediately preceding the inspection and even the Attendance Registers would be forged to show they are employed in the college for a long time. The hire charges for such Rent-a-Doc was as high as Rs 5 lakhs for fifteen days depending upon his reputation(!) and his acquaintance with the Inspection Team. No doubt the MCI team knew all along what was going on but was a shameless partner. No doubt there were reputed doctors in the medical colleges who would not accept such Rental-Doctors but there were some "professionals" who could be customarily rented every year. The joke was, the MCI team would come across the same doctor face to face in more than one college during the same year's inspection season! *"I no tell, You no tell"*, was the golden rule and everyone was laughing their way to the bank! The universal truth is, 'Those who have Gold, Make the Rules'! Such is the quality of medical education management in India. An apocryphal story goes like this: a doctor from Bihar goes to the US and when asked about liver disease, he could not, liver being the largest organ in the body! Needless to say, my admiration to the medical profession took a nose-dive though, it should be said, I did meet many doctors with high ethical values though they were in a minority.

My estimate was that Jalappa's Trust was investing about 70% of its donations in hospital equipment and qualified doctors while keeping the balance in its other "Trusts" to make under the table payments to MCI and political donations. However, I was an academic "observer" to these well-known corrupt practices and my limited task was to get the Trust DU status in which I succeeded in one year's time. As soon as this came through I left, though I was requested to continue with an indication I could lead it as its Vice Chancellor. A few months later, a highly respected former Vice-Chancellor of Rajiv Gandhi Health University and a person of high integrity became its VC after his retirement. Thus ended my brief but highly active and educative interlude with higher education. I never met Jalappa after that. But I would say he was a disciplinarian and also a person who cared for the poor compared to most other political leaders I came across. In the Kingdom of Blinds! He died in 2021 at the age of 95. I would still rate him as a good person with his heart in the right place.

THE SPEAKER OF KARNATAKA LEGISLAURE APPOINTS ME AS ADVISER TO THE JOINT LEGISLATURE COMMITTEE —BACK TO LAND ADMINISTRATION

A few days after my leaving Jalappa's Devaraj Urs Education Trust, I received a surprise call from the Speaker of Karnataka Legislative Assembly that he wanted me to meet him urgently in his office regarding some acrimonious discussions in the Assembly and he would send a car to fetch me. I was curious and told him I could come on my own steam and went. The Speaker whose name was also Krishna (no initials), was from Mysore district and a minister earlier with a rustic sense of justice, not belonging to major communities. During the previous few days there had been heated discussions in the Assembly and Council about encroachment of government lands and lakes in Bangalore city by developers, political leaders, officers and other powerful persons. The Speaker told me that he had constituted a Joint Legislature Committee of both houses to enquire into land-grabbing and AT Ramaswamy, a JD(S) MLA from Hassan district was to be JLC's Chairman. Usually, the Secretary to Legislature would be the Adviser to assist the JLC. However, unfortunately the Secretary of the Karnataka Legislature was under suspension and under an enquiry by a retired Judge for grabbing about an acre of Government land near his house! For this reason, but mainly in view of the complicated and specialized nature of the land problem, the Speaker felt that I should be the Adviser to JLC in view of my experience as DC. I expressed doubts about my suitability to work with a group of all-party MLAs and MLCs on the ticklish issue of land-grabbing in which many influential persons, often political leaders and MLAs themselves being involved. The Speaker said that was the reason why he wanted an independent person from outside government to be its Adviser and he had also mentioned it to the members of the JLC and all of them agreed. The JLC consisted of 18 members from Congress, BJP, JD(S), JD(U), CPM and the Kannada Paksha. The Speaker then sent for AT Ramaswamy and introduced me to him. He was in his late thirty's and was a BSc graduate from the University of Agricultural Sciences. I found him to be a pleasant person. Thus I joined duty at the Vidhana Soudha in 2005 after five years' interval.

AT Ramaswamy was an exceptionally hard working and honest person who did not entertain any pressure from any quarters—whether his own or other political parties or builders. I chose a few officers known to me from earlier days to assist. The JLC had powers to summon any Secretary to government including the Chief Secretary and to examine any file. As Adviser to the JLC, I exercised these powers and in any case all the officers were known to me and had respect for me and so I got full cooperation from them. I advised the Chairman to give wide publicity to the JLC and to issue a Press Note giving our phone numbers including mobile phones and invite members of the public to send information on public land encroachments by post, emails, phone, in person and even anonymously. Because of the wide publicity, the JLC received in a short period of three months over 1,100 written complaints apart from innumerable phone information. Eventually, the JLC worked for two years till November 2007 when the Assembly was dissolved because of the rift between the JD(S) headed by HD Kumaraswamy as CM and its coalition partner BJP's Yeddyurappa in "rotating" CMs! During this period the JLC met 40 times, made 90 spot inspections of land-grabbing, conducted over 100 internal meetings with 28 government departments and statutory bodies. I had also visited Hyderabad along with the Principal Secretary to Revenue Department, the brilliant Dr SM Jaamdar IAS, a Ph D in criminology who had spent thirteen years in Bagalkot to rehabilitate farmers losing lands and the Secretary of Parliamentary Affairs and Draftsman Bore Gowda to study the law and practice of controlling theft of public lands against which AP Government had taken the lead in passing the Land Grabbing (Prohibition) Act in 1980 itself. Following that visit, the Karnataka Land Grabbing (Prohibition) Bill, 2007 was prepared and was sent to Union Home Ministry for getting Presidential Assent. I had prepared two JLC reports which were approved by both houses of Legislature and sent to government for implementation. A large number of glaring land-grabbing were brought to the notice of JLC which we enquired. In all these cases there was wanton greed of grabbing public land, active collusion by government officials and judicial delay amounting to neglect in protecting public property in contrast to the eagerness to protect private property. In most of the land-grabbing instances, the JLC found that the officials who were in collusion were not proceeded against by the senior officials and the Ministers even protected them. *'Quis custodiet ipsos custodies?'—Who will guard the Guardians,* was the question asked by the Roman satirist Juvenal in the 2nd century CE. The hands of the Land-Grabbers in Karnataka are indeed very long and muscular! Land Mafia are India's Supermen. The justification of political leaders in Karnataka in protecting corrupt officials was: *He is corrupt alright, but he is OUR corrupt man!* It was like what President Harry Truman told CIA about the Nicaraguan dictator Somoza, *"Look, he's a bastard, but he's our bastard."* In Karnataka, if an officer commits small scale irregularities he would be in trouble. But if the illegalities are jumbo-size then, such crimes become "Policy Decisions" and you are very safe and rewarded big-time and your entire caste supports you!

The JLC identified about 34,000 acres of land-robbery in Bangalore Urban district of which about half was recovered. I prepared two Reports of the JLC which were discussed in full in the JLC meetings and were submitted to the Speaker who placed them before the Assembly and Council and were approved without any discussions! Meanwhile, the political situation changed and the coalition CM HD Kumaraswamy who, according to the understanding between JD (U) and BJP had to step down at the end of two years to make way for Yediyurappa, refused to do so. The BJP withdrew its support and the Assembly was dissolved and with it the JLC also ended. I have given various instances of land-grabbing in the two JLC Reports only to show the rot that had set in after *Solillada Sardar* Bangarappa's rule, followed by 11-7 Patel's Zombie regime and Fulbright Scholar Krishna's nepotistic administration and the fall from grace of a state once upon a time known for its mild and gentlemanly administrative culture. The JLC and I as its adviser could function well only because of the impartial courageous leadership of its Chairman AT Ramaswamy. Understandably, in the ensuing 2008 Assembly elections he was defeated even from his home constituency of Arkalgud!

IN AN UNGUARDED MOMENT, BS YEDDYURAPPA APPOINTS ME AS CHAIRMAN OF TASK FORCE FOR RECOVERY OF PUBLIC LANDS—MY FINAL REPORT 'GREED AND CONNIVANCE'

The JD(S)-BJP alliance did not last for more than two years as, at the end of the second year, the CM Kumaraswamy suffered from severe memory-blackout of his promise to step down for BJP to head the government. He also strongly felt there was no 'Gentlemen's Agreement' as neither party had any gentleman, with which all MLAs agreed! There was President's rule for six months and elections were held in May 2008 and for the first time the BJP got a near-majority of 110 seats while Congress secured 80 seats and the discredited JD(S) 28, yet again proving that Karnataka voters would reject one set of asinine leaders and get another replica by default in the musical chair democracy! With the support of 6 independent fleet-footed MLAs, Yediyurappa formed the first BJP ministry in Karnataka. (His luck was said to have improved enormously after he reverted to his 11-digit odd spelling of his name from the interim 12-digit YEDDIYURAPPA after the example of Jayalalith*aa* to single 'a'), thus proving the oddity of Indian leaders! After the submission of JLC's two reports, the government under President's rule had done nothing to recover the stolen public lands nor did anything to get the President's assent to the Land Grabbing (Prohibition) Bill. This was because the officers were busy playing golf for which purpose the 125-acre Challaghatta lake near the HAL airport was breached and given to the officers' golf club by the benign government!

Within a few weeks of the newly elected government coming to power, there was the now customary 'heated' discussion in the Legislature that land-grabbing was rampant and government did nothing about it. The new CM promised the Assembly that he would constitute a *Task Force* this time, instead of another committee, to implement the measures recommended in the JLC reports. The CM suggested that the Chief Secretary would head the Task Force. But the alarmed CS declined because fighting land-Mafia was dangerous business and they would remove him if he started removing land-grabs! So, one day I received a call from Baligar IAS who was Principal Secretary to CM whether I would consent to head the Task Force on a full time basis.

Baligar was a very fine officer of integrity and the CM was for once wise in choosing him as his official aide, though from his own community. With the fallen grace of politics and administration, the post of Secretary to CM became a crucial post next only to Chief Secretary. It is also noteworthy that excepting Veerendra Patil, the later Lingayat CMs chose persons of their community as Secretary to CM. SR Bommai, JH Patel and Yediyurappa—all chose Lingayat officers as Secretary to CM. It was a happy coincidence that both Mr Muddappa with Bommai and Baligar with BSY were officers of admirable integrity and rectitude.

However, I told Baligar that the Task Force would be effective only if it had the powers to summon officers and files, point out the law and ask them to act according to law just like the JLC had. Baligar solved the problem by simply asking me to prepare the draft Government Order myself including the enabling provisions of dealing with various departmental heads. This was quite a novelty because all government-appointed committees were only recommendatory and not proactive. But Baligar pointed out to me that what the CM wanted was a *Task Force—Karya Padé*—to perform the task, only just short of wielding AK-47s! He also told me that, if I chose, I could even include a senior police officer of DGP rank as member and a legal expert as full time member to point out the precise legal provisions under which the departmental heads must act. He told me that the Managing Director of the newly created Karnataka Public Lands Corporation with Rs 5 crore paid up capital, a senior dynamic IAS Officer, V Manjula, would be the Member Secretary of the Task Force. So, I agreed to be the Chairman of the Task Force. The members of the Legislature had said that land grabbing was a problem not only in Bangalore but in the entire state, especially in all the urban areas. Therefore, the Task Force had jurisdiction over all the 30 districts of Karnataka. It would cover not only all government lands belonging to departments such as Revenue, Forest, Animal Husbandry, etc. but also lands belonging to local elected bodies, statutory bodies and public sector undertakings. Thus, the Task Force started work and it received 1,508 complaints in its two years of work. I conducted meetings of all members of the Task Force once in two months and in total 8 such meetings were held during its 2-years existence. In addition, detailed review meetings were held at the district level. I had visited 16 of the 30 districts and had conducted review meetings with DCs and other district heads of departments.

I am giving these boring details because of what followed. After two years the Task Force was unceremoniously abolished in June 2011 by the then Revenue Minister Karunakara Reddy who, along with his brother Janardhana Reddy the Tourism Minister were the financiers for their party's central leadership and therefore beyond the control of the state chief minister and, to recover their election contribution, were actively engaged in the destruction of forests by illegal iron ore mining in Sandur taluk of Bellary district and export to China. This was exposed by Lok Ayukta Justice Santosh Hegde and UV Singh IFS, the Chief Conservator of Forests who headed the Enquiry Team in 2011. Because of this Rs 19,000 crore scam the CM himself had to resign, besides the Reddy Brothers, the 'Kings of Bellary' being dropped in August 2011 by the new government formed by Sadananda Gowda. The reason for the sudden, unceremonious sacking of the Task Force was the complaint by real estate Mafia such as Ozone Builders who were constructing a huge IT/BT Township by the side of Kempe Gowda International Airport by encroaching upon part of the Horticulture Department's farm and chasing away some Dalit cultivators through the Don Muthappa Rai and his son Rocky Rai (alias Rocket Rai), which the Task Force was enquiring into! During its working the Task Force identified 11 lakh acres of public land encroachment (valued at *Rs 19 lakh crores* at 'Guidance Value') and got removed about 47,000 acres. This was hardly 4% of the total area identified but it was a start. While the identification and removal of land-grabbing was still going on, the Task Force was abruptly abolished by the Revenue Minister to favour the land mafia.

EXSTENT OF LAND GRABBING IN KARNATAKA

During the two years the Task Force was allowed to function, the DCs and Heads of Departments in districts had already identified 11.07 lakh acres of public land illegally occupied. It was a detailed and thorough survey. It showed the names of land-grabbers village-wise, extent of encroachment by each, approximate value of the land and the date from which it was encroached. Thus, there was voluminous record in hard copy for each district which were kept in my office in Karnataka Public Lands Corporation. The market value of the 11 lakh acres under encroachment at a conservative value was Rs.19 *lakh crores* equal to 60% of Karnataka's GDP and four times its annual budget then!

But as could be expected, the land mafia put pressure on the Revenue Minister Karunakara Reddy and *instead of the encroachments being removed, it was the Task Force that was removed by the elected representatives!* This was the calibre of administration under the first BJP Ministry in Karnataka in 2011. I am not even referring here to the destruction of forests by illegal mining in Bellary district exposed by Lok Ayukta Justice Santhosh Hegde, Dr UV Singh IFS and the activist SR

Hiremath which is a *Karma Kanda* by itself. It caused the resignation of the CM Yediyurappa and his cronies, the Kings of Bellary. *[Of course, under our Adversarial system of Justice, not one has been sentenced even after eleven years after the Lok Ayukta Report.]*

NEED FOR AN URBAN PROPERTY OWNERSHIP RIGHTS (UPOR) IN BANGALORE

Most of the Government lands in Bangalore district have already been illegally converted into sites by middlemen working as proxy and agents of farmers or landless agricultural labourers and sold. This is because there is no proper survey, title-determination or protection of public lands. The only way to check this colossal corruption and theft of government land and untold misery to the ordinary citizens by costly litigation lasting generations making them bankrupt, is to have a City Survey done for Bangalore Metropolitan Region. The Revenue Department had belatedly attempted such a detailed survey, under the Urban Property Ownership Records Project in the Public-Private-Partnership mode, in the five cities of Mysore, Shimoga, Bellary, Mangalore and Hubl-Dharwad from 2009. However, though started in 2009, the UPOR made snail's progress. But a UPOR project is indispensable to Bangalore Metropolitan Region, following the Torren's system of 'Registration of Land' instead of the chaotic 'Registration of Deed', as in countries such as Australia. In Bangalore every square foot of land fetches anywhere from Rs 2,000 to Rs 22,000—an average of Rs 10,000—and therefore encroachment is rampant. 25% of Karnataka's total population of 6 crores and 49% of its total urban population of 2.3 crores live in BMRDA area. 40% of state's GDP and 65% of state's tax revenue is from BMRDA. BMRDA has 10 million motor vehicles for a population of 12.5 million. The short-sighted leaders and lethargic Bureaucracy and snail-paced Judiciary should realize that if Bangalore becomes unliveable because of undisciplined urban sprawl and vehicular pollution, the entire state collapses.

In the BMRDA area of 8,005 km^2, about 5 lakh acres (2,000 km^2) of government land is still available. Before long most of this land will be gone. Therefore, it is necessary that at least the government lands are taken up for survey and protected. It is the experience world over that the original city becomes the Central Business District and "Down-town" and people inevitably start living in suburbs. Therefore, people who live in area outside the now-existing BBMP but within BMRDA will require lands for housing, educational institutions, sports stadia, shops, non-polluting light industries for employment and other common facilities. If the still available 5 lakh acres of government land in BMRDA area disappears, government will have to acquire lands for such public purposes at high land cost and inevitable litigations. It is necessary that the Government anticipates such need and plans appropriate land use and protection of government lands.

PREPARATION AND PRINTING OF THE REPORT "GREED AND CONNIVANCE" BEFORE THE SUDDEN ABOLITION OF THE TASK FORCE

I knew about the impending abolition of the Task Force by the Revenue Minister in May 2011. Since more than one department's lands were involved, its termination should have gone before the cabinet according to the Rules, but in those days of Bellary's modern Vijayanagar Kings no rules were followed. A small time transport contractor from Bellary who was the *de-facto* Personal Assistant to Karunakara Reddy had been insisting my office staff to send maps showing village-wise location of government lands in Bangalore Urban district in colour obviously with the view of auctioning them out to the real estate Mafia. I had refused to send them and therefore knew that the Task Force would be wound up even though the task was not yet complete. So, I spent two weeks at home, preparing the report. My four year assignment in International Energy Initiative came in handy and I was able to prepare the entire report in my laptop. The report ran to about 200 pages and schedules. I gave it to the Member-Secretary of the Task Force who was the MD of the Karnataka Public Lands Corporation who took it to the Principal Secretary, Revenue Department who, reading it through got palpitations and declared government could not print it as it was highly critical. *So, I decided to print the report at my own cost.* The Marketing Consultancy Associates which was a subsidiary of government's Mysore Sales International, gave me an estimate of Rs 2,20,000 for 2,000 copies including many photographs which I paid and got it printed. On 31 May 2011 I received the Revenue Minister's order abolishing the Task Force. I sent copies of the Report to all members of the Task Force and to all MLAs, MLCs, MPs, Secretaries to Government and to the Private Secretaries of Ministers. I convened a Press Meet on 5 June which was very well attended and distributed copies to them. There was wide publicity in the media to my report for many days and the leading newspapers even wrote editorials on it. Strangely, when the media asked BSY who was in Mysore why the Task Force was terminated, he expressed his surprise and told them he would 'look into it' after returning to Bangalore! Of course nothing happened as the Reddy Brothers who were the Bellary Rajas in democratic India and, having become *Kuberas* after being born in a constable's family (they bought new Mercedes Benz cars for their swearing-in ceremony), and as Ministers destroyed the Sandur forests and exported iron ore illegally and made tons of black money and were the principal financiers in Karnataka for BJP's central leadership. Sushma Swaraj, who contested Sonia Gandhi from Bellary Parliamentary seat in 1999, was the "godmother" of the trio of Bellary including Sriramulu who was the gratuitous third Musketeer besides the two Bellary Princes, and she used to personally grace the annual *Varamahalakshmi Vratha* in Bellary every year from 1999 to 2010 and bless them. It was said that a kitty of Rs 300 crores was given to her at Rs 1 crore each for 300 Parliamentary Constituencies of BJP for the 2004 Lok Sabha elections. That is how Forests also contribute to India's vibrant democracy!

There was nothing the CM BSY could do against the Bellary Kings. However, an unexpected event occurred. The very next month, in July 2011, Justice Santosh Hegde, the Lok Ayukta of Karnataka gave his report on the Bellary Mining Scam of a royalty loss of Rs 19,000 crores by looting of forest land. BSY and both ministers had to resign. I consider my twenty months' full time work on Land-grabbing of Commons and my report with self-explaining title *Greed and Connivance*—Greed of political leaders and Connivance of Bureaucracy—and which I had to print at my own cost and which was appreciated by the public and media of Karnataka immensely, as my crowning achievement.

❖❖❖

After retiring in 2001, I had worked ten more years full time in government-related work. These were highly fruitful years and I could bring in my earlier years of varied experience to this last decade of work. In a sense, my most purposeful years as DC & DM, I relived in my last two assignments as Adviser to the Joint Legislature Committee and Chairman of the Task Force on Land Grabbing matters. It was *déjà vu*. As Chairman of the Task Force, I visited all the districts in Karnataka where I had not served. I re-acquainted with the Deputy Commissioners and Regional Commissioners who were highly affectionate towards me. I also met most of the other Heads of Departments whom I had not been familiar with in my pre-retirement days. This is an experience not given to any of the IAS officers. I remember the last lines of Nobel Eliot's *The Little Gidding:*

We shall not cease from exploration
And the end of all our exploring
Will be to arrive where we started
And know the place for the first time.

There are many highly philosophical explanations about what Eliot meant, such as he *probably intended to push his readers to undergo a cleansing so that they could be closer to God. Once they go through this process, then they will understand who they were when the process began. From there, humanity as a whole can keep moving forward.* In my own plebeian way, I interpreted it as *we should always be curious to know more and more and after forming reasonable convictions, again re-examine our experience, beliefs and knowledge and, if necessary, make further assessment of our beliefs, as new facts emerge, ad infinitum.* I am pleasantly surprised, I have not found any reasons to change my views on most matters from what I had in my DC days of 1970's. Except that officers and political leaders have become less honest, less courageous to fight for human values, even proudly corrupt and people have largely come to accept it as the new norm.

❖❖❖

CHAPTER 21

I Commit Contempt of Legislature

(And why it is necessary for more civil servants to do it !)

I have the honour of being one of very few IAS officers who have committed contempt of legislature. This is how it happened: My report on land-grabbing of public lands, *Greed and Connivance*, created widespread public discussion. The social and environmental activist SR Hiremath of Dharwad, who was instrumental in launching an agitation against the illegal mining in the forests of Bellary district, filed a PIL in the Supreme Court on my report and his *pro bono* advocate was Prashanth Bhushan. Meanwhile, the Governor of Karnataka Shri HR Bharadwaj, after seeing the discussion in the media and among the public, asked me to brief him on my report. I met him and while I had requested for fifteen minutes of his time, he spent two hours with me in going through my report in great detail.

In the Legislature, the matter of my Report of June 2011 was raised, and the ruling BJP government was now headed by Sadananda Gowda. BS Yediyuappa had resigned and the new CM was from Chikmagalur district where encroachment of forest lands by coffee planters was rampant and Gowda was a supporter of the planters as were all CMs. He took the stand that my report was not "approved" by government and therefore no official notice could be taken of it! This was lame because my report was in the public domain and a PIL was before the Supreme Court in which the government had been asked to submit para-wise reply. Besides, the Governor, after my briefing him, had written officially to the Chief Minister which read:

No.DO GS 88 EST 2011 dated 13-9-2011

"Dear Chief Minister,

You may be aware that the Government had constituted a Task Force for Recovery of Public Land and its protection in September 2009 under the Chairmanship of Shri V Balasubramanian, former Addl. Chief Secretary to Government of Karnataka. The Chairman of the Task Force had submitted a report to the Government in June, 2011 entitled "Greed and Connivance". When the Chairman of the Task Force met me, he had given me a copy of the report.

I have carefully gone through the report. It makes shocking revelations and it is an eye opener. The fact that more than 11,00,000 acres of Government land is under encroachment in the State is a very serious matter. The condition of lakes and water bodies in Bangalore and how they are systematically encroached or the sewage of the city let into these lakes has been brought out with illustrated cases in the report. In a subsequent letter, Shri Balasubramanian also ventured to quantify the value of land encroached and put it at Rs.19.5 lakh crores, more than the 2-G scam and Bellary Mining Scandal combined.

It is three months since the report has been submitted to the Government. I have also seen public disquiet in the media about the issues relating to encroachment of Government land and lakes. I would appreciate if you can let me know of the action taken by the Government on the findings and recommendations of the Task Force for Recovery of Public Land and its Protection as contained in its Chairman's report of 2011.

With warm regards,

Yours sincerely,

Sd/-
(H.R.BHARDWAJ)

Shri D.V.Sadananda Gowda,
Chief Minister of Karnataka,
VidhanaSoudha, Bangalore 560001 "

After receiving Governor's letter the Government could not pretend it had not received the Report. In fact, I had sent both the English and Kannada versions of it to all the Ministers, MLCs, MLAs, Secretaries to government, the Chief Secretary and the Secretary to CM. On receiving the Governor's letter, the government constituted three committees under the Additional Chief Secretary, the Principal Secretary of Revenue Department and the Chief Conservator of Forests to 'examine all aspects' of my report and take necessary action in usual officialese and clichés. Of course, nothing came of it as Committees are proverbially cold storages if not permafrosts. Government also had to prepare para-wise reply to the PIL filed in the Supreme Court. On the date of hearing I was present in the Supreme Court to assist Senior Counsel Prashant Bhushan along with SR Hiremath. After hearing the preliminary argument, the SC bench headed by Justice Altamas Kabir passed an order transferring the case to the Karnataka High Court as all the lands mentioned in my report were in Karnataka. Prashant Bhushan told the Court that even some of the sitting judges in the Karnataka HC were occupants of housing sites illegally received by them from the Karnataka Judicial Employees Cooperative Society as pointed in my report and therefore there will be a conflict of interest. However, the Court observed that if there was delay in the Karnataka High Court in hearing the case, the petitioner can again approach the Supreme Court.

In this background, the *Kannada Prabha* of Indian Express group requested me for an interview, especially regarding the role of the rich and powerful and the political leaders in land grabbing. One of the high-profile land grabbing mentioned in my report was about 62 acres of forest land in Kolar district which was in the possession of an MLA in the Congress party then. Along with the members of the Task Force and other officials I had visited the forest land in Kolar district and held detailed discussions on the spot with the officers and examined all the maps and records existing from 1920s. However, interestingly, just one day before my visit to Kolar, I received a phone call from one Diwakar, the Legal Adviser to the Chief Minister BSY, pretending to empathize with me and saying, *Why a senior person like you take the trouble to go to the remote forest, the local officers can themselves handle the matter!* When I told him that it is precisely because local officers were not even able to enter the land, that they had requested me to visit the land, he tried to dissuade me saying, the matter was "sub-judice". I had ascertained that there was no stay order from the High Court. So, I informed him that there was no legal infirmity and it was the bounden duty of the Task Force to help the district administration. This was the standard of legal advice being given to BSY and the functioning of the CM in helping the powerful land-grabbers!

My enquiry during the spot inspection revealed that even though the Assistant Conservator of Forests had passed an order for recovery of the land as early as 2007, the encroacher had preferred an appeal before the obliging Conservator of Forests who had ordered a "joint survey" by the forest department officials in the presence of the alleged land-grabber to ascertain the facts about the encroachment. He was ignorant about the *Godavarman* case and, what was clear, colluding with the encroacher. Predictably, the joint inspection never happened for four years as the encroacher would neither be present nor even allow the officials to enter the land which he had enclosed with high wall, like a fortress. During my spot inspection I found that the land was grown with fruit-bearing trees. On my instructions, the DC arranged for a joint survey again, this time getting the Deputy Director of Survey which showed the encroachment of forest land. Against this, the encroacher filed a Writ Petition in the High Court which ordered yet another joint survey! I asked the Survey Department to use the GIS (Geographical Information System), and Total Station instruments so that there will be no error in the survey. However, even after affixing the notice on the walls of the 'Garden Fortress' with a borewell in the middle of the forest, the encroacher was not present. The DCF Anil Kumar Rattan, IFS, was a highly conscientious officer and he had passed a 16-page detailed order establishing the extent of encroachment. Against this, the politically powerful encroacher again approached the High Court where it was pending. In India's Adversarial Justice system, it is possible to file multiple Writ Petitions before various courts at every stage and stymie the action of the state.

Meanwhile, fresh elections had taken place to the Karnataka Assembly in May 2013 and the encroacher had become an MLA after an interregnum of five years, this time from the ruling Congress Party, headed by Siddaramiah who, for a change, was from the not economically powerful 'Kuruba'—shepherd community. The popular daily, Kannada Prabha interviewed me in June 2013 about what the new government should do to recover the large extent of 11 lakh acres of government land under encroachment in the State. The forest encroachment in Kolar district was referred to by the reporter himself. The newspaper published this interview and mentioned the MLA by name. This was also widely covered by the media. The Assembly was in session and while proclaiming his innocence in the House, the MLA described me as Hitler and even broke down in copious tears! This theatrics so moved the other MLAs that the Speaker Kagodu Thimmappa referred the matter to the Privileges Committee of the Legislative Assembly, even though he had known me well as DC of Shimoga—he was from Sagar taluk in that district and was himself a member of the dramatis personae way back in 1972 holding public meetings for three days at the Shivappa Naika circle in Shimoga city protesting against my transfer—such are the principles of politicians when dealing with officers working in public interest! It was thought that encroachment of forest land was a legislator's privilege!

The next day there was even more acrimonious discussion on me in the Legislative Council! This was because, during the Kannada Prabha interview I had also referred to the vast encroachment of about 36,000 acres of pristine forest land in Chikmagalur district which had a high rainfall of 3,000 mm or 3 meters annually. This was in the heart of the Western Ghats and had rich coffee plantations. Chikmagalur district alone accounted for one-fourth of the total coffee production of India. I had visited coffee plantations in Chikmagalur on complaints of encroachments in July 2010 at the height of monsoon rains. It was an eye opener to me that while the area under coffee in the district was about 85,000 acres, the encroachment was 36,000 acres—as much as 40%! A small number of big planters had encroached huge extent of forest land adjoining their coffee plantations, some estates occupying over 700 acres of forest land each.

The *Kannada Prabha* had also published my comment that Sadananda Gowda who, as the MP from Chikmagalur, had led a delegation to the CM BSY and gave a petition demanding to restrain the Forest Department Officials from the 'high-handed action' against poor farmers to remove forest encroachments! The CM readily obliged the delegation by having his Secretary write to the Deputy Commissioner and Forest Department Officers *"Not to precipitate action"*. The background for this was, the Assistant Conservators of Forests in Chikmagalur district, especially in Koppa taluk where large scale encroachments by coffee planters had taken place, had booked 7,846 Forest Offence Cases against coffee planters and had even issued final orders for recovery in 1,193 cases though in no case the actual recovery had taken place. Many orders were appealed against before the Conservator of Forests in Chikmagalur who had conveniently kept them all pending for years. I had conducted two meetings of Forest Officers in the office of the Principal Chief Conservator of Forests in the headquarters of Forest Department in Bangalore, the *Aranya Bhavan*— with the *mantra* 'Wood Is Good' engraved prominently, which was attended, *inter alia,* by the Principal Chief Conservator of Forests and the Additional Chief Secretary in charge of Forests. In these meetings strict instructions were issued to the Forest Officers by the ACS and the PCCF to start removing large encroachments of over 5 acres. So, the coffee planters were understandably worried about the officers taking action. Hence, their meeting the CM BSY with Sadananda Gowda, the MP leading in the name of 'poor farmers' and the CM obliged.

After the issue of letter from the CM's office "not to take precipitative action" against forest encroachments, I pointed out to the Forest Department officers and to the government and CM's office that the dictionary meaning of "precipitative" action was, not to take action, *"unexpectedly, prematurely and without warning",* whereas in all the over 7,000 cases, written notices were given to the encroachers, opportunities given and in fact action was already delayed for years. But, the Forest Department Officers including the senior officers took refuge under the letter from CM's office for not taking any action and the blatant land grabbing by wealthy coffee planters have continued to this day. The fact that the CM or the Government have no powers to issue any such "stay orders" and only a Court of Law can issue such order went totally above the heads of officers. The deterioration of Rule of Law in India is precisely because the CM and the Ministers issue illegal stay orders, often orally, and these are slavishly obeyed by the officers who though have the legal powers but are cowards and do not act. The land mark Godavarman judgment of the Supreme Court was violated by the Forest Department in Chikmagalur wantonly. It is a myth that there is a *Long Arm of the Law*. In fact, there is no arm at all and the CMs cripple the administration to oblige the law breakers who donate funds for elections or otherwise for connivance and looking askance in return! Law is made physically handicapped by the Chief Ministers.

So, Sadananda Gowda gave in the Legislative Council a repeat performance of the earlier day's performance in the Legislative Assembly. He pleaded with the Chairman of the Legislative Council that he had only taken a delegation of poor farmers who had by mistake occupied some forest land! He also strongly submitted to the Chairman that the head of Task Force (referring to me by name) *"may be an honest person, but it should not go to his head"*! The Legislative Council also referred the matter to the Privileges Committee. But, after a few days, the Chairman of the Council's Privileges Committee, Madhusudan, MLC of the BJP informed me that as there was no substance in the complaint against me, the matter was dropped.

While the Privilege Committee of the Legislative Council dropped the enquiry against me without even calling me before it, that was not the case with the Privileges Committee of the Legislative Assembly. It issued a notice to me to appear before it. The Privileges Committee was headed by a senior Congress MLA from Dharwad district, Mr Koliwad who himself would later become the Speaker. Koliwad was quite nice to me. I narrated to the Committee all the facts relating to the encroachments and how it would not amount to any contempt of the Legislature in the remotest sense. I also pointed out to him that the very first recommendation in my Report was that a permanent Legislature Committee on the lines of Public Accounts Committee, Assurances Committee, the Committee on SC/ST, etc. should be constituted to protect public lands from land-grabbers. The Chairman opened my Report *Greed and Connivance* and read aloud the recommendation for the benefit of the members. He appreciated it and told the Legislature Secretary who was the Secretary of the Privileges Committee, to include my recommendation in the proceedings of the Committee. After an hour of discussion he said that the Committee found my efforts and Report on Encroachments impressive but, since a senior member of the Legislature (the concerned MLA was himself once the Speaker of the Assembly), the Committee had to take up the case for hearing. He also told me whether I would tell the Committee that my remarks in the interview were made "in the heat of the moment" so that the Committee can drop the matter! I was expecting such a move from the Privileges Committee as, for instance, in the Contempt of Court proceedings before the High Court the contemner usually expresses unconditional apology to the Court after which, their egos having been properly tickled, the Court drops the Contempt proceedings against the contemner with a frown and a strict warning! But, in my case I was very sure of the facts and the law. So, I politely told the Privileges Committee that my remarks were made with the cool of reason and not in any 'heat of the moment' and so there was no question of my saying anything to the contrary. The Chairman sighed and said, in that case he will have to call the complainant MLA before the Committee and hear him also along with me again to go into the details of the case. I told the Chairman this was perfectly agreeable to me and my advocate would also help me in defending my position as the Speaker Kagodu Thimmappa had agreed to my request that I may have the assistance of my legal counsel before the Privileges Committee. *[When I told my able counsel Mr Dhananjay I must pay his fees, he got offended and asserted that it was his 'privilege' to support a public cause!]*

Thus ended the contempt proceedings and I never heard from the Committee again. Later on I learned that the complainant MLA had written to the Privileges Committee that he was not keen on pursuing his complaint and give trouble "to an honest officer", as if he was magnanimous. Thus I lost a great opportunity to stand and explain on the floor of legislature how people in power consider it their right and privilege to do away with public property and commit a second contempt! However, throughout the month the episode went on and the media gave wide coverage to the problem of land grabbing in Karnataka. The newspaper *Kannada Prabha* whose publishing of the interview had caused the Privilege proceedings in the first place, ran on a daily basis a Question and Answer series on land grabbing with cartoons! But I was gratified that my publishing of the Report, though it cost me Rs.2,20,000, and the subsequent legislature proceedings due to my interview to the press created an awareness among the public about the magnitude of land grabbing and the role of the rich and powerful in the theft of commons.

SO WHAT HAPPENED TO THE FOREST LAND ENCROACHED UPON?

I was keeping in touch with this matter all through. It is the strategy of land-grabbers to entangle government in litigations in various courts. After some months, the HC passed an order for yet another 'joint survey' of the land, this time insisting that the Deputy Commissioner himself should be present personally during the survey and also the alleged encroacher. This was amusing because, the DC is not an expert on survey of lands. The DC could only grace the occasion by just being present with somebody to hold the umbrella above his head and this is what the HC wanted. As this rigmarole of 'Joint Inspection' of the encroached forest land was going on for over ten times and for a decade, to know how exactly the survey is done, I contacted a knowledgeable retired Joint Director of Land Records whom I had known in 2005 when I was the Adviser to the Joint Legislature Committee. What he explained to me was very interesting. In England the King allowed large scale transfer of village Commons to Manors from 16th century, especially when sheep farming became more profitable (often described as the 'biggest class theft of land'), and land so transferred had to be accurately measured. Hence, in 1620 Edmund Gunter, an English Clergyman and mathematician was commissioned to devise a measurement system. He prepared the 'Gunter's Chain' which consisted of 100 links of a chain made of brass and measuring exactly 22 yards. A length of 10 chains of 220 yards and 1 chain of 22 yards width made one acre of 4,840 sq.yards (220 * 22); for distance measurement of length, 10 chains made one Furlong (220 yards) and 8 furlongs made one mile of 1,760 yards. The length of the cricket pitch was determined in 1620 as one Gunter's chain of 22 yards and it has not been changed in 400 years! The first reference to cricket being played as an adult sport in England was in 1611, when two men in Sussex were prosecuted for playing cricket on Sunday instead of going to church! They were fined 12 pence each and made to do penance!

The Revenue Department under which Survey and Settlement was done, had employed surveyors who in turn appointed workers to do the physical work of carrying the Chains. These Chains were then made of galvanized steel from England (instead of the costly copper) and were heavy. When I told the JDLR about the recurring measurements of the 62 acres of forest land and the differing opinions between the forest department and survey department, he told me a very amusing history. The Gunter's chain of 22 yards of steel with brass rings for links was heavy. The workers in Mysore districts being undernourished and emaciated and finding it difficult to carry them unlike the well built

British workers or India's North-Western Provinces' workers, some senior officers of the Survey Department of India in Madras Province in course of time used the expedient of cutting the Gunter's Chain into half, having only 50 links measuring 11 yards instead of the standard 100 links and 22 yards, but still called it Gunter's Chain! Therefore, while the earlier maps would show the correct Gunter's Chain of 22 yards length, the later maps, if not carefully recorded that Half-Chain was used, would show only 11 yards as one chain and the boundary would be misunderstood as half! It was therefore likely that if the forest map showed its boundary at say 10 Chains from a land mark of a stream or rock-growth which would be 220 yards or 660 feet, the survey department, having used half chain, would show the boundary stopping at 330 feet! *[Incidentally, one Half-Gunter's Chain of 11 yards squared is 121 sq. yards and forty such chains would make one acre; and one such Half Gunter's Chain squared came to be called a "Gunta" in honour of Gunter and 40 Guntas making one acre!]*

As it was quite likely that the Survey Department officials who were doing the actual survey might have overlooked this elementary discrepancy which the JDLR told me, I telephoned the DC of Kolar, DK Ravi, whose presence the Court had ordered mandatory for surveying the land and explained the matter to him. I was not sure whether he took it seriously. It so happened that he was in the midst of various personal problems (about this in the following paragraphs) and he relied upon the subordinates to do the work. His report to the Principal Secretaries of the Revenue and Forest Departments said that the Forest maps were not "clear" and according to the Survey Department measurements the boundary of the concerned Forest in dispute stopped about 500 metres short of the boundary shown in the Forest Department map! The Principal Secretary of Forest Department, Mr Sivasailam was an IAS officer 1985 batch and twenty years junior to me. He was a meticulous and highly articulate officer who had understood that the Forest Department maps were the correct ones and wrote to his counterpart the Principal Secretary, Revenue Department that the Report of the DC of Kolar was 'wishy-washy' and a correct survey should be done. But, by this time the damage was done. The encroacher produced the DC's Joint Survey report before the District Judge at Kolar who held the order of the Forest Department as invalid. The Forest Department appealed against this before the High Court which also dismissed the appeal in February 2016. Thus ended the attempt to recover the forest land. *To repeat, Arrival of Truth is not the objective of Justice in India's Anglo-Saxon Adversarial system!* If only Joseph Marquis Dupleix of French Pondicherry had been more successful than Robert Clive of Madras,

India's judicial system would have been the very different 'Inquisitorial System' where Arrival of Truth is the Objective! The Ifs and Buts of history are often highly, intriguingly painful.

A DIGRESSION ON MR.DK RAVI, DC & DM OF KOLAR—THE 'MICHELIN' IMAGE BY THE MEDIA AND THE STARK REALITY EXPOSED BY CBI

This chapter would not be complete if I do not narrate what happened to DK Ravi the DC of Kolar who had conducted a defective survey which went against the Forest Department and public interest. In March 2015 Ravi committed suicide by hanging—the first of its kind in Karnataka's administrative history—in the 9th floor of his posh St Johns Woods Apartment, Koramangala rented by the government. After his stint in Kolar as DC, he was posted to Bangalore in the Commercial Taxes Department in October 2014. As suicide of a young IAS officer was a rare event, and he was just 35, understandably it created a media blitz and fire storm. The following were the screaming headlines in the media:

- It was a murder engineered by the real estate and sand Mafia and even some Ministers such as George and DK Shivakumar were involved;

- He was a friend of Dalits for whose welfare he had tirelessly worked which irked the major communities who got him transferred;

- In the Commercial Taxes department, he had raided the real estate company of a cabinet Minister and was planning a major raid on a famous real estate giant which was the reason for his murder;

The suicide was immediately politicised as there was Congress government of Siddaramaiah in Karnataka and a BJP government in the centre and all political parties and civil society jumped into the fray. As Ravi himself belonged to Okkaliga community, the JD (S) President announced that a Training Centre to coach IAS aspirants would be started in Bangalore in memory of Ravi! [In Karnataka's democracy, the JD (S) is considered as the Okkaliga's Party and BJP the Lingayats' favourite!] The NGOs did their bit by organizing a candle-light vigil for many days in Bangalore. Everyone demanded a probe by CBI. Even though the CBI was by this time a discredited organization (even Justice RM Lodha of the Supreme Court in the 'Coalgate Case' described it as a 'Caged Parrot' echoing its Master's Voice!), the hope obviously was, since the

Congress government was in power in the state the CBI, controlled by the BJP in the centre, would be highly objective in its investigation! The Human Rights NGOs who were till then the most vociferous critics of CBI, organized *bundhs* in Kolar and Bangalore demanding CBI investigation, thus suddenly becoming champions of CBI! The matter was taken to Sonia Gandhi who asked the CM to authorize the CBI to investigate, transferring the case from the state CID. This was done within a week. The CBI investigated the suicide case for eight months and submitted an 80-page report in November 2015. Concluding that it was a case of suicide and not murder, it made some very startling findings some of which leaked to the press being:

- Ravi was transferred from Kolar at his own request and, on his behalf, his father in law who was himself a second-rung Congress leader and also on the recommendation of the Dalit MP;

- He and his realtor friend Harikrishna had started in 2012 a real-estate company, R & H Property and had tried to purchase 50 acres of agricultural land belonging to Dalit landless persons in Sidlaghatta bordering Bangalore worth Rs 2 crores but as there was a prohibition of purchasing lands from Dalit grantees of government land, the land deal was not approved. The registered office of the firm was shown as 632, 25th Cross, 16th Main Road, Judicial Layout, Bengaluru-55 which was the residence of Harikrishna. An account was opened in the State Bank of Mysore, Yelahanka. His father-in-law Hanumantharayappa had given Rs 1 crore for investing in the land. Ravi had confided to Harikrishna that after making the venture a Rs.500-crore company, he would resign from the IAS. His batch-mate, a lady officer and her husband had also invested Rs.10 lakhs in the company;

- On December 7, 2014 morning Ravi's wife, upset with the fact that Ravi had been continuing his dalliance with the lady officer, sent a message on the Facebook to her asking her what would she do if somebody tried to wean away her husband from her. The lady officer forwarded the message to Ravi, causing a quarrel between the couple and his wife was compelled to send an apology to the lady officer.

- Since 2014, Ravi would visit the Spa in Taj Vivanta at Bangalore for body massage and became intimate with a masseuse, Ms Shelly from Nagaland to whose bank account he deposited Rs 30,000 on two occasions. According to Harikrishna, Ravi had once come down from Kolar to meet her in Orion Mall and took her to the resort Royal Orchard located in Yelahanka.

- From his Samsung Galaxy Note, iPhone and iPad it was found he had an infatuation on his already married lady-batch mate from 2009 but was dejected as it was unrequited. He had made repeated calls and messages to her throughout but they were not reciprocated. On his last day, at 9.50 am Ravi had sent a long message to her *about his love for her and that he has failed in his life and now would like to end it as he did not want to disturb her marriage and further that he had deleted all her pictures, messages in the mobile phone and that his last wish was she should come to hug and kiss his dead body. If at all there is a next life, we will be together, I am quitting, were his last words.*

The CBI investigation conclusively proved that there was no foul play of any kind and that Ravi committed suicide in despair due to the twin failure of business transaction and forbidden love. The media, the NGOs and the politicians found that their conspiracy theories had been their pure imagination. But no one apologized for misleading the public. Like the proverbial thief, being stung by scorpion while stealing and compelled to keep absolute silence, they kept quiet. Nobody apologized or applauded the CBI! The lazy-hasty media, naïve and motivated NGOs and habitually crooked politicians created a straw victim and the usually discredited FBI for once demolished it.

In the end it was a wasted life. Ravi was just 35. Hailing from a humble rural background, he was dazzled by the life style of most bureaucrats and wanted to join in. In 2012, within three years of joining the IAS, he floated a real-estate partnership, the *el dorado* of the get-rich-quick club of the land Mafia of Bangalore. But everything went wrong from the beginning as the 50-acre land deal failed. Normally, the life of an average IAS officer is a secure, sheltered existence. One need not do anything extra-ordinary to get along well. Ultimately, it is one's moral compass and a strong and committed philosophy that can see one through. One should have a moral strength not to cross boundaries. Or, in the alternative, one should have the immoral confidence from a political or a caste base to see through the tough choices and cross the Rubicon as many bureaucrats have done. At least two such corrupt officers ended as Chief Secretaries in Karnataka and one even became a cabinet minister taking oath to 'protect the Constitution' and getting police parade salutes on Independence and Republic Days! Contrary to the proverb, crime does indeed pay, *even when one is caught*. No doubt, the much praised, remarkably powerful Constitution does not allow the convicted felon to contest elections, but so what, if you can be leader of a political party, you can be king-maker and nominate Chief Ministers! Indians should learn the obvious lessons from Laloo Prasad Yadav's remarkable life! Most politicians took away citizens' money, but Laloo took money of cattle, meant for their fodder, which no other politician in the world has done. He continues to be the King-maker in Bihar's politics.

Ravi's dilemma was to turn back or to proceed. He could have reversed his steps to return to the normal, safe, comfortable, humdrum, unremarkable life of an IAS officer. Or he could have boldly made the Faustian bargain, crossed the Rubicon and amassed wealth and power and retired in luxury, holidaying in Kruger National Park with cabinet ministers for company, like some of his senior colleagues in Karnataka have done. Obviously he did not have the courage to do it either. This goes back to Aristotle's *Organon* (Logic) namely, *Principium tertii exclusi*— "there cannot be an intermediate between contradictories". Either you are corrupt or you are not-corrupt, there cannot be a middle way of being both *corrupt and also not-corrupt*. That is the Law of the Excluded Middle. Thus Ravi ended in suicide. He led a life of lie and ended a loser. In the end it was all a tragic, avoidable, waste. *(The Congress Party did not learn anything from this episode. In a by-election from a Bangalore city constituency in 2020, it chose Ravi's widow as its candidate, imagining that the Okkaligas will all vote for the 'martyred' Ravi but lost to the BJP candidate by over 57,000 votes. The Indian politicians have a congenital resistance to learning!)'*

❖❖❖

CHAPTER 22

Summing Up

"Yesterday I was a drop of semen,
Tomorrow I will be a handful of ashes"
—Marcus Aurelius, Meditations

RACE TO THE BOTTOM

Fifty years is a sufficient period to assess the traverse of administration. After all, starting from the 1857 Great Mutiny, the British Empire lasted in India just for ninety years disregarding the one hundred years' loose administration of the East India Co from 1757. My eyewitness assessment of Karnataka's administration during the past five decades is, it is a great Fall from Grace. I have worked in the regimes of Chief Ministers of various hues, from Veerendra Patil, Devaraj Urs, Gundu Rao, Ramakrishna Hegde, Bangarappa, JH Patel, HD Kumaraswamy, BS Yediyurappa, SM Krishna and Siddaramiah. I have also observed the functioning of Chief Secretaries from K Narayanaswamy in 1967 to all others till 2020. In my experience with 18 Chief Ministers and 27 Chief Secretaries in fifty years, a very clear fall in standards is obvious. Most commentators lament about the absence of 'Political Will' to give efficient administration. What they gloss over is the equally absent Administrative Will of bureaucracy. After the ethical tenures of RJ Rebello, GVK Rao, RA Naik, TR Satishchandran and JC Lynn, others acted more like Chief Clerks carrying out illegal orders of the Chief Ministers, always approved by a rubber stamp Cabinet. Permitting the 'Seconds Sale' in liquor, promoting corruption as in Classik Computers case, de-notification of BDA land acquisitions even after taking possession of land, destruction of forests and illegal mining, allowing land grabbing in lakes and public lands, regularizing illegal occupation and constructions, kidnapping MLAs as hostages and keeping them in Resorts, changing parties like chameleons changing colours—the race to the bottom has been supersonic with the 'neutral' higher bureaucracy being mute spectators and even participants. Dante

Alighieri said in his Inferno: *The hottest places in Hell are reserved for those who in time of moral crisis preserve their neutrality.* The 'Neutrality' of civil service is a myth, most are abettors and beneficiaries.

The most famous question asked of all Sherlock Holmes stories is, *Why didn't the dog bark?* When the famous racehorse Silver Blaze was stolen, the dog in the stable was silent. Holmes solves the mystery by deducing that the dog did not bark because the thief was a friend of the manor. Karnataka bureaucracy, from district level to the Principal Chief Conservator of Forests and the Chief Secretary, did not even whimper when forests in Bellary were wantonly destroyed for mining iron ore illegally because they were simply abetting the crime. It is not as if the bureaucracy is helpless. With the protection given in Articles 310 and 311 of the Constitution, no All-India Service officer can be removed by the state government. Point is, over a period of time, the bureaucracy in Karnataka has lost its moral anchor and backbone to stand up against the illegal acts of political bosses. You can always sabotage the illegal attempts of ministers by various checks and balances the law has given if only officers have courage. The most a CM can do is to transfer the officer which a stoic officer can convert to an opportunity to excel. There are some shining examples:

Chaturvedi Badrinath IAS was a 1957 batch officer of Tamil Nadu cadre. Because of his scholarly disposition and outspoken nature, his political bosses and senior officers did not like him and after sixteen years of service when he had to be promoted to Joint Secretary rank, he was posted as Director of Archives. With its dingy and dusty office in the 1909 *Grassmere* building in Egmore, Chennai to keep old documents and records, Archives is considered to be the dog house and punishment posting to humiliate an officer in all states. But Badrinath took steps to modernize and protect the original records, some of which as old as a 1640 Bible when the British East India Company was established in Madras, and he built the Archives Department into a modern institution as in advanced countries. Not only that. He used his time there to gather material for research and wrote five books, *Swami Vivekananda; Dharma—Hinduism and Religion in India; Finding Jesus in Dharma and Christianity in India; The Women of the Mahabaratha; The Question of Truth and The Mahabaratha.* These were hailed as remarkable in academic circles. After thirty years of service he took voluntary retirement to become a full time highly respected academic. In 2010 he was awarded the prestigious Sahitya Academy Award for his book *The Mahabaratha: An Enquiry into Human Condition.* He modernized the Department of Archives and Archaeology by appointing Malcolm Adisheshiah the renowned UNESCO Expert as adviser to the task which was a lasting contribution to that vastly important but badly neglected department by uncouth leaders and uneducated officers. Being literate is different from being educated. Many IAS officers are marginally educated.

Another 'punished' officer is **Ashok Khemka** of 1991 batch of Haryana cadre. He was a graduate from IIT, Kharagpur and a PhD from Tata Institute of Fundamental Research, an LLB in law, an MBA and an MA in Economics from IGNOU, New Delhi. He was a strict disciplinarian and was transferred 53 times in 28 years for just doing his duty in whatever job he held. In 2011 he was awarded the SR Jindal Prize for 'Crusade Against Corruption'. In 2013 when he was posted as a punishment to a lower post of Inspector General of Stamps and Registration, he exposed a land deal of under-valuation by Robert Vadra and ordered the cancellation of mutation of a 3.5 acre plot of land in Manesar-Shikohpur near Delhi which Vadra had sold to the leading real estate company, Delhi Land & Finance (DLF) for Rs 58 crores which was worth four times more even according to government's 'guidance value'. *[The joke then was, if you want to convert Rs.1 crore into Rs.100 cr take 'Robber' Vadra as your consultant; but, if you want to convert Rs.100 cr to Rs.1 cr take Vijay Mallya, the King of Bad Times as adviser!]* Khemka was promptly transferred by the then Congress Government. But he continued his crusade against corruption and successive governments including the BJP ruled ones kept on transferring him. His last transfer was to the customary Archives and Museums in 2019, his average tenure being 6 months 10 days in each post. Recently, Harper Collins published his biography, *Just Transferred,* [2020], with a photograph showing him sitting on a suitcase in a bus stand! It became a best-seller.

In Karnataka itself, there are many unsung heroes who have been harassed by transfers and worse. One such courageous officer was **Madana Gopal** (1984 IAS) who was suspended by Bangarappa in 1992 for taking on the Excise Contractors. **Harsh Gupta** (1997 IAS) had been the DC&DM of the Coffee Plantations district of Chikmagalur and later of Bidar, Mysore and Dakshina Kannada districts. He was shifted every six months because he took on the land-grabbers. In 2020 he was the 'Competent Authority' to enquire into the blatant Ponzi Scheme of IMA-Iliyas Monetary Authority—in which over 51,000 middle class people, mostly Muslims, were cheated of an estimated Rs 4,000 crores by enlisting the support of leaders and Ulemas, promising a monthly interest of 12% (144% annually!) in which two IPS Officers and a former Minister and 7-time MLA, Roshan Baig were arrested and being investigated by the CBI. Harsh Gupta was the Regional Commissioner of Bangalore Division when the IMA scam broke out and he was appointed with additional charge to ascertain and refund the dues of cheated depositors at the direction of the High Court. Within six months he was stripped of the post of Regional Commissioner by Yediyurappa because, as Regional Commissioner he conducted the election of Mayor of Bangalore City Corporation as provided by law but against the wishes of the CM. The 'honest' Chief Secretary even denied him an office, staff and a vehicle and the Court had to intervene!

Rashmi Mahesh (1996 IAS) was transferred 23 times in 19 years. On the basis of the audit of the Accountant General of Karnataka she unearthed the Rs.100 crore scam in the award of illegal contracts for six years in the prestigious Administrative Training Institute of Mysore and sent a detailed report to the Chief Secretary in 2014. But he did not take any action. Instead, when she told the media why she was attacked by a mob of affected illegal contractors who were also the employees of the Institute and suffered grievous hurt, the CS started disciplinary proceedings against her!

Roopa Moudgil IPS of 2000 batch was transferred 43 times in 21 years, the most noteworthy being her reporting the special treatment given to Jayalalithaa's constant companion *Chikkamma* Sasikala Natarajan in Bangalore's Parappana Agrahara Prison where an entire wing of 5 cells were kept at her disposal (1 for kitchen, 1 for visitors, 1 for relaxation besides two for other uses!) She was convicted for 4 years in the Disproportionate Assets case and had allegedly paid Rs.2 crore bribe to the DGP Prisons. The same DG of Prisons gave similar VIP treatment to the forgotten Abdul Kareem Telgi, the King of Fake Stamp-Paper scam (2006) estimated at Rs 20,000 crores and who was undergoing a 30-year sentence in the same prison where he was 'allotted' 3 fellow prisoners for hand and leg massage! On her report to government, a former Home Secretary Vinay Kumar IAS, a fine officer who was DC of Raichur when I was Divisional Commissioner, Gulbarga, was appointed to enquire into it who found the allegations to be true. But Roopa Moudgil was promptly transferred and on top of it was issued a notice by the office of the honest CM Siddaramiah for meeting the Press! Another fine officer, **Mathai** KAS, had served in the Air Force and joined the KAS in 2006. In 10 years of service he was transferred 27 times for various 'misdemeanours' such as reporting corruption and scams, the most important being the Rs.2,000 crores Advertising scandal in Bangalore city Corporation and the Rs.300 cr scam in Mandya Urban Development Authority. His salary was withheld illegally and he was denied a vehicle which prompted him to ride a bicycle to go to his office! His is the only case in India where a State Officer filed complaint against the Chief Secretary and seven senior

IAS Officers before the State Human Rights Commission for harassment.

On the other hand, at least two IAS officers whose houses were raided were made Chief Secretaries both superseding honest and senior officers. Such is the quality of administration given by CMs and Chief Secretaries in Karnataka! If a few citizens still have any iota of respect for government, it is because of the unsung heroic officers who fearlessly uphold the law. These are the crusaders who relentlessly march on regardless of whether they will ever reach the holy land. It does not matter where they end, what is important is the selfless journey which itself is the noble end. It is because of these Knights Templars that some democracy still survives here unlike neighbouring Pakistan, Bangladesh, Myanmar, Thailand or Nepal where the civil servants have been totally emasculated by the political leaders with the result in Pakistan, Bangladesh and Myanmar, which had the same civil services recruitment and protection as India before 1947, we witness the military take-over off and on and even when governments are democratically elected, the Prime Ministers are just nominees of the army. If the civil services will be similarly gelded and sterilized in India, here also we will have the OG (Olive Green) government. The academics, media and intelligentsia (many of them could not get through the UPSC examination for All India Services!) who paint all bureaucrats with the same tar brush do not realize what will happen to even the governance-deficit administration if the Bureaucracy is totally rendered epicene.

CHANGING SOURCES OF CORRUPTION IN KARNATAKA

Indira Gandhi self-servingly trivialized corruption saying, *Corruption is a Global Phenomenon.* India, with its Electoral Bonds and unchecked off-shore treasure islands shelter is a major player! Karnataka has seen three phases of corruption. The first was by political leaders and officials milking the proverbial PWD and Irrigation Department contractors till the 1970's. Investment in Irrigation and Power increased significantly during the 5-Year Plans which facilitated overestimates, false measurements, cost and time over-runs enabling huge corruption.

The second phase was special to Karnataka—the liquor barons funding political parties. Mysore State did not have any history of prohibition unlike the other states in India which were influenced by Mahatma Gandhi. In 1935, almost all states had Congress governments and most of them introduced restrictions on alcohol. But Mysore was a Part B State with a British Resident. Arrack, toddy and Indian Made 'Foreign' liquor were licensed from 1889. Since then liquor trade became an important source of government income and also corruption. But, in the 1980's there was an innovation in the form of "Seconds". To increase Karnataka's sales by exporting IMFL to other states, the export duty and tax was reduced to Rs.2 per litre compared to the higher duty for sale within the state. So, the liquor barons devised the simplest system of labelling the bottles "For Export" but selling it inside the state. Such sale was called "Seconds", the first being tax-paid for sale within state. This corrupt practice was rampant in the 1980s and it was estimated by the Taxation Task Force constituted by government that in one year alone, while 28 million litres of IMFL was officially sold in the state, almost two and a half times that quantity, 68 million litres, was additionally sold by way of "seconds". The liquor barons shared part of the loot with the political leaders with some "tips" going to government officers. Veerendra Patil stopped this in 1989 by nationalizing the wholesale of liquor through the state-owned Mysore Sales International controlling the movement of liquor from distilleries. But he was dismissed in one year and his successor Bangarappa aggravated corruption by appointing a former Excise Commissioner as the Chief Secretary, superseding three senior officers and also made him the Finance Commissioner, Chairman of MSIL, BDA and State Finance Corporation! As I have explained in detail in an earlier chapter, the same CM-CS combo placed orders for supply of 100 Apple-Macintosh computers, incompatible with the IBM-Microsoft system of the government, on a non-existent firm which never supplied the computers and the advance given to the middleman was shared with the CM! The CBI investigation showed that the amount was handed over at the official residence of the CM! But the case was dismissed by the High Court as it found that the deal was approved by the cabinet and the CM-CS duo alone could not be held responsible for a collective cabinet decision! The Rule of Law in India is, *Show me the Man, I will show you the Rule!* The 'Golden Rule' is, *Who has the gold, makes the Rules!*

The third phase of government-invented corruption started in late 1980's when Hegde's Janata Government legally permitted over 300 House Building Cooperative Societies to get large extent of land through government's land acquisition for distribution of sites to the houseless members of the HBCSs. Instead of giving sites to only their members, the politician-headed HBCSs distributed large number of sites to builders, contractors and political leaders ostensibly for "joint-development" of the sites for internal roads, layouts, drains, etc. Government acquisition of lands for the HBCSs was discontinued after strictures by the High Court. But then, 84 HC and SC judges had themselves acquired housesites of 60' x 90' and 80' x 120' dimension from the Karnataka Judicial Employees House Building Cooperative Society, to which they were not legally eligible as they are not 'Employees' of Karnataka Government, according to a judgment of the High Court itself. This was pointed out by JLC in its Report dated 26 July 2007 (pp 98-100). *In high places we invent virtues where none exists.*

With the Information Technology boom exploding in the new millennium, the population of Bangalore doubled to 12 million and with 10 lakh IT families with an average income of Rs.11 lakhs annually and Banks giving loans liberally, the boom in real estate by private sector skyrocketed. Land cost from 1970 to 2017 increased by *520 times*. This led to rampant land-grabbing by real estate mafia with officials' help. The government land under encroachment in the composite Bangalore district is 102,600 acres with the average Mode (Most Occurring Value) of Rs 5 crores per acre. According to the 2017 Koliwad Legislature Committee Report on Lake Encroachments in Bangalore Urban and Rural districts, out of 4,818 lakes, 3,333 were encroached upon to the extent of 12,042 acres. Inspite of the Reports of Joint Legislature Committee on land grabbing headed by AT Ramaswamy (2007), Task Force Report by me (2011) and Koliwad Committee Report (2017), no action was taken because political leaders, bureaucrats and realtors have a joint venture in land-grabbing. Even in Covid era the major real estate projects as identified by the Koliwad committee are continuing relentlessly as follows: Prestige Group (139 projects), Sobha (148 projects), Godrej Properties (125 projects), Mahindra Lifespace (104 projects), Brigade Group (64), Purvankara (64 projects), Rohan Builders (12 projects). All had their beginnings in 1980s. The most dangerous development is, the real estate mafia is no longer outside the government but inside the government itself.

KARNATAKA, THE 40% STATE

From being the gentlemanly state of 10% *Mamool,* Karnataka has made a great leap forward in the past fifty years. The Contractors are now washing the dirty linen of all, of the leaders, bureaucrats and themselves, in public that the 40% demanded of them is unbearable ! There should be a decency in bribing. After all, to instal potholes there has to be a road to start with which is rather difficult within 60%! To crown it all, an MLA has made a revelation that a 'Seer' in Delhi has told him, the CM chair is his if he can make an upfront, one-time capital investment of Rs 2,500 crores ! He also revealed, for ministership the going rate is a mere Rs 100 crores. Of course, from being a gentlemanly 10% *Mamool* state, to make progress to 40% is no doubt a big jump but it is nothing to the incomparable Bihar where in April 2022, an entire 500-

ton bridge was stolen away in three days! This introduces a new idiom, Robbing in Plain sight, in place of Hiding in Plain Sight! Karnataka has still a long way to go but it is catching up.

IS THERE A MEANING AND PURPOSE IN LIFE?

From my college days I have been an avid reader of Somerset Maugham. He was trained as a doctor but became a successful writer when, at the age of 23 his first novel, *Liza of Lambeth* was sold out in its first edition and he gave up medicine. He was orphaned at the age of ten. During the First World War he joined the Red Cross. He was also a part-time spy for the British Intelligence Service! He wrote about his life and philosophy when he was in his early sixty's while convalescing from tuberculosis in a sanatorium and titled it *The Summing Up* and published in 1938 though he lived upto 91 and died in 1965. It was therefore premature to have called it *The Summing Up*. However, I also read the book prematurely when I was just twenty and I was greatly impressed by it. He was an agnostic. His reasoning was simple. God cannot be both Almighty and All-Merciful. With all the evil and pain in the world, with small children dying painfully of meningitis, if God cannot stop it, he is not Almighty and if he can stop but does not, then he is not All-Merciful. Why then pray to a God who is not Almighty and All-merciful? A memorable passage from *The Summing Up* is:

The egoism of man makes him unwilling to accept the meaninglessness of life, and when he has unhappily found himself no longer able to believe in a higher power whose ends he could flatter himself that he subserved he has sought to give it significance by constructing certain values beyond those that seem to further his immediate welfare. Man has always sacrificed truth to his vanity, comfort and advantage. He lives not by truth but by make-believe, and his idealism, it has sometimes seemed to me, is merely his effort to attach the prestige of truth to the fictions he has invented to satisfy his self-conceit.

Maugham makes the point, it is possible for a person to do good to society without the help of believing in a Creator. What then is the point in believing in a Grand Design which has created *Plasmodium falciparum*—the Anopheles mosquito, Tubercle bacillus or Covid-19?

On the other hand, I also read Viktor Frankl's remarkable, *Man's Search for Meaning*, first published in 1946 and since then 12 million copies sold. He was a psychiatrist who survived the Nazi Concentration Camp during the World War II. His main thesis—Logotherapy—is, inspite of all the cruelty and meaninglessness of it all, individual lives can still have purpose and meaning. He gives his own will to survive as proof and his purpose having been to see his wife who was held in another camp and to publish his Logotherapy after his release. He never saw his wife as she was gassed without his knowing in another camp. But he did publish his theory after his release. In a memorable passage he says:

> *Everything can be taken from a man but one thing: the last of the human freedoms—to choose one's attitude in any given set of circumstances, to choose one's own way…..The way in which a man accepts his fate and all the suffering it entails, the way in which he takes up his cross, gives him ample opportunity— even under the most difficult circumstances—to add a deeper meaning to his life. It may remain brave, dignified and unselfish. Or in the bitter fight for self-preservation he may forget his human dignity and become no more than an animal. Here lies the chance for a man either to make use of or to forgo the opportunities of attaining the moral values that a difficult situation may afford him. And this decides whether he is worthy of his sufferings or not. Such men are not only in concentration camps. Everywhere man is confronted with fate, with the chance of achieving something through his own suffering….Life ultimately means taking the responsibility to find the right answer to its problems and to fulfill the tasks which it constantly sets for each individual. [Logotherapy is] "Live as if you were living already for the second time and as if you had acted the first time as wrongly as you are about to act now!"*

This is an important book which raises the basic question whether there is purpose and meaning for a human life. Frankl of course answers in the affirmative. His determination to live and to publish his manuscript and to see his wife (whom he thought was still alive) gave both purpose and meaning to his terrible years in the Concentration Camp. The contrast between Somerset Maugham's view about the meaninglessness of life and that of Frankl is remarkable. The Holocaust in which 6 million Jews died at the hands of Nazis, half of whom in the 27 main Extermination Camps and the huge 1,100 'sub-camps', is unimaginable. From these Camps only 450,000 Jews survived which included Frankl. But, the most abhorring aspect of the Holocaust was, in the Extermination Camps, there were *Kapos* who were Jewish Prison Supervisors appointed by German Guards, setting victim against victim. The *Kapos* were more cruel than the German guards themselves, towards their own Jewish brethren. The ingenuity of the German bestiality was, if a *Kapo* was not sufficiently harsh towards the prisoners, the *Kapo* himself would be stripped of his position and returned to be another common Jewish prisoner. To escape that danger, the *Kapos* were extra-ordinarily barbaric to their own Jewish prisoners. So, the question Frankl does not raise nor answer is, what was the purpose and meaning of life for a *Kapo*? Besides, unlike Frankl, six million Jews died by gassing, starvation, forced marches, frost-bite, typhus and sheer exhaustion from over-work. What was the meaning or purpose of life for those six million who died without dignity? In many camps the Germans used bulldozers to push the dead bodies into pits for mass cremation as sufficient land was not available to bury them. The German Generals who planned for the concentration camps had treated the Jewish prisoners as "Storage Problem"! Even the Pope Pius XII who knew in 1943 that Hitler was responsible for the Holocaust, did not condemn it and because of this he was known as "Hitler's Pope". What about the purpose and meaning of the life of *el Papa*—the Father of Christendom himself?

The purpose, the objective, may be just survival but it does not give much meaning. For landless agricultural workers who have no casual leave, earned leave or medical leave or pension, and who have to work to eat or starve if not able to work, what is the meaning of life? Einstein who escaped the Extermination Camps by leaving Germany in time, had the purpose of proving his scientific theories, including his elegant equation $E = MC^2$ which he formulated in 1905 and the first Plutonium fission test by Dr. Robert Oppenheimer and his team in July 1945. That was their purpose in life giving it meaning. But, the very next month, in August 1945 by exploding the first two atomic bombs in Hiroshima and Nagasaki 226,000 persons, almost all civilians, just evaporated. What happened to their purpose and meaning of life? As Viktor Frankl himself says, each person is unique and the purpose in life and meaning of life of each differs for each. In India with high poverty, incompetence and inequality as in many African countries, it only means, for a large mass of people, the only purpose and meaning in life is just to survive. It is a slow Extermination Camp without a visible barbed wire fencing. So, between Maugham and Frankl what stand can one take about the Meaning in Life? Maugham takes the extreme view that life has no meaning and man's idealism is a make-belief he has invented to satisfy his self-conceit. These are harsh words compared to the view of faith and hope of Frankl which he calls Tragic Optimism. The more I think about these two extremes the more it is difficult to fully agree or disagree with both the views. The Aristotelian binary of Yes or No and 'Exclusion of the Middle' does not apply here. Rather, one tends to agree with Buddhist monk Nagarjuna's Third Proposition, *Both True and Not True*, and also his Fourth Proposition, *Neither True, nor Not True*. This may sound quite confusing as the Brahmin Priests felt when they heard Buddha's reply to their question about existence of God, *I Neither Agree there is a God, Nor Disagree that there is a God*. This is because real life situations are quite complex and convoluted. In the psychological and social matter of Purpose and Meaning of Life, the variables are even more than in weather of Chaos theory and therefore there can be no one truth.

There is however one vital question which is seldom asked about the behaviour of the prisoners of Nazi Extermination Camps. Why was there no successful uprisings in the camps? Though there were one or two small revolts and even some escapes, there was no large scale uprisings in the camps. After the war a Nazi doctor of a Camp asked, Why did you people not revolt? You outnumbered the Guards one to hundred and there were over a thousand prisoners in Birkinau and the ten guards with weapons could have been overpowered by a hundred prisoners and would have died. In any case you were dying in the camp. Why did not a hundred Jews sacrifice their lives so others could escape? The ex-Nazi doctor himself answered, *Because you were weak, you are a weak race and we were right to exterminate you!*

This is a recurring theme with most conquered people, especially for Indians. Why did they not fight? Why did not the Hindus fight the small number of invaders riding their horses through Khyber and Bolan passes? It was the dharma of the Kshatriyas to fight. Even when Somnath temple was raided and looted seventeen times, making it the world's first ATM, the Brahmin priests did not preach resistance to the Maharajas and the Hindu population to wipe out the invaders of a different God. What purpose and meaning did they have for their living? Many of the Princes including from the "warrior" race of Rajasthan collaborated with the Mughals. This did not happen in China or even in Burma where they did not collaborate with the British. The last King of Burma, Thibaw Min, after the 3rd Anglo-Burmese War in 1885, was exiled in Ratnagiri, Maharashtra where he died in 1916 and was not allowed to see his country again. Did his life have any meaning or purpose?

HONEST OFFICERS AND PARATROOEPER'S PRAYER

From the high philosophy of Meaning to Life to humdrum bureaucracy: Honest and courageous officers need not be disheartened by the treatment they get from the CMs and Chief Secretaries. One is reminded of the touching *Paratrooper's Prayer*. André Zirnheld was born in 1913 and was killed in action in Libya in July 1942 during a raid behind enemy lines while serving as a parachutist in the Free French Army. He was a philosophy professor before the war. This was found in his pocket:

THE PARATROOPER'S PRAYER

I'm asking You God, to give me what You have left.
Give me those things that others never ask of You.
I don't ask You for rest, or tranquillity.
Not that of the spirit, the body, or the mind.
I don't ask You for wealth, or success, or even health.
All those things are asked of You so much Lord,
that you can't have any left to give.
Give me instead Lord what You have left.
Give me what others don't want.
I want uncertainty and doubt.
I want torment and battle.
And I ask that You give them to me now and forever Lord,
so I can be sure to always have them,
because I won't always have the strength to ask again.
But give me also the courage, the energy,
and the spirit to face them.
I ask You these things Lord, because I can't ask them of myself.

Walking the straight and narrow path, I had collected my fair share of 'enemies', both among politicians and among civil servants which latter must be surprising. Civil Servants are normally a placid, risk-averse, clever lot. Two of my IAS friends, for instance, made this pact: '*Whenever you meet a person, you praise me; whenever I meet one, I will praise you*'! This was a highly successful, 'win-win' situation in Game Theory, at no cost. Imagine, in a year's time how many admirers both would get with very little effort! But I was far from following this strategy. I rather revered the 19th century Scottish poet Charles Mackay's rebuke:

You have no enemies, you say?
Alas! my friend, the boast is poor;
He who has mingled in the fray
Of duty, that the brave endure,
Must have made foes! If you have none,
Small is the work that you have done.
You've hit no traitor on the hip,
You've dashed no cup from perjured lip,
You've never turned the wrong to right,
You've been a coward in the fight.

It is said that age not only makes a person mature but also mellows him. But I find this is not so in my case. I have hardened in my views with advancing age. I bristle at injustice, effrontery and corruption. I have been made to head the Transparency International, India, Bangalore. But due to corruption charges against some office bearers in its head office at Delhi, as India has a penchant for corruption, TI-I itself was blacklisted! In a reversal of Midas touch, even gold will become coal with Indian touch! But I have been sustained by my righteous anger which has been purifying me. Though the Task Force on Land-grabbing was abolished ten years ago, even now I receive phone calls from unknown villagers about land-grab by the rich and powerful though I can only tell them to bring it to the notice of the DCs. I even find appreciation from long-forgotten professional elite. One instance: On the last *Yugadi,* New Year day which also happened to be my 80th birthday, I was writing this memoir. My phone rang and showed the caller 'Unknown'. Anyway, I answered the stranger's call and was pleasantly surprised when the caller identified himself as RS Pappu, Advocate from Gulbarga. Greeting me on the new year's day, he said he used to appear before me in cases when I was DC of Gulbarga and that he remembered me on this day and wanted to greet me as he thought I was the only officer whom he still remembered worthy of greeting! It was touching that, expecting no benefit in return, he took the trouble to trace my phone and was giving me a call, fifty years after I left Gulbarga. Human mind is a powerful super-computer though Gary Kasparov might have lost to Deep Blue. So I could quickly retrieve him as the dark, tall, wiry lawyer, close to my age, who pronounced each word precisely and emphatically so that it registered in the person hearing it. I thanked him and reminisced a little about the old days. That call made my day, my year and even leant meaning to my civil servant's humdrum life. It was moving and I realized the meaning of heavy words such as Validation, Sanctity, Sacrament, Virtue, Honour, Dignity.

PECUNIA NON OLET—MONEY DOES NOT STINK

Once the Roman Emperor Vespasian of 1st century CE was counting his gold coins with his son Titus. Vespasian asked him, does he know where it came from? When Titus said No, Vespasian told him it was from the 'urine tax' collected from the public urinals in Rome where the merchants bought the urine for seasoning and softening leather used for soldiers' armour. His son threw away the coin in disgust. But Vespasian made him pick it up and asked him to smell it. When he said he could not get any smell, Vespasian told him, *"Pecunia non Olet'—* Money Does not Stink! How many of the corrupt 'Urine Money' officers and leaders would get such phone calls as I did? I have distilled contempt for corrupt leaders and corrupt bureaucrats whom I consider to be Nobel Eliot's spiritually dead *Hollow Men, filled with Straw, living in the Valley of Dying Stars and Worshipping False Idols.*

Aristotle long ago made a distinction between commodities necessary for life and other types of wealth, including money. The earning for necessaries, which is morally good, is considered as part of *"Oikonomia"*, "the household art of management" from which the English word "Economics" originated. To Aristotle, big money and artificial wealth is the means of "wealth-getting", or *"Chrematistics"*, which is both unlimited and morally degrading. For him the accumulation of money itself was an unnatural activity that dehumanizes those who practice it. Again, the 19th century American thinker Henry David Thoreau, often described as an Anarchist, gave this formula for Happiness:

$$H = MC \div D$$

in which **H** is Happiness, **MC** is Material Comforts and **D** is Desire. Happiness (H) increases if, for a given level of Material Happiness (MC), Desire (D) is kept low. But, if Desire keeps on increasing indefinitely, no amount of Material Comforts can keep pace with it and consequently Happiness disappears. MC is what Aristotle considered household requirements or articles or Necessities such as, for modern times, a modest house, a small car, books, a refrigerator, a colour TV and a good school for two or three children. When we find that Lok Ayukta has raided the houses of officers and find ownership of 3 houses, 4 sites, 1 Commercial Complex, two SUVs, 1 kg of gold, 20 kg of silver, 20 acres of land, Rs.1 crore of bank deposit, Rs.10 crores in Stocks and Shares, Rs.5 crore worth of Insurance Policies, Gold Ornaments (still under valuation!) etc, etc, then it would be clear that this is not what Aristotle termed as 'household art of management' or 'Economics', but pure Greed and Commerce which he despised.

The world of these corrupt officers is very small. They live the life of the well-frog in dark waters with slimy, creepy, cruddy creatures for company and have no idea of the wide sky, bright sun and blue waters. The only book they can ever read is their bank pass-book and the solitary card they can play in life is their credit card. They are ignorant of the fulfilled, examined life of the virtuous. They may even be happy. If ignorance is bliss, it is folly to be wise.

NON SERVIAM

When Satan was asked to serve God, he refused and said *Non Serviam* which means in Latin 'I do not serve you'. In course of time it has come to mean the rebellious philosophy of anarchists to defy authority. I have followed this philosophy within my limited reach in all my years and am proud of it. There is a French saying, *Whenever you lose, you die a little, whenever you win you are reborn.* But, winning and losing depends upon the maturity of mind and a 'considered and examined life'. Those who felt happy they had put me in place and had won, lived in mirages of Pyrrhic land, having small minds. It all goes back to John Stuart Mill's Qualitative Utilitarianism. It was Mill, the 19th century British Utilitarian-Liberal Philosopher who said, *"It is better to be a Man dissatisfied than a pig satisfied; better to be Socrates unhappy than a fool happy. And if the fool, or the pig, are of a different opinion, it is because they only know their own side of the question."* Mill, incidentally, joined as a Civil Servant in the British East India Company in 1823 at the age of seventeen and worked there till 1858 when it was abolished. My call to younger courageous colleagues is: Stand up and look high. Defy, blaspheme. Insult the corrupt for they are bullies, cowards and have no backbones. They live a lesser life and die many times before their death. March erect, arrogant, climb the waterfall, seldom is the fire-walk so cool. Remember Dylan Thomas:

> Do not go gentle into that good night,
> Old age should burn and rave at close of day;
> Rage, rage against the dying of the light....

Keep the head in the clouds but feet firmly on the ground, that is how giants are made. There is no Heaven or Hell waiting. Everything is mind. No soul, no mind, no after-life once the body stops. Only, the selfish gene finds successive bodies in your progenies. Learn the *Charvakas* and Richard Dawkins. Till one becomes a handful of ashes, walk the path of virtue. All Paths of Wealth lead but to the Grave. The journey is the joy. Be worthy of the suffering. Seize the day, seize the hour, *Carpe Diem!*

ADIEU.

❖❖❖